U0949562

Progress Report on China-ASEAN Expo

中国—东盟博览会发展报告

2010 第七卷
Volume Ⅶ

丛书编委会主任 李金早 沈北海 陈 武
Chairs of the Series Editing Committee Li Jinzao Shen Beihai Chen Wu

本卷编委会主任 陈 武
Chair of the Volume Ⅶ Editing Committee Chen Wu

主编 郑军健
Editor-in-Chief Zheng Junjian

GUANGXI NORMAL UNIVERSITY PRESS
广西师范大学出版社

Progress Report on China-ASEAN Expo

《中国—东盟博览会发展报告》编辑委员会

中国—东盟博览会作为国家层面的一个国际性展会，已经成为我国和东盟经贸合作的重要平台，中央将大力支持广西办好这个博览会。中国—东盟博览会要长期举办下去，要办出特色，办出实效。

——中华人民共和国主席 胡锦涛（2007年3月9日）

As a state-level international exposition, the CAEXPO has become an important platform for the economic and trade cooperation between China and ASEAN. Chinese central government will continue to grand full support to Guangxi to well organize the event. The CAEXPO should be a long-term program with distinctive characteristics and sound economic results.

—H.E. Hu Jintao, President of China
(March 9, 2007)

中国与东盟国家领导人寄语
中国—东盟博览会

Compliments of Heads of State/Government on the CAEXPO

中国和东盟10国政府共同主办中国—东盟博览会，搭建了互利共赢、合作发展的平台，推动了中国与东盟在贸易、投资、旅游等领域的实质性合作，是双方客商创造商机的舞台。

——中华人民共和国国务院总理　温家宝（2006年10月31日）

The CAEXPO, co-sponsored by the governments of China and the 10 ASEAN countries, forms a platform for win-win cooperation and development, which has promoted the pragmatic cooperation between China and ASEAN in the fields of trade, investment, tourism, etc. It is a platform for the enterprises of both sides to create business opportunities.

—H.E. Wen Jiabao, Premier of the State Council of China
(October 31, 2006)

中国—东盟博览会、中国—东盟商务与投资峰会已成为中国同东盟国家对话、交流、合作的有效平台。

——中国人民政治协商会议第十一届全国委员会主席 贾庆林（2010年10月19日）

The CAEXPO and the CABIS have become the effective platforms for the dialogues, exchanges and cooperation between China and the ASEAN countries.

—H.E. Jia Qinglin, Chairman of the 11th National Committee of the Chinese People's Political Consultative Conference (October 19, 2010)

中国—东盟博览会、中国—东盟商务与投资峰会已连续举办六次。东盟国家领导人多次出席，各国工商界踊跃参加。会议办出了实效，得到了肯定。

——中华人民共和国国务院副总理 李克强（2009年10月20日）

The CAEXPO and the CABIS, which have been held for 6 straight years, attract the repeat participation of ASEAN state leaders and business elites, reaping fruitful outcomes and gaining positive comments from all parties concerned.

—H.E. Li Keqiang, Vice Premier of the State Council of China (October 20, 2009)

中国—东盟博览会和中国—东盟商务与投资峰会是展示我国改革开放30年辉煌成就的重要窗口，已成为中国和东盟发展战略伙伴关系、促进互利合作共赢的重要平台，服务了国家周边外交战略，推动了中国—东盟自由贸易区建设。

——中华人民共和国国务院副总理 王岐山（2008年10月21日）

The CAEXPO and the CABIS are important showcases of China's tremendous achievements in the reform and opening-up in the previous 30 years. And as important platforms for China and ASEAN to develop their strategic partnership and to promote reciprocal cooperation for win-win results, the CAEXPO and the CABIS comply with China's diplomatic strategies and promote the CAFTA construction.

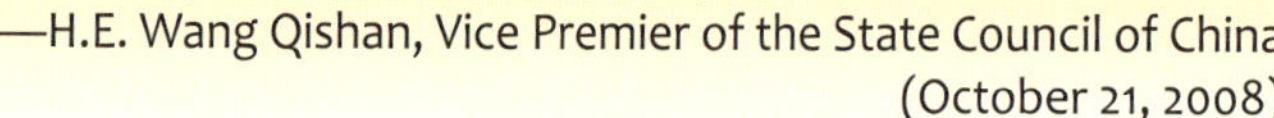

—H.E. Wang Qishan, Vice Premier of the State Council of China (October 21, 2008)

中国—东盟博览会要常办常新，越办越好。

——时任中华人民共和国副主席 曾庆红（2005年10月18日）

The CAEXPO shall be a grand event held on regular basis with new features and sound outcomes.

—H.E. Zeng Qinghong, the then Vice President of China (October 18, 2005)

中国—东盟博览会要一年比一年办得好，一年上一个台阶。

——时任中华人民共和国国务院副总理 吴仪（2004年11月2日）

The CAEXPO shall be better organized and achieve richer outcomes year on year.

—H.E. Madam Wu Yi, the then Vice Premier of the State Council of China (November 2, 2004)

中国—东盟博览会的成功举办，为促进中国—东盟自由贸易区建设，进一步深化中国与东盟战略合作伙伴关系搭建了一个重要平台。

——时任中华人民共和国国务院副总理 曾培炎（2007年10月27日）

The successful CAEXPO has built up a vital platform to accelerate the CAFTA construction and to further enrich the China-ASEAN strategic partnership.

—H.E. Zeng Peiyan, the then Vice Premier of the State Council of China (October 27, 2007)

中国—东盟博览会很成功，办得很好。

——文莱达鲁萨兰国苏丹　哈桑纳尔·博尔基亚（2006年10月31日）

The CAEXPO is well organized and very successful.

—His Majesty Sultan Haji Hassanal Bolkiah Mu'izzaddin Waddaulah, the Sultan and Yang Di-Pertuan of Brunei Darussalam (October 31, 2006)

中国—东盟博览会一年比一年成功，这不仅体现在参展商数量、签约额、交易额等数字上的增加，还表现在博览会影响力的不断增强，表现在东盟与广西、与中国的贸易往来日益频繁、关系日益密切。博览会已成为中国—东盟合作的重要机制，搭建了中国与东盟经贸合作的重要平台。

——柬埔寨王国首相　洪　森（2008年10月22日）

The CAEXPO is more and more successful, which is well evidenced by the growth of number of exhibitors, contractual volume of cooperation projects and trade volume, the increasing popularity and influence of this event and the ever-closer trading exchanges and bilateral links between ASEAN and Guangxi and China as a whole. The CAEXPO has become a major mechanism for cooperation between China and ASEAN, and formed an important platform for the economic and trade cooperation between the two sides.

—H.E. Samdech Hun Sen, Prime Minister of Cambodia (October 22, 2008)

十分高兴在中国—东盟博览会看到印尼的企业家和印尼商品，希望印尼工商界通过博览会继续加强与中国的经贸往来。

——印度尼西亚共和国总统　苏西洛·班邦·尤多约诺（2006年10月31日）

It is my pleasure to see enterprises and commodities from Indonesia at the CAEXPO and I hope that Indonesian business circle could further enhance trade ties with their Chinese counterparts via the CAEXPO.

—H.E. Dr. H. Susilo Bambang Yudhoyono, President of Indonesia (October 31, 2006)

中国—东盟博览会的连续成功举办使中国与东盟的战略伙伴关系得到进一步加强。衷心赞同将博览会继续举办下去，以促进东盟与中国的经济、贸易和投资合作，共同把中国—东盟地区建成一个繁荣的地区。

——时任老挝人民民主共和国总理　波松·布帕万（2009年10月20日）

The successful previous CAEXPOs have further strengthened the ASEAN–China strategic partnership. I sincerely agree to make this event a long–term program, to fuel the bilateral economic, trade and investment cooperation, thus to build a more prosperous ASEAN–China region.

—H.E. Bouasone BOUPHAVANH, the then Prime Minister of Lao PDR (October 20, 2009)

中国—东盟博览会使南宁在中国与东盟的政治、经济、文化交往中发挥着越来越重要的作用。

——时任马来西亚总理 阿卜杜拉·哈吉·艾哈迈德·巴达维（2006年10月31日）

Via the CAEXPO, Nanning now plays a more and more important role in the exchanges between China and ASEAN in politics, economy and culture.

—H.E. Yang Amat Berhormat Dato' Seri Abdullah bin Haji Ahmad Badawi, the then Prime Minister of Malaysia (October 31, 2006)

中国—东盟博览会是中国与东盟各国最好的交流合作平台，让参展商得到了实实在在的利益。

——时任缅甸联邦总理 登 盛（2008年10月21日）

The CAEXPO is the best platform for the exchanges and cooperation between China and ASEAN, which brings pragmatic profits for exhibitors.

—H.E. Lt-Gen Thein Sein, the then Prime Minister of Myanmar (October 21, 2008)

中国—东盟博览会是中国与东盟加强经贸往来的一个大舞台，促进了中国—东盟自由贸易区的建设。

——时任菲律宾共和国总统　格洛丽亚·马卡帕加尔·阿罗约（2006年10月31日）

The CAEXPO is a huge stage for China and ASEAN to enhance economic and trade exchanges, which thus accelerates the CAFTA construction.

—H.E. Madam Gloria Macapagal-Arroyo,
the then President of the Philippines (October 31, 2006)

中国—东盟博览会的举办为新加坡企业进入广西和中国市场搭建了良好的平台，新加坡完全支持博览会的举办。

——新加坡共和国总理　李显龙（2006年10月31日）

The CAEXPO shapes a sound platform for Singapore-based enterprises to access to the market of Guangxi and China as a whole, to which, Singapore offers full support.

—H.E. Lee Hsien Loong, Prime Minister of Singapore (October 31, 2006)

中国—东盟博览会给中国和东盟各国企业搭建了一个相互交流与合作的平台，促进了中国—东盟自由贸易区建设。

——时任泰王国总理　素拉育·朱拉暖（2006年10月31日）

The CAEXPO forms a platform for bilateral communication and cooperation among enterprises of China and ASEAN, and propels the CAFTA construction.

—H.E. Surayud Chulanont, the then Prime Minister of Thailand (October 31, 2006)

中国—东盟博览会将大力促进中国—东盟自由贸易区的形成，而这对中国与东盟则是共赢的。

——越南社会主义共和国总理　阮晋勇（2006年10月31日）

The CAEXPO will effectively accelerate the forming of the CAFTA, which will bring about win-win results for China and ASEAN.

—H.E. Nguyen Tan Dung, Prime Minister of Viet Nam (October 31, 2006)

特稿

在第七届中国—东盟商务与投资峰会开幕式上的主旨演讲

中共中央政治局常委、全国政协主席 贾庆林

（2010年10月19日）

尊敬的印尼副总统布迪约诺阁下，
尊敬的老挝副总理阿桑·劳里阁下，
尊敬的越南副总理张永仲阁下，
尊敬的东盟各国嘉宾，
各位来宾，女士们，先生们，朋友们：

金秋十月，丹桂飘香。在这美好的时节，我很高兴出席第七届中国—东盟商务与投资峰会。首先，我谨代表中国政府并以我个人的名义，对峰会的召开表示热烈的祝贺！对莅临峰会的东盟国家领导人和各位嘉宾表示诚挚的欢迎！

今年是中国—东盟自贸区全面实施的开局之年，也是中国—东盟战略伙伴关系再获丰收之年。一年来，双方高层交往密切，睦邻互信加强；各领域务实合作扎实推进，1至9月，双方贸易额达2113亿美元，同比增长44%；双方社会人文领域的交流合作广泛而活跃，在重大国际和地区问题上密切沟通与协调。充满生机和活力的中国—东盟睦邻友好合作，为我们各自国家发展提供了广阔空间和众多商机，也为亚洲率先实现经济回升向好和保持总体稳定作出了重要贡献。

女士们、先生们！

当前，国际政治经济格局加速调整，亚洲发展孕育着重大机遇。中国同东盟国家的前途命运日益紧密地联系在一起。在新形势下，巩固和加强中国—东盟战略伙伴关系，符合我们的共同利益，是我们的共同责任，也是我们的共同选择。中方将一如既往，坚定奉行与邻为善、以邻为伴的周边外交方针，同东盟加强战略互信，深化互利合作，扩大人文交流，密切在重大地区和国际问题上的沟通协调，促进我们各自国家又好又快发展，促进亚洲的和平、稳定、发展、繁荣。

从这个意义上讲，以“中国—东盟自由贸易区与区域经贸合作的展望”为主题的本届峰会，顺应了中国和东盟携手合作、共创未来的趋势和需求。我们希望峰会围绕主题，就进一步发挥中国—东盟自贸区作用，扩大双方经贸合作和相互投资，加强基础设施建设和互联互通，开展重大民生项目合作，促进双方中小企业交流合作，推动行业对接与合作，打造新的产业链，深化湄公河次区域开发、东盟—东部增长区等次区域合作等，集思广益、献计献策，推动中国—东盟互利合作进一步向广度和深度发展。

女士们、先生们！

今年是中国实施经济社会发展“十一五”规划的最后一年。五年来，我们励精图治，成功应对国内外各种重大风险和挑战，国家面貌发生了新的历史性变化。中国社会生产力快速发展，综合国力大幅提升，人民生活明显改善，国际地位和影响力不断提高，中国人民以自己的优异成绩谱写了中国特色社会主义事业的新篇章。

"十二五"时期是中国全面建设小康社会的关键时期，是深化改革开放、加快转变经济发展方式的攻坚时期。刚刚闭幕的中国共产党十七届五中全会描绘了未来五年中国发展的宏伟蓝图。我们将适应国内外形势新变化，顺应各族人民过上更好生活新期盼，以科学发展为主题，以加快转变经济发展方式为主线，深化改革开放，保障和改善民生，巩固和扩大应对国际金融危机冲击成果，促进经济长期平稳较快发展和社会和谐稳定，为全面建成小康社会打下具有决定性意义的基础。我们将坚定不移地走和平发展道路，恪守和平共处五项原则，同周边邻国和世界上其他国家平等相待、友好合作；将坚持相互尊重、求同存异，通过对话协商和平解决矛盾和分歧；将忠实履行自己应尽的国际责任和义务，向包括东盟国家在内的广大发展中国家提供力所能及的帮助。

女士们、先生们！

在东盟各国政府、商协会、企业界的鼎力支持和积极参与下，中国—东盟博览会、中国—东盟商务与投资峰会已成为中国同东盟国家对话、交流、合作的有效平台。在此，我谨对各位东盟国家领导人、企业家、专家学者付出的努力和作出的贡献表示衷心感谢。我深信，在大家共同努力下，中国—东盟博览会、中国—东盟商务与投资峰会将进一步办出特色、办出水平、办出成效，为推进中国—东盟自贸区深入发展，为不断开创中国—东盟睦邻友好合作新局面作出更大贡献。

最后，我衷心祝愿本届中国—东盟商务与投资峰会圆满成功！谢谢大家！

Keynote speech at the opening ceremony of the 7th CABIS

H.E. Jia Qinglin
Chairman of the National Committee of Chinese People's Political Consultative Conference (CPPCC)

(October 19, 2010)

Your Excellency Mr. Boediono, Vice President of Indonesia,
Your Excellency Mr. Asang Laoly, Vice Prime Minister of Laos,
Your Excellency Mr. Truong Vinh Trong, Vice Prime Minister of Vietnam,
Distinguished guests from ASEAN countries,
Ladies and gentlemen, friends:

In the golden month of October, I am very glad to be present at the 7th China-ASEAN Business and Investment Summit (CABIS). First of all, on behalf of the Chinese government and in my name, I extend the warm congratulation to the 7th CABIS, and the cordial welcome to the leaders of ASEAN countries and guests who are present at the summit.

This year marks the full implementation of the China-ASEAN Free Trade Area (CAFTA), and another harvest year of strategic partnership of China and ASEAN. Over the past year, both sides have intensified high level contacts and deepened the good-neighborly mutual trust. Cooperation in all fields pressed ahead, with the bilateral trade volume of the first nine months reaching US$ 211.3 billion, 44% higher year on year. The culture and people-to-people exchanges and cooperation of both sides are extensive and dynamic, communication and coordination have been increased on major international and regional issues. The good-neighborly and friendly cooperation between China and ASEAN, which is full of vitality and dynamism, has brought huge opportunities and broad space to the respective countries, and made an important contribution to Asia, which is taking the lead globally in the recovery and stability of its economy.

Ladies and gentlemen!

At present, we live at a time of accelerated adjustment in the international political and economic landscape and major opportunities in the development of Asia. The future and destiny of China and ASEAN countries are increasingly closely linked with each other. China would continue to pursue the policy of building friendship and partnership with neighbors and following this policy guideline, strengthen strategic mutual trust with ASEAN, which is in the interest of both China and ASEAN countries in the new situation. China will as usual carry out extensive and dynamic exchanges and cooperation in people-to-people and cultural fields and close communication and coordination on major international and regional issues, to boost the fast and smooth development of our respective countries, and the peace, stability, development, and prosperity of Asia at large.

In this sense, the 7th CABIS, with "Prospects on CAFTA and Regional Economic and Trade Cooperation" as its theme, has met the needs of China and ASEAN for common development and shared future. We hope the summit, while centering on the CAFTA, can have brainstorms and discussions on furthering the role of the CAFTA, expanding mutual investment and economic and trade cooperation, intensifying interconnection of infrastructure, carrying out major projects of livelihood, promoting small and medium sized enterprises cooperation, enhancing industrial matching and cooperation, creating new industrial chain, deepening the GMS development, and BIMP-EAGA cooperation, so as to enhance reciprocal cooperation between the two sides in more extended fields.

Ladies and gentlemen!

This year is also the last year of the 11th Five-year Plan of China to make its social and economic development. Over the past 5 years, we worked hard to cope with the major risks from home and abroad to make a historical change to our country. China has seen a rapid growth in the social production power, a significant increase of overall national power, much improved living conditions of the people, and an elevated international standing in the world. The Chinese people have written a new chapter in their history with their remarkable achievements.

The period of the 12th Five-year Plan will be the critical moment for China in its efforts to build an overall moderately prosperous society, to deepen reform and opening-up, and to accelerate the change of mode of economic development. The 5th plenary session of the 17th Congress of Chinese Communist Party, which concluded not long ago, has drawn a grand blue print for China in the coming five years. We will adapt to the domestic and international situations, meet the expectation of the people for better life, deepen reform and opening up, solidify and expand the fruits gained in tackling international financial crisis, promote long-term smooth and fast economic development and social harmony and stability, with scientific development as the theme and changing mode of economic development as the focus, so as to lay a decisive foundation for a moderately prosperous society. We will unswervingly adhere to the path of peaceful development, and the five principles of peaceful coexistence, to treat equally each other, develop good relations with neighboring countries and other countries in the world; we will try to solve problems and settle disagreements through dialogues and consultations on the basis of mutual respect and seeking common ground while reserving difference, we will be committed to our international duties and obligations and offer all helps and assistances that we can to the developing countries with ASEAN included.

Ladies and gentlemen!

With the great support and active participation of governments, chambers of commerce, and companies of the ASEAN countries, the CAEXPO and the CABIS have become the effective platform of dialogue, exchange and cooperation between China and ASEAN. Here, I would like to express my sincere gratitude to leaders, entrepreneurs, experts and scholars who have worked hard and made contribution to the success of the two events. I am convinced that with the joint efforts of all, the CAEXPO and the CABIS will be more characterized, more sophisticated and more successful and they will make more contributions to the advance of the CAFTA and the good neighbor and friendship between China and ASEAN.

Last but not least, I sincerely wish the 7th CABIS a complete success! Thank you all!

在第七届中国—东盟商务与投资峰会开幕式上的致辞

广西壮族自治区党委书记
广西壮族自治区人大常委会主任 郭声琨
（2010年10月19日）

尊敬的中共中央政治局常委、中国人民政治协商会议全国委员会主席贾庆林阁下，
尊敬的印尼副总统布迪约诺阁下，
尊敬的老挝副总理阿桑·劳里阁下，
尊敬的越南副总理张永仲阁下，
女士们，先生们，朋友们：

金秋十月，我们再次相聚南宁，隆重举行第七届中国—东盟商务与投资峰会。首先，我谨代表广西壮族自治区人民政府和全区各族人民，对峰会的召开表示热烈祝贺！对出席峰会的各位嘉宾表示诚挚的欢迎和衷心的感谢！

本届峰会是在中国—东盟自由贸易区如期建成、中国与东盟交流合作开启新的历史篇章的背景下召开的，具有特殊而重要的意义。峰会以“中国—东盟自由贸易区与区域经贸合作的展望”为主题，开展务实深入的对话和讨论，同时还将举办东盟国家领导人与中国企业家圆桌对话会以及一系列专题论坛和相关活动。这对于我们抓住自贸区建成的重大机遇，全面提升区域经贸合作水平，促进共同繁荣发展，将起到积极的推动作用。

女士们、先生们、朋友们！

中国—东盟商务与投资峰会已经连续成功举办了六届，取得了丰硕的成果，成为中国与东盟共同合作、共享机遇、共谋发展的重要平台。广西作为峰会的举办地，我们愿意以中国—东盟自由贸易区如期建成为契机，秉持互利共赢理念，按照业已达成的货物贸易、服务贸易、投资协议的安排，更加积极主动地与东盟各国工商企业界携起手来，进一步创新合作机制，丰富合作内涵，创造合作机遇，增强合作实效，共同开创中国—东盟自由贸易区更加美好的未来。

预祝第七届中国—东盟商务与投资峰会取得圆满成功！

谢谢大家！

Speech at the opening ceremony of the 7th CABIS

Guo Shengkun

Secretary of Chinese Communist Party Guangxi Committee

Chairman of Standing Committee of the People's Congress of Guangxi

(October 19, 2010)

Your Excellency Mr. Jia Qinglin, Chairman of the National Committee of CPPCC ,
Your Excellency Mr. Boediono, Vice President of Indonesia,
Mr. Asang Laoly, Vice Prime Minister of Laos,
Mr. Truong Vinh Trong, Vice Prime Minister of Vietnam,
Ladies and gentlemen, friends:

In the golden month of October, we once again meet with each other in Nanning for the 7th China-ASEAN Business and Investment Summit (CABIS). First of all, on behalf of the People's Government of Guangxi Zhuang Autonomous Region and the people of all ethnic groups in Guangxi, I would like to extend the warmest congratulation to the 7th CABIS, and the cordial welcome and heartfelt gratitude to all guests and participants of the summit.

To be held with the establishment of the CAFTA as scheduled and the new chapter of China-ASEAN exchanges and cooperation, the 7th CABIS is of special significance. Themed on "Prospects of CAFTA and Regional Economic and Trade Cooperation", the summit will carry out pragmatic and deepened talks and dialogues, and concurrently there will be a round table talk between the ASEAN leaders and Chinese businessmen held, as well as a series of events and activities, all of which will play a positive and important role in raising the level of regional economic and trade cooperation and promoting common development and prosperity on the basis of the founding of the CAFTA.

Ladies and gentlemen, friends, the CABIS has been successfully held for six consecutive years, producing rich outcomes. It has become an important platform to share opportunities for cooperation and development between China and ASEAN. As the host of the CABIS, Guangxi will take advantage of the establishment of the CAFTA, uphold the win–win and mutual benefit concept, follow the arrangement reached by the agreements of trade in goods, trade in services, and investments. It will work closely with ASEAN business communities to open a better future for the CAFTA by innovating cooperation mechanisms, enriching cooperation content, creating cooperation opportunities, and increasing cooperation effects.

I wish the 7th CABIS a complete success!

Thank you all!

在第七届中国—东盟博览会开幕式上的致辞

广西壮族自治区主席
中国—东盟博览会组委会副主任

（2010年10月19日）

尊敬的中共中央政治局常委、全国政协主席贾庆林阁下，

尊敬的印度尼西亚副总统布迪约诺阁下，

尊敬的老挝副总理阿桑·劳里阁下，

尊敬的越南副总理张永仲阁下，

尊敬的东盟各国领导人，

女士们，先生们：

今天，绿城南宁喜迎第七届中国—东盟博览会，这是中国—东盟自由贸易区建成后的首届博览会。我谨代表广西壮族自治区人民政府，向莅临本届博览会的各国领导人和各位嘉宾表示热烈的欢迎和诚挚的感谢！

七年前，中国—东盟博览会为中国—东盟自由贸易区建设应运而生。七年来，我们共同见证了博览会在各方的热情参与和大力支持下，连年迈上新台阶，每届取得新成效，已经成为自贸区建设的“助推器”，成为中国与东盟友谊合作的象征。今天，我们共同分享博览会的丰硕成果，共同分享自贸区建成的成功喜悦。

中国—东盟自贸区建成，这是中国和东盟的新机遇，是亚洲和世界的新机遇。广西作为博览会的承办方，作为中国面向东盟开放的前沿和窗口，我们愿与各方进一步发挥博览会的平台作用，不断拓展功能，促进博览会常态化、机制化，更好地推进自贸区的发展。我们愿与各方通过中国—东盟信息平台的建设，使之成为贸易、投资、文化、教育等多领域信息交流中心和“永不落幕”的博览会，更好地造福各国的企业和人民。我们愿与各方共同推进自贸区框架下的次区域合作，共推泛北部湾经济合作，共建南宁—新加坡经济走廊，共建跨境经济合作区，共创中国与东盟和谐共进、合作发展的新辉煌！

衷心祝愿本届博览会取得圆满成功！

谢谢大家！

Speech at the 7th CAEXPO opening ceremony

Ma Biao

Governor of Guangxi Zhuang Autonomous Region
Co-Chair of the CAEXPO Organizing Committee

(October 19, 2010)

Your Excellency Mr. Jia Qinglin, Chairman of the National Committee of CPPCC ,
Your Excellency Mr. Boediono, Vice President of Indonesia,
Your Excellency Mr. Asang Laoly, Vice Prime Minister of Laos,
Your Excellency Mr. Truong Vinh Trong, Vice Prime Minister of Vietnam,
Your Excellencies Leaders of ASEAN countries,
Ladies and gentlemen:

Today, the green city of Nanning is delighted to welcome the 7th China-ASEAN Expo (CAEXPO), the first CAEXPO since the founding of the China-ASEAN Free Trade Area (CAFTA). On behalf of the People's Government of Guangxi Zhuang Autonomous Region, I would like to extend the warm welcome and heartfelt gratitude to leaders of the countries concerned and the guests who are present at the 7th CAEXPO.

Seven years ago, the CAEXPO was born with the building of the CAFTA. For the last seven years, with the enthusiastic participation and active support from all parties, we have jointly witnessed the new progress made by the CAEXPO year by year, and the success of the CAEXPO has made it an important driving force behind the building of the CAFTA, and a symbolic of the China-ASEAN friendship and cooperation. Today, while we share the rich fruits of the CAEXPO, we also share the pleasure and success of the founding of the CAFTA.

The establishment of the CAFTA is not only the new opportunity for China and ASEAN, but also a new opportunity to Asia and the rest of the world. As the organizer of the CAEXPO, and the outpost and showcase of China opened toward ASEAN, we stand ready to advance the development of the CAFTA by furthering the role of the CAEXPO as an important platform, and increasing its function to regularize and mechanize the event. We also wish to work with relevant parties to build the China-ASEAN information platform, to make it an exchange center of information regarding trade, investment, culture, education and other fields and a CAEXPO that never closes as well, to bring more benefits to enterprises and people of countries concerned. We also wish to work with all parties to promote the sub-regional cooperation under the framework of the CAFTA, to advance the Pan-Beibu Gulf economic cooperation, to build the Nanning-Singapore economic corridor, to build the cross-border economic cooperation zone, and to create a bright future of harmonious advancement, cooperative development for China and ASEAN.

I sincerely wish the 7th CAEXPO a complete success!

Thank you all!

在第七届中国—东盟博览会开幕式上的致辞

中国商务部国际贸易谈判代表兼副部长 高虎城

（2010年10月19日）

尊敬的中共中央政治局常委、全国政协主席贾庆林阁下，
尊敬的印度尼西亚副总统布迪约诺，
老挝副总理阿桑·劳里，
越南副总理张永仲，
女士们，先生们：

今天，第七届中国—东盟博览会在绿城南宁开幕，我代表中国商务部，向支持和参与博览会的各国新老朋友表示热烈欢迎和衷心感谢！

中国与东盟是好朋友、好邻居、好伙伴。近年来，双方经贸关系不断取得新的进展。特别是经过双方十年努力，中国—东盟自由贸易区已于今年1月1日如期建成，标志着双方经贸合作进入到全面深入发展的新阶段。在自贸区建设的推进过程中，我们共同举办了六届中国—东盟博览会，通过这一平台，把投资贸易便利化的成果带给各国企业和人民，产生了互利共赢的积极的良好成效。

本届博览会将充分反映中国—东盟自贸区建设成果，内容更加丰富，针对性更强，将为双方企业和人民带来更多的实惠。

让我们以自贸区建成为契机，共同努力，在更大范围、更宽领域、更高层次加强合作，为促进本地区共同发展、共同繁荣作出新的贡献！

预祝第七届中国—东盟博览会圆满成功！

谢谢大家！

Speech at the opening ceremony of the 7th CAEXPO

Gao Hucheng

China International Trade Representative and Vice Minister of Commerce of China

(October 19, 2010)

Your Excellency Mr. Jia Qinglin, Chairman of the National Committee of CPPCC,

Your Excellency Mr. Boediono, Vice President of Indonesia,

Mr. Asang Laoly, Vice Prime Minister of Laos,

Mr. Truong Vinh Trong, Vice Prime Minister of Vietnam,

Ladies and gentlemen:

Today, the 7th China–ASEAN Expo (CAEXPO) opens in the green city of Nanning, on behalf of the Chinese Ministry of Commerce, I would like to extend the warm welcome and heartfelt gratitude to new and old friends from home and abroad who support and participate in the CAEXPO!

China and ASEAN are good friends, good neighbors, and good partners. In recent years, new progresses have been made in the bilateral economic and trade relations. In particular, with the joint efforts of both sides in the past decade, the China–ASEAN Free Trade Area (CAFTA) has been completed on January 1 this year as scheduled, marking a new stage of deep and full development in the bilateral economic and trade cooperation. During the course, we have co–sponsored 6 sessions of the CAEXPO, through which the fruits of investment and trade facilitation have been brought to enterprises and people of the countries concerned, generating a positive and mutually beneficial outcome.

The 7th CAEXPO will fully reflect the achievements of the CAFTA, with richer content and more customized services provided, which will bring more tangible benefits to enterprises and people of both sides.

Taking advantage of the founding of the CAFTA, let us strengthen cooperation at bigger range, in broader fields and on higher level, and make new contributions to promoting the common development and common prosperity of the region.

I wish the 7th CAEXPO a complete success!

Thank you all!

目录

第五章　创新展览大平台　传导自贸新商机

第六章　深化对话交流　扩大合作领域

第七章　飞歌传情　共话友谊

附 录

CONTENTS

前言

中国—东盟博览会组委会副主任兼秘书长
广西壮族自治区党委常委、自治区副主席　陈武

由中国国务院总理温家宝倡议、东盟10国领导人一致赞同、中国和东盟10国政府商务主管部门共同主办、广西壮族自治区人民政府承办的中国—东盟博览会已成功举办七届。经过七年的探索，博览会形成了集政治、外交、经贸、人文为一体，全方位与东盟开展合作的新模式，搭建了中国—东盟友好交流、经贸促进和多领域合作的重要平台，成为中国—东盟自由贸易区具有广泛影响力的国际盛会，为中国与东盟、发展中国家与发展中国家共同发展树立了典范。

一、中国—东盟博览会成效显著

七届博览会的成功举办，成效显著，体现在以下三个方面：

一是搭建了中国—东盟友好交流的平台，以政治外交影响力带动经贸等多领域合作。七届博览会共有38位中国和东盟国家领导人、1300多位部长级贵宾出席。会期举行多场双方领导人、部长、地方负责人之间的会谈，以及政界与商界高端对话，增进了政治互信，也推动了商家的务实合作，带动了文化、教育等多领域的交流活动。

二是搭建了经贸促进的平台，促进了双边经贸合作。博览会围绕中国—东盟自贸区建设进程以及中国和东盟国家的经济发展水平、资源禀赋、产业结构、行业特点而设置展览内容，高度集中了11国的企业、商品、项目、资金等方面的信息，将自贸区

的投资贸易便利化从政府层面推进到了企业层面，成为自贸区建设的“助推器”。七届博览会共有26.54万名客商参会，贸易成交额98.83亿美元，签约国际合作项目投资额417.52亿美元，签约国内合作项目投资额4027.92亿元，取得了良好的经贸成效。

2004年，首届中国—东盟博览会举办。中国和东盟双边贸易额提前一年实现了1000亿美元的目标。2007年，双边贸易额提前三年实现2000亿美元的目标。2010年，中国与东盟贸易额接近3000亿美元，同比增长37.5%。博览会发挥了经贸促进的作用，体现了自贸区的双赢效果，推动中国—东盟战略伙伴关系提升到一个更高的水平。

三是搭建了多领域合作的平台，为中国和东盟在经贸、人文等领域的合作提供机制保障。随着中国—东盟经贸合作不断扩大和深化，对双方在相关领域的合作提供了更多、更高的要求。例如，双方货物贸易快速增长，需要双方海关和质检加强合作，提高便利化水平。双方相互投资规模扩大，需要双方加强金融合作，给企业投资提供更好的支撑。双方贸易和投资的增长，都需要双方在交通、物流、通讯等多领域加强合作，完善基础设施支撑。同时，经贸合作要与工业、农业、科技、环保、减灾、卫生、教育、文化、旅游等多领域合作结合在一起，共同推进，才能深化双边全面合作，形成经济社会发展的持续推动力。

因此，七届博览会围绕贸易、投资、旅游、新闻、科技、港口、海关、质检、电信等多个领域，举办了180多个高层会议和交流活动，邀请各国各领域的政府官员、企业家、专家学者参会进行对话交流，研究解决上述领域相关问题的办法和机制，形成了相关领域的一系列合作机制，为经贸、人文等多领域的交流合作提供了机制保障。博览会还设立“魅力之城”专题，每届每个国家选派一个城市担任“魅力之城”，展示城市形象和发展商机，促进城市合作。每届博览会期间还举办南宁国际民歌艺术节等一系列文化体育交流活动，增进中国与东盟各国友好往来。

二、中国—东盟博览会建立了11国领导人亲自推动、11国政府共同主办、各国商界广泛参与的独具特色运行机制

中国和东盟国家领导人对博览会高度重视。胡锦涛总书记对办好博览会作出重要指示，强调：“中国—东盟博览会是国家层面的一个国际性展会”、“中央将大力支持广西办好这个博览会”，“要长期举办下去，要办出特色，办出实效”。温家宝、贾庆林、李克强、曾庆红、王岐山、吴仪、曾培炎等中央领导同志分别出席了历届博览会。柬埔寨首相洪森连续出席了五届，越南总理阮晋勇、老挝原总理波松、缅甸原总理梭温均连续出席了三届，其他东盟国家领导人也出席了历届博览会。自2003年第七次中国—东盟“10+1”领导人会议以来，博览会每年都被写入中国—东盟“10+1”领导人会议的《主席声明》，得到各国领导人的高度评价。

七年来，中国—东盟博览会建立了11国共办、独具特色的运行机制。

（一）成立了组委会，形成了“各部委支持办好博览会、博览会积极为各部委工作搭好平台”的工作机制

博览会筹办之初，就成立了由中国国务院分管领导担任名誉主任，中国和东盟10国政府经贸部长及东盟秘书长任共同主任的组委会。中方组委会由商务部、外交部、中国国际贸易促进委员会、国务院办公厅、中宣部、国家发展改革委、科技部、财政部、公安部警卫局、交通运输部、海关总署、国家质量检验检疫总局、国家旅游局、国家食品药品监督管理局、国务院新闻办公室等15个部委及广西壮族自治区人民政府组成，各部委从各自的职能出发，给予了博览会宝贵的支持和帮助。同时，各部委在博览会期间举办了各领域高层次论坛、会议及活动，博览会为各部委与东盟合作搭建了有效平台。

几年来，越南、老挝、泰国、印尼等东盟国家也建立了跨部门的组委会，在组织机构上为博览会成功举办提供了有力保障。

（二）建立了11国共办机制，体现互利共赢

共同主办是博览会的特色和基础。几年来，在11国共办方的共同努力下，博览会互利共赢的共办机制不断深化。我们建立了由各国经贸部长担任组委会共同主任、司局长担任副秘书长、处长为联络官的三级共办工作构架，形成了博览会高官会议、联络官会议等磋商机制、抽签决定国家专题展位排序的惯例，以及每届由1个东盟国家担任主题国，主题国领导人率团出席的机制。

通过以上措施，建立起平等尊重、共同主办、广泛参与的共办工作机制，使东盟国家能将其本国优势领域在博览会上加以充分展示，共同促进博览会的持续发展，为确保博览会的成功举办提供了保障。

（三）吸引了11国商协会和企业广泛参与，面向全球开放

几年来，中国和东盟各国商协会、企业界顺应时代发展潮流，积极通过博览会，深化了互利合作。我们邀请了41家中国和东盟商协会成为博览会的支持商协会，推进了中国—东盟自由贸易区建设和全面经济合作。

博览会不仅有中国和东盟各国的企业参与，而且还吸引了美国、日本、法国、德国、澳大利亚、加拿大等多个区域外国家，有效促进了区域外国家与中国和东盟国家的交流，进一步加深了相互了解，提升了中国和东盟作为一个整体在全球的影响力。

三、在新形势下，广西作为承办方，将继续举全区之力办好中国—东盟博览会，更好地服务中国—东盟友好合作

七年来，广西作为中国—东盟博览会的承办方，不断加强组织领导，加大工作力度，举全区之力，做好每届博览会的筹备工作。我们成立了由自治区主席任组长的博览会、商务与投资峰会（以下简称“两会”）广西领导小

组，还成立了由自治区有关厅局和相关单位组成的“两会”指挥中心，为博览会的成功举办提供了组织保障。

随着中国—东盟自由贸易区的建成，中国与东盟的合作进入了全面深入发展的新阶段。国家“十二五”规划纲要明确提出，要把广西建成与东盟合作的新高地，广西作为中国与东盟开放合作前沿和门户的作用将进一步得到发挥。我们要按照国家“十二五”规划要求，认真贯彻《国务院关于进一步促进广西经济社会发展的若干意见》、《广西北部湾经济区发展规划》，进一步承办好中国—东盟博览会，发挥广西的区位优势，为中国和东盟合作搭好平台。今后，要做好三个方面的工作：

一是进一步完善博览会承办工作的长效机制。我们将通过广西与东盟开放合作领导小组及其统筹协调办公室，进一步完善博览会承办工作机制，帮助企业界学习、了解、熟悉自贸区的有关政策、有关规则和各方面的知识，围绕交通基础设施、农业资源、工业优势产业、港口物流、旅游、共同市场建设、经济合作区、人力资源培训、文化、体育等多个领域，务实推进与东盟的合作。

二是继续举全区之力承办好中国—东盟博览会。广西将继续按照中国—东盟自由贸易区建设进程的要求，把博览会作为推进中国与东盟的合作，特别是中国—东盟自由贸易区建设的重要平台，继续举全区之力办出特色、办出水平。今后，我们将根据中国—东盟自由贸易区发展和中国与东盟合作的实际进程，举办更多的专业展，推动企业“走出去”，加强信息平台建设，把5天的博览会延伸为365天永不落幕的展会，让双方企业更好地分享中国—东盟自由贸易区带来的好处。积极扩大文化、教育、体育等多领域合作，把博览会的合作由经贸、投资领域为主的合作进一步扩展到多领域、多层次的合作。此外，继续发挥好中国与东盟合作“南宁渠道”的作用，吸引中国与东盟更多领域的合作机制落户南宁，服务中国与东盟全面合作。

三是进一步发挥好广西的区位优势和博览会的平台作用，服务中国—东盟友好合作。广西将进一步发挥博览会平台作用，进一步完善以交通为重点的基础设施建设，大力推动互联互通，大力实施《广西北部湾经济区发展规划》，加快建设中国—马来西亚（钦州）产业园区等重大项目，加快推进中越跨境经济合作区建设，继续推进大湄公河次区域合作、泛北部湾经济合作、“两廊一圈”合作、南宁—新加坡经济走廊建设，为服务中国—东盟友好合作作出新的贡献！

Foreword

Chen Wu
Vice Co-chair and Secretary General of the CAEXPO Organizing Committee
Member of the Standing Committee of the Chinese Communist Party (CPC) Guangxi Committee & Vice Governor of Guangxi Zhuang Autonomous Region

The China-ASEAN Expo (CAEXPO) was advocated by Premier Wen Jiabao of China and was applauded by the heads of state/government of the 10 ASEAN countries. Co-sponsored by the ministries of commerce/trade and industry of China and the 10 ASEAN member states and organized by the People's Government of Guangxi Zhuang Autonomous Region, the event has been successfully concluded with 7 sessions. Over the past 7 years, the CAEXPO has grown into a new model of comprehensive cooperation between China and ASEAN, which incorporates political, diplomatic, economic and cultural cooperation. The CAEXPO has built an essential platform for the friendly exchange, trade promotion and cooperation in various fields between China and ASEAN, and become an international event that exerts wide influence in the China-ASEAN Free Trade Area as well as an example of common development of China and ASEAN and that among developing countries.

I. Remarkable achievements

The previous 7 sessions have scored notable outcomes as follows:

It has shaped a platform for the China-ASEAN friendly exchange, and has driven economic and trade cooperation with its political and diplomatic influence. The previous 7 CAEXPOs attracted altogether 38 heads of state/government and over 1,300 ministerial VIPs of China and the 10 ASEAN countries. Bilateral meetings between leaders, ministers and local officials were held, and high-end talks between government officials and business communities were arranged. All the efforts have strengthened political mutual trust and promoted practical cooperation among businesses, also propelled the exchange and collaboration in culture, education and other relevant fields.

It has built a platform for business promotion, boosting bilateral economic and trade cooperation. The CAEXPO arranges its exhibitions by targeting the construction progress of the China-ASEAN FTA, the economic growth pace of China and ASEAN countries and resources, industrial mix and features of both sides. It has effectively accelerated the CAFTA construction, as it hubs enterprises, commodities, projects and capitals of the 11 countries, and extends the accessibility and familiarity of the CAFTA facilitations from government officials to enterprises. The previous 7 CAEXPOs drew 265,400 exhibitors and trade visitors, concluded a total trade volume of US$9.883 billion and contracted international and Chinese domestic investment cooperation projects worth US$41.752 billion and RMB402.792 billion respectively. The economic returns are impressive.

In 2004 when the 1st CAEXPO was held, the bilateral trade volume between China and ASEAN reached the goal of US$100 billion one year ahead of the schedule, and then the target of US$200 billion was met in 2007 three years earlier than the schedule. In 2010, the figure approached US$300 billion, up by 37.5% year on year. The CAEXPO promotes bilateral economic and trade cooperation, and helps elevate the China-ASEAN strategic partnership to a new high, evidencing that the China-ASEAN FTA is a win-win mechanism.

It has presented a platform for bilateral cooperation in various fields, providing institutional guarantee for the China-ASEAN cooperation in economy, trade, culture and other domains. Economic and trade cooperation between China and ASEAN is deepened and expanded, which raises higher demands on the bilateral collaboration in related sectors. For instance, the fast growing trade in goods requires closer cooperation between Customs and quality supervision authorities of both sides, thus to lift the level of facilitated trade; And the expansion of two-way investment needs the two sides to enhance financial cooperation, in a bid to provide better supports for investment cooperation among enterprises; The ever-increasing bilateral trade and investment expect much effective cooperation in transport, logistics and telecommunications and the strong support of perfect infrastructures. Meanwhile, economic and trade cooperation shall be integrated with the cooperation in industry, agriculture, science and technology, environmental protection, disaster reduction, health, education, culture, tourism and other fields, forging a joint force to deepen the comprehensive cooperation between China and ASEAN, and driving and sustaining their economic and social development.

To this end, the previous 7 CAEXPOs arranged over 180 high-end conferences and networking programs on trade, investment, tourism, journalism, science and technology, ports and harbors, Customs, quality supervision and telecommunications, and invited relevant government officials, entrepreneurs, experts and scholars to talk about the issues and problems encountered in bilateral cooperation and seek for solutions. A series of cooperative mechanisms were established, providing institutional guarantee for the bilateral exchange and cooperation in economic, trade and cultural domains. Additionally, the CAEXPO sets up the Pavilion of Cities of Charm to showcase the images and business opportunities of the 11 cities chosen by China and 10 ASEAN countries as their respective City of Charm, thus to promote cooperation among cities. Concurrently, cultural and sports exchange programs, inclusive of the Nanning International Arts Festival of Folk Songs, are held to propel the friendly exchanges between China and ASEAN.

II. The CAEXPO has established a unique operating mechanism that features full support of Chinese and ASEAN state leaders, co-sponsorship of 11 countries and active participation of business communities.

Chinese and ASEAN leaders attach keen importance to the CAEXPO. H.E. President Hu Jintao once stressed that the CAEXPO shall be made an international exposition jointly held by central governments, and the Chinese government shall grant full support to Guangxi in organizing this event. He also said, the CAEXPO shall be a long-term program that will witness new highlights and concrete profits year on year. H.E. Wen Jiabao, Premier of the State Council of China, H.E. Jia Qinglin, Chairman of the National Committee of the Chinese People's Political Consultative Conference, H.E. Li Keqiang, Vice Premier of the State Council of China, H.E. Zeng Qinghong, former Vice President of China, H.E. Wang Qishan, Vice Premier of the State Council of China, H.E. Madam Wu Yi, former Vice Premier of the State Council of China and H.E. Zeng Peiyan, former Vice Premier of the State Council of China all personally visited the CAEXPO. H.E. Samdech Hun Sen, Prime Minister of Cambodia has personally attended the CAEXPO for 5 consecutive sessions, and H.E. Nguyen Tan Dung, Prime Minister of Vietnam, H.E. Bouasone BOUPHAVANH, former Prime Minister of Lao PDR and H.E. Soe Win, former Prime Minister of Myanmar have presented 3 straight sessions, and heads of state/government of other ASEAN countries also made attendance in the CAEXPO. Since the 7th ASEAN-China Summit held in 2003, the CAEXPO has been talked in the Chairman's Statement for 8 times, receiving high credits of Chinese and ASEAN leaders.

Over the past 7 years, the CAEXPO has established a unique co-sponsoring mechanism that involves China and the 10 ASEAN member states.

(I) A Chinese organizing committee composed of competent Chinese ministries and commissions

An organizing committee was established at the very beginning, chaired by the ministers of commerce/trade and industry of China and the 10 ASEAN countries as well as Secretary General of the ASEAN. A vice premier of the State Council of China acts as the Honorary Chairman of it. The Chinese organizing committee constitutes of 15 ministries and commissions, including the General Office of the State Council, Ministry of Commerce, Publicity Department of the Central Committee of Communist Party of China (CCCPC), Ministry of Foreign Affairs, National

Development and Reform Commission, Ministry of Science and Technology, Ministry of Finance, Ministry of Public Security, Ministry of Transport, General Administration of Customs, General Administration of Quality Supervision, Inspection and Quarantine, National Tourism Administration, State Food and Drug Administration, State Council Information Office, China Council for the Promotion of International Trade (CCPIT), and the People's Government of Guangxi Zhuang Autonomous Region. All the ministries grant kind cooperation and assistance to the CAEXPO. Going forward, they also arranged high-end forums, conferences and programs on their respective field during the CAEXPO, to promote and enrich bilateral cooperation between China and ASEAN. The CAEXPO forges an efficient platform for the cooperation between Chinese ministries and ASEAN countries.

Certain ASEAN countries including Vietnam, Laos, Thailand and Indonesia also have established similar CAEXPO organizing committees, contributing great guarantee for the successful conclusion of the CAEXPO.

(II) The 11-country co-sponsorship to embody the objectives for reciprocal win-win outcomes

The co-sponsoring mechanism is a unique feature of the CAEXPO and the foundation for its success. For years, with the joint efforts made by the Co-organizers in China and the 10 ASEAN countries, the CAEXPO's reciprocal and win-win co-sponsoring mechanism is further cemented and deepened. We have established a 3-layer working mechanism of the organizing committee, i.e. the Co-chairs acted by ministers of commerce/trade and industry, Vice Secretaries General acted by directors general and Liaison Officers by division directors, negotiation mechanisms like the CAEXPO Senior Officials Meeting and Liaison Officers Meeting, and the allocation of National Pavilion through lots drawing. We have also established the Country of Honor mechanism, and state leader of the country concerned will head the government delegation to visit the event.

With these measures, we have established a co-sponsoring mechanism featuring equality, mutual respect, joint efforts in event preparation and active participation of relevant parties. And with such a co-sponsoring mechanism, ASEAN countries can effectively showcase their advantages and strength at the CAEXPO, which in turn promotes the sustained growth of the event and guarantees the success of each session.

(III) Open to the whole world, the CAEXPO captures keen interests of chambers of commerce and enterprises of China and the 10 ASEAN countries.

Over the past 7 years, Chinese and ASEAN chambers of commerce and enterprises have followed closely the global trend and deepened bilateral reciprocal cooperation via the platform of the CAEXPO. We have invited 41 chambers of commerce of both sides to be the CAEXPO Supporting Chambers of Commerce to accelerate the CAFTA construction and comprehensive economic cooperation between China and ASEAN.

In addition to the active participation of Chinese and ASEAN enterprises, the CAEXPO attracts businesses representing the United States, Japan, France, Germany,

Australia, Canada and other countries and regions outside CAFTA. The event has greatly boosted the exchange of those countries with China and ASEAN, further cementing mutual understanding, and improving the international influence of China and ASEAN as a whole.

III. In face of new condition, Guangxi, the CAEXPO Organizer, will pool all needed resources to well organize the event, in a bid to better serve the China-ASEAN friendly cooperation.

Over the past 7 years, as the CAEXPO Organizer, Guangxi has maintained concerted efforts and maximized all the resources of the province to prepare for the CAEXPO. Guangxi established the CAEXPO & CABIS Guangxi Leaders Group headed by the Governor and also the CAEXPO & CABIS Commanding Center that was composed of relevant departments and organizations to facilitate the event preparations.

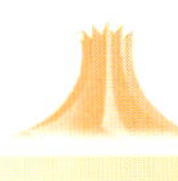

With the China-ASEAN FTA coming into force, the bilateral cooperation between China and ASEAN enters a new stage for overall development. China's 12th Five-year Plan defines the goal of building Guangxi as a new base for China's cooperation with ASEAN, therefore, Guangxi will be presented ample room to perform as a gateway to ASEAN. Guided by the Plan, we will practically implement the ***Opinions of the State Council of China on Further Promoting Economic and Social Development of Guangxi*** and the ***Guangxi Beibu Gulf Economic Zone Development Scheme***, and adopt effective measures to successfully organize the CAEXPO, thus to leverage the advantages of Guangxi and foster a sound platform for the China-ASEAN cooperation. More concerted efforts will be made in the following 3 aspects:

To perfect the long-term mechanism on organizing the CAEXPO: We will, via the Leaders Group for Guangxi-ASEAN Cooperation and its General Coordination Office, step up our efforts to optimize the CAEXPO working mechanism and help Chinese and ASEAN enterprises to understand in a better way the policies, rules and facilitations of the China-ASEAN FTA, practically propelling China's cooperation with the ASEAN countries in transportation infrastructures, agricultural resource, major industries, ports and harbors, logistics, tourism, building of common market, economic cooperation zone, human resource, culture, sport and other more fields.

To continue the utilization of all resources in Guangxi to ensure a more successful CAEXPO: In line with the demands raised by the CAFTA construction, Guangxi will anchor and expand the role of the CAEXPO as a crucial platform for the China-ASEAN cooperation, in particular, for fueling the CAFTA construction. The utilization of all resources in Guangxi will remain unchanged to make the CAEXPO a high-end and distinctive program as always. We will arrange more specialized exhibitions to match the CAFTA construction and progress of the China-ASEAN practical cooperation, to encourage and support enterprises' outward investment. We will also invest more efforts in building information platform, making the 5-day CAEXPO an exposition that works all year around, thus allow the Chinese and ASEAN enterprises to enjoy more effectively the benefits of CAFTA. Aggressive endeavor will also be made in expanding cultural, educational and sport cooperation to enrich and upgrade the role of the CAEXPO, which was originally centered on trade and investment cooperation. Furthermore, we will leverage the Nanning Channel for China–ASEAN cooperation to attract more cooperation mechanisms to settle in Nanning, to provide better service for the comprehensive cooperation between China and ASEAN.

To better utilize Guangxi's geographical advantages and the CAEXPO as a cooperation platform for more fruitful friendly cooperation between China and ASEAN: Guangxi will bring into full play the CAEXPO as a platform for cooperation, perfect infrastructure construction, especially the transportation facilities, and promote connectivity, and press ahead with the implementation of ***Guangxi Beibu Gulf Economic Zone Development Scheme***. Specific measures will include construction of major projects, inclusive of the China (Qinzhou)–Malaysia Industrial Park and the China–Vietnam Transborder Economic Cooperation Zone, acceleration of the Greater Mekong Sub–regional Cooperation, Pan–Beibu Gulf Economic Cooperation, Two Corridors & One Rim Cooperation and Nanning–Singapore Economic Corridor, being more contributable to the China–ASEAN friendly cooperation.

本届概述

2010年1月1日，中国—东盟自由贸易区全面建成，这是中国—东盟关系的一件大事。对于肩负着推动中国—东盟自贸区建设重任的中国—东盟博览会而言，中国—东盟自由贸易区全面建成既是荣耀，也是进一步发展的动力。中国—东盟博览会的使命并未因此而终止，而是要站在一个新的历史起点上，更加深入地推进中国—东盟自由贸易区建设，促进中国—东盟友好合作。

2010年10月19日至10月24日，第七届中国—东盟博览会在中国广西南宁成功举办。中国和东盟国家领导人、部长级贵宾、国际组织代表、各国商协会会长、世界知名企业家共同出席此次盛会，表明了各方抓住中国—东盟自由贸易区建成的重大机遇，发挥中国—东盟博览会平台作用，加强全面合作，深化互利共赢的共同愿望，增强了各方继续共同推进中国—东盟自由贸易区建设，深化战略伙伴关系，实现共同发展、共同繁荣的信心和决心。本届中国—东盟博览会在促进中国—东盟友好交流、提高经贸实效、拓展多领域合作等方面，迈上了新的台阶。

2010年10月19日，第七届中国—东盟博览会在广西南宁隆重开幕

The 7th CAEXPO grandly opens in Nanning of Guangxi on October 19, 2010

一 谱写中国—东盟友好交流新篇章

在中国—东盟自由贸易区如期建成背景下举办的第七届中国—东盟博览会不仅是经贸盛会，也是政治、外交的舞台，在加强全面合作、深化共办共赢、促进双方战略伙伴关系等方面取得了新的成效，全方位深化和促进了中国与东盟友好交流合作。

中共中央政治局常委、全国政协主席贾庆林，东盟国家4位领导人和中外191位部长级贵宾出席，东盟10国、东盟秘书处、中国国内36个省区市以及法国、德国、加拿大等区域国家和地区组团参会，联合国工发组织负责人出席盛会。其中，印度尼西亚作为第七届博览会的主题国，派出了132人的代表团参展参会，除了副总统布迪约诺外，还包括12名部级官员。各国领导人的高度重视，既很好地促进了中国和东盟各国的友好交流，也有利于11国从政府层面来推动经贸以及其他各个领域的交流与合作。

出席第七届中国—东盟博览会的各国政要对中国—东盟博览会给予高度评价。贾庆林主席说，中国—东盟博览会已成为中国同东盟国家对话、交流、合作的有效平台。印度尼西亚副总统布迪约诺表示，在中国—东盟自由贸易区建成之际举办的第七届博览会具有特殊的意义，不仅为双方商家企业展示产品、宣传形象、结识新伙伴提供了便利，创造了商机，而且也将推动东盟与中国在竞争日益激烈的全球市场中进一步加强经济合作，最终实现共赢。

会期举行了一系列活动，增进了了解和互信，促进了中国与东盟的伙伴关系。其中，贾庆林主席会见了印尼、老挝、越南3国领导人，与东盟其他国家和东盟秘书处代表团团长进行了集体会见；广西壮族自治区领导分别拜会或会见东盟国家领导人、东盟各代表团团长和友城代表团；中外领导人和各代表团团长还出席了中国—东盟博览会开幕式、中国—东盟商务与投资峰会开幕式、主题国国家馆开馆仪式、巡视展馆、中国—东盟自由贸易区建设成就展、南宁国际民歌艺术节暨第七届中国—东盟博览会开幕晚会、中国—东盟商务区各国商务联络部办公楼移交仪式等重要活动，进一步密切了双方友好交流。第七届博览会在促进双方友好合作方面形成了新的亮点：

一是交流层次更加丰富。本博览会除了有国家领导人之间的会见，还安排了东盟国家政要与企业家、国内省市领导的对话交流活动。例如，海南省领导与新加坡的部长级官员举行了会谈，马来西亚贸工部副部长会见了国内有关企业负责人。

二是交流渠道进一步拓宽。会期增加了商协会之间的交流及行业对接活动，推动商界合作。还围绕文化、新闻、体育等领域，举行了一系列交流活动，增进了解，促进友好往来。

2010年10月18日，中国—东盟自由贸易区建设成就展在广西南宁举行

Achievement Exhibition on CAFTA Construction in Nanning, Guangxi, China on October 18, 2010

三是城市间交流更加务实。创新了“魅力之城”活动的形式和内容，举办了“魅力之城”宴会、专场推介会、“魅力之城”移交仪式等。广西钦州市作为中国“魅力之城”，与各国城市增进友谊，开展务实合作，扩大了广西北部湾经济区的国际影响力。

二　展会内容创新　经贸成效再创新高

第七届中国—东盟博览会根据自贸区建成的新需求，优化展览内容，在继续办好农业展、金融展的基础上，增加服务贸易专题，新增珠宝展，新设东盟品牌展区、食品展区和木材家具展区，得到了企业的欢迎，企业踊跃参展，参展企业质量明显提升，经贸成效再创新高。

一是展位供不应求，重复参展率显著提高。中国国内企业、东盟国家申请及使用商品展位均创历届新高，外国展位数居国内同类展会前列。博览会专业化水平和市场认知度进一步提升。其中，国际经济合作展、工程机械与运输车辆、包装机械的重复参展率分别达到90%、82%和52%。柬埔寨重复参展率达到76%、新加坡达到55%，缅甸达到45.9%。招商组展工作更专业化和市场化，行业对接进一步加强。中国国内自行报名和行业协会组织参展等市场手段组展的展位数量占展位总数的80%，远高于政府组展的比例。东盟10国在本国展区设立了品牌展区、食品展区和家具展区，35家东盟知名品牌企业参加品牌展，成为本届博览会专业买家关注的焦点。服务贸易专题吸引参展单位49家，使用展位160个，展示了金融、物流和文化教育三个重点领域。本届博览会还积极拓展工商会、专业行业商协会及中介机构等合作渠道，继续深化与东盟共办方、支持商协会的合作，挖掘更多资源，推动招商组展的专业化。

二是采购商团组的行业采购特色突出，团组配对覆盖率达到100%。采购商团组较往届明显增加。除了中国和东盟国家外，法国、德国、澳

第七届中国—东盟博览会商品贸易专题东盟商品展区
The 7th CAEXPO ASEAN Commodity Section

大利亚、美国、加拿大和日本等区域外国家和地区数量更多、质量更高的采购商团组参会，团组数量比上届增加50%。博览会通过组织采购团巡馆、商贸对接等更具针对性的活动，以及制作采购商和投资商标志、徽章等方式，促进了企业间的互动。

三是贸易配对更有针对性，客商满意度普遍提高。会期举办了三场大型贸易对接会，东盟国家和国内各省区市采购团与参展企业进行了对接，采购企业总数达到了376家。会期将东盟各国采购团的采购对接活动集中举办，活动吸引了众多国内参展企业积极参与。各采购团和参展企业均对此次采购对接活动表示满意。本届博览会还首次邀请联合国机构举办采购说明会，国内外企业表现出极大兴趣。

四是专业展取得良好成效。本届博览会农业展展示了中国、马来西亚、日本、新西兰等国家和地区的众多名优产品和品牌企业，特别是台湾岛内企业成规模参展，展位数超过100个，展示了台湾特色水果、茶叶、特色食品等，成为一个亮点。农业展商品成交9544.7万美元，同比增长70.5%。珠宝展吸引了全国各大珠宝产业基地代表产品踊跃参展，贸易成交额达到1200万美元，举办了国际彩色宝石名人论坛，搭建了珠宝业合作的新平台。

五是行业对接更加务实。会期举行了两场东盟主要参展行业的工作会议——中国—东盟博览会食品与农产品商协会工作会议和中国—东盟博览会木材与木制品商协会工作会议，这是博览会首次举办中国—东盟行业合作工作会议。双方相关行业商协会及重要企业代表共同商讨以博览会为平台，进一步开展行业合作，并在条件成熟后酝酿新的专业展。

六是商品贸易成交活跃，成交量大幅提高。本届博览会交易总额达到17.12亿美元，比2009年增长3.5%。其中，东盟国家商品贸易成交额7.17亿美元,同比增长154%；国内商品贸易成交额9.85亿美元。东盟出口到中国的贸易额明显增长，同比增长12.3%。东盟国家和国内大部分省区市成交量明显上升。作为本届博览会主题国，印尼的商品贸易成交额比2009年增长了85倍，新加坡增长了23倍，越南和泰国分别增长了727%和45%。天津、福建、安徽、山西、黑龙江、贵州、甘肃、宁夏、内蒙古等中国国内省区市的商品贸易成交额成倍增长。

七是中国与东盟加强投资合作的共识进一步落到实处。会期举行了中国—东盟博览会投资合作工作会议，东盟各国投资促进部门和东盟秘书处参加了会议。与会各方共同商讨通过博览会平台，加强本国投资促进部门、地方政府和产业园区间合作，重点做好中国企业“走出去”和东盟国家投引资项目的对接。东盟方对第七届博览会继续加强开展投资合作的工作表示高度赞赏。

八是投资促进活动更具针对性。会期共组织了46场投资推介、投资促进和项目对接活动，活动涉及行业领域更广，层次更深，专业性务实性更强，邀请渠道拓宽，企业参与积极性普遍增强，活动现场气氛更活跃。东盟各国投资推介会广受欢迎。东盟方充分肯定国家推介会是推动双方在投资领域合作的有效平台。投融资项目对接会现场对接效果明显。100多家中国实力雄厚的对外投资企业、股（权）投资机构、项目咨询机构以及东盟投资促进机构和投资商参会，500多个投融资项目实现对接。

九是投资合作更有成效。会期共签订国际经济合作项目135个，总投资额66.9亿美元，比上届增长3%。其中，中国与东盟签约的投资合作项目58个，总投资额26.63亿美元，分别占国际经济合作项目的43%和38%。项目数量多，涉及农业、制造业、商贸物流、旅游开发、矿产开采及加工、交通能源设施建设等更多领域，合作质量进一步提升。本届博览会签署中国国内经济合作项目156个，总投资674.46亿元，比上届增长9%。

第七届中国—东盟博览会上举行的中国湖南—东盟产业合作对接会

The Industrial Cooperation Meeting Between Hunan(China) and ASEAN at the 7th CAEXPO

三　推动中国—东盟多领域合作走向纵深

第七届中国—东盟博览会紧扣“自贸区与新机遇”的重点主题，同期举办第七届中国—东盟商务与投资峰会，举办9个高规格会议、论坛和系列文化体育交流活动，在务实推动中国—东盟全方位、多层次、宽领域合作方面取得良好成效。

第七届中国—东盟商务与投资峰会以“中国—东盟自由贸易区与区域经贸合作的展望”为主题，进一步推进务实合作。中国和东盟国家领导人出席并发表了演讲。会期举行了东盟国家领导人与中国企业家CEO圆桌对话会、中国—东盟商会领袖论坛和物流、机械、矿业等行业论坛，形式更加新颖，交流更加深入。中共中央政治局常委、全国政协主席贾庆林评价说，在东盟各国政府、商协会、企业界的鼎力支持和积极参与下，中国—东盟博览会、中国—东盟商务与投资峰会已成为中国同东盟国家对话、交流、合作的有效平台。

本届博览会期间举办的第二届中国—东盟金融合作与发展领袖论坛围绕“深化合作机制，构建中国—东盟自由贸易区互利共赢金融发展新格局”的主题，就进一步拓展自贸区金融合作平台，构建自贸区互利共赢金融发展新格局，更好地服务于区域内各领域合作，推动区域经济一体化，进行了深入交流，通过了《论坛共识》。论坛首次增设的中国—东盟银行家圆桌会议形成了《中国—东盟银行家圆桌会议倡议》。中国人民银行行长助理李东荣表示，金融论坛作为中国—东盟开展更紧密的金融合作而搭建的一个新平台，促进了中国—东盟金融领域合作有序深入开展，进一步丰富、拓展了中国—东盟博览会的平台作用。

中国—印度尼西亚能源论坛务实促进了中国和印尼能源合作。论坛探讨了中国—东盟自贸区建成背景下双方的能源合作，双方企业还围绕加强石油天然气、可再生能源、电力和煤炭等方面互利合作的内容进行

2010年10月19日，第七届中国—东盟商务与投资峰会在广西南宁开幕

The 7th CABIS held in Nanning, Guangxi on October 19, 2010

了深入讨论，签署了《印尼巴厘岛塞露坎巴湾电厂股东合资协议书》等多项合作协议。

本届博览会为中国与东盟在更多领域开展合作提供了广阔平台。会期还举办了中国—东盟社会发展与减贫论坛、首届中国—东盟红十字论坛、第三届中国—东盟智库战略对话、中国—东盟海事磋商机制第六次会议、第三届中国—东盟电力合作与发展论坛暨中国—东盟电力经贸合作洽谈会、2010中国—东盟国际口腔医学交流与合作论坛、“加强国际司法交流与合作，促进区域经济发展与繁荣”研讨会等。各场论坛规格高，均有中国和东盟国家部长级官员、国家直属企业负责人、国际知名专家学者出席。论坛的举办体现了各方抓住中国—东盟自由贸易区建成的新机遇，深化合作的共同愿望；进一步完善并深化了博览会已形成的磋商合作和对话机制，进一步发挥了中国—东盟合作“南宁渠道”的作用。

本届博览会“魅力之城”继续把中国—东盟友好合作从国家层向进一步延伸到城市层面。“魅力之城”专题活动更加丰富多彩，更加深入务实。会期，各国领导人和代表团团长分别巡视了“魅力之城”展区，举办了“魅力中国·钦州之夜”宴会，11国魅力之城结为“友谊之城”，推进了中国与东盟国家城市之间的合作；举办了“魅力之城”专场推介会，开展务实合作，扩大了“魅力之城”与企业的合作；推出了博览会魅力之城“护照”，以民众喜闻乐见的形式介绍11国“魅力之城”；博览会为每个“魅力之城”设计了印章，专门举办了第八届博览会中国“魅力之城”移交仪式，体现在充满机遇的自贸区环境下，城市之间友好交流、互利共赢的愿望，也象征着中国—东盟博览会“魅力之城”的传承与发展。会期，东盟各国客商还到本届博览会中国“魅力之城”钦州市进行了考察。

本届博览会举行了丰富多彩的文化体育交流活动，促进了文化体育

“魅力之城”展区
Pavilion of Cities of Charm

流光溢彩的第十二届“大地飞歌”南宁国际民歌艺术节

The 12th Nanning International Arts Festival of Folk Songs & Inauguration of the 7th CAEXPO

交流。会期举办了南宁国际民歌艺术节暨第七届中国—东盟博览会开幕晚会，打造中国—东盟文化艺术交流的盛宴；举办高尔夫名人邀请赛、网球联谊活动、中国—东盟汽车拉力赛暨中国—东盟媒体汽车拉力赛，成为中国与东盟各国加强体育交流、增进沟通与了解的重要平台；举办青年艺术品创作等活动，深入推进中国与东盟青年在文化等领域的交流与合作。丰富多彩的文化体育交流活动，增进了中国和东盟各国人民的友谊，进一步拓宽了双方合作领域，促进了双方合作。

四　展示自贸区共赢成果　彰显自贸区辉煌成就

与第七届中国—东盟博览会与中国—东盟商务与投资峰会同期举办的中国—东盟自由贸易区建设成就展，对中国—东盟自由贸易区的建设历程与成就进行了生动展现，得到了各方的好评。

展览由中国—东盟自贸区成就展区，中国—东盟博览会、中国—东盟商务与投资峰会成就展区和艺术展区组成，以时间发展为主线，以图片、图表、文字、音视频等形式呈现，全面反映中国与东盟各国在中国—东盟自贸区的建设过程以及在政治、经济、文化、社会等方面取得的巨大成就。

在中国—东盟自贸区成就展区，中国—东盟自贸区建设历程和辉煌成就得以充分展示。历程部分回顾了自贸区建设的大事，从1991年中国与东盟开始对话合作，到2010年1月1日中国—东盟自贸区如期建成，各阶段主要事件逐一展现。成就部分主要展示中国—东盟自贸区深化双方战略伙伴关系、务实推动双方的经贸合作以及拓展加深双方多领域合作、催生并巩固了众多的合作机制等方面取得的成就，包括在中国—东盟自贸区逐步实施降税的背景下，双方在货物贸易、服务贸易、双向投资以及农业、信息通讯、人力资源开发、交通、能源、文化和旅游、公共卫生等11个重点领域广泛合作的成果，充分反映中国与东盟携手合作、互利共赢的大好局面。

成就展的“两会”展区集中展示了中国—东盟博览会、中国—东盟商务与投资峰会在推动中国—东盟自贸区建设等方面的重要作用。该展区通过历届国家领导人和部长级贵宾出席图片，博览会开幕式模型，“魅力之城”展示，历届博览会经贸成效数据以及商务与投资峰会、各主题论坛和高规格专业论坛等精彩内容，充分展示了2004年首届中国—东盟博览会和中国—东盟商务与投资峰会举办以来，“两会”对深化区域合作、推动中国—东盟自贸区建设，促进中国与东盟商企合作，以及推动中国与其他国家和地区友好交流、多领域合作发挥的巨大作用。“两会”展区匠心独运地把七届博览会的开幕式场景制作成微缩模型，再现经典瞬间。

艺术展区是成就展特殊而又重要的组成部分，其通过艺术的形式展示了中国与东盟的交流与合作。艺术展共展出中国和东盟艺术家创作的400多件作品，包括书法、美术、摄影、篆刻和少儿作品等。这些作品内容多以中国—东盟自贸区建设进程和成就为题材。中国和东盟10国领导人寄语博览会为内容的书法长卷是其中的最大亮点，展示了博览会对中国—东盟自贸区建设的独特贡献以及自贸区的美好未来。本次展览东盟10国均有艺术家参与创作，参加创作的东盟国家艺术家共有66位，占全部艺术家的近三成。

社会各界对自贸区成就展高度关注。据不完全统计，参观人数达十多万人。马来西亚贸工部副部长拿督贾谷·东加·沙甘说，成就展办得很好，可以使人们清楚地了解到自贸区及博览会一步步成长的历程。印尼工商会馆中国委员会副秘书长施锦场认为，中国—东盟自贸区建设成就展集中展示了中国—东盟自贸区建设的成果，反映中国与东盟互利共赢，进一步增强了大家共建中国—东盟自贸区的决心。

中国—东盟自由贸易区建设成就展艺术展区

Artwork Show of the CAFTA Achievements Exhibition

五　中外媒体关注热度不减　博览会品牌知名度不断提升

中国—东盟博览会不仅是中国与东盟各国经贸交流的盛会，也是一场全球媒体的盛会。第七届中国—东盟博览会期间，中外媒体聚焦南宁，进一步提升了中国—东盟博览会的品牌知名度和影响力。

第七届中国—东盟博览会继续受到海内外主流媒体和专业媒体的高度关注。参与本届博览会报道的中外媒体层次高、数量大、记者人数多。据统计，共有199家中外媒体、1458名记者参会报道第七届博览会，到会记者人数比2009年增加39名。其中，东盟媒体72家88人，创国内同类活动参与的东盟媒体之最。与会媒体发稿量大、报道集中，高潮迭起。据不完全统计，媒体累计发稿9900多篇；网络报道页面9460篇，网络相关新闻转载与链接页面85万余条。

中国中央媒体及港澳主流媒体报道力度大，质量高。《人民日报》推出博览会特刊，刊发博览会重点稿件。新华社通过文字、摄影、音视频等对博览会进行全方位立体报道。中央电视台派出30人的报道团队参加本届博览会的宣传报道工作。《国际商报》推出“中国—东盟博览会专版”。《香港文汇报》、《香港商报》、《澳门日报》等为博览会开辟专栏。

东盟媒体及区域外媒体高度关注，重点报道。文莱、印尼、菲律宾、泰国、越南等东盟国家以及日本、希腊等国家的84家主流媒体，均在头版头条或重要版面刊登、发表博览会相关新闻报道。泰国《星暹日报》刊登了《第七届中国—东盟博览会揭幕　贾庆林出席并宣布开幕》、《水润花开 共享硕果》等大量文章对第七届博览会进行了重点宣传报道。菲律宾《商报》发表了《中国—东盟博览会落幕　10万民众“触摸”东盟风情》等文章。马来西亚《光华日报》等东盟媒体也进行了大量报道。

第七届中国—东盟博览会现场直播时间长，影响面广。中央电视台

第七届中国—东盟博览会上媒体云集
Media at the 7th CAEXPO

新闻频道、第四频道、中央人民广播电台、中国国际广播电台、广西电视台、广西人民广播电台、广东人民广播电台、越南之声、越南广宁省广播电视台等主要媒体均对博览会开幕式进行了现场直播，把博览会的盛况及时向广大观（听）众传播。人民网、新华网、中国网络电视台、国际在线、中国新闻网等10家网站也强势出击，以图文、视频等方式对博览会开幕式、东盟国家领导人与企业家圆桌对话、中国—东盟商会领袖论坛等博览会重要活动进行网络直播，在互联网上形成强大声势。

多种语言直通东盟，形成立体传播态势。中国国际广播电台派出23人采访团队，用文莱语、柬埔寨语、印尼语、老挝语等东盟10国语言和中文、英语播发博览会新闻，并在北美、柬埔寨、老挝等国家落地播出。中国新闻社对外通稿被东盟各国、美国、澳大利亚以及港澳台地区的媒体广泛采用，中国新闻社还向东盟国家主流媒体提供英语、泰语、越南语、柬埔寨语等专版报道，在海外产生重大影响。国际在线推出英、印尼、老挝、马来、缅甸、菲律宾、泰国、越南等8个语种的专题报道，全面报道博览会盛况。

广西媒体各展所长，突破创新宣传形式。《广西日报》、广西电视台、广西人民广播电台、广西新闻网等区直媒体相继开设专刊专栏，组织策划“创新及亮点系列、重点贵宾和企业专访系列、专业性宣传系列、博览会论坛宣传系列”等系列宣传报道活动，全方位、多角度开展宣传报道，全面提升博览会的影响力。

第七届中国—东盟博览会深受与会媒体、记者好评。《人民日报》在报道中评论称，作为中国—东盟自由贸易区建成后首次举办的博览会，第七届中国—东盟博览会充分反映了自贸区的建设成果，内容更丰富，针对性更强，成效更显著，为双方企业和人民带来了更多实惠。新华社在报道中评论称，中国—东盟博览会已成为世界通往中国—东盟自贸区的最佳桥梁。柬埔寨《华商日报》记者张戈西说：“在中国—东盟自贸区如期建成的背景下，第七届中国—东盟博览会的举办具有特殊意义。从东盟各国赶来参会的贵宾们带来的贸易投资成果，更让今年的博览会有了更多的实质性的内容。”马来西亚《光华日报》记者周圣栋说：“中国—东盟博览会的成功举办是整个中国与东盟国家的成功，自贸区的建立更是促进双边经济贸易的里程碑，将成为跨时代的一个经济合作计划，为两边人民创造无限的商机。”

六　发挥平台效应　带动广西经济发展

中国—东盟博览会连续七届在广西南宁成功举办，在促进中国—东盟友好合作的同时，对提升广西对外开放水平和拉动广西经济发展的作用进一步显现。

第七届中国—东盟博览会推动广西在更多领域和更深层面参与国际国内区域合作。本届博览会期间，广西壮族自治区领导与东盟国家领导人、各国代表团、友好城市代表团等举行了17场会见，就共建广西北部湾经济区，共促泛北部湾经济合作、大湄公河次区域合作、南宁—新加坡经济走廊，共同服务中国—东盟自贸区发展，达成广泛共识。

钦州作为中国“魅力之城”在本届博览会上成果喜人。会期，钦州市代表团拜会了马来西亚贸工部副部长等东盟国家部长级官员和东盟国家商协会会长，与东盟国家、韩国、香港、台湾等地的众多知名企业实现了“无缝”对接，与国内其他省市的商贸代表团进行了全方位交流。会期钦州举办了商机推介会、4场产业专场推介会、商务研讨会、钦州活动日、钦州之夜等活动，每场活动都高朋满座，带来无限商机。博览会期间钦州签订了51个项目，总投资238亿元人民币，并与东盟10国的“魅力之城”结为“友谊之城”。5天内，马来西亚（钦州）产业园项目由提出迅速提升为两国商务部门共同推进的项目，韩国（钦州）产业园的建设有了实质性进展。

第七届中国—东盟博览会为广西各地市与东盟国家和中国省区市之间交流合作搭建了良好平台，进一步推动了广西各地经济发展。本届博览会期间，防城港市领导拜会了越南领导人。文莱、柬埔寨、马来西亚、菲律宾、新加坡、越南等国家的代表团顺访了南宁、桂林、玉林、钦州、百色、防城港、崇左，考察有关企业和投资合作项目。会期还举办了中国凭祥—越南同登跨境经济合作区工作商讨会、桂琼战略合作重点工作计划协议签署仪式等，促进了广西与东盟国家和国内省区市之间的合作。

本届博览会扩大了广西与友城间的交流与合作，推动建立更多友城。菲律宾友城宿务省、日本友城熊本县、韩国友城忠清北道分别派出

“魅力中国·钦州之夜”活动
Night of Qinzhou

中国凭祥—越南同登跨境经济合作区工作商讨会

Pingxiang (China) - Dong Dang (Vietnam) Cross Border Economic Cooperation Zone Working Meeting

代表团参会，并组织企业参展。会期，友城代表团拜会了广西壮族自治区领导，积极参与各项活动，进一步加强了与广西的友好交流与合作。广西也通过会见和座谈等方式积极推动缔结更多东盟国家友城。

第七届中国—东盟博览会使得广西对外资的吸引力进一步增强。第七届博览会投资合作签约项目中，广西签订利用外资项目84个，总投资44.26亿美元，分别比上届增长42.3%和17.1%；中国国内21个省区市和中央直属企业对广西的投资合作项目146个，投资总额671亿元人民币，比上届增长10.8%。

第七届中国—东盟博览会进一步促进了广西会展业发展。在博览会巨大的品牌效应、辐射效应的驱动下，本届博览会期间和博览会后，广西各地先后举办了第七届梧州国际宝石节、2010年中国—东盟现代农业展示交易会、第十八届中越商品交易会、第七届中小企业商机博览（中国·玉林）等展会，推动了各地市的对外开放和经济社会发展。

第七届中国—东盟博览会带来了巨大的人流、物流、信息流、资金流，给南宁市相关行业带来了明显的经济效益。博览会期间，主要接待宾馆客房收入同比稳步增长，81家主要接待宾馆、酒店的平均入住率为49.21%，客房收入3114万元，同比增长13.63%，累计接待住客8.72万人次。客货运输繁忙活跃，五大公路客运站累计出发和到站车次44508次，旅客37.34万人次，发送旅客47.56万人次；铁路旅客15.37万人次，发送15.62万人次。物流量明显提高，铁路、民航进出南宁市的货物量分别达到91.5万吨和1050吨，同比分别增长1.63%和8.47%。南宁吴圩国际机场累计起、降航班1010次，比2009年同期增长3.7%，经由航空抵达和发送的旅客人数分别达到5.93万人次和5.84万人次，分别比2009年同期增长12.8%和9.2%。接待游客再创新高，达到30.91万人次，同比增长71.29%，为历届博览会之最。

The 7th China-ASEAN Expo

Overview

The on-scheduled establishment of the China-ASEAN Free Trade Area (CAFTA) on January 1, 2010 is of great significance for the development of the China-ASEAN relations. The completion of the CAFTA is not only a glory for the China-ASEAN Expo (CAEXPO), which has always been dedicating itself to promoting this task, but also a new driving force for its own future development. Therefore, the CAFTA establishment is not an end of the CAEXPO's mission, but a new beginning for itself to further promote the CAFTA construction and to inject new vigor for the China-ASEAN friendly cooperation.

The 7th CAEXPO has been successfully concluded in Nanning, Guangxi, China on October 19-24, 2010. Chinese and ASEAN heads of state/government, VIPs at ministerial-level, representatives of international organizations, chairpersons/presidents of chambers of commerce and trade associations and world renowned entrepreneurs show presence at the event, reflecting the confidence and decision of all the parties concerned to seize the great opportunity brought by the CAFTA establishment to enrich their strategic partnership, so as to achieve common development and prosperity. To this end, the 7th CAEXPO has effectively promoted the friendly exchanges, economic outcomes and bilateral cooperation in various fields.

I. A new chapter for China-ASEAN friendly exchanges

The 7th CAEXPO, which is held against the backdrop of the due establishment of CAFTA, is not only a grand economic and trade event, but also a stage for politics and diplomacy. It has further enhanced bilateral comprehensive cooperation, strengthened the CAEXPO co-sponsoring mechanism for win-win results and promoted bilateral strategic partnership, and thus deepened the bilateral friendly exchanges and cooperation in an all-rounded way.

H.E. Jia Qinglin, Member of the Standing Committee of the Political Bureau of the Communist Party of China (CPC) and Chairman of the National Committee of the Chinese People's Political Consultative Conference (CPPCC) and state leaders of 4 ASEAN countries as well as 191 VIPs at ministerial level personally visit the 7th

CAEXPO. Business professionals from the 10 ASEAN member states, the ASEAN Secretariat, 36 Chinese provinces and municipalities as well as countries/regions outside China–ASEAN region like Germany and Canada participate in the event. Leader of the United Nations Industrial Development Organization (UNIDO) also attends the event. It is worth noting that, the 7th CAEXPO welcomes 132 participants including Vice President Boediono and 12 ministerial–level officials from Indonesia, which is the Country of Honor of the year.

Great importance granted by state leaders of the countries concerned not only further promote China–ASEAN friendly exchanges, but also better enhance the bilateral exchanges and cooperation in the fields like economy and trade from government level.

Participating state leaders and VIPs make high credits on the 7th CAEXPO. Chairman Jia Qinglin said that the CAEXPO has become an effective platform for the dialogues, exchanges and cooperation between China and the ASEAN countries. Vice President Boediono of Indonesia said that the 7th CAEXPO is of particular significance, as it is held at the occasion of the CAFTA establishment. It has not only provided convenience and opportunities for enterprises of both sides to showcase products, promote company images and establish new business links, but also advance the bilateral economic cooperation in the increasingly competitive international market, so as to achieve win–win results.

A series of programs/activities are held during the fair period, enhancing mutual understanding and trust and also advancing the partnership of the two sides. Chairman Jia has bilateral meetings with state leaders of Indonesia, Lao PDR and Vietnam respectively, and has a group meeting with heads of the delegations of other ASEAN countries and the ASEAN Secretariat. Top leaders of Guangxi Zhuang Autonomous Region have audiences with state leaders of the ASEAN countries and meet with heads of delegations of other ASEAN countries and sister cities/provinces. In addition, Chinese and ASEAN state leaders and other heads of government delegations show their presence at major events, including the opening ceremonies of the 7th CAEXPO and the 7th CABIS, pavilion tours to the CAEXPO exhibitions, the Achievement Exhibition of CAFTA Construction, the Nanning International Arts Festival of Folk Songs & Gala Show for the Inauguration of the 7th CAEXPO and the Handover Ceremony of Business Liaison Offices of China–ASEAN Business Park, further enhancing bilateral friendly exchanges with highlights as follows:

1. More diversified forms of bilateral exchanges: Apart from meetings of state leaders, dialogues between high–ranking officials of the ASEAN countries and Chinese provincial/municipal leaders or entrepreneurs are also arranged during the fair period. For example, leader of Hainan Province of China has a dialogue with Singaporean minister, and Malaysian Deputy Minister of International Trade and Industry has a meeting with relevant Chinese entrepreneurs.

2. Widened channels of bilateral exchanges: The 7th CAEXPO, for the first time, introduces the networking programs for major chambers of commerce/trade associations of different industrial sectors, promoting business cooperation. Additionally, a series of exchanging programs for other fields like culture, press and sports are also arranged, as did previously, further strengthening mutual understanding and friendly

cooperation.

3. More tangible city-to-city exchanges: The showcase of Cities of Charm is innovative and enriched. Besides the traditional programs, Qinzhou City, the 7th CAEXPO City of Charm of China held reception banquet, promotion conference and handover ceremony. As a core of Guangxi Beibu Gulf Economic Zone, Qinzhou, via the CAEXPO, has deepened friendship with its ASEAN counterparts, enhancing its influence in the world.

II. More innovative business promotion programs boost the economic and trade outcomes to a new high

To meet the new demands created by the CAFTA establishment, the 7th CAEXPO has optimized its exhibition contents and arranged more diversified business promotion programs. Apart from the traditional Agricultural Exhibition and Financial Exhibition, the 7th CAEXPO has newly introduced the Pavilion of Trade in Services, Jewelry Show, ASEAN Brand Galleria, Foodstuffs Show and Wood Furniture Show, which receive positive feedback from the participating enterprises. With the participation of more quality enterprises, the economic and trade outcomes of the 7th CAEXPO have hit a new historical high.

1. Booth demands are far more than the planned supply, with more repeat exhibiting enterprises. The number of Chinese booth applicants and that of ASEAN both hit new records. The number of booths used by foreign exhibitors outstands among similar trade fairs/expositions in China. It is worth noting that 90% of exhibiting enterprises of the International Economic Cooperation Exhibition are repeat exhibitors. Repeat exhibitor rate of the Engineering Machinery Exhibition is 82%, the Foodstuff Processing & Packaging Machinery Exhibition, 52%, and 76%, 55% and 45.9% exhibiting enterprises from Cambodia, Singapore and Myanmar respectively are repeat exhibitors of the CAEXPO.

More exhibitors and trade visitors/buyers are organized by professional exhibition companies and trade associations in specific sectors. Booths used by enterprises that directly register with the CAEXPO Secretariat or are organized by chambers of commerce and trade associations account for 80% of the total, much more than those organized by government departments. The 10 ASEAN countries have set up Brand Galleria, Foodstuff Show and Furniture Show at their own Pavilion of Commodity Trade. Among them, the Brand Gallerias, with the participation of 35 ASEAN brand enterprises, have attracted the eyeballs of professional buyers. 49 enterprises use 160 booths of the Pavilion of Trade in Services, showcasing services in 3 major fields, i.e. finance, logistics and culture & education.

The 7th CAEXPO has actively enhanced its partnership with chambers of commerce and industry, trade associations and exhibition agents, and deepened its cooperative relations with its ASEAN Co-sponsors and Supporting Chambers of Commerce, to explore more channels for the invitation of exhibitors and trade visitors in a more professional way.

2. Sourcing groups' procurement intentions are more targeted, and 100% of them are provided with business matching services. The number of sourcing groups is

sharply increased this year. Apart from those from China and ASEAN, more sourcing groups and buying missions come from France, Germany, Australia, U.S., Canada and Japan, with more brand enterprises. The total number of sourcing groups is 50% more than that at the previous session. By attending a series of programs arranged by the CAEXPO Secretariat, including visiting specific exhibitions and suppliers, taking part in business matching programs, the buying missions, wearing special buyers' or investors' badges, have more effective interactions with exhibitors.

3. Business professionals are more satisfied with the effective trade matching services provided at the 7th CAEXPO. 3 large–scaled trade matching programs are arranged during the fair period. ASEAN and Chinese buying missions, up to 376 enterprises, have had one–to–one business talks with the exhibiting enterprises. The business matching program tailored for ASEAN sourcing groups have also attracted the active participation of Chinese exhibiting enterprises. Besides, UN Sourcing Conference is held at this event for the first time, which has draw keen interests of enterprises from China and other countries.

4. Professional exhibitions have gained rich outcomes. The Agricultural Exhibition has showcased brand enterprises and products from China, Malaysia, Japan, and New Zealand. It is worth noting that enterprises from Chinese Taipei use over 100 booths to exhibit distinctive local fruits, tea and foodstuffs, which has become a highlight of the fair. Total trade volume has reached USD 95.447 million, 70.5% more than that of the previous year. Besides, the Jewelry Show, which attracts major Chinese jewelry production bases, has hit a total trade volume of USD 12 million. The concurrent International Colored Gemstone Celebrity Forum has built a new platform for cooperation in the sector.

5. More pragmatic business matching programs are arranged for specific industrial sectors. Two working meetings targeting two major ASEAN industries, i.e. the Working Meeting for Food & Agro–based Products Associations and the Working Meeting for Timber & Wood Product Associations, are held during the fair period. It is the first time that working meetings of such kind are held at the CAEXPO. Relevant associations and chambers of commerce as well as leading enterprises have in–depth discussions on using the CAEXPO as a platform to further enhance cooperation and organizing professional exhibitions at the CAEXPO when condition permits.

6. Trade volume is increased sharply. The total trade volume of the 7th CAEXPO has topped USD 1.712 billion, an year–on–year increase of 3.5%, among which, USD 717 million is concluded by ASEAN enterprises, up 154% than that of the previous session, and USD 985 million by Chinese enterprises. ASEAN countries and most Chinese provinces and municipalities have witnessed a large increase of their own trade volume. Indonesia, as the Country of Honor this year, has a trade volume 85 times of the previous session, and Singapore, 23 times. The trade volumes of Vietnam and Thailand are increased by 727% and 45% respectively. Chinese provinces and municipalities including Tianjin, Fujian, Anhui, Shanxi, Heilongjiang, Guizhou, Gansu, Ningxia and Inner Mongolia also have folded increases of trade volumes.

7. China and ASEAN's consensus on enhancing investment cooperation is further materialized. The CAEXPO Working Meeting on Investment Cooperation is held during the fair period. Participants include officials of the investment promotion

agencies of the 10 ASEAN countries and the ASEAN Secretariat, to discuss on enhancing cooperation among investment agencies, local governments and industrial parks via the CAEXPO as a platform. All parties concerned agree to enhance project matching between Chinese investors and ASEAN project holders. The ASEAN side has highly credited on CAEXPO's efforts in promoting two-way investment.

8. More effective investment promotion programs have been arranged. 46 in-depth investment promotion seminars/conferences and project-matching programs are held during the fair period, which have drawn the active involvement of enterprises from different channels. National investment promotion conferences of the ASEAN countries are well received by the audience, shaping effective platforms for promoting two-way investment cooperation. The Project Financing/Investing Seminar also harvests rich fruits. With the participation of over 100 Chinese leading enterprises with foreign investment, equity investment institutions and project consultation organizations as well as ASEAN investment promotion agencies and investors, over 500 financing projects have found their investors.

9. Investment cooperation is more fruitful. 135 international economic cooperation projects have been concluded during the fair period, with a total investment volume of USD 6.69 billion, up 26.63% than that of the previous sessions. Among them, 58 are concluded between Chinese and ASEAN enterprises, with an investment volume of USD 2.663 billion, respectively accounting 43% and 38% of the total international cooperation. Those concluded projects cover a wide range of fields, including agriculture, manufacturing, trade logistics, tourism development, mineral resources exploring and processing, transportation and energy facility construction and so on. Besides, 156 Chinese domestic economic cooperation projects are signed, with a total investment volume of RMB 67.446 billion, an year-on-year increase of 9%.

III. Promote China-ASEAN in-depth cooperation in various fields

With CAFTA & New Opportunities as the Theme of the Year, the 7th CABIS, 9 high-end conferences/forums and a series cultural and sports programs have been concurrently held with the 7th CAEXPO, effectively promoting the bilateral cooperation in different fields and at different levels.

The 7th CABIS, with CAFTA & Regional Economic Cooperation Prospect as the theme, has further pragmatic cooperation between the two sides. Chinese and ASEAN state leaders respectively address the summit. Roundtable dialogues between ASEAN state leaders and Chinese entrepreneurs, China-ASEAN business summit forum and forums on logistics, machinery and minerals have been arranged during the 7th CABIS. Chairman Jia Qinglin said that with the full support and active participation of the governments, chambers of commerce/trade associations, business communities of the countries concerned, the CAEXPO and the CABIS have become the effective platforms for the dialogues, exchanges and cooperation between China and the ASEAN countries.

The 2nd China-ASEAN Summit Forum on Financial Cooperation & Development (Financial Forum) held during the 7th CAEXPO, with the theme of "Deepening Cooperation Mechanism, Constructing a New Framework of Reciprocal Financial Cooperation within CAFTA", has become a more effective platform for financial cooperation and established a new framework for the development of the industry within the China–ASEAN region, which have facilitated bilateral cooperation in other fields and advanced the regional economic integration. With in–depth exchanges and discussions, the Financial Forum has approved the Consensus on the 2nd China–ASEAN Summit Forum on Financial Cooperation and Development.

The China–ASEAN Bankers Roundtable Meeting has been held during the Financial Forum for the first time. Mr. Li Dongrong, Assistant Governor of the People's Bank of China said that the Financial Forum has fully played its role as a new platform for enhancing bilateral cooperation in the field, which intensified the CAEXPO as platform for bilateral cooperation in various fields.

The China–ASEAN Energy Forum, as one of the high–ended forums held during the fair period, has pragmatically enhanced the energy cooperation between the two sides. Apart from energy cooperation after the CAFTA establishment, enterprises of the two sides have also had in–depth discussions on reciprocal cooperation in petroleum and natural gas, renewable energy, power and coal. The forum has witnessed several agreements concluded, including a shareholders joint venture agreement on a power plant in Bali, Indonesia.

The 7th CAEXPO has become a platform for bilateral cooperation in various fields. Other high–ended conferences/forums that are held during the fair period include the China–ASEAN Social Development & Poverty Reduction Forum, the 1st China–ASEAN Red–Cross Forum, China–ASEAN Conference on Maritime Consultative Mechanisms, the 3rd China–ASEAN Power Cooperation & Development Forum & China–ASEAN Power Economic and Trade Cooperation Fair, the China–ASEAN Forum on Dentistry and Seminar on Strengthening International Judicial Exchanges and Cooperation, Promoting Regional Economic Development and Prosperity.

All of them have attracted the attendance of Chinese and ASEAN high–ranking officials at ministerial level, leaders of state–owned enterprises directly under the central government and world renowned experts and scholars, which reflects common wishes of all the parties concerned to seize the opportunities brought by the CAFTA establishment to strengthen bilateral cooperation. Through these conferences/forums, the CAEXPO negotiation and dialogue mechanisms have been further improved, and the Nanning Channel has played a more important role in promoting China–ASEAN cooperation.

The Pavilion of Cities of Charm has better finished its mission to extend the bilateral friendly cooperation at state level to that among the cities. More wonderful and diversified programs have been arranged: Chinese and ASEAN state leaders and heads of government delegations have respectively inspected the Pavilion; the City of Charm of China has held a reception banquet for its ASEAN counterparts; Cities of Charm of China and the 10 ASEAN member states have established friendship between each other, promoting city–to–city cooperation; the promotion conferences of the Cities of Charm have pragmatically advanced bilateral cooperation and enhanced that between relevant governments and enterprises; introductions to the Cities of Charm have been printed on their respective "Passport", which are very popular among the audience; a specific Stamp has been designed for each of the Cities of Charm; and a handover ceremony has been held between the current and the next City of Charm of China. All of these programs fully reflect the common wish of the cities concerned to enhance friendly exchanges and achieve win–win results. Besides, ASEAN business professionals have visited Qinzhou, the City of Charm of China.

Colorful cultural and sports programs have been arranged during the fair period, promoting bilateral exchanges in the field. The Nanning International Arts Festival of Folk Songs & Gala Show for the Inauguration of the 7th CAEXPO has presented a feast of China–ASEAN arts exchanges. CAEXPO Golf Masters' Invitational, CAEXPO Tennis Game and the China–ASEAN International Touring Assembly & China–ASEAN Journalists Rally have become important platforms for the two sides to enhance sports exchanges and mutual understanding. Youth Arts Performance has advanced cultural exchanges and cooperation among the young people between the two sides. All of these programs have better strengthened the friendship between the peoples of the two sides and bilateral cooperation in various fields.

IV. Showcase the CAFTA win–win fruits and splendid achievements

The CAFTA Achievements Exhibition, which was held concurrently with the 7th CAEXPO and the 7th CABIS, has vividly showcased the history and achievements of CAFTA construction, thus gained positive comments from the visitors.

The Exhibition is composed of several sections for displaying CAFTA construction achievements, CAEXPO & CABIS achievements, and artwork show. Via diverse forms including pictures, graphs, texts and audio & video, it runs through the whole development course of CAFTA construction and the development of the two major events, reflecting the splendid achievements gained in the CAFTA construction, as well as various fields including politics, economy, culture and society in both China and the 10 ASEAN member states.

In the section for CAFTA achievements, its history and marvelous fruits are well present. It reviews the milestone events, one after another, of the CAFTA construction, from the initiated dialogue partnership in 1991, till the on–scheduled CAFTA establishment on Jan. 1, 2010. And the Achievement Section mainly showcases the CAFTA achievements in strengthening bilateral strategic partnership, in pragmatically promoting the trade & commercial cooperation, in deepening and enriching bilateral cooperation in more fields, as well as in cultivating and consolidating many cooperation mechanisms. Against the backdrop of the gradually–implemented CAFTA tariff reduction program, both sides have gained rich fruits in the cooperation in 11 key fields including commodity trade, trade in services, two–way investment, agriculture, ICT, human resource development, transportation, energy, culture, tourism and public health, etc. This section well presents the fruitful China–ASEAN cooperation for win–win results.

The CAEXPO & CABIS Section displays the prominent role of these two major events in promoting the CAFTA construction. It showcases the pictures of heads of state/government and VIPs at the previous events, the miniatures of CAEXPO opening ceremonies and Cities of Charms, the economic and trade outcomes of the previous CAEXPOs, as well as pictures of the previous sessions of CABIS, various theme conferences and high-end forums, evidencing that since year 2004 when the 1st CAEXPO and the 1st CABIS were held, these two major events have effectively promoted the regional cooperation, the CAFTA construction, the trade collaboration, as well as the friendly exchanges and cooperation in various fields between China and the rest of the world. And the most worth noting part of this Section is that the CAEXPO opening ceremonies are vividly showcased in the form of miniatures.

As a special and significant part of the CAFTA Achievements Exhibition, the artwork show exhibits the China-ASEAN exchanges and cooperation in the form of fine arts. It presents over 400 artwork pieces by artists of both sides, including calligraphy, fine arts, photograph, carving and artwork pieces by children, which mainly take the CAFTA construction progress and achievement as their focus and themes. The long calligraphy scroll about the compliments of state leaders of China and the 10 ASEAN countries to the CAEXPO is the biggest highlight, embodying the unique contribution of the event to the CAFTA construction and CAFTA's bright future. The Exhibition has attracted the participation of 66 artists from the 10 ASEAN countries, who account for 30% of the total.

The Exhibition has drawn keen attention of the people from different walks of life. According to incomplete statistics, the Exhibition attracts over 100,000 visitors. H.E. Y.B Dato' Jacob Dungau Sagan, Deputy Minister of International Trade and Industry of Malaysia said that the Exhibition is very successful, which help people know the history of the CAFTA and the CAEXPO clearly. Mr. Sutikno Sanusi, Vice President of the Indonesia Chamber of Commerce-China Committee believed that the Exhibition has fully showcased the CAFTA achievements, reflected the common wish of China and ASEAN to achieve mutual benefits and win-win results, and further strengthened the determination of the two sides to jointly well build the CAFTA.

V. Wide range coverage by Media around the world further enhances the CAEXPO recognition

The CAEXPO is not only a grand event for economic and trade exchanges between China and the ASEAN countries, but also a grand gathering of media around the world. During the 7th CAEXPO, media from home and abroad gather in Nanning, further enhance the recognition and influence of the event.

The 7th CAEXPO has, as always, drawn eyeballs of Chinese and foreign mainstream and professional media, attracting a large number of journalists/correspondents. Statistics show that 1458 journalists/correspondents (39 ones more than that of the previous year) from 199 media around the world cover the event. Among them, 88 are from 72 ASEAN media, which creates a record of the event of such kind that attracts the coverage of ASEAN. According to incomplete statistics, over 9900 reports have been released on newspapers, magazines and television stations and 9460 news articles have been reported on websites, along with over 850,000 entries of relevant internet reprints or links.

The Chinese central media and mainstream media from Hong Kong SAR and Macao SAR have invested great efforts in covering the 7th CAEXPO. People's Daily has published a special issue on the event. Xinhua News Agency has reported the event with news articles, pictures and videos. The China Central Television (CCTV) has sent a 30-member-group to report the 7th CAEXPO. International Business Daily has promoted a special page on the event. Wenweipo, Hong Kong Commercial Daily and Macao Daily have also opened special columns on the event.

Media from ASEAN and other countries have also made full coverage on the 7th CAEXPO. CAEXPO-related news articles have been published on the front or important pages of 84 mainstream media from Brunei Darussalam, Indonesia, Philippines, Thailand, Vietnam, Japan and Greece. Thailand's Siam Daily has published a large number of reports on the 7th CAEXPO, including Chairman Jia declaring the open of the event and the theme of the opening ceremony. Philippines' Chinese Commercial News has published news articles on the 7th CAEXPO, crediting on the event that allows Chinese average people experience ASEAN's folk custom in China. Other ASEAN media like Malaysia's Kwong Wah Yit Poh have also made theme coverage on the event.

The 7th CAEXPO is lively broadcasted by more media of China and ASEAN. CCTV-News, CCTV-4, China National Radio (CNR), China Radio International (CRI), Guxangxi Television, Guangxi Radio, Guangdong Radio, Voice of Vietnam and Quang Nihn Radio have lively broadcasted the 7th CAEXPO opening ceremony to the local people. In addition, 10 internet media, including people.com, xinhuanet.com, China Net Television (CNTV), CRI Online and Chinanews.com, through live web casting in the forms of pictures and videos, have superbly highlighted major programs of the 7th CAEXPO like the opening ceremony, the roundtable meeting between ASEAN state leaders and Chinese entrepreneurs and the China-ASEAN Business Summit Forum.

The 7th CAEXPO has been covered by many languages. CRI has dispatched a 23-member-team to report the event in Malay, Cambodian, Indonesian, Lao, English and Chinese, which are land broadcasted in the North America, Cambodia, Laos and other countries. China News Service Website's press report has been widely used by the media from the ASEAN countries, U.S., Australia, Hong Kong SAR, Macao SAR and Chinese Taipei. Besides, it has provided English, Thai, Vietnamese and Cambodian special reports for the mainstream media of the ASEAN countries, exerting a great influence outside China. CRI Online has also promoted special reports in 8 languages including English, Indonesian, Laos, Malay, Myanmar, Filipino, Thai and Vietnamese to cover the grand event.

Local media in Guangxi have fully played their own strength to promote the 7th CAEXPO from different angles. Media like Guangxi Daily, Guangxi Television, Guangxi Radio and Guangxinews.com have developed special volumes, pages or programs to report the highlights, interview VIPs and participating enterprises and cover forums/conferences during the fair period, promoting the 7th CAEXPO in an all-rounded way and increasing the influence of the event.

VI. The 7th CAEXPO has boosted the economic development of Guangxi

The CAEXPO has been concluded successfully in Nanning, Guangxi for 7 straight years, which has not only enhanced the China–ASEAN friendly cooperation, but also further promoted Guangxi's opening–up and economic development.

The 7th CAEXPO has provided a platform for Guangxi to involve in the regional cooperation in various fields. During the fair period, leaders of Guangxi have had 17 meetings with state leaders of the ASEAN countries and delegations from sister cities and other countries, reaching consensus on jointly building the Guangxi Beibu Gulf Economic Zone to enhance Beibu Gulf economic cooperation, GMS cooperation, Nanning–Singapore Economic Corridor for the development of CAFTA.

Qinzhou, as the City of Charm of China, has achieved remarkable outcomes. During the fair period, Qinzhou government has meetings with ASEAN VIPs at ministerial level like Deputy Minister of International Trade and Industry of Malaysia and presidents/chairmen of the chambers of commerce and trade associations. It has face–to–face talks with renowned enterprises from ASEAN, Hong Kong SAR, Chinese Taipei and Republic of Korea, as well as in–depth discussions with business delegations of other Chinese provinces or municipalities.

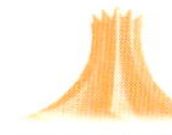

Besides, Qinzhou has held a series of programs during the fair period, including a briefing conference on Qinzhou business opportunities, 4 industrial promotion conferences, a business seminar, Qinzhou Day and Night of Qinzhou, each of which has attracted active participation of the business professionals and brought about abundant business opportunities. Qinzhou has concluded 51 projects, with a total investment volume of RMB 23.8 billion, and become the City of Friendship of the Cities of Charm of the 10 ASEAN countries. Within only 5 days, Malaysia (Qinzhou) Industry Park has gained support from the Ministry of Commerce of China and Korea (Qinzhou) Industrial Park has made pragmatic progress.

The 7th CAEXPO has provided a sound platform for the cities of Guangxi to enhance cooperation with the ASEAN countries and other Chinese provinces and municipalities. During the fair period, leader of Fangchenggang city has had an audience with Vietnamese state leader. Delegations from Brunei Darussalam, Cambodia, Malaysia, Philippines, Singapore and Vietnam have made survey trips to relevant enterprises and investment cooperation projects in Nanning, Guilin, Yulin, Qinzhou, Baise, Fangchenggang, Chongzuo. In addition, a working meeting of the Pingxiang (China) – Dong Dang (Vietnam) cross border economic cooperation zone and a signing ceremony of agreement on Guangxi–Hainan working plan have been held during the fair period, advancing Guangxi's cooperation with ASEAN countries and other Chinese provinces.

The 7th CAEXPO has also helped enhance exchanges and cooperation between Guangxi and its sister cities and establish new sistership with more foreign cities or provinces. Sister cities like Cebu of Philippines, Kumamoto of Japan and Chungcheongbuk of ROK have grouped enterprises to join the 7th CAEXPO as exhibitors and trade visitors. Delegations of sister cities have had meetings with leaders of Guangxi and actively participated in the programs of the CAEXPO, further enhancing their exchanges and cooperation with Guangxi. And Guangxi has also actively built new sistership with more ASEAN countries via the CAEXPO as a platform.

The 7th CAEXPO makes Guangxi a more attractive investment destination. During the fair period, 84 projects of Guangxi have found foreign investors, attracting a total investment volume of USD 4.426 billion, respectively increased by 42.3% and 17.1%. Besides, the province has concluded 146 projects with 21 Chinese provinces/ municipalities, with a total investment volume of RMB 67.1 billion, 10.8% more than that of the previous year.

The 7th CAEXPO has further promoted the development of Guangxi convention & exhibition (C & E) industry. Driven by the brand effect of the CAEXPO, local cities of Guangxi have held different expositions and trade fairs during and after the fair period, including the 7th Wuzhou International Gemstone Festival, the China–ASEAN Modern Agricultural Exhibition, the 18th Sino–Vietnam Trade Fair and the 7th SME Opportunity Fair, advancing the opening–up and economic and social development of these cities.

Huge flows of people, goods, information and capital brought about by the 7th CAEXPO have helped relevant sectors of Nanning gain rich economic returns. During the 7th CAEXPO, major hotels in Nanning have witnessed a steady increase in room revenue. 81 major hotels have accommodated 87,200 persons, hitting an average occupancy rate of 49.21%, receiving room revenue of RMB 31.14 million, a year–on–year increase of 13.63%.

Both passenger and freight transport are very busy. 5 major long–distance bus stations have experienced 44,508 times of arrival and departure, carrying 373,400 person times, and the railway station, 153,700 person times.

91.5 tons of goods are delivered by train and 1050 tons by air, respectively increased by 1.63% and 8.47%. 1010 flights are taken off or landed at the Nanning International Airport, 3.7% more than that of the same period of last year. 59,300 persons arrive in Nanning and 58,400 people depart here by air, respectively increased by 12.8% and 9.2%. The number of tourists reaches 309,100, up by 71.29%, hitting a new record.

10+1
第七届
盟博览会
THE 7th
EXPO

第一章

1 自贸区元年万象新 十一国携手办盛会

——第七届中国—东盟博览会的筹备

2010年中国—东盟自由贸易区如期全面建成，标志着双方经贸合作进入全面深入发展的新阶段。

中国—东盟自由贸易区是由发展中国家组成的最大自由贸易区，是中国和东盟着眼长远作出的一项互利的制度安排，给双方带来的是更多机遇，是更大的市场和更优化的资源配置条件。中国—东盟自由贸易区建成以后，双方贸易投资增长加快，经济融合程度加深，企业、人民切实受益，成效显著。

第七届中国—东盟博览会在此背景下举办，具有重要意义。

2010年6月26日，中国国家主席胡锦涛在加拿大会见印度尼西亚总统苏西洛，并邀请苏西洛总统出席第七届中国—东盟博览会。中央领导和有关部委的关怀、指导、支持，极大地鼓舞了广西承办好第七届中国—东盟博览会的信心和决心。

东盟10国政府部门、东盟秘书处、东盟各国主要商协会对第七届中国—东盟博览会筹备工作高度重视，与中方加强合作，完善共办机制，共同做好各项筹备工作。

广西壮族自治区继续举全区之力承办中国—东盟博览会，坚持高标准、高水平、高要求，全区上下增强责任感、使命感，全力以赴，奋勇拼搏，各项筹备工作更加机制化、常态化，搭好平台，进一步服务好中国—东盟友好合作。

CHAPTER ONE

Welcome the Newly-established CAFTA, China and ASEAN to Co-sponsor CAEXPO

—Preparations of the 7th CAEXPO

China-ASEAN Free Trade Area (CAFTA), established on schedule in 2010, marks a new stage for both sides in economic and trade cooperation.

The CAFTA which is the largest free trade area made up of developing countries, an institution arrangement of long term mutual benefits made by China and ASEAN, has brought about more opportunities and bigger market and more optimized resource allocation. With the establishment of CAFTA, the bilateral trade has seen faster growth, deepened economic integration, more benefits for enterprises and people, making remarkable achievements.

In this context, the 7th China-ASEAN Expo (CAEXPO) bears great significance.

On June 26, 2010, Chinese President Hu Jintao met with Indonesia President Susilo Bambang Yudhoyono in Canada, and invited him to attend the 7th CAEXPO. With the guidance and support granted by the Chinese central government and relevant ministries, Guangxi, as the host of the 7th CAEXPO, has been greatly encouraged and boosted in holding the event.

The governments of the 10 ASEAN countries, ASEAN Secretariat, and major chambers of commerce of the 10 ASEAN countries have attached great importance to the 7th CAEXPO, working together with the Chinese side to improve the co-sponsorship and to prepare for the event.

Guangxi Zhuang Autonomous Region, where the 7th CAEXPO is convened, continuously spares no efforts to hold the event, with high standard, high level and high requirements as the guideline, all relevant departments and agencies work hard with responsibility to make all preparation work more systemized, offering a platform for better serving the friendly cooperation between China and ASEAN.

一　第七届中国—东盟博览会举办的背景

2010年，中国—东盟自由贸易区如期全面建成。这是中国推动对外开放战略和区域经济一体化战略的一个里程碑，也是中国—东盟经贸合作进入全面深入发展新阶段的标志。第七届中国—东盟博览会在这一背景下举办，意义重大。

（一）中国—东盟自由贸易区如期全面建成

根据2002年11月签署的《中国—东盟全面经济合作框架协议》设定的目标，2010年中国和东盟将全面建成自由贸易区。经过七年的共同努力，双方先后签署了《货物贸易协议》、《服务贸易协议》和《投资协议》，从而中国—东盟自由贸易区全面建成的目标如期实现。

从2010年1月1日起，中国和东盟六个老成员，即：文莱、菲律宾、印尼、马来西亚、泰国和新加坡之间，有超过90%的产品实行零关税。中国对东盟平均关税从9.8%降到0.1%，东盟六个老成员对中国的平均关税从12.8%降到0.6%。东盟四个新成员，即越南、老挝、柬埔寨和缅甸，也将在2015年实现90%零关税的目标。除了货物贸易之外，双方服务部门的开放水平也有进一步的提升，投资政策和环境得到法律制度的保障，从而更加稳定和透明。随着中国与东盟之间基本实现自由贸易，资金、资源、技术和人才等生产要素的流动效率会显著提高，双方之间经济一体化程度将会达到前所未有的水平。

为纪念中国—东盟自由贸易区如期建成，2010年1月7日上午，中国—东盟自由贸易区论坛暨中国—东盟自由贸易区建成庆祝仪式在中国广西南宁举行。中国全国政协副主席黄孟复，中国十届全国人大常委会副委员长蒋正华，老挝常务副总理宋沙瓦·凌沙瓦，广西壮族自治区党委书记、自治区人大常委会主任郭声琨，广西壮族自治区主席马飚、中国商务部副部长易小准、东盟国家部长级贵宾用金钥匙共同开启了中国—东盟自由贸易区合作大门。

（二）中国—东盟经贸合作进入全面深入发展新阶段

中国—东盟自由贸易区全面建成以后，双方贸易投资增长加快，经济融合程度加深，企业和人民切实受益，成效显著。

2010年1—7月，中国与东盟进出口总额1610亿美元，同比增长49.6%。其中，中方出口767.3亿美元，进口842.7亿美元，同比分别增长43.2%和56.1%。东盟对华出口增速比从中国进口增速高出13个百分点。中方逆差75.4亿美元。来自中国的进口有效促进了东盟国家扩大就业和经济发展。中国对东盟投资快速增长，2010年上半年，中国对东盟新增非金融类直接投资金额12.2亿美元，同比增长125.7%。东盟已成为中国企业赴海外投资兴业的主要目的地之一。

实践证明，中国—东盟自由贸易区是互利互惠的，符合双方利益。在这新形势下，中国与东盟各国将一起进一步落实《中国—东盟全面经济合作框架协议》，提升双方经贸合作的规模和水平。在双方90%以上的货物相互实现零关税的基础上，进一步提高服务贸易的相互开放水平，实施好《中国—东盟投资协议》，保障和促进双向投资合作进一步发展。中国—东盟博览会将发挥更加重要的平台作用。

2010年1月7日，中国—东盟自由贸易区建成庆祝仪式暨自贸区论坛在广西南宁开幕

On January 7, 2010, the celebration of the China-ASEAN Free Trade Area (CAFTA) establishment & the opening ceremony of CAFTA Forum held in Nanning, Guangxi

二　中央领导关怀和国家有关部委指导支持

第七届中国—东盟博览会的筹备工作得到了党中央、国务院的关怀指导，得到了中央有关部委的大力支持。

（一）中央领导的关怀，极大地鼓舞了广西承办好第七届中国—东盟博览会的信心和决心

2010年6月26日，中国国家主席胡锦涛在加拿大多伦多会见前来出席二十国集团领导人第四次峰会的印度尼西亚总统苏西洛，并邀请苏西洛总统出席第七届中国—东盟博览会。

胡锦涛强调，中方高度重视发展同印尼的战略伙伴关系，愿以建交60周年为契机，深化各领域务实合作，不断开创中国印尼战略伙伴关系新局面。中方建议双方保持高层交往良好势头，欢迎苏西洛总统来华出席上海世博会和中国—东盟博览会；扩大深化经贸合作，中方愿扩大对印尼的投资，支持中国企业继续积极参与印尼基础设施建设等重大项目，鼓励中国游客赴印尼旅游；共同办好“中印（尼）友好年”有关活动，巩固两国人民传统友好纽带；加强在国际和地区事务中的协调和配合，为建立更加公正合理的国际政治经济秩序作出努力。

胡锦涛指出，中国愿意看到一个更加团结、稳定、繁荣的东盟，将一如既往支持东盟共同体建设和一体化进程，坚定支持东盟在东亚合作中发挥主导作用。中国—东盟自由贸易区全面建成，是双方关系史上的重要里程碑。中国愿意同东盟加强合作，共同维护和建设好中国—东盟自由贸易区，加快推进基础设施互联互通，深化金融领域合作，扩大社会人文交流，推动中国东盟关系不断迈上新台阶。

苏西洛表示，印尼同中国战略伙伴关系发展很好，两国政治、经济、安全等领域合作不断深化，人民传统友谊进一步加深。中国是印尼的朋友和伙伴，印尼方真诚希望加强同中国的合作，进一步提升两国合作水平。他完全

2010年6月26日，中国国家主席胡锦涛在多伦多会见前来出席二十国集团领导人第四次峰会的印度尼西亚总统苏西洛

Chinese President Hu Jintao at the meeting with Indonesian President Susilo Bambang Yudhoyono at the 4th G20 summit in Toronto, Canada on June 26, 2010

同意胡锦涛关于发展两国关系的重要意见，表示印尼愿意同中国保持高层交往，欢迎中国企业赴印尼在基础设施、旅游等领域投资，进一步拓展两国贸易，共同举行两国建交60周年纪念活动。他还表示，中国同东盟关系十分重要，双方要共同保证中国—东盟自由贸易区顺利实施。

党中央、国务院对广西经济社会发展十分关心。从2010年初至第七届中国—东盟博览会开幕前，温家宝、贾庆林、习近平、李源潮等中央领导同志分别到广西考察指导工作，充分肯定近年来广西各项建设取得的成绩，对广西经济社会发展作重要指示，极大地促进了广西各项工作，鼓舞了广西承办好第七届中国—东盟博览会的信心和决心。

（二）中央有关部委继续加大力度，指导和支持办好第七届中国—东盟博览会

国务院办公厅、商务部、外交部等中国—东盟博览会组委会成员单位和有关部委，紧扣中国—东盟自由贸易区如期建成的新形势，加大工作力度，支持做好第七届中国—东盟博览会筹备工作。

2010年2月上旬，国务院副秘书长丘小雄，商务部党组副书记、商务部副部长高虎城，商务部副部长易小准，外交部部长助理胡正跃等国务院和中央部委领导在北京分别听取了中国—东盟博览会秘书处关于第七届中国—东盟博览会筹备工作的汇报，表示支持办好第七届中国—东盟博览会，并对筹备工作及博览会长远发展提出意见。

2010年4月7日，商务部在北京召开第七届中国—东盟博览会筹备会议，全面部署第七届中国—东盟博览会展览工作。商务部相关司局和全国各省（自治区、直辖市）商务主管部门负责人出席会议。商务部党组副书记、商

务部副部长高虎城在会上强调，要以中国—东盟自贸区建成为契机，充分认识在新的历史起点上办好中国—东盟博览会对于深化中国与东盟经贸合作的重要意义，继续把中国—东盟博览会作为中国企业开拓东盟市场的重要平台，在服务国家战略、为国内企业开拓东盟市场方面做好服务。广西壮族自治区党委常委、自治区副主席陈武在会上说，广西作为承办方，将继续举全区之力，进一步做好第七届中国—东盟博览会各项筹备工作，为服务国家战略、服务中国—东盟自贸区作出更大贡献。

2010年4月7日，第七届中国—东盟博览会筹备工作会议在北京召开

The preparatory meeting for the 7th China-ASEAN Expo (CAEXPO) held in Beijing, China on April 7, 2010

2010年7月26日，国务院新闻办公室举行中国—东盟经贸关系进展暨第七届中国—东盟博览会、第七届中国—东盟商务与投资峰会新闻发布会。这是国务院新闻办公室连续第七年举办中国—东盟博览会的新闻发布会。商务部副部长高虎城，广西壮族自治区党委常委、自治区副主席陈武，中国国际贸易促进委员会（以下简称中国贸促会）副会长张伟向中外媒体记者介绍了中国—东盟自贸区建成半年来中国—东盟经贸关系进展，以及第七届中国—东盟博览会、第七届中国—东盟商务与投资峰会等筹备工作情况。国务院新闻办新闻局副局长陈文俊主持新闻发布会。东盟国家驻华使馆商务参赞或代表，商务部、中国贸促会以及广西壮族自治区有关部门负责人出席新闻发布会。作为中国—东盟自由贸易区全面建成后举办的新一届盛会，第七届中国—东盟博览会和商务与投资峰会受到中外新闻媒体的高度关注。共有新华社、人民日报、中央电视台、越南之声广播电台等49家中外媒体81名记者参加本次新闻发布会，其中，国外媒体6家，港澳台媒体8家。

2010年7月30日—8月1日，商务部合作司在云南省西双版纳州召开第七届中国—东盟博览会国际经济合作展区筹备工作会议。来自全国27个省市商务主管部门的代表及部分中央企业代表共60余人参加了会议。会议对前六届

2010年7月26日，中国—东盟经贸关系进展暨第七届中国—东盟博览会、第七届中国—东盟商务与投资峰会新闻发布会在国务院新闻办公室举行

Press conference on the progress of China-ASEAN economic and trade relations & preparations for the 7th CAEXPO and the 7th CABIS held at the Information Office of State Council of China on July 26, 2010

中国—东盟博览会国际经济合作展区的成效给予肯定，对第七届中国—东盟博览会国际经济合作展区筹备工作进行了部署。

2010年9月20日，中国—东盟博览会、中国—东盟商务与投资峰会组委会会议在北京召开。自治区党委常委、自治区副主席、中国—东盟博览会组委会副主任兼秘书长陈武，商务部副部长陈健，中国贸促会副会长、中国—东盟商务与投资峰会组委会副主任于平出席会议并讲话。

国务院办公厅、中宣部、外交部、国家发展改革委、科技部、财政部、公安部警卫局、交通运输部、海关总署、国家质量监督检验检疫总局、国家旅游局、国家食品药品监督管理局、国务院新闻办公室等组委会成员单位的负责同志出席会议。

陈武在讲话中介绍了中国—东盟博览会、中国—东盟商务与投资峰会成功举办六届以来取得的显著成效，通报了本届盛会筹备工作进展情况。他说，第七届中国—东盟博览会、商务与投资峰会是在中国—东盟自贸区如期建成、贯彻落实中央关于加快经济发展方式转变的工作部署、深入实施新一

2010年9月20日，第七届中国—东盟博览会、第七届中国—东盟商务与投资峰会组委会会议在北京召开

The conference of the 7th CAEXPO and the 7th CABIS Organizing Committee held in Beijing on September 20, 2010

轮西部大开发战略的背景下举办的关键一届，既有新的机遇，也有新的挑战。广西将继续举全区之力做好各项筹备工作，通过博览会和峰会这一平台，进一步深化中国与东盟合作，更好地服务国家周边外交战略。

陈健在主持会议时说，办好中国—东盟博览会是一项长期性的任务。我们要认真贯彻胡锦涛总书记关于“中国—东盟博览会要长期举办下去，要办出特色、办出实效”的指示精神，在中国—东盟自贸区建成后，坚持把博览会越办越好，常办常新。他动员各成员单位多为如何长期办好博览会出主意、想办法，进一步加大对广西承办工作的支持，共同努力，继续办好中国—东盟博览会、商务与投资峰会。

于平在讲话中说，面临新的形势，中国—东盟商务与投资峰会要继续发挥作为中国与东盟进行高层对话、深化双方经贸合作的平台作用，坚持“务实、创新、可持续发展”的办会思路，不断创新办会形式，丰富办会内容，增加峰会的务实成果，把峰会完善成为促进中国与东盟商务与投资合作的长期有效机制。

会议审议了第七届中国—东盟博览会、商务与投资峰会重要活动安排及新增的展览和活动内容。本届博览会新增服务贸易专题，将举办中国—东盟自贸区建设成就展、农业展、珠宝展、金融展及金融论坛、东盟品牌展和食品展、木材家具展等。

会议研究了第八届中国—东盟博览会和商务与投资峰会的工作，讨论了第八届博览会的重点主题，建议结合2011年中国—东盟建立对话关系20周年活动设计相关内容。

各成员单位的有关负责同志在发言中表示，将结合本单位实际，继续对广西的承办工作给予大力支持和帮助，共同努力巩固、发展好中国—东盟博览会和商务与投资峰会平台，为服务国家周边外交战略、推动中国—东盟自贸区建设作出新的贡献。

三　东盟十国强力推动共办

东盟10国政府部门、主要商协会和企业对第七届中国—东盟博览会筹备工作高度重视，与中方加强合作，完善共办机制，共同做好各项筹备工作。

（一）东盟十国加大共办力度

2010年4月9日，商务部在南宁召开第七届中国—东盟博览会高官会，来自中国和东盟10国各共办方及东盟秘书处的代表就第七届中国—东盟博览会筹备工作进行深入研讨并达成共识。

会议由中国商务部亚洲司司长吕克俭、东盟秘书处经济一体化合作司高级官员蓬猜共同主持并分别讲话。中国商务部合作司商务参赞石资明在高官会上发言，对充分利用博览会重要平台，进一步加强中国与东盟投资合作工作表示大力支持。中国—东盟博览会秘书处秘书长郑军健通报了第七届中国—东盟博览会、主题国以及博览会期间重大活动安排的工作设想；中国—东盟博览会秘书处副秘书长李文杰就第七届博览会交通、住宿和展场餐饮等客户服务安排作了发言；中国—东盟博览会秘书处副秘书长农融就第七届博览会招商招展和展务工作安排作了发言；中国—东盟商务与投资峰会秘书处负责人通报了第七届中国—东盟商务与投资峰会工作安排。

东盟方通报了本国领导人或代表团团长拟出席第七届博览会情况、组展

2010年4月9日，第七届中国—东盟博览会高官会议在广西南宁举行

The Senior Official Meeting of the 7th CAEXPO held in Nanning of Guangxi on April 9, 2010

招商工作情况、“魅力之城”甄选工作情况、重点展示行业/展品、投资项目收集工作情况等，并就博览会的筹备工作提出了建设性意见。

会议各方一致认为，博览会是中国与东盟经贸合作、推动中国—东盟自贸区建设和落实自贸区成果的重要平台，中国—东盟自由贸易区建成后博览会的平台作用将更加得以凸显。各方将继续共同培育、维护、发展好这一共同主办的国际性大型展会，一致认为做好贸易配对工作，提高经贸实效是博览会的核心业务。

东盟各国表示，博览会共办工作是本国经贸主管部门工作重点，将进一步研究制定相关政策和措施，逐步形成跨部门的合作机制，积极引导和鼓励本国品牌和知名企业参展。东盟方充分肯定了中方提出的第七届博览会工作要点。东盟国家均表示将至少维持第六届博览会参展规模，并进一步提高参展企业质量，引导参展行业集中在本国的优势产业上。部分东盟国家如印尼、新加坡共办部门代表还表示将扩大参展规模。马来西亚等国对设立本国“品牌展区”等工作设想和有关活动进度安排予以支持，并表示将按照上述设想和建议做好相关筹备工作。东盟方对以博览会为平台进一步加强中国与东盟的投资合作表示支持。本次高官会首次邀请东盟国家投资主管部门官员与会，并在会期举办了投资合作工作会议。

会议确定印尼将出任第七届中国—东盟博览会主题国。东盟各国表示赞同第七届中国—东盟博览会选择“自贸区与新机遇”为重点主题，并加大对博览会的宣传，提高博览会的知名度。文莱因航班缘故未出席本次高官会，但表示将全力支持第七届中国—东盟博览会筹备工作。

7月13日至8月2日，由中国商务部主办，中国—东盟博览会秘书处承办的中国—东盟自由贸易协定研修班在广西南宁开班。培训对象主要为文莱、柬埔寨、印度尼西亚、老挝、马来西亚、缅甸、菲律宾、泰国及越南等东盟国家经贸主管部门官员和东盟秘书处官员。邀请中国—东盟合作方面的官员和专家学者授课。此次研修班内容紧扣中国—东盟自贸区、紧扣中国—东盟

2010年7月13日，中国—东盟自由贸易协定研修班在南宁正式开班

The Seminar on China-ASEAN Free Trade Agreements opened in Nanning, China on July 13, 2010

博览会，重点宣讲自贸区的理论、通关实务和博览会的实践，还邀请马来西亚投资官员与广西官员同台讲解本国本地区的投资合作范例，并现场学习了天津经济技术开发区招商引资的好经验。此次研修班的举办，加强了中国商务部与东盟各国经贸主管部门的联系，促进了第七届博览会的筹备工作。

2010年9月上旬，“中国—东盟博览会合作媒体广西行”活动举行。东盟10国的14位记者参加了此次采访活动，每个东盟国家均派记者参加。期间，东盟10国记者联合采访了广西壮族自治区人民政府副秘书长魏然，以及广西商务厅、广西北部湾经济区规划建设管理委员会办公室、广西外事办以及中国—东盟博览会秘书处等机构负责人，以及柬埔寨、缅甸、老挝驻南宁领事馆官员和有关企业。在南宁期间，商务部国际司专家为东盟媒体记者讲授了中国—东盟自由贸易区相关知识。各国记者还赴广西钦州市参加了钦州市确定为第七届中国—东盟博览会中国“魅力之城”新闻发布会，参观了钦州港经济开发区和钦州保税港区。各国记者还到广西百色市和贵港市进行了采访。

（二）印度尼西亚担任第七届中国—东盟博览会主题国，积极筹备主题国活动

第七届中国—东盟博览会主题国是印度尼西亚。印度尼西亚政府高度重视，专门成立了由贸易部牵头，文化旅游部、投资署共同组成的主题国联合工作组，与博览会秘书处加强合作，积极开展主题国各项筹备工作。

在参展参会的组织方面，印度尼西亚贸易部扩大参展规模，重点组织手工制品、农产品、食品、橡胶、棕榈油等企业参展，并继续包馆。为扩大博览会在印度尼西亚企业界的影响，印度尼西亚贸易部还与博览会秘书处联合署名，共同印制符合印尼需要的博览会宣传资料，向印尼各行业商会发放，在印尼开展博览会专场推介活动。

在投资促进方面，印尼投资协调署与印尼贸易部、博览会秘书处密切配合，扎实落实博览会投资促进各项工作。印尼投资协调署还指定官员专门负责博览会的相关工作。

印中友协、印尼中华总商会、印尼工商会馆中国委员会等商协会积极动员会员企业参加第七届博览会，帮助博览会秘书处派发各类宣传资料，并采取会议介绍、电子直邮、网络链接和新闻报道等形式，向各会员企业和媒体推介博览会，组织更多的企业参展参会。

中国驻印尼大使馆及经商处全力支持印尼担任第七届博览会主题国，在主题国筹备工作方面给予了支持和帮助。

四　广西继续举全区之力承办

（一）积极争取各方支持

广西壮族自治区党委、自治区人民政府高度重视第七届中国—东盟博览会承办工作。自治区党委书记郭声琨，自治区主席马飚，自治区党委常委、自治区副主席陈武等自治区领导多次利用赴京出差或出席会议的机会，拜会国务院和有关部委有关负责人，争取对中国—东盟博览会承办工作的支持，并率团出访东盟国家，推动东盟国家共同办好中国—东盟博览会。

2009年11月1—8日，广西壮族自治区主席马飚率广西政府代表团展开东盟合作之旅，出访了马来西亚、菲律宾。自治区政府秘书长王跃飞陪同考察。访问历时8天，出访主题突出、任务重大。在第六届中国—东盟博览会刚刚落下帷幕、中国—东盟自由贸易区即将建成之际，马飚率团访问马来西亚、菲律宾两国，目的在于推动到访国与广西共同办好中国—东盟自由贸易区论坛和第七届中国—东盟博览会，共同推进区域合作和中国—东盟自贸区建设，加强双边以经贸为重点的多领域合作，携手抵御国际金融危机。

访问期间，马飚拜会了马来西亚总理纳吉布、菲律宾副总统德卡斯特

2009年11月5日，广西壮族自治区主席马飚率团出访菲律宾并与菲律宾商界举行座谈会

H.E. Ma Biao, Governor of Guangxi Zhuang Autonomous Region, led a delegation to visit the Philippines and had talks with local business community on November 5, 2009

罗；会见了我驻马来西亚、菲律宾两国大使，亚洲开发银行等重要地区组织领导人，马、菲两国相关部门及地方负责人；与两国重要商协会领袖和重要客商进行了座谈，与到访两国在多个合作领域达成了一系列共识。马飚还发出热情邀请，邀请大家到广西出席中国—东盟自贸区论坛、自贸区建成庆典活动、2010年泛北部湾经济合作论坛，以及第七届中国—东盟博览会和商务与投资峰会。

2010年1月13日，以广西壮族自治区党委书记、自治区人大常委会主任郭声琨为团长的广西代表团启程对泰国、新加坡进行为期8天的访问。广西代表团这次出访主题明确，使命重大。代表团拜会了到访国领导人、重要经济部门及当地知名企业，并举办经贸座谈会、签约仪式等活动。这次访问对于加强广西与到访国的高层往来，巩固双方传统友谊；在中国—东盟自贸区建成背景下，深化双方在各领域的务实合作；探讨继续共同办好中国—东盟博览会、中国—东盟商务与投资峰会，共同应对新的经济形势，实现互利共赢等方面，都具有重要意义。

1月14日，广西壮族自治区党委书记、自治区人大常委会主任郭声琨在泰国首都曼谷拜会了泰国总理阿披实。宾主双方进行了坦诚友好的会谈，就共同关心的问题交换了意见，达成了高度共识。郭声琨建议双方加强以下三方面的合作。一是推动政府间的合作与交流，为双方企业家和投资者创造更好的投资环境和更优的投资条件。二是推动双方在农业、文化、教育、旅游、物流等领域深化合作。尤其要通过扩大语言教育的交流合作，增进双方传统友谊；通过举办丰富多彩的文化交流活动，隆重庆祝中泰建交35周年。三是双方共同办好今后的中国—东盟博览会及商务与投资峰会等活动。第七届中国—东盟博览会将围绕“自贸区与新机遇”这一主题，促进中国和东盟各国全方位、多层次、宽领域的合作。希望泰国政府继续支持广西办好第七

2010年1月13日，广西壮族自治区党委书记、自治区人大常委会主任郭声琨率广西代表团对泰国进行访问

H.E. Guo Shengkun, Secretary of Communist Party of China (CPC) Guangxi Committee, led a Guangxi delegation to visit Thailand on January 13, 2010

届中国—东盟博览会，欢迎泰国政府、工商界、企业界人士积极参会。广西将为泰国企业界参展参会提供更多的便利、更周到的服务。

阿披实就进一步深化双方合作提出三点建议。一是继续加强农业领域的合作，推动更多泰国农产品通过广西凭祥口岸进入中国。二是进一步加强和改善物流体系建设。双方继续共同努力，加强交通基础设施建设；并在运输、海关、检验检疫方面加强沟通合作，推动双边互联互通和通关便利化，促进双方在贸易、投资等领域的发展。希望南宁至曼谷的直航航班能持续开办下去，以更好地促进双方人员交往，进一步扩大贸易来往。三是加强文化、教育、旅游等领域的交流合作。尤其要重视语言教学的合作交流，掀起双方人员互学对方语言的高潮；并通过举行各种文化交流活动，庆祝泰中两国建交35周年。泰国政府将一如既往地全力支持在广西南宁办好第七届中国—东盟博览会及商务与投资峰会。

1月19日，率团访问新加坡的广西壮族自治区党委书记、自治区人大常委会主任郭声琨拜会了新加坡总理李显龙。双方进行了坦诚友好的会谈，就共同关心的问题交换了意见，达成了高度共识。郭声琨建议新加坡在南宁设立领事机构，以更便于广西与新加坡在人员、物流、旅游等方面的往来；希望新加坡继续支持办好中国—东盟博览会、中国—东盟商务与投资峰会。新加坡是东盟国家的领头羊，在进一步加强区域合作、共同应对国际金融危机中，新加坡发挥着不可替代的作用；建议共同推进南宁—新加坡经济走廊建设。目前南宁—新加坡经济走廊已经得到中国交通运输部、铁道部和商务部的支持，这个经济走廊如果能建成，将会进一步带动整个区域的发展。

2010年1月19日，广西壮族自治区党委书记、自治区人大常委会主任郭声琨在新加坡拜会了新加坡总理李显龙

H.E. Guo Shengkun, Secretary of CPC Guangxi Committee, at the meeting with H.E. Lee Hsien Loong, Prime Minister of Singapore in Singapore on January 19, 2010

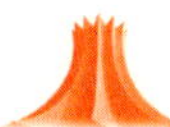

李显龙表示，支持双方开展人力资源培训方面的交流合作，希望广西的官员在新加坡能够学有所成、有所收获，能够和新加坡人分享想法、观念，并了解到一些新加坡解决问题的方法；支持新加坡的企业家和广西的企业家开展合作，到广西投资兴业。希望新加坡企业家到广西考察项目的时候，能得到广西各级政府的全力支持；支持广西利用新加坡作为中转，进一步推动区域的进出口贸易；建议进一步增加双方的互访，加强沟通与联系，深化双方的合作；支持每年一度在广西南宁举办的中国—东盟博览会。无论是从地缘优势，还是从区域合作来看，进一步加强和广西合作都是一个很自然、很必然的过程，新加坡的企业都很愿意来参加博览会，新加坡的政府也会一如既往地支持博览会。

5月25—27日，广西壮族自治区主席马飚率广西代表团访问印尼。期间，马飚一行分别与印尼贸易部长冯慧兰、东盟秘书处副秘书长巴加斯·哈普索罗及印尼工商会中国委员会和印尼中华总商会的主要负责人举行了会谈，就第七届中国—东盟博览会、泛北部湾经济合作、中国—印尼经贸合作区、加强广西与印尼经贸与投资合作等议题进行了广泛交流并达成许多共识。

5月25—27日，广西壮族自治区党委常委、自治区副主席陈武率团访问文莱，期间分别拜会文莱王储比拉及工业与初级资源部部长叶海亚、国家工商会代理会长卡玛鲁汀等，并现场考察广西在文水稻试验种植合作项目。在与文方会谈中，陈武表示希望进一步深化广西与文莱在项目投资及农业技术等领域的合作，并介绍了2010年拟在广西举办的第七届中国—东盟博览会及泛北部湾经济合作论坛等重要活动。

9月9—14日，以广西壮族自治区主席马飚为团长的广西代表团对越南社会主义共和国的正式友好访问。马飚拜会了越南国家主席阮明哲、总理阮晋勇、国会主席阮富仲、副总理阮善仁等越南国家领导人，会见了越南外交部等8个部门的部长、副部长，会见了谅山等4个与广西交界省的主要领导，就许多重大问题进行了深入沟通，达成了广泛共识。

（二）加强组织领导

1. 郭声琨指出，“两会一节”意义重大，举全区之力确保成功。2010年国庆期间，郭声琨、马飚、陈武、余远辉、林念修等自治区领导研究部署第七届中国—东盟博览会、中国—东盟商务与投资峰会筹备工作。郭声琨书记对第七届中国—东盟博览会筹备工作作出重要指示。

郭声琨指出，2010年是中国—东盟自贸区建成的第一年，办好第七届博览会、商务与投资峰会具有特殊意义，有利于巩固自贸区成果，深化与东盟的友好关系，尤其是2010年博览会的主题国印尼，是东盟10国中人口最多、影响力较大的国家，办好2010年“两会”，可以有效消除个别东盟国家对自贸区零关税的疑虑和担忧，增强东盟10国与我国继续共同推进自贸区建设的信心，进一步深化我国与东盟的战略伙伴关系。

郭声琨希望指挥中心工作人员发扬前六届“两会”精神，增强责任感和使命感，全力以赴，奋勇拼搏，再接再厉，做好2010年“两会一节”冲刺阶段的各项筹备工作。全区各地市、各部门要支持配合“两会一节”工作，继续举全区之力，确保取得圆满成功，为服务国家战略，带动广西经济社会发展作出新的贡献。

2. 成立广西与东盟开放合作领导小组及其统筹协调办公室。2010年2月22日上午，广西与东盟开放合作领导小组统筹协调办公室揭牌仪式在广西国际博览事务局举行。广西壮族自治区党委常委、自治区副主席、广西与东盟开放合作领导小组副组长陈武为广西与东盟开放合作领导小组统筹协调办公室揭牌。仪式结束后，广西与东盟开放合作领导小组统筹协调办公室召开了第一次工作会议。

2010年2月22日，广西与东盟开放合作领导小组统筹协调办公室揭牌仪式在广西国际博览事务局举行

On February 22, 2010, the inaugural ceremony of Coordinating Office of Leading Group of Opening and Cooperation between Guangxi and ASEAN held at the CAEXPO Secretariat

在中国—东盟自贸区建成的新形势下，广西壮族自治区党委、自治区人民政府高度重视加强广西与东盟的全面开放合作工作，成立了广西与东盟开放合作领导小组，自治区党委书记郭声琨、自治区主席马飚亲自担任领导小组组长。统筹协调办公室作为广西与东盟开放合作领导小组常设的服务性工作机构，将在统筹协调、信息沟通、项目推动方面发挥作用，为各市、各部门与东盟的合作做好服务。这对巩固自贸区建设的成果，统筹好广西与东盟开放合作的各项工作，加快推进广西与东盟开放合作重大项目全面落实有着重要的意义。

陈武在会上要求统筹协调办公室尽快运作起来，更好地把各方面的资源调

动起来，统筹各方面的合作，在以往的基础上，把广西与东盟的交流合作由经济领域扩大到非经济领域，全面深化广西与东盟的开放合作，并使之机制化、常态化，提高工作效率，确保广西与东盟全面开放合作更上一个新台阶。

广西壮族自治区人民政府副秘书长、广西与东盟开放合作领导小组统筹协调办公室主任魏然在会上通报了统筹协调办公室工作机制和广西与东盟合作的行动计划。广西与东盟开放合作领导小组的25个成员单位领导参加了揭牌仪式和工作会议。

广西与东盟开放合作领导小组统筹协调办公室的工作机制包括：

一是日常工作机制。包括信息收集、简报工作、文秘和档案管理三大内容。

二是联席会议机制。对于涉及多个部门的复杂合作项目，通过召开有关部门参加的联席会议，协调和推进广西与东盟合作项目（或事项）的落实。

三是督促检查机制。由办公室常驻副主任牵头逐项跟踪督促各部门、各市对东盟开放合作具体项目（或事项）的落实，定期调查了解工作完成情况并及时向领导小组报告。

四是调研规划机制。组织相关调研、学习、规划、策划等活动，在自贸区及东盟各国的有关政策和市场研究、广西与东盟多领域合作研究等方面，形成一系列研究报告、行动计划、发展规划等，为领导小组决策提供科学依据。

以上机制旨在搭建广西与东盟开放合作的信息沟通和项目跟踪落实的平台。通过建立以上四个机制，将解决信息沟通和项目落实的问题。

3. 召开“两会”广西领导小组会议。2010年9月27日上午，第七届中国—东盟博览会、中国—东盟商务与投资峰会广西领导小组会议在南宁召开，听取“两会”筹备工作汇报，研究部署有关工作。广西壮族自治区主席、“两会”广西领导小组组长马飚主持会议并讲话。他强调，要抢抓中国—东盟自贸区建成的新机遇，继续举全区之力办好中国—东盟博览会和商

2010年9月27日，第七届中国—东盟博览会、中国—东盟商务与投资峰会广西领导小组会议在南宁召开

The conference of Guangxi leading group of the 7th CAEXPO and the 7th CABIS held in Nanning, China on September 27, 2010

务与投资峰会，深化广西与东盟全方位、多层次、宽领域的合作，展现广西对外开放的新形象。

广西壮族自治区党委常委、宣传部部长、“两会”广西领导小组副组长沈北海，自治区党委常委、南宁市委书记、“两会”广西领导小组副组长车荣福，自治区党委常委、自治区副主席、“两会”广西领导小组副组长陈武，自治区副主席林念修出席会议。

马飚充分肯定了“两会”筹备工作进展。他说，第七届中国—东盟博览会、中国—东盟商务与投资峰会是在中国—东盟自由贸易区建成后举办的第一届盛会，意义重大。现在距“两会”开幕只有20多天时间，各级各部门要进一步增强紧迫感和责任感，抢抓中国—东盟自贸区建成这一新机遇，继续举全区之力办好中国—东盟博览会、商务与投资峰会，深化广西与东盟全方位、多层次、宽领域的合作，展现广西对外开放的新形象。

马飚强调，当前要抓紧进驻指挥中心集中办公，尽快落实关键岗位人员。要抓紧制定各类工作方案、细案和应急预案，并反复演练。要进一步加强与国家部委的联系，跟踪落实好各部门和各兄弟省领导的邀请工作。要做好自贸区成就展、博览会开幕式等重大活动的组织策划。要做好采购商、投资商的邀请和经贸配对工作。要加强展览现场管理，既要严格执法，又要文明执法。要做好安全保卫工作，确保万无一失。要做好接待工作。要加强宣传策划，营造良好氛围。要加强供水、供电、卫生、消防以及道路桥梁等基础设施保障工作。要做好经费、人力和车辆保障。要做好南宁市市容市貌整治工作。要做好2011年博览会的策划。要加强领导，落实责任，确保各项筹备工作顺利推进。

出席会议的还有广西壮族自治区政府秘书长王跃飞等“两会”广西领导小组成员，“两会”指挥中心各工作部负责人，以及各有关单位负责人。

（三）万众一心举盛会

作为广西的一件盛事，中国—东盟博览会不仅是政府推动，更是全民参与、凝聚了广西各族人民心愿和力量的盛会。

2010年7月13日上午，广西国际博览事务局与广西艺术学院举行签约仪式，共同签署《共建创新型实践型艺术人才培养教学研究基地合作协议》，并举行基地揭牌仪式。广西壮族自治区政协副主席黄格胜，中国—东盟博览会秘书长、广西国际博览事务局局长郑军健出席签约和揭牌仪式。广西艺术学院是广西唯一一所国家独立设置的具有硕士授予权的艺术高校。近年来，广西艺术学院师生参加了六届博览会的开幕式工作，参与了博览会礼品、纪

念品的设计制作，为博览会提供了必不可少的支持和帮助，取得了很好的成效。博览局也为广西艺术学院的师生提供了良好的实践、创作平台，双方互惠互利，交流和友谊不断加深，合作硕果累累。教学研究基地建立后，双方在宣传推介、展览形象设计、博览会开幕式、国际论坛的组织实施、人力资源等方面的合作将进入一个更高层次的新阶段，将为中国—东盟博览会长效发展和广西艺术人才培养作出更大的贡献。

9月2日，中国—东盟博览会秘书处和钦州市人民政府联合举行新闻发布会，正式对外宣布：第七届中国—东盟博览会中国“魅力之城”确定为广西钦州市。围绕“魅力之城”，钦州积极策划了一系列宣传推广活动，如邀请东盟各国的媒体记者到钦州采风、考察等。经贸活动方面，主要是在博览会期间，举行钦州招商推介会，举办当届、历届中国—东盟“魅力之城”市长交流会、博览会支持商协会招待酒会、中国驻东盟10国商务参赞联谊会以及钦州活动日，希望通过这一系列活动，增强客商、东盟各国对钦州的认识，充分挖掘钦州的魅力，展示钦州的商机。

9月18日上午，第七届中国—东盟博览会、中国—东盟商务与投资峰会“携手共进30天”活动启动仪式在南宁国际会展中心举行。广西壮族自治区主席马飚宣布活动启动。自治区党委常委、宣传部部长沈北海，自治区党委常委、南宁市委书记车荣福，自治区党委常委、自治区副主席陈武，自治区党委常委、秘书长余远辉、柬埔寨王国驻南宁总领事英洪，越南社会主义共和国驻南宁总领事阮英勇，缅甸联邦驻南宁总领事敏隋，泰王国驻南宁总领事安特蓬，老挝人民民主共和国驻南宁总领事潘坎·尹他波里，菲律宾共和国驻广州总领事馆代表等东盟国家外交使节，广西壮族自治区政府秘书长王

2010年9月18日，第七届中国—东盟博览会、中国—东盟商务与投资峰会“携手共进30天”活动启动仪式在南宁国际会展中心举行

The 7th CAEXPO and the 7th CABIS 30-day Countdown Ceremony held at Nanning International Convention and Exhibition Center on September 18, 2010

跃飞，广西区直有关部门负责人，以及各界代表共300多人参加启动仪式。马飚宣布第七届中国—东盟博览会、中国—东盟商务与投资峰会“携手共进30天”启动，本届“两会”筹备工作进入最后冲刺阶段。

陈武在致辞中表示，在中国—东盟自贸区如期建成的新形势下，我们要加大创新力度，提高服务水平，让企业通过中国—东盟博览会这一平台，更好地享受自贸区建成后带来的无限商机。目前第七届中国—东盟博览会、商务与投资峰会筹备工作进展顺利，博览会活动内容将更加丰富、更加务实。广西将继续举全区之力办好盛会，各级各部门将以更大的热情、更高昂的斗志、更饱满的精神状态，全力以赴，确保第七届中国—东盟博览会和商务与投资峰会取得圆满成功。

东盟国家外交使节代表、参展参会企业代表、博览会战略合作伙伴代表也在仪式上发言，共同表达了美好愿景。

9月，博览会秘书处举办的中国—东盟博览会主题口号、诗词楹联征集活动圆满结束。本次征集活动由中国—东盟博览会秘书处举办。截至9月10日，共收到应征作品共3000多条，其中主题口号应征作品1000多条、副主题口号应征作品2198条；诗词、楹联应征作品1000多首。征集活动历时一个月，参赛作者来自全国24个省（自治区、直辖市），近自广西，远至哈尔滨、上海、昆明……香港特区和东盟国家人士也积极投稿。应征者中有国家公务员、在校大中专学生、企业职工，也有教师、军人、退休干部，以及文联、楹联学会会员等，其中业余创作人员占了很大比例，充分反映了广大应征者对中国—东盟自贸区和中国—东盟博览会的热情关注，对征集活动的积极参与。新加坡的作者还用不太熟练的中文完成了作品创作；来自四川地震灾区的应征者在参赛同时，字里行间寄托了对自贸区和博览会美好将来的憧憬，一件件作品，透着一股志在参与、重在参与、不计较比赛名次的认真劲头。

10月11日，第七届中国—东盟博览会指定接待宾馆授牌仪式举行。此举旨在继续做好第七届博览会乃至今后各届博览会的接待服务工作，进一步规范“中国—东盟博览会指定接待宾馆”称号的使用，培育和形成博览会接待品牌宾馆（酒店）。经过重新核发，有12家宾馆（酒店）获得“第七届中国—东盟博览会指定接待宾馆”称号。

10月11日，由广西知名书法家集体创作、以中国和东盟10国领导人寄语博览会为内容的书法长卷，由广西文联副主席韦苏文代表创作者赠送给中国—东盟博览会秘书处。在赠送仪式上，中国—东盟博览会秘书处秘书长郑军健接过了这一艺术精品。

该书法长卷是专门为第七届中国—东盟博览会的重要组成部分“自贸

区成就展”创作的。作品总长9米，宽1.8米，以中国和东盟国家领导人对中国—东盟博览会的寄语为书写内容。中国国家主席胡锦涛关于办好博览会的指示书于长卷的首要位置。长卷还书写了文莱苏丹哈桑纳尔、柬埔寨首相洪森、印尼总统苏西洛、老挝时任总理波松、马来西亚时任总理巴达维、缅甸时任总理登盛、菲律宾时任总统阿罗约、新加坡总理李显龙、泰国时任总理素拉育和越南总理阮晋勇等领导人对博览会的寄语。

该卷作品由广西书法家协会副主席、书法家韦克义，书法家刘炳清、王精、林建勋、刘德宏、刘炳玉、黄大业、陈小冰、甘文峰、彭洋、冯华春等11人集体创作。书体汇集了行草隶篆不同类别，风格庄重舒展，豪放凝重，又不失灵巧娟秀。卷容华美，气势宏大，给人以强烈的视觉冲击力。字里行间倾注了书法家们对中国—东盟博览会的满腔热忱。

10月13日，第七届中国—东盟博览会首席战略合作伙伴签约仪式暨新闻发布会在南宁举行。广西壮族自治区主席马飚亲手将“中国—东盟博览会首席战略合作伙伴”证书交到新加坡丰隆亚洲有限公司总裁张冬贵的手中。这是国外企业首次成为中国—东盟博览会首席战略合作伙伴。广西壮族自治区党委常委、自治区副主席陈武出席仪式并代表中国—东盟博览会组委会接过丰隆亚洲的赞助支票。

第七届中国—东盟博览会的战略合作伙伴有中国移动广西公司、中国有色矿业集团、广西投资集团、广西农垦集团4家知名企业，合作伙伴有中国银行等43家企业。

2010年10月13日，第七届中国—东盟博览会战略合作伙伴签约仪式暨新闻发布会在广西南宁举行

The signing ceremony and press conference of the 7th CAEXPO Strategic Partner held in Nanning, China on October 13, 2010

10月14日，中国—东盟博览会秘书处与龙州县委、县政府联合召开广西龙州天琴作为2010中国—东盟博览会国家政要和贵宾指定礼品的交接仪式暨

新闻发布会。龙州天琴是壮族骆越先民的文化遗产，是壮族乐器中最古老的乐器之一，至今已有1000多年历史。龙州天琴经过精心改良，琴音清亮、圆润、甜美悦耳，琴身将壮族铜鼓、绣球、青蛙等壮族文化元素融为一体，具有较高的演奏性、观赏性与收藏性。

10月15日上午，第七届中国—东盟博览会、第七届中国—东盟商务与投资峰会志愿者培训上岗志愿者徽章揭幕仪式在广西民族大学举行。共有1170名志愿者到场参加此次培训。仪式上，全体志愿者庄严宣誓，立志为即将召开的第七届中国—东盟博览会、中国—东盟商务与投资峰会提供热情周到的服务。

仪式上还进行了志愿者徽章的揭幕。专门设计的这套志愿者徽章，用时尚的徽章对志愿者每天的服务进行评价、认可和鼓励。这套徽章共分为两组11枚，方形的一组包括“一起加油”、“坚持不懈”、“我服务 我快乐”等内容，提醒志愿者在奉献中保持乐观的心态；圆形的一组为本届志愿者服装的图案，上面分别有1—3颗星，代表志愿者的等级，将根据志愿者服务表现颁发带有“星”的徽章，以此激励每一个在岗的志愿者，始终如一地做好每一项服务。

10月15日，第七届中国—东盟博览会、中国—东盟商务与投资峰会指挥中心信息通讯技术保障组组织自治区通信管理局、自治区工信委、中国电信广西公司、中国移动广西公司及中国联通广西分公司等五家单位在南宁国际会展中心开展了2010年“两会”信息通讯技术保障应急综合演练。演练从实

2010年10月15日举行的“两会”信息通讯技术保障应急综合演练

On October 15, the information and communication technology emergency drill was held to ensure the success of the 7th CAEXPO and the 7th CABIS

战角度出发，检验了应急通信队伍的快速响应、跨专业联动、有效应对及快速保障的能力。这次演练出动移动监测车2辆，全球眼设备1套，应急指挥车1辆、卫星通信车1辆、应急通信车3辆，光缆抢修设备3辆，近100名应急工作人员参加了演练。

10月17日，第七届中国—东盟博览会国家政要和贵宾礼品交接仪式暨新闻发布会在南宁举行。由郑军里、柒万里等11位广西知名画家联袂创作的三环艺术瓷器、景德镇艺术瓷器、《繁花似锦——中国—东盟10国名花·名家真迹》成为第七届中国—东盟博览会赠送给各国政要和贵宾的礼品。以中国及东盟10国国花为主题的《繁花似锦——中国—东盟10国名花·名家真迹》，寓意中国与东盟多元文化在自贸区建成大背景下交汇融合，百花齐放。艺术家们还为三环艺术瓷器及景德镇艺术瓷器创作了具有中国田园特色的画作，表达了对中国和东盟10国人民友谊长青的美好祝愿。

10月17日，中国—东盟博览会秘书处、广西邮政公司举办了“2010中国—东盟博览会特许纪念品”新闻发布会，发布《相聚博览会 共建自贸区》主题纪念邮票珍藏册等4款特许纪念品。

广西各级各部门以饱满的热情、高昂的斗志、全力以赴，奋战在各行各业各条战线上，高标准、严要求地完成各项筹备任务，用自己的实际行动，为中国—东盟自由贸易如期建成后的新一届博览会出谋划策、添砖加瓦，确保盛会圆满成功。

第二章

2 水润花开　共享硕果
——第七届中国—东盟博览会开幕

2010年10月19日，第七届中国—东盟博览会在南宁国际会展中心隆重开幕。

中国和东盟国家领导人、部长级贵宾、国际组织负责人、商协会会长、企业家出席盛会，表明了各方抓住中国—东盟自由贸易区建成的重大机遇，发挥博览会平台作用，加强全面合作，深化互利共赢的共同愿望，增强了各方继续共同推进自贸区建设，深化战略伙伴关系，实现共同发展、共同繁荣的信心和决心，也反映出博览会和商务与投资峰会的影响力和吸引力。

会期举行了双方领导人、部长、地方负责人之间的会见，以及政界与商界高端对话。各国领导人、部长、代表团团长巡视了展馆。主题国印度尼西亚举办了国家馆开馆仪式、印度尼西亚领导人与中国企业家圆桌对话会、印度尼西亚国家推介会等主题国系列活动，深化了共办共赢。

本届中国—东盟博览会开幕式以“水润花开，共享硕果”为主题，形象地表达出博览会的“合作之水”从涓涓细流到滔滔江河，浇灌着自贸区的广袤大地，滋润万物，结出了累累硕果的深刻寓意。

Efforts of All Fruits for All

—The 7th CAEXPO Opens

On October 19, 2010, the 7th CAEXPO opened with grand ceremony in Nanning International Convention and Exhibition Center.

Present at the event were heads of state/government of China and the 10 ASEAN nations, VIPs at ministerial level, heads of international organizations, heads of chambers of commerce and entrepreneurs of China and the ASEAN countries, showing the common wish of all sides to take advantage of the CAFTA and CAEXPO for comprehensive cooperation and deepened mutual benefits. It also enhanced the confidence and determination of all sides to further advance the CAFTA construction for deepened strategic partnership and common development and prosperity, as well as the influence and attraction of CAEXPO and China–ASEAN Business and Investment Summit (CABIS).

Concurrently with the CAEXPO, a series of programs were also held, such as meetings of state leaders, ministers, heads of local governments; high–end dialogues of political and business communities, inspections of VIPs to the CAEXPO exhibition halls, including state leaders, ministers, heads of delegations of China and the ASEAN countries. Indonesia, the Country of Honor of the 7th CAEXPO, staged the opening ceremony for its national pavilion. Indonesian state leader had round–table dialogue with Chinese CEOs, and other events such as Indonesia promotion conference were held to deepen the co–sponsorship and win–win outcome.

The opening ceremony of the 7th CAEXPO is themed on "Efforts of All, Fruits for All", vividly illustrating the development of the "Water of Cooperation" from droplets into giant rivers, which is watering the vast territory of the CAFTA and bears great fruits.

CHAPTER TWO

一　中国和东盟国家参加中国—东盟博览会

2010年10月19—24日，第七届中国—东盟博览会在中国广西南宁举行。本届博览会是中国—东盟自由贸易区如期全面建成后举办的新一届盛会，对于进一步促进中国—东盟友好合作、推动中国—东盟自由贸易深入发展，实现本区域的共同发展、共同繁荣，具有重要意义。

（一）中国和东盟政要出席第七届中国—东盟博览会

在中国—东盟自由贸易区如期全面建成的背景下，本届博览会受到了中国和东盟各国的高度重视。11国政府均派出了高规格的代表团出席第七届中

第七届中国—东盟博览会开幕式盛况
The grand opening ceremony of the 7th CAEXPO

国—东盟博览会及同期举办的第七届中国—东盟商务与投资峰会。

中共中央政治局常委、全国政协主席贾庆林，本届博览会主题国印尼副总统布迪约诺，老挝副总理阿桑·劳里，越南副总理张永仲，柬埔寨国务兼商业大臣占蒲拉西，文莱工业和初级资源部部长叶海亚，缅甸商务部部长吴丁乃登，马来西亚国际贸易和工业部副部长贾谷·东加·沙甘，菲律宾贸易与工业部副部长克里斯托伯，泰国商业部部长助理威拉萨·金那拉，新加坡贸工部兼新闻通讯艺术部政务次长陈振泉等出席本届博览会、商务与投资峰会。

中国商务部国际谈判贸易代表兼副部长高虎城、国家质量监督检验检疫总局局长支树平、国家发展与改革委员会副主任张国宝、外交部副部长张志军等中国有关部委领导出席本届博览会、商务与投资峰会。据统计，出席本届博览会、商务与投资峰会的部长级贵宾有191人。其中，东盟及其他国家部长级贵宾53人。

（二）中国和东盟商家和世界知名企业参展参会

本届博览会参展企业2200家，各国大企业和品牌企业比上届增多，展位需求量大，供不应求。本届博览会总展位数4600个，比上届增长15%。其中，中国内地及港澳台地区使用展位3379个，外国企业使用展位1221个，其中东盟10国展位1178个，均创历届新高。印尼、老挝、马来西亚、缅甸、泰国、越南等六个东盟国家包馆。东盟10国均组织本国品牌企业参展，东盟品牌展区成为本届亮点。东盟各国还在本国展区内按行业布展，突出展示农产品食品、木材家具、轻工工艺、珠宝等行业产品，有效提高了本届博览会的

第七届中国—东盟博览会的东盟国家展区
The 7th CAEXPO ASEAN Commodity Section

专业化水平。

本届博览会市场吸引力和影响力提升反映在几个方面：本届博览会国内外企业重复参展率明显提高，外国展位数连年提升，博览会的外国展位数目前在中国国内展位中居于前列，博览会已经成为东盟等外国企业开拓中国市场的重要渠道。

本届博览会专业观众39130人，比上届增长2%。其中来自美国、法国、日本、韩国和港澳台地区的专业观众有所增加。参展参会规模进一步扩大。

（三）中外媒体积极参会报道

第七届中国—东盟博览会、中国—东盟商务与投资峰会继续受到国内外主流媒体和专业媒体的重视。到会采访的记者比往年又有增加，达到199家共1458名记者，比上届增加39名。其中，国外媒体72家共106名记者（含东盟媒体88人）；港澳台媒体16家共41名记者。

人民日报、新华通讯社、中央人民广播电台、中央电视台、中国国际广播电台、中国新闻社、中国日报等中国中央级媒体派出阵容强大的记者队伍报道此次盛会。

印尼、菲律宾、泰国、文莱、越南等东盟国家以及日本、希腊等国家媒体派出记者到会采访。香港凤凰卫视、文汇报、香港商报、澳门日报等港澳台地区媒体也派出记者报道了此次盛会。参加采访报道的媒体和记者数量多，规模大，体现了各方对本届博览会的高度关注。

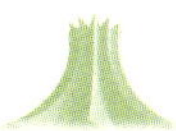

二 第七届中国—东盟博览会开幕式

金风送爽硕果飘香，绿城南宁嘉宾云集。2010年10月19日下午，第七届中国—东盟博览会在南宁国际会展中心朱槿花厅隆重开幕。

在中国—东盟自贸区如期建成的背景下，第七届中国—东盟博览会的举办具有特殊意义。本届开幕式以“水润花开，共享硕果”为主题，形象地表达出博览会的“合作之水”从涓涓细流到滔滔江河，浇灌着自贸区的广袤大地，滋润万物，结出了累累硕果的深刻寓意。

当天下午，数万朵象征灿烂辉煌的向日葵，把南宁国际会展中心朱槿花厅装扮得恢宏喜庆。中国与东盟各国的标志性建筑图案镶嵌在环廊四周的12朵大向日葵之中。整个开幕式现场让人置身花的海洋，给人带来美好的希望。

2010年10月19日，第七届中国—东盟博览会开幕式在广西南宁举行

The 7th CAEXPO opening ceremony held in Nanning, Guangxi on October 19, 2010

中共中央政治局常委、全国政协主席贾庆林宣布第七届中国—东盟博览会开幕

H.E. Jia Qinglin, Chairman of the National Committee of Chinese People's Political Consultative Conference (CPPCC), declares the opening of the 7th CAEXPO

开幕式主席台的背景像展开的双翼，也像厚重的史书，象征自贸区和博览会翻开了新的一页，展翅腾飞，进入新的发展时期。寓意随着中国—东盟自贸区的建成，中国—东盟博览会站在新的起点，迎来新的机遇，开始谱写新的篇章。

在这个花团锦簇、充满希望和生机的金色朱槿花厅，中国和东盟国家领导人、部长、地方政府行政长官、国际组织负责人、世界知名企业家、商协会会长以及区域经济研究专家与参展会客商齐聚一堂，共同见证第七届中国—东盟博览会开幕的精彩时刻。

“一进会场，我们就被满场的向日葵花海给吸引住了，它让我们感受到光明和希望。我们坚信，中国和东盟各国之间的经贸大戏会越唱越火热，自贸区的明天会越来越美好！”这是广西农垦集团有限公司董事长刘刚在开幕式现场的感言，也代表了出席开幕式各方嘉宾的心声。

14时，开幕式正式开始。开幕式由本届博览会主题国印度尼西亚贸易部部长冯慧兰主持，印度尼西亚副总统布迪约诺、广西壮族自治区主席马飚、中国商务部国际贸易谈判代表兼副部长高虎城分别致辞。

布迪约诺说，经过近20年的时间，中国已经成为东盟各国可以信赖的伙伴，在许多事务上发挥重要作用。作为目前全球第二大和发展速度最快的经济体，中国为东盟创造了很多机遇，只要双方携起手来，就能成为推动世界经济发展的强大力量。东盟与中国发展双边关系最重要的支柱就是中国—东盟自贸区。自贸区的建成，标志着双方的战略合作伙伴关系迈入了新纪元，区域一体化进程也迎来了一个新的里程碑。第七届中国—东盟博览会的举办，让中国和东盟双方有很好的机会，来庆贺和分享合作与友谊的成果。要保证这些成果，最重

印度尼西亚副总统布迪约诺在第七届中国—东盟博览会开幕式上致辞

H.E. Boediono, Vice President of Indonesia addresses the 7th CAEXPO opening ceremony

要的措施就是继续支持中国—东盟自贸区的建设，正像2010年中国—东盟博览会的主题所言，我们要用自贸区产生的新机遇，进一步来推进自贸区的建设。

马飚说，7年前，中国—东盟博览会为中国—东盟自由贸易区建设应运而生。7年来，我们共同见证了博览会在各方的热情参与和大力支持下，连年迈上新台阶，每届取得新成效，已经成为自贸区建设的“助推器”，成为中国与东盟友谊合作的象征。广西作为博览会的承办方，作为中国面向东盟开放的前沿和窗口，愿与各方进一步发挥博览会作用，不断拓展功能、完善机制，通过中国—东盟信息平台建设，使之成为贸易、投资、文化、教育等多领域信息交流中心和“永不落幕”的博览会，更好地服务于自贸区发展和造福各国的企业和人民。我们愿与各方共同推进自贸区框架下的次区域合作，共推泛北部湾经济合作，共建南宁—新加坡经济走廊，共建跨境经济合作区，共创中国与东盟和谐共进、合作发展的新辉煌。

广西壮族自治区主席马飚在第七届中国—东盟博览会开幕式上致辞

H.E. Ma Biao, Governor of Guangxi Zhuang Autonomous Region addresses the 7th CAEXPO opening ceremony

高虎城说，经过双方10年努力，中国—东盟自由贸易区已于2010年1月1日如期建成，标志着双方经贸合作进入到全面深入发展的新阶段。在自贸区建设的推进过程中，我们共同举办了六届中国—东盟博览会，通过这一平台，把投资贸易便利化的成果带给各国企业和人民，产生了互利共赢的良好成效。本届博览会将充分反映中国—东盟自贸区建设成果，内容更加丰富，针对性更强，将为双方企业和人民带来更多的实惠。让我们以自贸区建成为契机，共同努力，在更大范围、更宽领域、更高层次加强合作，为促进本地区共同发展、共同繁荣作出新的贡献。

中国商务部国际贸易谈判代表兼副部长高虎城在第七届中国—东盟博览会开幕式上致辞

H.E. Gao Hucheng, China International Trade Representative and Vice Minister of Commerce of China, addresses the 7th CAEXPO opening ceremony

剪彩仪式前播放的短片，回顾了中国—东盟自贸区建设的历程，反映了博览会对自贸区建设推动作用，描绘自贸

印度尼西亚贸易部部长冯慧兰主持第七届中国—东盟博览会开幕式

H.E. Madam Ibu Mari Elka Pangestu, Indonesian Minister of Trade, hosts the 7th CAEXPO opening ceremony

区美好明天。短片结束后，14个晶莹剔透、造型独特的“成果之杯”缓缓升起，“成果之杯”由三层水晶杯堆叠而成。

14时36分，随着中共中央政治局常委、全国政协主席贾庆林宣布第七届中国—东盟博览会开幕，剪彩仪式开始。由贾庆林主席与第七届中国—东盟博览会主题国印度尼西亚副总统布迪约诺、老挝副总理阿桑·劳里、越南副总理张永仲、柬埔寨国务兼商业大臣占蒲拉西、文莱工业和初级资源部部长叶海亚、缅甸商务部部长吴丁乃登、中国商务部国际贸易谈判代表兼副部长高虎城、马来西亚国际贸易和工业部副部长贾谷·东加·沙甘、菲律宾贸易与工业部副部长克里斯托伯、泰国商业部部长助理威拉萨·金那拉、新加坡贸工部兼新闻通讯艺术部政务次长陈振泉、广西壮族自治区党委书记郭声琨、东盟秘书处东盟市场一体化合作司司长苏柏什等各国贵宾为开幕式剪彩。

14位剪彩嘉宾手捧象征自贸区成果的果汁，共同倾入主席台前的“成果之杯”，表达中国和东盟11国共享自贸区成果、共庆自贸区丰收的喜悦。金色的花瓣在主席台周围伸展开来，一朵巨大的向日葵在舞台上盛情绽放，与大厅环廊上的数万朵向日葵交相辉映，预示着博览会和自贸区的明天将更加灿烂、更加辉煌。色泽鲜艳的“苹果”从会场上空纷纷扬扬飘落下来，一群身着中国与东盟各国民族服装的少女向现场嘉宾送上印有“博览会让自贸区明天更美好”字样的“苹果”。伴随着漫天飞舞飘扬的礼花、彩带以及雷鸣般的掌声，第七届中国—东盟博览会正式拉开序幕。

在延续博览会“合作之水”概念的前提下，本届开幕式主题定为“水润花开，共享硕果”，以共享成果为剪彩创意，受到出席开幕式嘉宾的普遍赞誉。

“每一年的中国—东盟博览会都会给人不同的惊喜，”越南驻南宁总领事阮英勇评价说，“今年的开幕式别出心裁，用开花结果来寓意中国和东

中国与东盟国家领导人在第七届中国—东盟博览会开幕式上剪彩
Leaders of China and the ASEAN countries jointly inaugurate the 7th CAEXPO opening ceremony

盟各国的友好合作以及自贸区的建设硕果累累，主题创意很好，比喻恰如其分，抒发了中国和东盟国家人民的美好情怀。开花结果，这是一个无限的循环，自贸区的明天会越来越辉煌。”

缅甸农产品食品加工出口协会会长佐敏温说：“同前几届相比，本届开幕式富有特色，特别是中国和东盟各国领导人共同倾倒成就果汁的创意很新颖，寓意东盟国家与中国的友谊会更加深厚，合作机会的机遇更多，博览会和自贸区的明天会更好。”

“这是具有深层次含义的。自贸区正式建成是我们期待已久的成果。本届博览会领导人剪彩所用的果汁就是自贸区成果和博览会‘合作之水’交融而成的精华。中国—东盟自贸区就好比含苞待放的花蕾，每一届博览会的成功举办，都在浇灌着自贸区合作之花不断开放，结出硕果。我们对自贸区建成后办好博览会的意义也有了更深刻的体会。” 中国著名东南亚商务专家、中国—东盟商务理事会主管中方秘书处常务副秘书长许宁宁对本届开幕式的创意给予高度评价。

出席第七届中国—东盟博览会开幕式的还有：国家质量监督检验检疫总局局长支树平、国家发展与改革委员会副主任张国宝、外交部副部长张志军、全国政协副秘书长王胜洪，广西壮族自治区领导马铁山、陈际瓦、沈北海、车荣福、温卡华、陈武、黄道伟、余远辉、吴恒、刘新文、莫永清、覃瑞祥、荣仕星、文明、陈章良、杨道喜、林念修、高雄、李康、梁胜利、林国强、蒋济雄、李达球、蒋培兰、黄格胜、黄日波、彭钊、李彬，广西壮族自治区人民检察院检察长张少康，自治区党委组织部部长周新建，以及国际组织负责人、世界知名企业家、商协会会长、区域经济研究专家与参展参会客商代表共1300多人。

出席第七届中国—东盟博览会开幕式的各国嘉宾

Guests at the 7th CAEXPO opening ceremony

三　中外贵宾巡视展馆

2010年10月19日，中共中央政治局常委、全国政协主席贾庆林在国家有关部委领导及广西壮族自治区党委书记、自治区人大常委会主任郭声琨，自治区主席马飚陪同下，来到南宁国际会展中心，巡视了第七届中国—东盟博览会投资合作专题展区、"魅力之城"展区和先进技术专题展区，详细了解各展厅的参展情况。

在投资合作专题展区，贾庆林与中国铝业公司、中国有色矿业集团有限公司、北京建工集团有限责任公司的负责人亲切交谈，鼓励他们利用好中国—东盟博览会这一良好平台，加强与各方尤其是东盟国家在基础设施建

2010年10月19日，中共中央政治局常委、全国政协主席贾庆林巡视第七届中国—东盟博览会展馆

H.E. Jia Qinglin, Chairman of the National Committee of CPPCC, at the 7th CAEXPO exhibition halls on October 19, 2010

设、资源开发和加工等领域的合作，形成全方位、多层次、宽领域的经济合作格局，实现互利共赢，取得更大成就。

在巡馆时，贾庆林不时在印尼、柬埔寨等充满异国风情的展馆、展台前停下脚步，细细欣赏展品的独特造型和演员的动人歌舞，并对此报以亲切的微笑和鼓励的掌声。

作为本届博览会中国“魅力之城”的广西钦州市，其展厅以“扬帆起航”的海轮形象呈现在大家面前，展现未来的钦州将成为新兴自由港、产业合作基地和国际海湾城，吸引了贾庆林的目光。2007年6月，贾庆林曾来到钦州市，就推进广西北部湾经济区开放开发进行调研。在钦州展厅，贾庆林认真观看了钦州市的宣传短片，听取了钦州市委主要领导的简要汇报，对钦州市作为中国—东盟自贸区前沿城市的独特魅力表示赞赏，对广西北部湾经济区在短短几年里发生的巨大变化感到欣慰。他深情地说，祝贺你们以“钦州速度”创造了“北部湾奇迹”！广西壮族自治区领导马铁山、陈武、余远辉、梁胜利等陪同巡馆。

10月19—20日，东盟各国领导人、代表团团长也分别巡视了第七届博览会展馆。

10月19日，印尼副总统布迪约诺一行在广西壮族自治区主席马飚，自治区党委常委、宣传部部长沈北海等领导的陪同下，来到印尼“魅力之城”梭罗市展馆门口，共同参加在这里举行的主题国印尼馆开馆仪式。开馆仪式结束后，布迪约诺一行在马飚、沈北海等领导的陪同下，饶有兴趣地巡视了代表梭罗市文化特色的皮影戏及蜡染和面具。随后，布迪约诺一行在沈北海陪

2010年10月19日，印度尼西亚副总统布迪约诺巡视第七届中国—东盟博览会展馆

H.E. Boediono, Vice President of the Republic of Indonesia at the 7th CAEXPO exhibition halls on October 19, 2010

同下巡视了中国“魅力之城”钦州展馆、先进技术展馆、印尼国家商品馆。在印尼国家商品馆，布迪约诺一行驻足了解印尼参展商品内容，了解项目推介情况，并同参展人员交谈并亲切握手。

10月19日，老挝副总理阿桑·劳里一行在广西壮族自治区党委常委、统战部部长黄道伟的陪同下，从3号入口进入南宁国际会展中心巡视。在老挝“魅力之城”甘蒙馆，阿桑·劳里介绍了甘蒙在矿产资源、旅游开发、交通建设等方面的情况，黄道伟听后盛赞甘蒙是个美丽的地方。在中国“魅力之城”钦州展区，阿桑·劳里对这个古代海上丝绸之路起点的城市充满了兴趣，仔细听取了钦州坭兴陶、林浆纸业及保税港区等内容的介绍。在老挝商品展区，阿桑·劳里不忘推荐老挝的红木家具和啤酒，并对木薯淀粉产品及纺织品展区进行了巡视。巡馆结束时，黄道伟表示，他计划带领一批广西的企业家到老挝考察投资置业，共享中国—东盟博览会带来的商机。

2010年10月19日，老挝副总理阿桑·劳里巡视第七届中国—东盟博览会展馆

H.E. Asang LAOLY, Vice Prime Minister of the Lao People's Democratic Republic at the 7th CAEXPO exhibition halls on October 19, 2010

10月19日，越南副总理张永仲来到南宁国际会展中心，在广西壮族自治区党委常委、政法委书记温卡华的陪同下巡馆。张永仲一行首先来到越南“魅力之城”大叻，向参展的越南企业家挥手致意，了解越南商品参展情况，并多次现场题词，鼓励越南企业加强与中国企业的交流与合作，进一步扩大双方经贸往来。张永仲还参观了中国“魅力之城”钦州展区，饶有兴趣地观看钦州具有浓郁传统特色的陶瓷展品。张永仲在现场接受越南媒体的采访时表示，要继续加大越南与广西的经贸合作和交流，特别是在农业开发、基础设施建设、自然资源开发等领域深化合作，实现互利共赢。

2010年10月19日，越南副总理张永仲巡视第七届中国—东盟博览会展馆

H.E. Truong Vinh Trong, Vice Prime Minister of the Socialist Republic of Vietnam at the 7th CAEXPO exhibition halls on October 19, 2010

10月19日，柬埔寨国务兼商业大臣占蒲拉西一行在广西壮族自治区人大常委会副主任覃瑞祥的陪同下，参观了中国—东盟博览会投资合作、魅力之城展厅以及农业先进适用技术展厅。这是占蒲拉西第七次参加中国—东盟博览会。在柬埔寨商品展区，占蒲拉西驻足了解柬埔寨的大米、家具、珠宝、食品等参展商品，与参展商人亲切交谈，询问参展情况。占蒲拉西说，柬埔寨的商人对参加中国—东盟博览会非常有兴趣，也很主动，希望通过博览会这个平台，找到更多更大的商机。在柬埔寨“魅力之城”磅湛展区，身穿民族服装的柬埔寨人为贵宾献上了编织得非常厚实的茉莉花串，并表演了根据吴哥窟壁画整理出来的阿普萨拉舞。磅湛位于湄公河西岸，是柬埔寨人口最多、面积最大的农业大省，资源丰富，风光美丽，磅湛展区再现了古吴哥文化。占蒲拉西一行还参观了紧邻的中国“魅力之城”钦州展区，并与钦州参展人员合影。

2010年10月19日，柬埔寨国务兼商业大臣占蒲拉西巡视第七届中国—东盟博览会展馆

H.E. CHAM Prasidh, Senior Minister and Minister of Commerce of the Kingdom of Cambodia at the 7th CAEXPO exhibition halls on October 19, 2010

2010年10月20日，文莱工业和初级资源部部长叶海亚巡视第七届中国—东盟博览会展馆

H.E. Pehin Dato Awang Haji Yahya, Minister of Industry & Primary Resources of Brunei Darussalam at the 7th CAEXPO exhibition halls on October 20, 2010

10月20日，文莱工业和初级资源部部长叶海亚在广西壮族自治区副主席杨道喜的陪同下，参观了南宁国际会展中心各展馆。叶海亚部长一行首先来到“魅力之城”钦州展区，详细了解已经正式投产的中国石油广西钦州千万吨炼油项目，并对钦州石化产业园和保税港区发展建设表示赞赏。叶海亚希望文莱和中国能在能源领域进行深入的洽谈及合作。随后，叶海亚部长一行来到科技专题展区，他对广西在机电一体化和现代化农业装备等领域的先进水平表示出浓厚兴趣，并仔细参观展馆内的柳州高华机械有限公司生产的焊接、冲压等模具设备。最后，叶海亚一行来到位于会展中心二楼的东盟商品馆，看到来自东盟各国琳琅满目的展品，叶海亚部长竖起了大拇指，并对第七届中国—东盟博览会的成功举办表示衷心的祝贺。

10月19日，缅甸商务部长吴丁乃登一行在广西壮族自治区政协副主席李达球的陪同下，来到位于南宁国际会展中心2号展厅东侧门的缅甸馆进行巡馆。在缅甸馆，吴丁乃登向李达球介绍了缅甸的纺织业、煤炭业、农业、林业、水产业等，他说，缅甸的很多项目都是缅方企业与中方企业一起合作，希望双方企业多接触，成为好朋友。随后，在参观“魅力钦州”展区和“先进技术”展区时，吴丁乃登一行饶有兴致地听取了海上丝绸之路和钦州拟打造成国际海

2010年10月20日，缅甸商务部长吴丁乃登巡视第七届中国—东盟博览会展馆

H.E. U TIN NAING THEIN, Minister of Commerce of the Union of Myanmar at the 7th CAEXPO exhibition halls on October 20, 2010

湾新城的介绍，并对广西自主研发的高新技术机电一体化和现代农业装备等表现出了浓厚的兴趣。最后，吴丁乃登与李达球来到缅甸商品展区，参观了玉石展等，并共同为缅甸商品展区剪彩。

10月20日，马来西亚国际贸易与工业部副部长拿督贾谷·东加·沙甘一行在广西壮族自治区政协副主席蒋济雄的陪同下，巡视了博览会马来西亚商品馆和“魅力之城”展厅，双方领导共同为马来西亚商品馆剪彩。在马来西亚商品馆，贾谷·东加·沙甘饶有兴致地参观了马来西亚的食品、保健品、机电、手工艺品等各个展位，并与参展商人亲切交流，询问参展情况。来自沙捞越州的贾谷·东加·沙甘对家乡的参展企业倍感兴趣。在沙捞越的食品企业展位前，贾谷·东加·沙甘和蒋济雄兴致勃勃地品尝了清真锅巴、泡菜等食品，连声称赞“好吃”，并鼓励参展商大力开拓中国市场。在马来西亚“魅力之城”吉隆坡展区，贾谷·东加·沙甘仔细倾听工作人员介绍“魅力之城”所展示的主题，他希望通过这些展示，能吸引更多的中国人到马来西亚旅游和投资。在“魅力之城”钦州展区，钦州市领导热情地向贾谷·东加·沙甘一行介绍了钦州在国际航运中的发展思路，贾谷·东加·沙甘对钦州的发展前景表示赞赏。

2010年10月20日，马来西亚国际贸易与工业部副部长拿督贾谷·东加·沙甘巡视第七届中国—东盟博览会展馆

H.E. Dato' Jacob Dungau Sagan, Vice Minister of Trade & Industry of Malaysia at the 7th CAEXPO exhibition halls on October 20, 2010

10月19日，菲律宾贸工部副部长克里斯托伯一行在广西壮族自治区人大常委会副主任文明的陪同下，巡视了第七届中国—东盟博览会菲律宾馆。在菲律宾展馆里，克里斯托伯驻足在一个展示椰子油的展台前，向参展商了解产品的情况后说，要利用好中国—东盟博览会这个平台，把菲律宾的特色商品推向广阔的中国市场。在广西农垦展台，两个硕大的南瓜引人注目。克里斯托伯以为是模型，当听说这是实物，其种子经过中国神舟五号太空飞船携

2010年10月19日，菲律宾贸工部副部长克里斯托伯巡视第七届中国—东盟博览会展馆

H.E. Adrian S.Cristobal, Jr, Vice Secretary of Trade & Industry of the Republic of the Philippines at the 7th CAEXPO exhibition halls on October 19, 2010

带上太空、再经过培育才结出来的大南瓜时，他说：“这太神奇了”。克里斯托伯还观看了其他国家的展馆展区。对于中国—东盟博览会吸引了这么多参展商前来参展，他表示，菲律宾今后将会组织更多的商家前来参会。

10月20日，泰国商业部部长助理威拉萨在广西壮族自治区政协副主席李彬、泰国驻南宁领事馆总领事安特蓬先生等陪同下，兴致勃勃来到南宁国际会展中心。在博览会泰国馆门前，两位赤足而盛装的泰国姑娘手捧花钵翩翩起舞，把芬芳鲜艳的玫瑰花瓣撒向光临展馆的贵宾。进入泰国馆，首先是泰国茉莉香米的展位，展台上的电饭锅里已煮好满满一锅雪白的茉莉香米饭。威拉萨见状饶有兴趣地抄起锅铲，加入鸡蛋、火腿肠、肉松、胡萝卜等配料炒起米饭来，随后分送给李彬等陪同人员及现场观众品尝。大家纷纷夸赞泰国香米就是香。巡视完泰国馆，威拉萨一行又高兴地来到位于二号展馆的

2010年10月20日，泰国商业部部长助理威拉萨巡视第七届中国—东盟博览会展馆

H.E. Veerasak Jinarat, Assistant Minister of Commerce of the Kingdom of Thailand at the 7th CAEXPO exhibition halls on October 20, 2010

“魅力之城”展厅，参观了本届博览会泰国“魅力之城”清莱展位。威拉萨向李彬表示，感谢广西政府给予泰国代表团的热情接待，作为博览会主办方之一的泰国商业部将会一如既往地支持中国—东盟博览会。

10月19日，新加坡贸工部兼新闻通讯艺术部政务次长陈振泉在广西壮族自治区政协副主席黄日波的陪同下，巡视了第七届中国—东盟博览会展馆。陈振泉首先在“魅力之城”新加坡展区了解布展情况。随后，在中国“魅力之城”钦州展厅听了钦州市发展情况介绍。陈振泉感叹：“钦州发展速度快，变化很大！”陈振泉还参观了先进技术展和新加坡企业展、商品展。在新加坡商品展区，陈振泉热情地和参展商打招呼，向他们了解参展内容和项目推介情况。在接受记者采访时，陈振泉表示：“今年的博览会与去年相比规模更大、形式更丰富，这也预示着中国与东盟之间的合作更上一层楼。今年是中国和新加坡建交20周年，同时也是中国—东盟自由贸易区正式启动的第一年，因此今年的中国—东盟博览会在新加坡得到了踊跃的响应，参展企业为历届最多，相信今后双方的各领域合作还会更加紧密。”

2010年10月19日，新加坡贸工部兼新闻通讯艺术部政务次长陈振泉巡视第七届中国—东盟博览会展馆

H.E. Sam Tan Chin Siong, Parliamentary Secretary for Trade and Industry of the Republic of Singapore at the 7th CAEXPO exhibition halls on October 19, 2010

四　主题国活动

（一）主题国开馆仪式

2010年10月19日上午，第七届中国—东盟博览会主题国印度尼西亚开馆仪式在南宁国际会展中心隆重举行。印尼副总统布迪约诺，广西壮族自治区主席马飚出席仪式并共同剪彩。

印尼贸易部部长冯慧兰，印尼工业部部长希塔亚，印尼国企部部长穆斯塔法·阿布巴卡，自治区领导沈北海、陈武、刘新文、蒋济雄等出席开馆仪式。

布迪约诺在致辞中热情洋溢地推介“魅力之城”梭罗。他说，我非常赞同梭罗市当选本届中国—东盟博览会“魅力之城”。梭罗确实能表现印尼形象，宣传印尼贸易。在梭罗这个城市里，有各种各样的民族，有很多非常勤

2010年10月19日，第七届中国—东盟博览会主题国印度尼西亚开馆仪式在南宁国际会展中心举行

On October 19, 2010, Indonesia, Country of Honor of the 7th CAEXPO, held the inaugural ceremony for the Pavilion of Indonesian City of Charm at the Nanning International Convention and Exhibition Center

奋的手工艺制造商，他们来自不同省份，有着自己的宗教和文化背景，能聚在一起做生意，这就是印尼健康民族发展的象征，也能代表中国—东盟博览会的团结合作精神。

布迪约诺指出，2010年是印尼与中国建交60周年，印尼总统苏西洛和中国国家主席胡锦涛把2010年定为两国友好年。我们将以此为契机，进一步发展两国战略合作伙伴关系。2008年，印中两国双边贸易额已经增长到300亿美元。现在印尼与中国发展战略性合作伙伴关系正在迈出第二大步伐，即在3至5年内达到双边贸易额500亿美元。我们将与中国继续搭建友好之桥，尤其在文化、媒体方面加强合作。希望有更多的中国游客来印尼访问，也希望有更多的印尼游客到中国访问。

仪式结束后，布迪约诺、马飚等兴致勃勃地参观了“魅力之城”梭罗展厅。精美的木雕，艳丽的蜡染……印尼传统手工艺品让嘉宾们连连称赞。布迪约诺乘兴将一个木雕脸谱送给马飚，马飚欣然接过，表示将送到广西民族博物馆陈放，让更多的中国人民、广西人民认识和了解印尼文化。

（二）印度尼西亚领导人与中国企业家圆桌对话会

2010年10月19日下午，印度尼西亚副总统布迪约诺与中国企业CEO圆桌对话会在南宁举行。广西壮族自治区主席马飚、中国商务部国际贸易谈判代表兼副部长高虎城、中国贸促会副会长王锦珍出席会议并致辞。印尼贸易部部长冯慧兰主持对话会。印尼工业部部长希达悦、印尼国企部部长穆斯塔法·阿布巴卡尔、印尼驻华大使易慕龙出席会议。

布迪约诺在演讲中说，多年来印尼政府已经为加强印尼与中国双边关系奠定了良好基础。随着中国—东盟自贸区的建成，印尼政府将继续努力为广

2010 年 10 月 19 日，印度尼西亚副总统布迪约诺与中国企业 CEO 圆桌对话会在南宁举行

On October 19, 2010, H.E. Boediono, Vice President of the Republic of Indonesia at the round table meeting with CEOs of Chinese enterprises in Nanning

大国外企业到印尼投资发展提供良好的环境。作为东南亚最大的国家，印尼要实现可持续发展，维持发展竞争力，同时减少地区不平衡，重中之重就是要不断更新、加强硬件和软件，特别是要加强交通通讯基础设施建设，建立有效的物流系统和知识系统，确保融入全球发展趋势当中。希望更多的中国企业关注印尼，参与到印尼的发展建设当中。

马飚在致辞中说，广西与印尼隔海相望，友谊与合作源远流长。近年来，广西与印尼各级政府和企业界的友好交流越来越密切，合作成果越来越显著。中国—东盟自由贸易区的如期建成，为广西进一步扩大与印尼各省和工商企业界的合作带来了新的机遇。广西愿以此为契机，全面深化同印尼工商企业界的交流与合作，为促进中国与印尼的经贸关系、促进区域共同繁荣发展作出新的更大贡献。

高虎城在致辞中说，2010年是中国和印尼两国建交60年，又是中印两国的友好年，在两国领导人的关心和共同努力下，两国经贸合作取得了很好的发展。2010年是中国—东盟自贸区全面建成的第一年，自贸区对中印双边贸易的拉动作用初步显现。我们应当继续鼓励双方的企业扩大贸易投资，继续提供各种便利，不断提升双方经贸合作的水平，不断拓展双方经贸合作的领域，造福两国人民。

王锦珍在致辞中说，中国和印尼两国资源丰富，经济互补性强，市场巨大，而且企业间有着发挥互惠互利合作的共同愿望，多年来在两国政府支持和企业努力下，双边经贸合作获得了长足的发展。中国贸促会将努力推动两国企业抓住中国—东盟自贸区建成的新机遇，进一步促进双边经贸关系，提升合作水平。

中国技术进出口总公司总裁唐毅，中国机械进出口集团总裁王旭升，中国进出口银行业务部副总经理李文，中国技术进出口总公司副总裁单伟，华为技术有限公司亚太地区副总裁马悦，中国寰球工程公司副总裁王卓岩等中国企业代表参加会议，与印尼国家领导人及有关部门领导、企业的代表展开了热烈、务实、友好的对话。

（三）印度尼西亚国家推介会

2010年10月21日上午，印度尼西亚国家推介会在南宁国际会展中心举行。推介会由印尼投资协调署和印尼贸易部出口发展总司主办，印尼贸易部出口发展总公司总司长赫斯蒂、广西壮族自治区人大常委会副主任刘新文出席推介会。

刘新文指出，2009年，虽然受国际金融危机影响，中国与印尼的双边贸

2010 年 10 月 21 日，印度尼西亚国家推介会在南宁国际会展中心举行

The Promotion Conference of Indonesia held at Nanning International Convention and Exhibition Center on October 21, 2010

易额仍达到280多亿美元，印尼继续成为中国在东盟的第四大贸易伙伴。印尼也是中国在东盟投资最多的国家之一和对外承包工程的重要市场。广西十分重视发展与印尼的经贸关系。广西与印尼的合作已全面展开，双边贸易持续快速增长，双向投资发展势头良好。当前，广西进入了经济快速发展、扩大开放合作的新时期，正抓紧实施《广西北部湾经济区发展规划》和深入推进西部大开发，广西北部湾经济区已逐步具备重要国际区域经济合作区的雏形。通过印尼国家推介会，相信广西与印尼将迎来更大的合作局面。

赫斯蒂表示，中国—东盟是个巨大的市场，自贸区为印尼的发展铺开了道路，特别是进出口方面，中国是印尼的友好合作伙伴。东盟是中国投资者的主要投资区域，而印尼有丰富的资源，有很多受过良好教育的年轻劳动力，政府出台了许多优惠政策。希望能与中国建立更好的合作关系，互利共赢；印尼能为中国提供很多机会和资源，在信息、制造业、技术方面都有很大的合作前景。

五 中国和东盟国家领导人会见

2010年10月19日，中共中央政治局常委、全国政协主席贾庆林在广西南宁分别会见了前来出席第七届中国—东盟博览会、商务与投资峰会的印度尼西亚副总统布迪约诺、老挝副总理阿桑·劳里、越南副总理张永仲，并集体会见了柬埔寨、文莱、缅甸、马来西亚、菲律宾、泰国、新加坡等国政府代表团团长和东盟秘书处代表。

在会见布迪约诺时，贾庆林说，中国和印尼是友好邻邦。建交60年来，特别是2005年两国建立战略伙伴关系以来，双边关系呈现成熟、快速、稳定的良好发展态势。双方政治上相互支持信任，各领域务实合作成果丰硕，民间交往日益扩大，在国际地区事务中保持了良好的协调与配合。中方高度重视发展同印尼友好互利关系，愿同印尼方一道努力，全面推进两国战略伙伴关系，造福两国人民。

2010年10月19日，中共中央政治局常委、全国政协主席贾庆林在广西南宁会见印度尼西亚副总统布迪约诺

On October 19, 2010, H.E. Jia Qinglin, Chairman of the National Committee of CPPCC, at the meeting with H.E. Boediono, Vice President of the Republic of Indonesia in Nanning, China

布迪约诺表示，印尼中国关系经历60年的发展取得全面进展。印尼方愿不断提升两国战略伙伴关系，深化经贸、能源、文化、教育等各领域的交流与合作。布迪约诺说，东盟—中国自贸区建成以来，成果惠及双方人民，东盟与中国的关系也更加紧密。印尼方愿与中方共同努力，落实好东盟—中国自贸协定，不断扩大两国贸易和相互投资规模。布迪约诺还对中国共产党十七届五中全会胜利召开表示祝贺。

在会见阿桑·劳里时，贾庆林说，近年来中老关系呈现蓬勃发展势头。2009年，两党两国最高领导人一致同意建立全面战略合作伙伴关系，双边关系迈上新的高度。双方高层交往频繁，战略互信日益巩固，双边贸易额连年快速增长。中方愿同老方密切协作，保持高层交往势头，开拓经贸投资、基础设施、农业开发、科教人文等领域务实合作，不断充实和丰富中老全面战略合作内涵。

阿桑·劳里积极评价老中关系。他说，老中关系发展顺利，双方战略互信不断加深，经贸、基础设施、农业、教育文化等各领域合作不断拓展，成果丰硕。老挝人民为中国人民取得的伟大发展成就感到由衷高兴，热烈祝贺中国成功举办上海世博会。他强调，老挝党、政府和人民坚定支持中国的和平统一大业，继续坚定奉行一个中国政策。

2010年10月19日，中共中央政治局常委、全国政协主席贾庆林在广西南宁会见老挝副总理阿桑·劳里

On October 19, 2010, H.E. Jia Qinglin, Chairman of the National Committee of CPPCC, at the meeting with H.E. Asang LAOLY, Vice Prime Minister of the Lao People's Democratic Republic in Nanning, China

2010年10月19日，中共中央政治局常委、全国政协主席贾庆林在广西南宁会见越南副总理张永仲

On October 19, 2010, H.E. Jia Qinglin, Chairman of the National Committee of CPPCC, at the meeting with H.E. Truong Vinh Trong, Vice Prime Minister of the Socialist Republic of Vietnam in Nanning, China

在会见张永仲时，贾庆林说，进入新世纪，在“长期稳定、面向未来、睦邻友好、全面合作”十六字方针指引下，中越友好关系取得积极进展。中越增进互信，扩大合作，符合双方共同利益，对本地区的和平、稳定与发展也具有重要意义。中方愿与越方共同努力，增进互信，加强交流，深化合作，排除干扰，推动中越全面战略合作伙伴关系不断向前发展。

张永仲表示，越中关系发展良好，各领域合作不断取得新进展。越方高度重视发展越中友好合作关系，愿与中方携手努力，推动两国战略合作伙伴关系不断迈上新台阶。张永仲热烈祝贺中国共产党十七届五中全会胜利召开，表示中国经济社会的全面发展和应对国际金融危机的成功经验给越南及各国带来机遇和信心。

在谈到中国—东盟关系时，贾庆林表示，全面加强同东盟的睦邻友好和互利合作，是中国政府坚定不移的政策，也是中国周边外交的优先方向。中国—东盟关系的发展，不仅给中国和东盟各国人民带来了实实在在的利益，也有力地促进了地区的和平稳定与发展。2010年初，中国—东盟自贸区全面建成，双方经贸合作进入了一个全面快速发展的新阶段。

贾庆林强调，在经济全球化的今天，中国的发展离不开亚洲，亚洲的发展也离不开中国。无论中国如何发展强大，我们同东盟相互尊重、平等相待、睦邻友好、互利合作、共同发展的方针政策不会变化。2011年中国同东盟将迎来建立对话关系20周年，双方将举办一系列庆祝和纪念活动。希望双方抓住这一历史契机，不断增进政治互信，大力促进各领域友好交流和务实合作，推动中国–东盟战略伙伴关系取得更大发展。

贾庆林还表示，中国—东盟博览会是双方交流和开展多领域合作的重要平台。本届博览会的主题是“自贸区与新机遇”，希望各国充分利用博览会平台，进一步扩大经贸合作，实现双方的互利共赢和共同发展。

六　广西壮族自治区领导人拜会东盟国家领导人及会见其他贵宾

2010年10月19日晚，广西壮族自治区党委书记、自治区人大常委会主任郭声琨在南宁会见前来出席第七届中国—东盟博览会和商务与投资峰会的印尼副总统布迪约诺一行。

郭声琨代表广西壮族自治区党委、政府和广西各族人民，对布迪约诺副总统一行的光临表示欢迎。他说，2010年是中国印尼建交60周年，印尼又是2010年博览会主题国。这次博览会和峰会能够取得圆满成功，与印尼作为主题国所做的大量工作和精心安排是分不开的，对此表示衷心感谢。

郭声琨说，中国和印尼有着长期友好的传统友谊，广西和印尼也有着深厚友谊和友好合作。我和马飚主席曾先后访问贵国，都得到了热情接待，并达成了很多共识。在双方高层推动下，双方合作内容不断丰富，合作领域不断拓宽。郭声琨建议，今后双方应进一步加强合作，一是继续共同推动和办

2010年10月19日，广西壮族自治区党委书记、自治区人大常委会主任郭声琨在南宁会见印度尼西亚副总统布迪约诺

On October 19, 2010, H.E. Guo Shengkun, Secretary of the Chinese Communist Party Guangxi Committee at an audience with H.E. Boediono, Vice President of the Republic of Indonesia in Nanning

好中国—东盟博览会、中国—东盟商务与投资峰会。二是进一步加强经贸合作，包括项目合作及文化旅游等方面的合作。广西农垦在印尼建立的经贸合作区已经得到很大发展，我们还将鼓励和动员更多的广西企业到印尼投资。三是支持广西与印尼东爪哇省建立友好区省关系。四是欢迎印尼在南宁设立领事和商务机构。我们将提供一切方便，同时给予各方面支持，使得双方沟通渠道更加畅通，双方合作更加便捷。

布迪约诺代表印尼代表团全体成员对广西方的热情接待和周到安排表示感谢，并希望能更加充分地利用好两国当前的有利发展机遇，进一步巩固和发展双方的良好关系。他说，广西发展前景十分广阔，南宁是一个非常有活力的城市，希望有更多印尼的商家来广西、来南宁投资合作，共同发展。布迪约诺表示，印尼是个很大的市场。要进入东盟，就要先进入印尼。而要在印尼发展得好发展得快，就要比别人来得早。他非常支持和赞赏郭声琨关于进一步加强广西和印尼在各个领域合作的建议，支持广西与印尼东爪哇省建立友好区省关系，并将认真研究在南宁设立领事馆等事宜。

广西壮族自治区领导沈北海、陈武、余远辉参加会见。

10月19日晚，广西壮族自治区党委书记、自治区人大常委会主任郭声琨在南宁会见前来出席第七届中国—东盟博览会和商务与投资峰会的老挝副总理阿桑·劳里一行。

郭声琨代表广西壮族自治区党委、政府和5000多万各族人民对阿桑·劳里副总理的到来表示热烈欢迎，对老挝政府重视发展中老关系和加强与广西的交流合作，连续7年由高层领导亲自率团出席中国—东盟博览会和商务与投资峰会表示衷心感谢。

2010年10月19日，广西壮族自治区党委书记、自治区人大常委会主任郭声琨在南宁会见老挝副总理阿桑·劳里

On October 19, 2010, H.E. Guo Shengkun, Secretary of the Chinese Communist Party Guangxi Committee at an audience with H.E. Asang LAOLY, Vice Prime Minister of the Lao People's Democratic Republic in Nanning

郭声琨说，中老两国人民有着深厚的传统友谊。广西和老挝一直都是好同志、好邻居、好伙伴、好朋友。近年来，广西和老挝双方高层互访频繁，老挝高层领导每年都率团出席中国—东盟博览会和商务与投资峰会或来广西访问。我去年曾两次访问老挝，得到了老挝党和政府的热情接待，拜会了朱马里主席和波松总理等国家领导人，就共同关心的问题达成高度的共识，友谊得到深化，合作进一步拓宽。广西的企业到老挝投资越来越多，很多企业家十分看好老挝的投资环境和资源优势。此外，双方在教育和文化、干部培训方面的合作也迈出了可喜的步伐。总的来说，老挝和广西在各方面的合作都是愉快的、成功的。希望双方进一步加强在经贸、文化、教育和纪检监察等方面的合作，特别是加大农业领域的合作力度，取得更大的实效，使双方的合作越来越广泛，效果越来越明显。

阿桑·劳里说，老中两国、两党之间的友谊源远流长。一直以来，广西都给予老挝很大的帮助和支持。中国—东盟博览会和商务与投资峰会的举办十分成功，内容丰富，形式多样，值得我们很好考察和学习借鉴。老挝的森林、矿产、旅游等资源丰富，可以和广西加强交流合作，双方实现优势互补，共同发展。希望有更多的广西企业到老挝投资发展，推动老挝和广西进一步拓宽合作领域，深化双方传统友谊，达到互利共赢的效果。

广西壮族自治区领导陈武、黄道伟、余远辉参加会见。

10月20日，广西壮族自治区党委书记、自治区人大常委会主任郭声琨在南宁会见前来出席第七届中国—东盟博览会和商务与投资峰会的越南副总理张永仲一行。

2010年10月20日，广西壮族自治区党委书记、自治区人大常委会主任郭声琨在南宁会见越南副总理张永仲

On October 20, 2010, H.E. Guo Shengkun, Secretary of the Chinese Communist Party Guangxi Committee at an audience with H.E. Truong Vinh Trong, Vice Prime Minister of the Socialist Republic of Vietnam in Nanning

郭声琨说，张永仲副总理率团参加第七届中国—东盟博览会和商务与投资峰会，充分体现对越中关系的高度重视和对广西、对博览会的大力支持。这次博览会在经贸方面取得广阔领域的合作，和张永仲副总理出席会议以及越南代表团的努力是分不开的。

郭声琨说，双方秉持“十六字”方针和“四好”精神，中越两国是好朋友、好兄弟，对于广西来说更是好上加好、亲上加亲。通过中国—东盟博览会这个平台，我们每年相互见面、沟通，就大家共同关注的问题达成共识，双方的合作是愉快的、成功的。在经贸方面，越南已连续11年成为广西的第一大贸易伙伴。在项目合作方面，双方企业都加快了进入对方投资领域的步伐。在教育文化旅游等方面，双方合作取得丰硕成果，双方互派留学生逐年增多，目前越南在广西的留学生达3000多人。在政府交流方面，高层互访频繁，交流活动呈现多层次、多元化、群众化，特别是2010年8月举行的中越青年大联欢活动，规模之大、层次之高、内容之丰富，对两国青年来说都是前所未有的，进一步增进了中越青年的了解和友谊，使中越老一辈领导人亲手缔造的中越友谊得到巩固、发展、深化。这些交流活动使我们成为最亲的朋友。我们要进一步加强双方的交流和合作，拓展农业合作领域，巩固经贸合作良好势头，推动工业项目的优势互补，特别是在高速公路和铁路建设方面，使双方的合作越来越成熟，越来越深化，效果越来越显著。

张永仲说，广西和越南山连山、水连水，又是同志加兄弟，特别是中越青年大联欢活动给越南人民留下深刻印象。中国—东盟博览会和商务与投资峰会的规模一年比一年大，效果一年比一年显著，已经成为中国与东盟各国广泛交流、经贸合作的良好平台。2010年，越南在博览会设置190个展位，展示的产品很丰富，找到许多商机。近年来，广西经济增速越来越高，经济总量越来越大，发展质量越来越好。希望广西继续加大在越南的投资，越南各省将和广西加强沟通和互访，进一步推动双方在各领域进行全方位的交流与合作。

广西壮族自治区领导温卡华、陈武、余远辉参加会见。

10月20日，广西壮族自治区党委书记、自治区人大常委会主任郭声琨在南宁会见前来出席第七届中国—东盟博览会和商务与投资峰会的柬埔寨国务兼商业大臣占蒲拉西。

郭声琨说，占蒲拉西阁下是广西的老朋友、好朋友，也是我个人的老朋友、好朋友。您创造了参加中国—东盟博览会和商务与投资峰会的“七连冠”，是博览会最坚定、最全面的支持者之一。博览会期间，在同贾庆林主席的见面会上，您代表东盟国家作的发言非常有价值，对广西的工作和贡献

2010年10月20日，广西壮族自治区党委书记、自治区人大常委会主任郭声琨在南宁会见柬埔寨国务兼商业大臣占蒲拉西

On October 20, 2010, H.E. Guo Shengkun, Secretary of the Chinese Communist Party Guangxi Committee at an audience with H.E. CHAM Prasidh, Senior Minister and Minister of Commerce of the Kingdom of Cambodia in Nanning

给予了充分肯定，提出了共同办好博览会的很多好建议，对此表示衷心感谢。希望柬埔寨继续支持第八届博览会和商务与投资峰会，诚挚邀请洪森首相和占蒲拉西阁下继续参加博览会。

占蒲拉西对广西的热情接待和周到安排表示感谢。他说，见到郭书记就像见到了朋友和兄弟。博览会为企业创造了和各方交流合作的机会和平台，这次柬埔寨参展参会人员达到200多人，创造了新的纪录。广西发展潜力巨大，前景十分美好，柬埔寨将继续支持广西办好博览会和商务与投资峰会，也希望广西加大力度促进广西企业到柬埔寨投资，尤其在农产品加工、农业产业发展等方面加大投资合作力度。

郭声琨对占蒲拉西提出的合作建议表示赞同，表示要共同落实合作共识，推进具体合作项目。重点在农业产业、经贸合作、产业项目、文化旅游等方面加大合作力度，动员广西乃至中国的企业家到柬埔寨投资发展。特别要抓紧推进在柬埔寨的广西国宏公司大米加工厂、吴哥实景演出《微笑的高棉》等项目进度。

广西壮族自治区领导余远辉、覃瑞祥参加会见。

10月19日晚，广西壮族自治区党委书记、自治区人大常委会主任郭声琨在南宁会见了前来出席第七届中国—东盟博览会和商务与投资峰会的新加坡贸工部兼人力部政务部长李奕贤和贸工部兼新闻通讯艺术部政务次长陈振泉。

郭声琨代表广西壮族自治区党委、政府和5000多万各族人民，对李奕贤一行到来表示热烈欢迎，对新加坡政府重视发展中新关系和加强与广西的交流合作，大力支持广西承办好博览会和商务与投资峰会表示衷心感谢。

郭声琨说，我在2010年元月份访问新加坡时，留下了深刻而美好的印象，并与新加坡领导人就共同关心的问题达成了共识。双方的合作愉快而富有成效，在经贸方面，虽然今年仍然受到国际金融危机的影响，但是进出口贸易总额仍在增长；在文化交流和教育培训方面，广西送出一大批干部去新加坡培训，这种交流合作是深层次的，带来的影响是深远的；在港口物流和旅游方面的合作也成效显著。今后，双方应进一步加强在经贸、投资、港口物流等领域的务实合作，推进双方在教育培训、旅游业、城市建设、社会管理和土地资源利用等方面的交流与合作，实现优势互补，资源共享，携手发展。广西将营造更优的环境，提供更好的服务，使新加坡企业在广西留得住，有回报，发展得好。

李奕贤表示，广西和新加坡尽管处在不同的发展阶段，但也处在共同的世界贸易环境里，遇到共同的贸易发展问题。新加坡愿意与广西加强交流与合作，实现共同发展。南宁的发展空间很大，来南宁参加博览会和投资峰会的新加坡企业不断增加，希望他们能够找到发展的新机遇。2010年是新加坡和中国建交20年，双方有很好的合作机遇和宽广的合作空间，比如海港物流、制造业等方面都可以进一步加强合作。李奕贤希望有更多的新加坡企业到广西考察投资，也欢迎广西的朋友继续到新加坡考察。

广西壮族自治区领导余远辉、杨道喜、黄日波参加会见。

10月20日，广西壮族自治区党委书记、自治区人大常委会主任郭声琨在南宁会见了前来出席第七届中国—东盟博览会和商务与投资峰会的马来西亚贸工部副部长贾谷·东加·沙甘。

郭声琨说，贾谷·东加·沙甘副部长率团参加第七届中国—东盟博览会和商务与投资峰会，体现了马来西亚政府对中国、对广西的深厚友情和对博览会的大力支持，给博览会增添了新的光彩，也为博览会的成功举办奠定了良好的基础。

郭声琨说，近年来，中国政府非常关注广西的发展，广西经济社会发展迈上了新台阶，与东盟的合作也取得了明显的成效。广西经济总量不断增大、经济质量不断提高和整个发展环境不断改善，为广西与马来西亚的合作创造了良好的条件。我们希望与马来西亚分享良好的发展机遇，在多领域开展合作。一是共同建设好、利用好博览会平台，为双方的企业和工商界进行沟通合作提供帮助。2011年的第八届中国—东盟博览会的主题国是马来西亚，相信有马来西亚政府和贾谷·东加·沙甘副部长的支持，第八届中国—东盟博览会将会办得更加精彩、更加成功、更加务实。二是在农业等方面开展产业合作。广西和马来西亚都有较好的农业发展条件，双方加强优势互补，一定能实现双赢。三是在文化教育旅游方面加强合作，进一步推动双方高层互访，结成友好省区，为今后双方沟通联系架起桥梁，进一步深化双方

在各领域的务实合作。

贾谷·东加·沙甘说，第一次率团到南宁参加中国—东盟博览会和商务与投资峰会，感觉双方企业之间合作潜力巨大。我们热情邀请广西企业到马来西亚投资发展，相信马来西亚和广西在各领域的合作将有一个美好的未来。马来西亚作为2011年第八届中国—东盟博览会的主题国，愿与中方一道，把中国—东盟博览会办成双方开展互利合作的最佳平台，使第八届中国—东盟博览会取得更大的成功、更好的成效。

广西壮族自治区领导余远辉、陈章良、蒋济雄参加会见。

此外，广西壮族自治区党委书记、自治区人大常委会主任郭声琨在南宁还分别会见了前来出席第七届中国—东盟博览会、中国—东盟商务与投资峰会相关论坛的国家质检总局局长支树平，安徽省省长王三运，中国农业银行党委副书记、监事长车迎新，中国电力企业联合会原党组书记、常务副理事长谢振华，北京银行董事长闫冰竹等。

10月19日下午，广西壮族自治区主席马飚在南宁会见前来出席第七届中国—东盟博览会和商务与投资峰会的印度尼西亚副总统布迪约诺一行。

马飚代表广西壮族自治区人民政府对布迪约诺副总统率团出席第七届中国—东盟博览会、商务与投资峰会表示欢迎和感谢，对印尼作为本届博览会主题国成功举办的一系列活动表示祝贺。他说，副总统阁下在第七届中国—东盟商务与投资峰会上的精彩演讲，充分体现了对中国与印尼两国传统友谊的高度重视，以及对于中国—东盟自贸区建成后进一步加强交流合作的诚挚愿望。

马飚指出，广西与印尼有着很强的互补性，合作潜力巨大，发展前景美好。建议印尼进一步支持广西农垦集团在印尼建设的中国—印尼经贸合作区项目，同时进一步加强双方在能源、农业、渔业、旅游、制造业、教育、卫生、体育等各领域的交流合作。相信此次副总统阁下访问广西必将促使更多的广西企业关注印尼，深化对印尼的认识与了解。广西将为在桂投资的印尼企业做好服务，并鼓励和组织更多广西企业到印尼投资，共同推进中国与印尼友好交流与经贸合作迈上新的台阶。

布迪约诺对广西方面的热情接待表示感谢，对马飚主席提出的加强印尼与广西经贸往来的建议表示赞赏。他说，在桂投资的印尼企业界人士和在桂学习的印尼留学生是深化印尼与中国友好交流的基础。希望进一步加强广西和印尼各省市的友好交往，进一步密切双方经贸联系，拓展商贸投资领域，加大印尼和广西的企业家之间的互访和相互投资力度，深化印尼与中国人民的理解和友谊，抓住中国—东盟自贸区建成的新机遇，实现合作共赢、共同发展。

印尼贸易部部长冯慧兰、印尼工业部部长希达悦、印尼国企部部长穆斯塔法·阿布巴卡尔、印尼驻华大使易慕龙等会见时在座。

10月21日下午，广西壮族自治区主席马飚在南宁会见出席第七届中国—东盟博览会、中国—东盟商务与投资峰会的老挝副总理阿桑·劳里一行。

2010年10月21日，广西壮族自治区主席马飚在南宁会见老挝副总理阿桑·劳里

On October 21, 2010, H.E. Ma Biao, Governor of Guangxi Zhuang Autonomous Region at an audience with H.E. Asang LAOLY, Vice Prime Minister of the Lao People's Democratic Republic in Nanning

马飚代表自治区政府对阿桑·劳里率团出席盛会表示欢迎，对老挝长期以来大力支持广西承办好中国—东盟博览会和商务与投资峰会表示感谢，对万象建城450周年表示祝贺。马飚说，近年来广西与老挝的交往日益密切。中国—东盟博览会在广西举办，老挝每届都派国家领导人出席，体现了老挝对广西的支持和友谊。随着中国—东盟博览会在广西的连续举办，更多广西企业加深了对老挝的了解，为进一步推动和加强广西与老挝的经济贸易交流合作打下了良好基础。

马飚指出，随着中国—东盟自由贸易区2010年1月如期建成，广西与老挝的交流与合作站在了全新的历史起点上。希望双方继续保持高层交往的良好势头，进一步发挥中国—东盟博览会和商务与投资峰会的重要平台作用。广西愿与老挝进一步加强在经贸、农业、旅游等领域的务实合作，将组织更多企业到老挝发展，也欢迎老挝企业来桂发展。相信随着老挝驻南宁总领事馆以及商务办事机构的启用，必将为推动广西与老挝企业深化了解、谋求合作发挥重要作用。

阿桑·劳里对广西方面给予老挝代表团参展参会提供的大力帮助表示感谢。他深情地回忆起革命时期中国和广西对老挝的支持和帮助。他说，老挝与中国的传统友谊源远流长。老挝成立35周年以来在经济社会发展上取得的

巨大成就与中国的帮助密不可分。希望双方关系在未来得到更好发展。随着中国—东盟博览会连年在广西举办，老挝与广西的交往日益密切，交流与合作不断深化。随着中国—东盟自贸区的建成，老挝与中国、广西的友好合作关系必将进一步加强。老挝将一如既往地支持广西承办中国—东盟博览会和商务与投资峰会。希望广西政府组织更多的本地企业到老挝考察投资，组织更多的游客到老挝观光旅游。

老挝工贸部部长南·维亚吉，广西壮族自治区党委常委、自治区副主席陈武，自治区党委常委、统战部部长黄道伟等参加会见。

10月19日晚，广西壮族自治区主席马飚在南宁会见前来出席第七届中国—东盟博览会和商务与投资峰会的越南副总理张永仲一行。

马飚代表广西壮族自治区党委、政府对张永仲率团到访表示欢迎，对越南大力支持广西承办好中国—东盟博览会、商务与投资峰会表示感谢。他说，2010年9月，广西政府代表团访问越南，得到了越南国家领导人的亲切接见和热情款待，深深感受到越南党和国家高度重视发展中越两国传统友谊，高度重视中越经贸交流与合作。

马飚指出，越南已连续11年成为广西最大的贸易伙伴，双方合作潜力巨大。他希望越方继续支持广西承办中国—东盟博览会和中国—东盟商务与投资峰会，双方共同推进中越跨境经济合作区建设，共同推动南宁—河内经济走廊、南宁—新加坡经济走廊建设以及泛北部湾经济合作，进一步加强在经贸、教育、旅游、交通等各领域的交流与合作。

张永仲对第七届中国—东盟博览会、商务与投资峰会的成功举办表示祝

2010年10月19日，广西壮族自治区主席马飚在南宁会见越南副总理张永仲

On October 19, 2010, H.E. Ma Biao, Governor of Guangxi Zhuang Autonomous Region at an audience with H.E. Truong Vinh Trong, Vice Prime Minister of the Socialist Republic of Vietnam in Nanning

贺，并转达了越南总理阮晋勇的问候。他说，广西在不久前成功举办了越中两国青年大联欢活动，给越中两国人民尤其青年一代留下了难忘印象，对推动越中友好关系具有重要意义。马飚主席随后率团访问越南，与越南国家领导人进行会谈，取得了一系列的合作共识。越方将加强与广西的沟通协作，尽快落实这些共识，进一步巩固发展友好合作关系。祝愿越中两国传统友谊万古长青。

越南驻华大使阮文诗、越南政府办公厅副主任乔廷树、越南外交部副部长裴青山、越南工贸部副部长阮成边、越南驻南宁总领事阮英勇，广西壮族自治区党委常委、政法委书记温卡华等会见时在座。

10月20日下午，广西壮族自治区主席马飚在南宁会见前来参加第七届中国—东盟博览会、中国—东盟商务与投资峰会的柬埔寨国务兼商业大臣占蒲拉西一行。

马飚代表广西壮族自治区党委、政府对占蒲拉西表示欢迎，对柬埔寨长期以来支持广西承办中国—东盟博览会和商务与投资峰会表示感谢。他说，柬埔寨连续7年派高层领导率团出席中国—东盟博览会和商务与投资峰会，充分体现了柬埔寨对巩固和加强中柬传统友谊的高度重视。令人欣喜的是，如今越来越多的柬埔寨企业产品在博览会上展销，越来越多的中国和广西企业认识和了解柬埔寨王国，并逐年加大对柬埔寨的投资力度，中国—东盟博览会在推动中国与东盟各国经贸合作交流平台作用日益显现。

马飚指出，广西和柬埔寨有着很强的互补优势。近几年来双方经济贸易交流与合作不断拓展。随着中国—东盟自贸区的建成，双方交流与合作的领域将进一步拓展，水平将进一步提升，实效将进一步增强。希望柬埔寨继续支持广西承办中国—东盟博览会和商务与投资峰会，推动办会机制常态化。

2010年10月20日，广西壮族自治区主席马飚在南宁会见柬埔寨国务兼商业大臣占蒲拉西

On October 20, 2010, H.E. Ma Biao, Governor of Guangxi Zhuang Autonomous Region at an audience with H.E. CHAM Prasidh, Senior Minister and Minister of Commerce of the Kingdom of Cambodia in Nanning

相信柬埔寨商务部驻南宁办事机构的设立，将为两国企业和投资者加强沟通了解和对接搭建起更加便利的桥梁，推动双方在农业、旅游、工业、物流、商贸、教育等方面的合作深入开展。

占蒲拉西说，中国人民是柬埔寨人民的好朋友。中国经济发展和巨大的市场对柬埔寨经济贸易发展意义重大。每次到广西参加中国—东盟博览会，都可以感受到广西的飞速发展和巨大变化。随着中国—东盟自贸区的全面建成，双方贸易额将进一步增长。他说，柬埔寨永远支持广西承办好中国—东盟博览会。希望更多的中国和广西企业到柬埔寨投资发展。相信在双方的积极努力下，柬埔寨与中国的经贸交流与合作将向更高层次和更宽领域迈进。希望广西继续支持柬埔寨驻南宁商务办事机构的建立与发展。

广西壮族自治区人大常委会副主任覃瑞祥参加会见。

10月19日晚，广西壮族自治区主席马飚在南宁会见前来出席第七届中国—东盟博览会、中国—东盟商务与投资峰会的缅甸商务部部长吴丁乃登一行。

马飚代表广西壮族自治区人民政府对吴丁乃登出席盛会并访问广西表示欢迎，对缅甸和缅甸商务部长期以来大力支持广西承办好中国—东盟博览会和商务与投资峰会表示感谢。他说，中国—东盟博览会及商务与投资峰会连续举办七届，一直得到缅甸的大力支持和积极参与，每届均派高层官员率团参会。近年来，广西与缅甸不断巩固发展传统友谊，双方高层互访频繁，经贸交流与合作不断加深。2010年1至8月广西与缅甸进出口总额达1038万美元。

马飚指出，广西与缅甸合作互补性强，发展合作潜力巨大。希望缅甸商务部继续支持广西承办好中国—东盟博览会和商务与投资峰会，进一步巩固双方良好的合作基础，进一步推进双方在经贸、能源、农业、旅游、教育等各个领域的务实合作。广西欢迎更多的缅甸产品进入广西，同时也将鼓励和推动更多的广西企业到缅甸投资。

吴丁乃登感谢广西方面的热情接待。他说，近年来，缅甸与广西的交流与合作不断加深。尤其连续举办七届的中国—东盟博览会，为中国与东盟经贸交流合作发挥了沟通桥梁的作用，包括缅甸在内的东盟各国在中国的贸易投资额逐年增大。随着缅甸驻南宁总领事馆和商务中心的建成使用，相信缅甸与广西的经贸交往合作将迈上新的台阶。希望广西为缅甸商人在广西投资搭建更好的平台，接收更多的缅甸商人到广西学习汉语，面向缅甸加强农业技术培训。

广西壮族自治区政协副主席李达球等参加会见。

10月21日上午，广西壮族自治区主席马飚在南宁会见参加第七届中国—东盟博览会、中国—东盟商务与投资峰会的文莱工业和初级资源部部长叶海亚一行。

马飚代表自治区政府对叶海亚的到来表示欢迎，对叶海亚部长和文莱工业和初级资源部长期以来大力支持广西承办好中国—东盟博览会和商务与投资峰会、高度重视发展与广西的交流与合作表示感谢，对文莱国家商务联络部（办事处）在南宁东盟商务区正式启用表示祝贺。

马飚说，近年来广西与文莱的高层往来十分密切，有力地促进了双方各领域的交流与合作，双方在经贸、农业、旅游等方面的合作成果明显。2010年1至8月广西与文莱进出口总额达164万美元，同比增长68.1%。在中国—东盟自由贸易区建成运行的背景下，进一步巩固和发展双方友好合作关系具有十分重要的意义。希望部长阁下和文莱工业与初级资源部继续关注、支持中国—东盟博览会和商务与投资峰会，继续推动更多的文莱企业前来参会，进一步推动双方在经贸、旅游、渔业、港口等多领域的务实合作。

叶海亚感谢广西方面热情周到的安排。他说："作为广西人民的老朋友，我到广西就像回家一样。"中国—东盟博览会已经在广西连续举办7届，每年他都来，但每次来都能感受到新发展、新动向，所以每次到广西都是一次愉快的体验。很高兴看到文莱与广西的进出口贸易额在不断增加，文莱的清真食品2010年还首次在博览会上展出。希望能够更好地借助中国—东盟博览会的平台，不断深化和拓展与广西的合作。文莱工业和初级资源部愿意继续巩固和发展与广西的传统友谊和友好合作。

文莱驻中国大使张慈祥，广西壮族自治区副主席杨道喜等参加会见。

10月20日下午，广西壮族自治区主席马飚在南宁会见前来出席第七届中国—东盟博览会、中国—东盟商务与投资峰会的菲律宾贸易与工业部副部长艾德里安·克里斯托伯一行。

马飚代表自治区党委、政府对克里斯托伯表示欢迎，对菲律宾贸工部长期以来大力支持广西承办中国—东盟博览会和商务与投资峰会表示感谢。他说，广西与菲律宾有着长期传统的友谊。近年来，双方高层互访越来越多，经贸交流合作越来越紧密，双方在经贸、农业、旅游、友城交往等各个领域的交流与合作取得了显著成果。2010年1至8月，广西与菲律宾进出口总额达4704万美元，同比增长145.7%。此外，广西还与菲律宾缔结了6对各级友好城市，双方开展了丰富多彩的友好交往活动。

马飚表示，随着中国—东盟自贸区的建成，广西与菲律宾之间的交流与合作进入了一个新的阶段。双方合作潜力巨大，前景美好。广西愿与菲律宾进一步加强工业、物流、商贸、港口、农业、渔业、旅游等各领域的交流与合作。希望菲律宾贸工部继续支持广西承办中国—东盟博览会和商务与投资

峰会；继续共同推进泛北部湾经济合作；尽快在南宁设立总领事馆，为双方经贸合作和人员往来搭建更加便利的平台。

克里斯托伯高度评价本届中国—东盟博览会的筹备能力和接待水平。他说，对于东盟成员国来说，中国—东盟博览会不仅是促进东盟与中国贸易和投资的重要平台，也是东盟成员国之间交流合作的重要平台。在过去7年里，菲律宾和其他东盟国家都积极参与中国—东盟博览会，充分证明了中国—东盟博览会取得的巨大成功。菲律宾与广西有着很强的互补性，尤其体现在农业方面。2010年12月，广西农业代表团将赴菲律宾访问，我们将借此机会更好地学习和借鉴广西先进的农业技术。希望广西派出更多的代表团到菲律宾考察投资，双方进一步探讨扩大合作。

广西壮族自治区人大常委会副主任文明、菲律宾驻广州总领事金举深等参加会见。

10月20日上午，广西壮族自治区主席马飚在南宁会见前来参加第七届中国—东盟博览会、中国—东盟商务与投资峰会的菲律宾宿务省省长格温多琳·加西亚一行。

马飚代表自治区党委、政府对加西亚出席第七届中国—东盟博览会和商务与投资峰会表示欢迎，对宿务省首次在博览会上布展表示感谢和祝贺。他说，今年宿务省首次在中国—东盟博览会上布展，充分体现了加西亚省长和宿务省对博览会的支持和进一步加强双方友好关系的重视。相信加西亚省长再次访问广西必将进一步巩固和发展广西与宿务两省区的传统友谊，推动两省区经贸交流与合作。

在简要介绍广西经济社会发展和中国—东盟博览会举办情况后，马飚指出，广西高度重视发展与宿务省的友好关系。随着两省区今年正式建立友好关系，双方友好交往进入了新的阶段。广西愿意为宿务省更多企业前来参会参展提供帮助，扩大双方经贸合作成效。同时愿意进一步深化旅游、港口物流、海洋运输、教育等各领域的合作，进一步拓宽双方交往渠道，推动双方交流合作迈上新台阶。

加西亚对第七届中国—东盟博览会、商务与投资峰会的成功举办表示祝贺，对广西政府给予的热情款待表示感谢。她说，很高兴再次来到广西访问。在一年当中两次来到这里，充分证明广西是宿务省最重要的友好省区之一。宿务与广西2010年正式建立友好省区关系，这是两省区交流与合作中的重要里程碑。相信依托现有良好基础，两省区交流与合作一定能够取得更大的成绩。宿务十分愿意在教育、港口建设领域与广西商讨具体合作，热切希望宿务到南宁的直航航班尽快开通，进一步加强两地人民的交往，深化传统友谊与交流合作。

广西壮族自治区党委常委、自治区副主席陈武等参加会见。

10月21日上午，广西壮族自治区主席马飚在南宁会见参加第七届中国—东盟博览会的柬埔寨磅湛省省长洪能一行。

马飚代表自治区政府对洪能率团参会表示欢迎，对磅湛省成为本届博览会魅力之城表示祝贺，并请洪能转达对柬埔寨首相洪森的崇高敬意和美好祝福。他说，中国和柬埔寨有着非常深厚的传统友谊，近年来得到不断巩固和发展。作为广西的"荣誉公民"，洪森首相连续出席了5届中国—东盟博览会，是东盟国家当中出席博览会次数最多的领导人。2009年广西代表团访问柬埔寨期间，洪森首相还在百忙之中安排了接见。多年来，我们深深感受到柬方领导人高度重视中柬两国牢不可破的传统友谊，深深感受到柬方对博览会的高度重视和全力支持，以及对广西的深厚感情。

马飚指出，中国—东盟博览会作为中国与东盟交流合作的重要平台发挥了重要作用。广西在承办过程中成为面向东盟开放合作的前沿和窗口。广西和磅湛优势互补，合作潜力大，前景非常好。希望以此次磅湛省代表团访问广西为契机，双方共同探讨在经济、贸易、农业、渔业、旅游等各领域的合作，努力实现互利共赢、共同发展。

洪能转达了洪森首相对广西领导人和对广西人民的问候，对广西方面给予磅湛省代表团的热情接待表示感谢，对第七届中国—东盟博览会的成功举办表示祝贺。他说，他是首次率团访问广西，代表团成员充分感受到广西经济社会的快速发展，也坚信中国—东盟博览会的成功举办必将推动东盟10国与中国在经贸、旅游、文化、投资等方面的合作取得更大的发展。柬埔寨与中国有着长期传统的友好关系。作为柬埔寨的大省，磅湛省将继续支持广西承办好中国—东盟博览会，推动柬埔寨与广西的交流与合作。希望广西政府支持更多的本地企业到磅湛省考察投资，进一步加强两省区的交流与合作。

磅湛省副省长骆林泰，广西壮族自治区副主席杨道喜等参加会见。

10月19日晚，广西壮族自治区主席马飚在南宁会见日本熊本县知事蒲岛郁夫、议长小杉直率领的熊本县代表团一行。

马飚代表广西壮族自治区党委、政府对熊本县代表团到访广西表示欢迎，对熊本县长期以来给予广西发展的大力支持表示感谢。他说，广西自1982年与熊本县缔结友好关系以来，双方在政治、经济、文化、旅游、新闻、教育等多个领域开展了丰富多彩的交流活动，取得了丰硕的成果，增进了两地人民的了解与友谊。迄今为止，双方相互来往的团组超过400个，互访人员超过4000人。熊本县接收广西赴熊本进修、留学各类人员近300人。

在简要介绍广西经济社会发展和第七届中国—东盟博览会的有关情况后，马飚指出，广西十分珍惜与熊本县近30年的传统友谊。希望双方在多年友好交往的基础上，不断巩固和发展双方在经贸、教育、旅游、医药、卫生等各领域的交流与合作，不断开拓友好交往的新局面。

蒲岛郁夫感谢广西方面给予熊本县代表团的热情周到的接待。他说，短短一年后再次来到广西，充分感受到广西在过去一年中的飞速变化，这种发展速度令人惊叹，发展成绩令人钦佩。本届中国—东盟博览会期间，在展位供不应求的情况下，熊本县还增加了展位，充分体现了熊本县与广西28年友好交往结下的深厚情谊和进一步密切经贸往来的意愿。随着中国—东盟商务区日本园等项目的建成开放，必将进一步促进熊本县与广西各领域的友好合作，推动双方经济社会共同发展。

广西壮族自治区人大常委会副主任刘新文等参加会见。

此外，广西壮族自治区主席马飚在南宁分别会见商务部国际贸易谈判代表兼副部长高虎城，国家质检总局局长支树平，国家发改委副主任、国家能源局局长张国宝，安徽省省长王三运，中国电子信息产业集团有限公司总经理刘烈宏，中国铝业公司总经理熊维平，中国铝业股份有限公司总裁罗建川，中国出版集团党委书记、副总裁王涛，印尼中华总商会总主席纪辉琦，香港广西总商会会长邓清河，韩国忠清北道代表团，韩国SK集团大中华区首席副总裁韩文錤，台湾优良商品协进会理事长林玮轩等出席第七届中国—东盟博览会、中国—东盟商务与投资峰会的中外嘉宾。

本届博览会期间，还举行了多场中外政要、部长级官员、地方政府领导和企业家的会见和对话活动，促进了政商高端对接和多层次的交流。如，中国海南省副省长李国梁会见了新加坡贸工部兼新闻通讯艺术部政务次长陈振泉一行。马来西亚贸工部副部长拿督贾谷・东加・沙甘与中国中信建设有限责任公司、宁波风神风电科技有限公司负责人举行了会谈。马来西亚贸工部副部长拿督贾谷・东加・沙甘、菲律宾贸工部副部长克里斯托伯分别会见了中国—东盟博览会秘书处秘书长郑军健。博览会期间还安排了东盟国家政府相关部门与广西各地市、各厅局的对接，博览会支持商协会会长与中国各省区市代表团的多场次、多形式的对接洽谈，多层次交流活动更加丰富。

第三章

3 自贸区建成展新机　区域合作谋跨越

——第七届中国—东盟商务与投资峰会开幕

中国—东盟自由贸易区于2010年1月1日全面建成，是区域经济一体化具有里程碑意义的大事，有力地促进了中国与东盟市场的一体化进程。

在这一新形势下，第七届中国—东盟商务与投资峰会赋予新的使命，那就是推进和落实中国—东盟自贸区协议，进一步深化区域经贸合作。

为此，第七届中国—东盟商务与投资峰会围绕中国—东盟自由贸易区建成后区域经贸合作的前景、机遇和挑战进行探讨和展望，并继续发挥高层对话、经贸合作的重要平台作用，增加会议的务实成果，完善其促进中国与东盟商务与投资合作的长效机制。

第七届中国—东盟商务与投资峰会主题是“中国—东盟自由贸易区与区域经贸合作的展望”，议题和活动包括开幕式、印度尼西亚共和国副总统布迪约诺与中国企业CEO圆桌对话会、中国—东盟商会领袖论坛、2010中国—东盟矿业合作论坛暨展示会、中国—东盟经贸与物流合作论坛、中国—东盟轻工产品展览会、商务早餐会等。

2010年10月19日，第七届中国—东盟商务与投资峰会在南宁成功举办。中国和东盟国家领导人、政府高官、商协会领袖、专家学者以及国际组织、区域组织代表等1500多名嘉宾、代表出席会议。

CAFTA New Opportunities for Regional Cooperation

—The 7th CABIS Opens

The CAFTA has been fully established on January 1, 2010, a milestone in the regional economic integration, powerfully enhancing the process of the market integration between China and ASEAN.

Under the new circumstance, the 7th CABIS has carried new mission, which is to advance and implement the agreements of the CAFTA, thus to deepen the regional economic and trade cooperation.

To this end, the 7th CABIS has carried out exploration and prediction on the prospects, opportunities and challenges of regional economic and trade cooperation in the context of the CAFTA establishment. The event has continuously played the role as a platform for high-level dialogues, economic and trade relations, generating practical outcomes and improved the long term mechanism for boosting business and investment cooperation between China and ASEAN.

The theme of the 7th CABIS is "Prospects of CAFTA and Regional Economic and Trade Cooperation", and a number of events were held, including the opening ceremony, round-table dialogue conference of Indonesian Vice President Boediono and CEOs of Chinese enterprises, China-ASEAN Summit Forum for Chambers of Commerce, 2010 China-ASEAN Mining Industry Cooperation Forum and Exhibition, Forum on China-ASEAN Regional Economic and Trade and Logistics Cooperation, China-ASEAN Light Industrial Products Exhibition, business breakfast meeting, etc.

On October 19, 2010, the 7th CABIS was successfully held in Nanning, with 1,500 participants including state leaders of China and ASEAN, senior officials, heads of chambers of commerce, scholars and researchers from China and the ASEAN countries, as well as representatives of international and regional organizations.

CHAPTER THREE

一　第七届中国—东盟商务与投资峰会主题和议题

（一）主题："中国—东盟自由贸易区与区域经贸合作的展望"

中国—东盟自由贸易区2010年1月1日建成，给中国—东盟之间的经贸合作和区域发展带来重要影响。本次商务与投资峰会将围绕对中国—东盟自由贸易区建成后的区域经贸合作前景、机遇和挑战进行讨论和展望。

第七届中国—东盟商务与投资峰会会场
Venue of the 7th CABIS

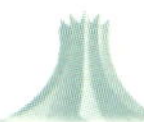

（二）印度尼西亚共和国副总统布迪约诺与中国企业CEO圆桌对话会

邀请印度尼西亚共和国副总统布迪约诺与中国和东盟企业家，围绕双边经贸关系特别是双方高度重视的重大合作项目开展建设性对话，促进政府与企业的沟通，加强企业之间的互动，为项目的顺利建设打下良好基础。

（三）中国—东盟商会领袖论坛

为整合中国与东盟商会资源，构建中国—东盟商会网络和平台，形成固定的中国与东盟联合对话机制，推动中国与东盟工商界进一步加强交流，增进了解，在商务与投资峰会期间举办中国—东盟商会领袖论坛，以推动中国—东盟商会开展全方位、宽领域、多层次的务实合作，促进区域经济共同繁荣和发展。

（四）2010中国—东盟矿业合作论坛暨展示会

在新的区域合作形势下，中国—东盟矿业合作将迎来前所未有的机遇。此次论坛作为中国—东盟商务与投资峰会系列活动，将为中国与东盟矿业搭建一个新的交流与合作平台，旨在推动中国与东盟矿业的共同发展。

（五）中国—东盟经贸与物流合作论坛

中国—东盟自由贸易区建成后，区域货物和商品流通将更加快捷高效，在机遇和挑战共存的市场环境下，如何创造性地开展区域内物流合作，探讨区域性物流体系的形成，将成为企业界关心的焦点。

（六）中国—东盟轻工产品展览会

该展览会是在南宁举办的首个与市民日常生活密切相关的轻工产品展销会，重点突出展示与市民日常生活密切相关的轻工产品，通过对当前轻工业材料和产品的规模展示和集中交易，整合和优化泛北部湾区域和东盟10国轻工业采购资源。

（七）商务早餐会

为加强中国和东盟企业的直接交流与互动，举办了商务早餐会提供场地和机会以便双方企业开展企业推介、商务配对、样品展示等活动。

二　第七届中国—东盟商务与投资峰会开幕式

2010年10月19日下午，第七届中国—东盟商务与投资峰会在广西人民会堂隆重开幕。中共中央政治局常委、全国政协主席贾庆林，印度尼西亚副总统布迪约诺，老挝副总理阿桑　劳里，越南副总理张永仲，广西壮族自治区党委书记郭声琨，中国商务部国际贸易谈判代表兼副部长高虎城，中国外交部副部长张志军，中国贸促会副会长王锦珍等出席开幕式。广西壮族自治区主席马飚主持开幕式。

2010年10月19日，第七届中国—东盟商务与投资峰会在广西人民会堂隆重开幕

The opening ceremony of the 7th CABIS held in Guangxi People's Hall on October 19, 2010

贾庆林在开幕式上发表主旨演讲。他指出，2010年是中国—东盟自贸区全面实施的开局之年，也是中国—东盟战略伙伴关系再获丰收之年。一年来，双方高层交往密切，睦邻互信加强，各领域务实合作扎实推进，社会人文领域合作广泛而活跃，在重大国际和地区问题上密切沟通与协调。

贾庆林表示，当前，国际政治经济格局加速调整，亚洲发展孕育着重大

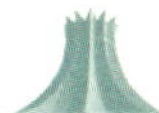

2010 年 10 月 19 日，中共中央政治局常委、全国政协主席贾庆林在第七届中国—东盟商务与投资峰会开幕式上发表主旨演讲

On October 19, 2010, H.E. Jia Qinglin, Chairman of the National Committee of the Chinese People's Political Consultative Conference delivers a keynote speech at the opening ceremony of the 7th CABIS

机遇。中国同东盟国家的前途命运日益紧密地联系在一起。在新形势下，巩固和加强中国—东盟战略伙伴关系，符合我们的共同利益，是我们的共同责任，也是我们的共同选择。中方将一如既往，坚定奉行与邻为善、以邻为伴的周边外交方针，同东盟加强战略互信，深化互利合作，扩大人文交流，密切在重大地区和国际问题上的沟通协调，促进各自国家又好又快发展，促进亚洲的和平、稳定、发展、繁荣。希望这次峰会围绕主题，就进一步发挥中国—东盟自贸区作用，扩大双方经贸合作和相互投资，加强基础设施建设和互联互通，开展重大民生项目合作，促进双方中小企业交流合作，推动行业对接与合作，打造新的产业链，深化湄公河次区域开发、东盟、东部增长区等次区域合作，集思广益、献计献策，推动中国—东盟互利合作进一步向广度和深度发展。

贾庆林指出，刚刚闭幕的中国共产党十七届五中全会描绘了未来五年中国发展的宏伟蓝图。中国将适应国内外形势新变化，促进经济长期平稳较快发展和社会和谐稳定，为全面建成小康社会打下具有决定性意义的基础。中国将坚定不移地走和平发展道路，恪守和平共处五项原则，同周边邻国和世界上其他国家平等相待、友好合作；将坚持相互尊重、求同存异，通过对话协商和平解决矛盾和分歧。中国—东盟博览会、中国—东盟商务与投资峰会已成为中国同东盟国家对话、交流、合作的有效平台。深信在大家共同努力下，中国—东盟博览会、中国—东盟商务与投资峰会将进一步办出特色、办出水平、办出成效，为推进中国—东盟自贸区深入发展，为不断开创中国—东盟睦邻友好合作新局面作出更大贡献。

布迪约诺在致辞中表示，中国—东盟商务与投资峰会已经成为促进东盟与中国商务合作的重要平台。东盟是中国投资者最大的投资目的地，如期

2010年10月19日，印度尼西亚副总统布迪约诺在第七届中国—东盟商务与投资峰会开幕式上致辞

On October 19,2010, H.E. Boediono, Vice President of the Republic of Indonesia addresses the opening ceremony of the 7th CABIS

建成的中国—东盟自贸区将使东盟对中国的投资更具吸引力。随着经济的发展，印尼期待着实现融入世界经济的目标。要实现这一目标，我们将升级基础设施，包括道路、桥梁、港口、铁路等。这次峰会将为印尼和中国以及其他东盟国家企业间的合作敞开大门。希望通过这次峰会，中国与东盟10国能够携手合作，能够提出建设性的举措，改善双方经贸关系，实现互利共赢。

广西壮族自治区党委书记、自治区人大常委会主任郭声琨和中国贸促会副会长王锦珍在开幕式上分别致辞。

郭声琨说，本届峰会开展务实深入的对话和讨论。这对于抓住自贸区建成的重大机遇，全面提升区域经贸合作关系的水平，促进共同发展和繁荣，将起到积极的推动作用。广西作为峰会的举办地，愿意以中国—东盟自贸区建成为契机，秉持互利共赢理念，按照业已达成的货物贸易、服务贸易、投资协议的安排，更加积极主动地与东盟各国工商企业界携起手来，进一步创新合作机制，丰富合作内涵，创造合作机遇，增强合作实效，共同开创中国—东盟自由贸易区更加美好的未来。

2010年10月19日，广西壮族自治区党委书记、自治区人大常委会主任郭声琨在第七届中国—东盟商务与投资峰会开幕式上致辞

On October 19, 2010, H.E. Guo Shengkun, Secretary of the Chinese Communist Party Guangxi Committee, addresses the opening ceremony of the 7th CABIS

王锦珍说，我们高兴地看到，在双方政府的大力支持和企业的共同努力下，中国与东盟之间的经贸联系越来越紧密，合作越来越多，发展越来越好。中方有信心和东盟各国共同抓住机遇，应对挑战，为积极打造一个开放程度更高，相互合作更密切，发展前景更广阔的自由贸易区共同作出努力。峰会将继续为双方商界提供商务交流、产品展示、项目合作、信息共享的平台。希望中国和东盟工商界人士广泛交流，为实现务实合作，实现本地区共同繁荣而努力。

出席开幕式的还有中国质检总局局长支树平，国家发改委副主任、能源局局长张国宝，全国政协副秘书长王胜洪，广西壮族自治区领导马铁山、陈际瓦、车荣福、温卡华、陈武、黄道伟、余远辉等。

2010年10月19日，中国国际贸易促进委员会副会长王锦珍在第七届中国—东盟商务与投资峰会开幕式上致辞

On October 19, 2010, H.E. Wang Jinzhen, Vice Chairman of China Council for the Promotion of International Trade (CCPIT) addresses the opening ceremony of the 7th CABIS

2010年10月19日，广西壮族自治区主席马飚主持第七届中国—东盟商务与投资峰会开幕式

On October 19, 2010, H.E. Ma Biao, Governor of Guangxi Zhuang Autonomous Region, hosts the opening ceremony of the 7th CABIS

来自东盟各国代表团和商协组织的负责人，中国政府有关部门和各省（区、市）的领导，外交使节、国际和区域组织的代表，中国和东盟政界、企业界知名人士以及有关专家学者和媒体记者共1500多人参会。其中，中国和东盟国家外交、商务、工贸等政府部门的部长和国家工商会会长等部级官员200多人。中国内地20多个省、自治区、直辖市均由省领导率团参会。300多名中外媒体记者到场报道此次盛会。

三　第七届中国—东盟商务与投资峰会专题会议

（一）印度尼西亚共和国副总统布迪约诺与中国企业CEO圆桌对话会

2010年10月19日下午16：30—17：30，本届圆桌对话会于南宁市广西人民会堂五楼会议厅举行。

印度尼西亚共和国副总统布迪约诺率70人代表团出席，中国国际贸易促进委员会副会长王锦珍在会上致辞，广西壮族自治区主席马飚作了总结发言。印尼方对话嘉宾包括：印度尼西亚共和国贸易部部长冯慧兰，印度尼西亚共和国工业部部长希达悦，印度尼西亚共和国国企部部长穆斯塔法·阿布巴卡尔，印度尼西亚共和国驻中华人民共和国大使易慕龙，印度尼西亚共和国国家出口发展署主席海丝蒂·印达·克蕾丝娜里尼，印尼国家电力公司总裁达荷兰·伊斯坎，印度尼西亚共和国国营电信公司总裁里那迪·福曼赛亚，印度尼西亚共和国国家石油公司液态天然气部门主管哈里·卡由利阿托。中方对话嘉宾包括：中国技术进出口总公司总裁唐毅，中国机械进出口集团总裁王旭升，中国进出口银行业务部副总经理李文，华为技术有限公司亚太地区副总裁马悦，中国技术进出口总公司副总裁、中技—中南联合体代表单伟，中国寰球工程公司副总裁王卓岩。对话嘉宾围绕双边经贸关系特别是双方关注的重大合作项目开展建设性对话，促进政府与企业的沟通和双方合作企业之间的互动，为互利合作创造更有利的氛围和条件。中国和印尼政府高官、工商会负责人、企业家、专家学者以及国际组织和区域组织代表共250多人出席圆桌对话会。60多名中外媒体记者到场报道对话会。

印度尼西亚副总统布迪约诺在发言中介绍了印尼的基本情况和近期发展目标，他说，中国—东盟自由贸易区的建立有非常重要的意义。印尼政府将会继续努力建立一个适当的框架和机制，为企业的发展提供有益的环境。为了实现可持续发展，保持竞争力，减少地区间的不平衡，印尼政府工作的重中之重是更新印尼的硬件和软件基础设施并加快它们的发展。特别是要把

2010 年 10 月 19 日，印度尼西亚副总统布迪约诺与中国企业 CEO 圆桌对话会在广西南宁举行

On October 19, 2010, H.E. Boediono, Vice President of the Republic of Indonesia at the round table dialogue with CEOs of Chinese enterprises in Nanning

印度尼西亚副总统布迪约诺在圆桌对话会上发言

H.E. Boediono, Vice President of the Republic of Indonesia speaks at the round table dialogue

建设交通和通讯的基础设施及高效的物流系统和服务放在首位。印尼正在融入整个地区和全球的发展中，在这个过程中我们需要确保国与国之间交流的畅通。印尼政府不断提高基础设施建设的财政预算，提供风险共享和激励制度，印尼财政部设立了印尼基础设施保障基金，为优质的项目提供保证金；新的土地征用制度规定政府先征得土地再出售给企业；还有印尼财政部与国际金融公司（IFC）、日本国际合作银行（JBIC）和亚洲开发银行（ADB）共同开发的印尼基础设施融资项目和新办的政府投资公司。

中国商务部国际贸易谈判代表兼副部长高虎城在发言中指出2010年是中国印尼两国建交60周年，又是“中国印尼友好年”。在两国领导人关心和双方共同努力下，近年来，两国经贸合作取得了丰硕成果。2008年，双边贸易额达315亿美元，提前两年实现了300亿美元目标。2009年，双边经贸合作经受住国际金融危机的考验并取得新的发展。双方基础设施建设领域合作成果显著，中国企业承建的泗马大桥、风港燃煤电站和阿萨汉水电站陆续竣工，第一批1000万千瓦电站融资问题圆满解决，合作项目已全面开工，目前总体进展顺利。至今，中方已累计向印尼方提供18亿美元优惠出口买方信贷，用于建设印尼经济发展急需的电站、大桥、大坝和公路等基础设施项目。中国企业对印尼投资增长迅速，2010年1—8月新增直接投资1.87亿美元，同比增长近40%，印尼已成为中国企业赴海外投资的主要目的地之一。2010年是中国—东盟自贸区全面建成的第一年。2010年以来，中国—东盟自贸区对中国印尼贸易的积极拉动作用已初步显现。中方统计，2010年1—9月双边贸易额约304亿美元，同比增长56.3%，印尼对华出口也实现57.7%的高速增长。自贸区建成的头8个月，中国从印尼进口的纺织品、天然橡胶、水果和煤炭金额同比分别增长42%、55%、116%和261%。这充分说明了中国—东盟自贸区是一个互利双赢的安排，双方政府应鼓励双方企业，进一步利用好自贸区提供的各种便利，继续提升双边经贸合作的水平。中国印尼经贸合作为两国和两国人民带来了实实在在的利益。两国经贸合作潜力巨大，进一步提升合作规模和水平是大势所趋。只要双方共同努力、精诚合作，就一定能给两国经贸合作不断带来新的活力，造福两国人民。

中国国际贸易促进委员会副会长王锦珍在致辞中指出中国和印度尼西亚都是发展中的大国，各有不同的丰富资源，市场巨大。中国是印尼第三大贸易伙伴国，中国与印尼提前两年实现双方确定的2010年双边贸易额300亿美元的目标。2010年，中国—东盟自贸区全面建成后，1—8月,中国和印尼的进出口总额近270亿美元,增长近60%。贸易结构呈现良好的互补性。在相互投资和经济合作方面，增长速度也进一步加快。作为中国最大的贸易投资促进机构，中国贸促会愿意与印尼工商会、印尼中华总商会等商协会组织及各级政府机构一起，为加强两国企业间的交流牵线搭桥，提供优质、直接、有效的服务。本次圆桌对话会的目的，就是探讨两国企业如何充分利用中国—东盟自贸区建设的契机，进一步促进双边经贸关系，并提高合作水平。出席今天圆桌对话会的企业家来自金融、电力、铁路、通讯、石油等领域，这些企业在推动中国和印尼经贸合作方面起到了积极和重要作用。相信布迪约诺副总统与以上企业家的对话和交流必将对提高中国与印尼的经贸合作水平产生重要的现实意义。

（二）首届中国—东盟商会领袖论坛

2010年10月20日9：30—11：30，首届中国—东盟商会领袖论坛在南宁明园饭店5号楼二楼多功能厅举行。

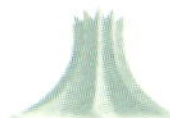

2010年10月20日，首届中国—东盟商会领袖论坛在广西南宁举行
The 1st China-ASEAN Business Leaders Forum held in Nanning on October 20, 2010

本届论坛是中国—东盟商务与投资峰会举办7年来的第一届商会领袖论坛，也是自中国—东盟自由贸易区建成以来的首届商会领袖论坛。近200位中外嘉宾与会。会议分两节进行，第一节会议由印尼工商会馆中国委员会副秘书长施锦场主持，演讲嘉宾有：中国贸促会副会长于平，中国国际商会常务理事、中国物流与采购联合会副会长、华南城主席郑松兴，老挝国家工商会副会长乔汤·帕塔玛冯，中国物流与采购联合会首席顾问丁俊发，越南工商会副会长段维姜，柬埔寨中华总商会会长高华，新加坡制造商联合会副会长李雪民，印尼工商会馆中国委员会秘书长熊德龙。第二节会议由中国—东盟商务理事会中方常务副秘书长许宁宁主持，演讲嘉宾有：缅甸国家工商会副会长翁伦、泰国工业联盟副主席曼孔、马来西亚中华总商会中央理事梁家兴、马中经贸总商会会长拿督黄汉良、菲华联谊总会理事长施清胆、印尼中华总商会主席纪辉琦、广西壮族自治区副主席林念修。15位演讲嘉宾以密切双方工商企业界的交流与合作、推进区域物流体系的形成为主题发表演讲，与大家就共同关注的经济热点、贸易、投资问题进行交流和研讨。论坛的举办，有利于进一步推动中国与东盟工商界加强交流，增进了解，整合中国与东盟商会资源，构建中国—东盟商会网络和平台，形成固定的中国与东盟联合对话机制，推动中国与东盟商会开展全方位、宽领域、多层次的务实合作，促进区域经济共同繁荣和发展。与会嘉宾一致通过《中国—东盟商会领袖论坛备忘录》。会上，还安排中国湖南省永州市市长龚武生介绍湖南永州市情况，为国内省份走进东盟提供绝佳机会。

中国国际商会常务理事、深圳华南城有限公司董事长郑松兴发言说，中国—东盟自贸区的建成后，货物贸易、服务贸易和投资市场相互开放，中国与东盟经贸合作开始上升至一个新的历史水平。中国—东盟自贸区在制度层面问题解决之后，加快广西北部湾经济区和东盟各国商贸物流基础设施建设与对接，已成为当前最迫切的任务。因为区域经济是一种聚集经济，是人流、物流、资本流等各种生产要素聚集的规模生产，但各种要素的聚集是为了商品的扩散，如果没有发达的商业流通体系作为保障，生产出来的产品就会堆积在狭小的空间里，难以实现其价值，甚至不可能产生大规模的生产活动，影响区域经济的运转。因此，在区域经济发展过程中，高效、完善的物流系统，对促进区域经济的快速运行起着基础性的保障作用。同时，这同中国和广西壮族自治区政府要求广西北部湾经济区建成面向东盟开放合作的物流基地、商贸基地、加工制造基地、信息交流中心、交通枢纽中心和区域金融中心的定位，也是完全一致的。

柬埔寨中国商会会长高华在发言中说，参加中国—东盟商会领袖论坛，各国商会领袖齐聚一堂，交流情况、互通信息、探索发展思路，这是一次极好的加深友谊、共谋合作与发展的机遇。中国—东盟自由贸易区全面启动的新形势，不可否认地成为中国企业进入东盟市场和中资商协会实现新的作为两者结合的最佳机遇和重要契机。中国企业应充分利用好东盟国家现有商协会组织的优势，集合商界精英的力量，汇聚更多的资源和人才，以商会作为信息交流和沟通的平台，将市场需求、商界权益与政府的政策、行为融会贯通，促进跨国界、跨行业、跨企业的经贸活动，达到互利共赢的目的。

印度尼西亚中华总商会总主席纪辉琦在演讲中说，历届中国—东盟商务与投资峰会规模不断扩大，层次不断提高。现今，它已成为中国与东盟极为重要的交流平台，其影响力更是已经悄悄渗透到世界各国，是一个名副其实的世界性大会。中国—东盟自贸区已经建成，并初步显示出强大的生命力，然而我们不应该忘记它目前还犹如一个新生的婴儿，它需要自贸区各国政府、社会各界的细心呵护。不同性质的机构、组织对自贸区负有不同的责任。在自贸区的新机遇与挑战下，商会要清楚地为自己重新定位。各国商会不再只局限于服务本国企业家，各国商会应当有机地连成一个整体，增加往来，积极互动，相互推介项目，并相互提供各国最新经贸资讯与政府政策；为各国企业家的经贸活动提供便利与协助；积极承担桥梁作用，创造机会，为本国与自贸区企业家的交流与合作提供平台，促进项目对接，优化企业分工；帮助引导本国其他企业参与自贸区经贸活动；要勇于向政府反映企业家的心声，并积极协助政府为创建一个良好的经贸、投资环境而奋斗。

印尼工商会馆中国会馆秘书长熊德龙在演讲中指出，参加中国—东盟商会领袖论坛的代表都是各行各会的精英，有银行界、工商界、物流界等。众多精英欢聚一堂，可以用一句中国话来形容——麻雀虽小，五脏俱全。中国有13亿人口，印尼有2.5亿多人口，包括新加坡、菲律宾、马来西亚等，总共

有18亿—19亿的人口，这个市场的内需非常大，就好像打麻将不求人，我们的内需空间很大。建议往后中国和东盟国家在旅游、金融、农业和工业发展上，大家互利互补，取得双赢。希望中国和东盟各位领袖和各位商会，和国际报业集团保持联系，希望能够定期在东盟任何一个国家看到相关报道，这样也会为大家的事业发展创造更多的商机。

老挝国家工商会副会长乔汤·帕塔玛冯在演讲中指出，中国和东盟各国商会必须在各级别、各领域扩展双边经贸合作；同时促进中国和东盟各国全方位的深化合作，交流互鉴和共同发展。关注以下几个方面的问题：第一，要建立信息分享中心，各国商会可以及时地发布商业信息、介绍商业伙伴、提供咨询服务、开展培训，组织展览会和研讨会等，以此为企业间合作牵线搭桥；第二，中国和东盟各国政府应当改善物流设施，促进道路和铁路建设，改善水运和航运等物流条件，还要发展通讯技术。上述措施，将有助于我们共建区域共同市场，尤其有利于贸易、物流和旅游合作，也有利于中国和东盟各国的商业发展和共同利益。

马来西亚中国经济贸易总商会总会长拿督黄汉良在演讲中说，中国—东盟自由贸易区的落实是实现东盟和中国合作的划时代大事，是亚洲人办好自己事务的具体表率。事实证明，自贸区对各国都有好处。拥有19亿人口的中国大市场肯定给各国商家带来空前的商机和挑战。民间商会的角色就更加重要，要配合政府落实推动利民的政策。东盟各国经济发展不一，各国经济结构也不同，商家之间的经济利益关系，形成矛盾心理存在。商会要领导各国商家把握商机，指导方向，顾全大局，深入了解各国的商情和潜力，调整业务结构，甚至加速企业转型以适应扩大了的新市场。商会可以组织会员参与各国的商业交流，加强市场的调查研究，做到商家互补共赢。各国可进行企业合作联营，努力扩大规模后，走出东盟，迈向国际，促进世界经济一体化、区域化和国际化。

马来西亚中华总商会中央理事梁家兴在演讲中说，中国—东盟自贸区内进出口贸易货物应免收进口税。区域内的商家拥有整个19亿人口的中国—东盟自贸区市场。自贸区内零关税也有利于鼓励商家在自贸区内投资，然后把产品促销到自贸区内的其他国家。中国企业可以到自然资源丰富的国家开厂投资，然后再将产品营销，这样就能确保企业有充足天然资源的供应，同时也能保证产品价格的稳定。商会的作用体现在举办洽谈会，扩展各国的商家在别国找到合适的贸易和投资伙伴。商会可组织贸易投资访问团到别国去访问考察、开拓商机，也可接待访问团，并安排本国的商家和来访的商家进行交流和洽谈合作。

缅甸国家工商会副会长翁仑在演讲中说，中国是缅甸第二大贸易伙伴，也是很大的一个投资来源地，特别是随着自贸区的运行，这样的贸易往来今后还会继续扩大。此外，在2010年，东盟也成为中国第四大贸易伙伴，自2008年以来双方贸易有巨大的增长。中国—东盟自贸区的建立将推进双方在技术经济方面的合作，同时也促进双边贸易共同发展，加强双方在非商业领域的合作，这也将促进实现商品的自由流动，在整个地区实现经济更自由的合作。缅甸国家工商会的主要作用是推动保护商业部门的利益，同时推动他们更多了解政府关于商业的政策，以便促进中小企业更好的发展，促进投资和贸易。缅甸国家工商会非常了解和熟悉国家在经济方面、贸易方面有关的政策，致力于推动国家采取更加有利于商业发展的政策，同时也积极推动政府和企业之间的合作。

菲华联谊商会副理事长施清胆在演讲中说，中国日益成为东盟的重要投资来源地。中国的开放经济为东盟提供了重要的市场。中国已经取代美国成为东盟第三大贸易伙伴。据预测，在未来3—5年内，中国将会成为东盟最大的贸易伙伴。我们充分肯定中国取得经济快速发展。随着中国影响力的不断扩大，我们将中国视为我们发展的伙伴而不是竞争者。为了更好地发挥自己的作用，各国商协会应当加强和本国会员企业的合作，加强和政府的合作以及加强和国外商协会的合作。 通过加强和会员企业的合作，商协会可以有效促进中国—东盟间的经济贸易合作，促进国内企业提升竞争力，实现区域市场和国际市场的共同繁荣。

泰国工业联盟副会长李锡龙在演讲中说，东盟和中国之间一直都有着很好的合作，泰国也从这个合作当中收获了很多利益。泰国作为东盟成员国的一员，从2010年的关税减到零之后，以及从东盟的经济共同体的建设当中收获了很多的利益。中国—东盟自贸协定的执行，有助于逐步扫除贸易障碍，促进双边贸易。中国—东盟自贸区有许多的优势可以发挥，主要体现在以下几个方面：一是有助于扩大市场；二是自贸区有助于各国工业领域的专业化分工；三是东盟和中国之间的基础设施合作。

新加坡制造商联合会副会长、新加坡经贸代表团团长、东方石油（新加坡）有限公司总裁李雪民在演讲中说，广西是中国与东盟国家展开经贸联系的桥头堡，中国—东盟博览会作为中国—东盟自由贸易区建设的“助推器”，在中国—东盟经贸合作中发挥了重要作用，第七届博览会将以“自贸区与新机遇”为重点主题，特色更加鲜明。新加坡工商界一直关注自由贸易区的发展，也十分重视中国—东盟博览会这一平台。我会已连续五年组织新加坡经贸代表团，出席中国—东盟博览会。2010年组团出席第七届博览会，就是要帮助新加

坡企业进一步了解自贸区的发展状况，建立更加广泛的商务联系，把握自贸区全面建成的契机，促进与中国及其他东盟国家企业更广泛的交流与合作。

越南工商会副会长段维姜在演讲中说，东盟已经成为了一个很好的经贸推动和促进发展平台，成为一个非常具有竞争力的实体。在全球经济一体化过程中，中国—东盟的合作机制发挥了重要的作用，促进了地区经济复原和发展。在此基础上，我们应当携手共进，共同打造一个富有生机的东盟商贸和生产中心。自贸区的建成，为东盟各国的经济发展提供了难得的机遇，东盟各国在技术合作方面的合作前景广阔。中国—东盟的合作在世界上发挥了越来越重要的作用。2010年举办的第一届中国—东盟商会领袖论坛意义重大，是中国在为东盟各国经贸交流机制上的一个重要创新。

（三）2010中国—东盟矿业合作论坛暨展示会

2010中国—东盟矿业合作论坛暨展示会于2010年9月6—7日在南宁国际会展中心举行。作为商务与投资峰会系列活动之一，此次论坛为中国与东盟矿业界的合作搭建了一个新的交流与合作平台，推动了双方资源开发领域的新合作。

1. 政界高规格出席。中国国土资源部副部长汪民，广西壮族自治区党委书记、自治区人大常委会主任郭声琨，广西壮族自治区主席马飚，自治区党委常委、自治区副主席陈武，自治区党委常委、秘书长余远辉，自治区副主席林念修，国际地质科学联合会委员、前主席张宏仁，菲律宾自然资源与环境部副部长杰米尔斯·多利诺，柬埔寨工业矿产能源部副国务秘书凯奇，中国贸促会副秘书长刘凤华，东盟矿业协会联合会会长本杰明等领导出席了

2010年9月6—7日，首届中国—东盟矿业合作论坛暨展示会在南宁举行

2010 China-ASEAN Mining Cooperation Forum and Exhibition held in Nanning on September 6-7, 2010

论坛的有关活动。柬埔寨、缅甸、老挝、泰国、越南五个东盟国家矿产局，中国有色矿业集团、中国铝业、中国五矿集团、国家开发银行、中国进出口银行、中信证券、中国建设银行、加拿大多伦多股票交易所、香港交易及结算所等均派高层出席论坛有关活动。

2. 业界高度参与。中国和菲律宾、柬埔寨、缅甸、老挝、泰国、越南等六个东盟国家矿业主管部门负责人和代表在开幕式发表了讲话，14位中外企业家在高峰论坛上演讲，11位专家在矿业学术论坛上演讲，16位高层管理人员在矿业投融资论坛上发表演讲。矿业展览会设中国矿业展示区、东盟10国国家矿业展示区、广西矿业展示区、越南煤炭集团、中国铝业、广西有色金属集团、金川集团、柳工、中信大锰、至尊珠宝等特装展位，展出效果良好。中外500多家企业报名参会。

3. 活动内容丰富。本次矿业论坛是第七届中国—东盟商务与投资峰会系列活动之一，也是中国与东盟国家矿业界首次举办的矿业会议，于9月6—7日在南宁国际会展中心举行，共进行了开幕式、项目签约仪式、高峰论坛、矿业学术论坛、矿业投融资论坛、矿业项目专场推介会、矿业展览会、欢迎宴会、午餐会等多项活动。

4. 合作成效显著。本届矿业论坛参会代表达600多人，其中东盟国家150多人，展出面积2900多平方米，共签订13个合作项目，总投资额近70亿元人民币，贸易意向成交4.2亿元人民币，取得了丰硕的成果。其中广西有色金属集团有限公司与香港FDC矿业集团有限公司就柬埔寨罗连省罗文铁矿采选开发合作项目达成了20亿人民币签约金额，是13个签约项目中数额最大的一项。万象矿业有限公司、广西地润矿业投资有限公司、广西有色冶金有限公司等企业就老挝、缅甸等境外的矿业项目分别签订了合作协议。

5. 搭建了新的平台和机制。本届矿业论坛的成功举办，标志着在2010年1月1日中国—东盟自由贸易区正式建成后，中国与东盟矿业界已形成合作的共识和愿望，建立起一个新的洽谈途径和交流合作平台与机制。东盟矿业协会联合会会长菲利普·罗姆德兹，印尼中华总商会常务主席、印尼科技能源有限公司董事长陈泳志，老挝国家工商会执行董事、老挝澜沧矿产有限公司总经理沙曼·安内卡，缅甸地质协会秘书长古国琼，泰国工业联盟首席执行主任查恩，国际地质科学联合会前主席张宏仁，国际矿业企业工作委员会公共事务总监邹星应邀率团出席。中国有色金属集团副总经理严弟勇，中国铝业公司执行董事、副总裁刘祥明，菲律宾菲莱克斯矿业集团董事长埃内斯托·维拉卢拉，广西有色金属集团董事长李阳通，金川集团有限公司董事长汪海洲，广晟有色金属股份有限公司董事长叶列理等业界组织、行业集团和

2010 中国—东盟矿业合作论坛签约仪式现场

Contract signing ceremony of 2010 China-ASEAN Mining Cooperation Forum

大型矿业企业负责人亲自率团参展参会，开展项目对接、洽谈业务，带动了中国和东盟矿业界的踊跃参会，进一步了深化区域矿业互惠共赢的合作，为推动中国与东盟矿业的共同发展打下良好的基础，前景广阔，意义深远。

此外，出席论坛的各国矿业部委官员通过这一平台介绍了本国矿业优势和鼓励政策，中国国土资源部副部长、中国地质调查局局长汪民在致辞中说，中国和东盟国家拥有丰富的矿产资源，在矿业领域互补性强，矿业合作具有良好的基础和广阔的前景。在双边领域，国土资源部与东盟国家矿业主管部门保持着良好的双边合作关系，人员互访频繁，开展了包括相邻区域重要成矿带编图、成矿规律对比研究等领域的多项地质矿产合作研究项目。在多边领域，国土部积极参与“10+3”框架下与东盟在地质矿产领域的合作。自2007年起，积极参加“10+3”矿业高官磋商会，并在会后积极争取条件，为东盟国家地质矿产管理和技术人员开展培训和研讨，分享成功经验，增进了解和互信。中国矿业企业对东盟国家开展了矿业领域的投资合作，成功实施了一批矿业勘查开发项目，促进了所在国的经济发展。在全球经济发展新时期，应把握机遇，锐意进取，尽快建立起多层次、多渠道的具有鲜明特色的矿业合作长效机制，拓宽合作领域，提高合作水平，推动矿业资源勘查开发合作迈上新的台阶，以矿产资源的可持续利用，促进和保障经济社会的可持续发展，最大限度地实现优势互补和互利共赢。

菲律宾环境与自然资源部副部长杰米尔斯·多利诺在致辞介绍了本国的矿产优势和在建项目，一是菲律宾有广泛的丰富矿产资源战略位置，具备有经验的技术资源、有效法律体系和有效的矿业环境政策，矿产资源丰富，而且也因为多种类的金属和非金属而知名，特别是黄金、铜、镍、烙铁和锰，土地面积大约是3千万公顷，900万公顷有潜在的丰富的矿产资源，只有1.4%得到勘探和开采。二是菲律宾位于东南亚，同时接近中国、日本和韩国，具有亚洲战略性的位置。三是菲律宾有能力、有经验的矿产工作人员包括工程师、矿产工业学家能够满足本地的需求，加以有效的法律体系、清晰的矿业环境政策和矿业法令，为投资者营造良好投资环境。

柬埔寨工业矿产资源部副国务秘书凯奇在演讲中介绍，柬埔寨是拥有丰富矿产，包括金、铁矿、铜、铅、锌、红宝石、蓝宝石、硅土、高磷土、石灰等，来自澳大利亚、中国、越南、韩国及柬埔寨国内的公司，已经获取了许可执照来更好地研究和开发矿产资源。2010年颁布矿产资源的管理和开发方面的法律法规之后，相关矿业法律法规得到更好的贯彻，能够完善柬埔寨的矿产资源的管理和开发。鼓励和希望跟多投资者和企业来柬埔寨寻求投资合作机会。

老挝能源矿产部地矿司司长同帕在演讲中说，在老挝能源矿产方面的发展仍然处于初级阶段，由于缺乏投资、缺乏技术和经验，只有几个能源矿产公司，这些公司规模大多数都是非常小的。非常欢迎各国投资者来老挝开展在矿产领域的合作和投资。目前关于矿产资源和开发管理方面的法律法规，以及矿产资源方面人力和经验的开发正进一步完善。同时，老挝政府非常关注中国和老挝在能源矿产方面合作的机会和战略伙伴关系，并以此为推动器，它能够更好促进两个国家紧密合作关系。

缅甸矿产部矿产局局长温庭在发言中介绍，缅甸在1988年采取了市场经济政策，旨在不断解除中央的控制，鼓励私营部门的开发和投资，同时鼓励外商企业投资，通过简化进出口的程序促进对外贸易。在公平和互利的基础上，欢迎外国资本投资缅甸，并且能够让合理的经济回报寄回本国。缅甸相关的矿业法律，所有的自然矿业资源不管是在土地上还是在大陆架上都是国有的。缅甸鼓励外国和本地的投资者来投资于矿业行业。

泰国工业部初级工业与矿产局副局长萨内·尼优泰在演讲中说，泰国遵循东盟的经济共同体蓝图的合作框架，关注于技术、环境、贸易、投资方面的合作，在过去几十年，泰国积极参与东盟“10+3”框架之内的合作，特别是在地质科学方面和矿业数据方面都有很密切的合作。目前泰国寻求矿业合作发展新的领域，希望与中国加强矿业技术和基础合作。建议与东盟各国不仅是在矿业方面，包括在人力、金融以及实体的资源方面加大相互利用，从而相互受益。

越南地质与矿产局副局长郑春边在发言中介绍说，越南有5000多个矿藏以及矿石资源，同时包括60多种不同的矿产资源，在过去几年中，越南大量拓展与其他国家的合作包括全球与地区性的合作，在地质与采矿领域积极的发展，很多地质矿物组织也来到越南进行矿产资源的勘探和评估工作，而

且很多的矿物勘探和矿产公司也纷纷从不同的国家赶到越南来，对这个地区的矿产资源以及法律环境进行研究，寻找进的合作机会，在矿产领域进行投资。根据目前的矿产法以及未来将要新出台的矿产法，越南将会鼓励外国机构以及外国个人来合作，在开放的政策下，越南已经做好准备来欢迎任何的外国组织和外国个人来越南合作、来越南投资。

（四）中国—东盟经贸与物流合作论坛

2010年10月20日下午14：30—17：30，中国—东盟经贸与物流合作论坛在广西人民会堂举行。由商务与投资峰会秘书处和北京中物联物流规划研究院具体承办。

论坛分两节进行。第一节会议主持嘉宾是中国物流与采购联合会副会长兼秘书长崔忠付，演讲嘉宾包括：中国商务部国际经贸关系司副司长孙元江，中国海关总署监管司司长郝崇福，中国交通运输部国际司副司长杨赞，中国铁道部运输局副局长苏顺虎，中国广西钦州市市长肖莺子，中国物资储运协会会长姜超峰，泰国立法政大学教授、亚行GMS物流发展规划项目负责人鲁斯·班睦雍，中美总商会董事约翰·克拉克，新加坡叶水福集团中国首席执行官吴荣昇。第二节会议主持嘉宾是广西物流与采购联合会会长张福利，演讲嘉宾包括：中国物流与采购联合会副会长兼秘书长崔忠付，中国苏

中国—东盟经贸与物流合作论坛会场
China-ASEAN Trade and Logistics Cooperation Forum

州物流中心有限公司副总裁姚武，中国工业经济联合会副会长、中国华南国际工业原料城执行董事、首席顾问许扬，文莱国家工商会副会长卡玛鲁汀，新加坡劲升逻辑有限公司中国区总经理陈福成，新加坡全球海事港口服务公司总裁詹姆斯·冯，嘉里大通物流有限公司西区总经理向曦。共有近600名的国内外物流企业CEO、金融机构高级管理人员、制造业、流通业负责物流和采购事务的高级管理人员与会，其中中方代表近500人，区内代表350人左右，区外代表150人，东盟国家以及来自日本、香港等国（地区）代表达100多人。到场报道的中外新闻媒体记者达100多人，各大网络现场直播，广西电视台全程录播。

中国商务部国际经贸关系司副司长孙元江说，中国—东盟自贸区总体发展势头良好，但目前仍存在一些问题：一是贸易便利化水平有待提高；二是自贸区的利用率不高；三是对东盟市场的了解不足。很多企业不了解东盟各国的法律法规、产业结构、资源布局及消费者习惯等，也没有意识到通过内部自贸区和与各大国的自贸区整合，东盟已经成为一个统一的大市场。企业可以借助东盟与日本、韩国、澳大利亚等国家的自贸协定开拓更多市场。物流业直接影响着企业从自贸区政策中获实际利益的多少，物流成本占经济总量的比重越小，对经济的实际贡献越大。建议：第一，大力推进贸易便利化工作，发挥自贸区作用。第二，加强开展基础设施合作和互联互通建设。第三，加强与东盟的行业对接和产业合作。我们要学会尊重当地企业和民众的利益，要注意对当地产业的带动和扶持，要对当地环境、社区和劳工履行必要的社会责任。

中国海关总署监管司司长郝崇福在演讲中说，海关的传统职能主要有四个，监管、征税、缉私和统计。非传统安全、反恐、反偷渡、环境安全和食品卫生安全等也是海关这几年来不断发展的职能。近年来由于恐怖主义抬头，非传统安全的威胁越来越大，所以世界海关组织在2005年通过了一个保证贸易链安全和便利的框架。当今海关不仅要提供通关便利，还要确保贸易链安全。中国海关和其他国家海关的合作是在WTO的框架及世界海关组织通过的保证贸易链安全和便利的框架下进行的。只有各国之间海关合作不断的加强，货物通关的便利才会更多。

中国铁道部运输局副局长苏顺虎在发言中介绍当前中国铁路集装箱运输和中国—东盟集装箱多式联运发展的情况。首先是要抓住黄金机遇。2002年以来，党中央和国务院做出了加快铁路发展的重大战略部署，国家有关部门和地方政府对铁路发展给予了大力的支持。二是通过坚持改革创新，集装箱铁路运输取得了长足的发展。三是加强沟通与合作，加快中国—东盟集装箱运

输领域的发展。随着中国和东盟合作不断深化，双方的经济贸易和物流需求呈快速增长的态势，中国—东盟集装箱领域也正迎来大发展的有利时期。多式联运是货运发展的方向，充分发挥集装箱在多式联运的作用是大趋势，也符合低碳经济的客观要求。要实现这个目标，既需要中国铁路进一步提升自身的服务能力，更离不开东盟各国政府及经贸和物流界同行大力支持。

广西壮族自治区钦州市市长肖莺子在发言中介绍了钦州的情况和优势，并建议：共同推进南方亿吨大港建设合作。加强在港口基础设施建设、码头经营、航运服务、物流配送、港口信息化、修造船舶等方面的合作。共同推进产业发展合作。共同打造货畅其流的物流体系和高效、务实的产业平台，重点推进中国—东盟（钦州）国际农产品交易中心、中国—钦州（东盟）国际商贸城等一批大型专业市场和综合物流加工区的建设。共同推进贸易便利化合作。加强口岸服务硬件和软件建设，推进一站式通关。积极发展离岸贸易和离岸金融等业务，进一步减少交易障碍。共同推进人才、信息等交流合作。双方多组织管理人才、商家互访考察交流，加强中国—东盟自由贸易区相关政策和自由港政策体系的研究，不断提升合作层次和合作水平。

中国物资储运协会会长姜超峰在发言中指出，中国—东盟自贸区的主要特点是贸易便利化，贸易便利化的主要支持是融资和物流的便利化，没有这两项，企业资金流转和贸易的最终完成都会有障碍。贸易融资是基于商品交易中的存货、预付款和应收账款等资产的融资，借款人以销售收入为还款来源，银行以借款人的存货、预付应收账款为贷款的保证。贸易融资是用存货作为质押进行借款，然后用预付款和应收款质押来进行贷款，再用销售收入来归还这个贷款，银行可以在全封闭状态对资金运行进行全封闭的监管。贸易融资推进了贸易的便利，首先是扩大贸易量，第二是节约贸易时间，第三是简化企业资质评审程序，增加了贸易安全系数。中国—东盟自贸区金融物流业务才刚刚开始，好比一张白纸，这张白纸有赖于我们的同行同仁做以下一些工作：统一业务的标准，甚至是国际性的统一标准，统一业务流程、统一单证、统一计算机系统和统一格式。如果这几个统一都达到了，我们“10+1”金融物流业务就能够顺利地开展起来。

泰国立法政大学教授、亚行GMS物流发展规划项目负责人鲁斯·班睦雍在发言中指出，物流对于进一步提高一个地区的经济融合是非常重要的。一个地区要形成具有竞争力的贸易，必须要有一个全面清晰的计划发展物流和通讯设施。大湄公河次区域的规模虽不算大，但其更加注重发展经济走廊，如昆明和曼谷之间的经济走廊，还有连接昆明、曼谷与河内的经济走廊，这几年通过一系列基础设施的发展计划，到2015年，硬件方面的互联互通能达

2010年10月20日，中国—东盟经贸与物流合作论坛在广西南宁举行

China-ASEAN Trade and Logistics Cooperation Forum held in Nanning on October 20, 2010

到一个很高的程度。物流的具体工作不单由一个行政部门主管，往往有多个政府机构参与其中，如运输部、海关总署和商务部等，所以需要有一个联动机制。须在各国国内和国家之间建立一个强有力的协调机制，还需要统计与物流相关的数据，如有人说中国物流的成本是GDP的20%，在泰国这个比例是18%，其他的国家如何呢？这是一个需要加强合作的方面。

中美总商会代表约翰·克拉克在发言中说，中国—东盟自贸区的平均关税在10年内要降到0%—5%，区域内贸易和投资限制将被取消。中国—东盟自贸区将会是世界上最大的自贸区，它会有19亿的消费者，生产总值是6万亿美元，自贸区内的贸易总量会达到4.5万亿美元。东盟和中国的出口结构互补性很强，原来在中国进行生产的一些行业和企业可能会转移到东盟国家。对东盟国家来说，与中国竞争是比较困难的，所以最佳的方案是与中国合作，这样的贸易关系能够使中国和东盟一起成长。中国向东盟国家的出口占出口总量的8.3%，东盟向中国的出口只占其总量的3.9%，目前日本、欧洲、美国三大市场在中国和东盟的出口当中分别占52%和50%，中国—东盟自贸区的建立将减少这些国家对日本、欧洲和美国的依赖。

新加坡叶水福集团中国首席执行官吴荣昇在发言中指出，中国之所以能成为一个世界工厂，廉价的劳动力和技术工人只是原因之一。这几年中国不断地投资建设基础设施，如码头、机场、互联网平台和通关EDI等，让中国制造的产品非常有竞争力。根据世界银行曾经做的一份报告，如果东盟国家能够提高在码头，还有互联网方面的能力和竞争力，能够使东盟贸易增加7.5%，也就是能增加220亿美元的收益。应该探讨如何把“10+1”精神用来生产顶级的产品，如该怎样好好地利用FTA来发展汽车行业，马来西亚有很多

的橡胶，马来西亚可以专注做轮胎，一些玻璃和汽车零部件由其他国家来生产，再把零部件运到中国、越南、泰国或马来西亚最后组装成汽车，中国可以把重点放在组装左行驶类的汽车，泰国的重点可以是右行驶类的汽车。

嘉里大通物流有限公司西区总经理向曦在演讲中说，经过30年的发展，嘉里大通物流在大中华地区和港澳地区拥有200家自由的服务网点，在东盟八个国家有规模和实力非常雄厚的分公司和很好的物流基础设施。我们在泰国曼谷湾有自己的港口和几十万平方米的仓储设施，我们强大的物流服务网络是为了更好地利用中国—东盟自由贸易区建立后的巨大物流商机和贸易发展，为中国—东盟自贸区的发展提供一个良好的服务网络基础。原来的分段式运输要求在每个国家都要有一个代理人，而且由于跨境多，对各个国家的法律、运输、海关以及贸易条款不是很熟悉，双方在交易货物时要各自承担本国的关务和运输安排费用，既费时成本也非常高。对于消费者来说，只用与一家物流商交易，运输时间非常短，成本也非常低。通过全方位一体化的运输，不仅大大降低了物流成本，而且大大提高了效率，缩短了货物在途时间，也为客户解决货物质押资金问题提供了很大的方便。

中国物流与采购联合会副会长兼秘书长崔忠付说，中国—东盟自由贸易区的建成，促进了中国和东盟各个国家的经济发展，扩大了双边贸易额和投资规模，推动了区域内各国之间的物流、资金流和信息流的融合与发展，提高了本地区的整体竞争力，为区域内各国人民创造了更多福祉。与此同时，中国—东盟自贸区的建立，有利于推动东盟经济一体化，对世界经济增长也有积极作用。然而，当前中国与东盟中小企业在国际贸易中仍存在诸多不便与困难。面对中国—东盟自由贸易区建立带来的众多贸易机会，中小企业由于自身能力的不足而无法得到更多的发展机会。在新的经济形势下，如何让更多的中小企业更容易地参与到国际贸易中来，是最大化提升中国与东盟经济实力和增强彼此在经济全球化中的应对能力的关键。

苏州物流中心有限公司副总裁姚武在发言中介绍，苏州工业园区利用苏州3.4%的土地和5.2%的人口，创造了苏州15%的GDP，说明苏州工业园区正逐渐发展成为苏州的一个新的社会经济发展增长极。2010年1—8月工业园区进出口产值488亿美元，保税区产值是538亿美元。苏州工业园区先试先行，探索创新，其中有全国首个中外合作办学试点、虚拟空港模式试点、全国海关模式试点、全国第一家内陆型综合保税区试点和先进性技术发展试点等。正是因为高端制造业和工业园区的快速发展，苏州现代物流业得到了很大发展。通过虚拟口岸的打造，苏州为商贸的发展提供了更好的保障。

华南国际工业原料城执行董事、中国工业经济联合会副会长许扬在发言中指出，广西南宁具备构建中国商贸物流中心的有利条件，因为具备了构建商贸园区的地缘优势、交通优势和产业优势。南宁华南城的建设目标就是将其打造成中国—东盟商品的最佳展示平台和方便快捷的商贸物流平台。南宁华南城的使命和产业特点是工业原料和制成品的展示批发中心、仓储运输配送中心、展览交易中心、实体市场和虚拟市场相结合展示的交易平台以及娱乐和居住相结合的配套设施。整合社会资源，把服务和培育市场放在首位，降低制造业和商贸流通的采购成本和交易成本，提高企业的创新能力和市场反应能力，提高企业和地区的竞争力。正在建设中的南宁华南城2010年已经举办了中国—东盟轻工产品展览会，马飚主席亲自到会剪彩并宣布开幕。我们有品牌中心、物流中心、设计中心、会展中心、仓储中心、金融中心、采购服务中心、网上交易平台、行业协会、办公场所、质量检测中心和行政服务中心为工商和税务提供法律保险等服务。

文莱国家工商会副会长卡玛鲁汀在发言中介绍，文莱将建立国际物流的中心，覆盖整个地区物流的转运，将连接东南亚很多港口及国家和地区，包括欧洲和澳大利亚等。文莱将会发展成为东南亚发展的一个重要中心，将会和新加坡、曼谷加强合作。中国—东盟自贸区在2010年1月1日正式建成，是一个有19亿人口的巨大市场，这促使东盟成为世界供应链的一个重要环节。东盟是中国第四大贸易伙伴，根据官方数据，中国和东盟的双边贸易额在2008年达到了2311亿美元，文莱国家工商会将在促进文莱同中国货物之间的来往方面做出努力。

新加坡劲升逻辑有限公司中国区总经理陈福成在演讲中说，口岸和物流贸易是一个非常复杂的流程，在买方和卖方之间可能有20%—30%的企业机构在不断地交换信息和发指令，大部分是重复的。上世纪80年代时，面对金融危机和经济衰退，新加坡政府组织的一个委员会建议用IT手段来提升新加坡的贸易竞争力。每个经济体、国家或省市区，如果想要提高竞争力，需考虑五个方面，码头作业系统、港口社区系统、通关系统、出口加工区管理系统和贸易便利化系统。如果这五个系统能做到数据共享和流通，就能大大减少成本，节约时间。几年前东盟10国启动了一个东盟单列窗口项目，东盟国家间的进出口业务可以通过一个平台把出口数据发送到进口国，进口国可以重用大约50%—70%不等的数据，减少非常庞大的贸易成本。如果中国和东盟间的贸易也可以和东盟单列窗口有连接，数据在这个平台上共享，不仅可以大大减少成本，也可以使贸易更加地便捷。

新加坡全球海事港口服务公司总裁詹姆斯·冯在发言中介绍，中国现在正在开放中，并注重发展西部地区。将物流工业对外资开放，促进这个行业

内部的竞争，会使中国面对很多挑战，如在基础设施方面。还要促进信息产业发展，提高质量标准，相关法律的执行也非常重要。新加坡和中国可以通过一些合作来共同来推动自贸区，包括思想的交流及共同培训和研发。通过合作来提高人力资源素质，这样才能支持新的政府的项目，推动物流行业的发展。

中国物流与采购联合会首席顾问、中国贸促会物流行业分会会长丁俊发在发言中阐述了打造中国—东盟物流运作平台的必要性与迫切性。一是中国—东盟贸易量急剧增加，经济处于上升期。二是高物流成本成为东盟各国经济发展、提高国际竞争力的严重障碍。三是中国—东盟一体化有利于消除贸易壁垒，促进东盟各国经济快速发展。四是提出了打造中国—东盟一体化物流运作平台的思路——“12345”战略。“1”即制定一个中国—东盟物流发展一体化规划，统一行动，分阶段实施。“2”即打通两轴。一轴为海上物流通道，二轴为陆路物流通道。“3”即建设物流服务一体化的三层架构：政府或行业协会的联盟、公共服务平台、物流节点建设。“4”即四联发展。其一，多种运输方式联运，做到无缝连接；其二，产学研联手，打组合拳；其三，制造业、农业、商业与物流业联动，加快物流产业的市场化、专业化、国际化、现代化；其四，商流、物流、信息流、资金流联结，发挥积聚效应。“5”即打好五大战役或叫五大工程。其一，成立东盟物流联盟，确定运作机制，制定总体规划，打造国际物流服务平台；其二，着力打造公共服务的三大平台：物流基础设施平台，物流公共信息平台，物流产业政策平台；其三，培育物流企业，尤其是重点培育一批具有国际竞争力的企业集团，进入国际市场；其四，建设物流一体化运作标准化工程，降低物流成本，推进物流的现代化；其五，加强物流人才教育工程建设，可以考虑利用现有的学校教育，也可以考虑建立新的物流人才培育基地。

（五）中国—东盟轻工产品展览会

本届轻工产品展览会由中国—东盟商务与投资峰会秘书处联合有关方面共同承办。本届轻工产品展览会规划展览面积1.5万平方米，614个标准展位，共有参展企业365家，其中来自东盟国家的企业有60多家，来自台湾地区的参展企业有100多家，来自珠三角地区有70多家。展会会场共设有七大展区，分别为东盟特色商品展区、香港产品展区、台湾产品展区、华南城组团展区、工艺礼品展区、数码通信展区及政府组团展区。在为期5天的展会中，现场签约额为2.4亿元人民币，意向签约额为9.5亿元人民币，中外参观人数达到33.5万人次。

2010 年 10 月 20 日，中国—东盟轻工产品展览会在广西南宁华南城会展中心隆重开幕

On October 20, 2010, the opening ceremony of China-ASEAN Light Industrial Products Exhibition held at the Exhibition & Convention Center of South China City (Nanning)

（六）商务早餐会

2010年10月20日，第七届中国—东盟商务与投资峰会举行商务早餐会。广西壮族自治区主席马飚、中国贸促会副会长于平出席商务早餐会并致辞。中外政界、商界以及国际和区域组织200多位代表出席早餐会。为加强中国和东盟企业的直接交流与互动，早餐会提供场地和机会以便双方企业开展企业推介、商务配对、样品展示等活动。

2010 年 10 月 20 日，第七届中国—东盟商务与投资峰会举行商务早餐会

The 7th CABIS Business Breakfast Meeting held on October 20, 2010

四　第七届中国—东盟商务与投资峰会的特点和成果

（一）秉承服务国家周边外交战略的办会理念，继续保持政治外交高规格，充分发挥作为中国与东盟进行高层对话的平台作用

当前，国际政治经济格局加速调整，亚洲发展孕育着重大机遇。中国和东盟国家领导人在中国—东盟商务与投资峰会开幕式讲话中普遍认为，在新形势下，中国同东盟国家的前途命运日益紧密地联系在一起，中国与东盟10国应携手合作，巩固和加强中国—东盟战略伙伴关系，符合彼此的共同利益，也是双方的共同责任和共同选择。本届中国—东盟商务与投资峰会以“中国—东盟自由贸易区与区域经贸合作的展望”为主题，顺应了中国和东盟携手合作、共创未来的趋势和需求。中外国家领导人希望有关各方通过此次峰会平台，围绕主题，集思广益，献计献策，就进一步发挥中国—东盟自贸区作用，扩大双方经贸合作和相互投资，改善双方经贸关系，实现互利共赢，提出建设性举措，推动中国—东盟互利合作进一步向广度和深度发展。中国和东盟领导人充分利用此次出席中国—东盟商务与投资峰会的机会展开对话，对中国—东盟携手合作，巩固和加强中国—东盟战略伙伴关系表示高度重视并达成一致共识，成为采访这次峰会的媒体尤其是境外媒体的关注焦点，再一次表明了加强中国与东盟之间区域合作的重要性和迫切性以及进一步深化合作的必要性。

（二）紧扣主题，以推进和落实自贸区协议作为重点，达成广泛共识

推进和落实自贸区协议在中国—东盟自贸区发展中具有重要的积极意义。本届中国—东盟商务与投资峰会的主题为“中国—东盟自贸区与区域经贸合作的展望”，按照业已达成的《货物贸易协议》、《服务贸易协议》、《投资协议》的安排，加大创新力度，提高服务水平，让企业更好地享受贸易和投资便利化，享受更多商机，更加积极主动地与东盟各国工商企业界携

起手来，进一步创新合作机制，丰富合作内涵，创造合作机遇，增强合作实效，共同开创中国—东盟自由贸易区更加美好的未来。

（三）以促进区域内行业合作为重点，加强务实合作，行业间互动卓有成效

促进中国与东盟行业合作是中国—东盟自贸区实现共赢的重要支撑。本届中国—东盟商务与投资峰会围绕主题，设置系列专题活动，涉及石油、电力、电信、金融、工程承包、矿业、物流、路桥、机械等诸多领域，与会者就整合资源、互补优势，建立和完善双方行业间合作机制，积极、务实、全面地加强双方行业合作，深入地展开互动，初步形成合作意向，为下一步工作奠定良好的合作基础。我们有理由相信，合作各方将以此次会议为契机，促进双方行业合作进入新的阶段，为自贸区内本国经济繁荣作出贡献。

（四）创新会议活动和内容，通过创新举办系列专题活动建立起区域行业合作机制，实效性强

为了实现促进中国—东盟商务与投资峰会由“论”向务实合作方向发展的目标，本届中国—东盟商务与投资峰会对会议活动和内容进行创新，争取通过行业合作论坛建立起区域行业合作机制。实践证明，本届中国—东盟商务与投资峰会分别举办圆桌对话会、商会领袖论坛、矿业行业合作论坛、经贸和物流合作论坛等活动，已经有效地建立起政府与企业圆桌对话机制，商协组织工作机制，矿业合作工作机制以及物流合作工作机制等，为中国与东盟开展高层次、深领域的合作提供有力保证。

（五）区域内外政界、工商界人士参会积极性创新高，进一步凸显中国—东盟商务与投资峰会日益提升的吸引力、影响力和生命力

2010年是中国—东盟自由贸易区建成的第一年，中国和东盟国家领导人、部长级贵宾、国际组织代表、各国商协会会长、世界知名企业家以及商界代表1500多人共同出席本届中国—东盟商务与投资峰会，部长级贵宾有200多人，其中，东盟及其他国家部长级贵宾60多人。法国、加拿大、美国、南美洲等区域外客商对此次会议的举办高度关注，纷纷报名参会。湖南永州市派出100多人的工作组在峰会上作专场推介。区域内外政界、商界人士掀起参加商务与投资峰会新高潮，表明了各方抓住中国—东盟自由贸易区建成的重大机遇，发挥峰会平台作用，加强全面合作，深化互利共赢的共同愿望，增强了各方继续共同推进自贸区建设，深化战略伙伴关系，实现共同发展、共同繁荣的信心和决心。

（六）以项目为载体，展会结合，相得益彰

在本届中国—东盟商务与投资峰会早餐会、矿业合作论坛、物流合作论坛、商会领袖论坛等平台上，安排企业推介、样品展示，设置洽谈专区，积极开展投资和贸易促进活动，充分利用各种资源进行投资、贸易配对。除此之外，中国—东盟商务与投资峰会秘书处还与有关方面共同举办了首届中国—东盟轻工业产品展览会，这是中国—东盟商务与投资峰会继创办中国—东盟地方特色产品展览会之后又一个务实行动。这些活动以项目为载体，为中国与东盟工商界企业寻找商机，达成合作提供方便，展中有会，会中有展，展会结合，相得益彰。

第四章

自贸区建设成就辉煌 累累硕果见证大发展
——中国—东盟自由贸易区建设成就展

21世纪初，为顺应经济全球化和区域经济一体化的潮流，中国和东盟各国领导人高瞻远瞩，作出了建设中国—东盟自由贸易区的英明决策。实践证明，2010年中国—东盟自由贸易区全面建成后，给双方企业和人民带来了实实在在的好处，达到了共赢的效果。

为反映中国—东盟自由贸易区建设成就，在第七届中国—东盟博览会期间，同期举办中国—东盟自由贸易区建设成就展。

中国商务部官员、东盟国家驻南宁领事馆官员以及中国和东盟各国各界代表500多人出席了成就展开馆仪式。成就展内容丰富，国际性强，以图片、图表、文字、音视频等形式，反映自贸区建设的进程、各方面取得的成就，以及自贸区前景展望，包括反映中国—东盟博览会和中国—东盟商务与投资峰会对促进自贸区发展的成果展示。

其中，艺术展区由中国和东盟艺术家以及少年儿童以自贸区及中国与东盟的友好合作为题材，创作了一批书法、美术、摄影、篆刻等作品，艺术地反映了自贸区合作共赢的主题，也很好地反映了中国与东盟在文化等领域合作的成就。共有330位中国和东盟国家书画艺术家参与创作，其中东盟国家艺术家有66位，占20%。

会期，数万中国和东盟各界人士参观了成就展，中央政治局委员、中宣部部长刘云山、马来西亚贸工部副部长拿督贾谷·东加·沙甘等贵宾参观后给予高度赞誉。

CAFTA's Great Achievements

— CAFTA Achievements Exhibition

In the early 21st century, to meet the demand of global and regional economic integration, heads of state/government of China and the ASEAN countries have jointly made the brilliant decision to build the CAFTA. With the due establishment of the CAFTA in 2010, enterprises and people of both sides have been practically benefited, achieving a win-win result.

With an aim to reflect the accomplishments made by the CAFTA, during the 7th CAEXPO, the CAFTA Achievements Exhibition was held concurrently.

500 people including officials of the Chinese Ministry of Commerce, officials of consulates general of some ASEAN countries in Nanning, and representatives from all walks of life of China and ASEAN attended the opening ceremony of the exhibition. With a variety of genres such as pictures, graphics, texts, audio and videos, the exhibition has displayed the whole course of the CAFTA construction, the accomplishments made in many respects, its prospects, as well as the achievements made by the CAEXPO and the CABIS in promoting the development of the CAFTA.

The artwork show, one of the sections of the exhibition, displayed a number of works of calligraphy, fine arts, photography, carvings, with the theme of CAFTA and friendly cooperation between China and ASEAN. It well reflects the win-win theme of the CAFTA and the achievements made in the cooperation in cultures and other fields between China and ASEAN. A total of 330 artists displayed their works, of which 66 were from the ASEAN countries, 20% of the total.

During the CAEXPO, tens of thousands of visitors from China and ASEAN countries visited the exhibition, including H.E. Liu Yunshan, Head of Publicity Department of the Central Committee of Chinese Communist Party and Dato' Jacob Dungau Sagan, Vice Minister of Trade & Industry of Malaysia, who all sang high praise of the exhibition.

CHAPTER FOUR

一　中国—东盟自由贸易区建设成就展的意义

2010年1月1日，惠及19亿人口的中国—东盟自由贸易区如期全面建成。中国—东盟自由贸易区给双方企业和人民带来了实实在在的好处，达到了共赢的效果。为了很好地反映这些成就，在第七届中国—东盟博览会期间，同期举办中国—东盟自由贸易区建设成就展。

中国—东盟自由贸易区建设成就展是中国商务部、东盟10国经贸主管部门、东盟秘书处共同主办，广西壮族自治区人民政府承办的第七届中国—东盟博览会的重要组成部分。中国—东盟自由贸易区建设成就展于2010年10月20日至11月8日在广西民族博物馆二层中厅举行。

2010年是中国—东盟自由贸易区如期建成的第一年，为充分展示中国与东盟各国在共同推动中国—东盟自由贸易区建设中的巨大成就，进一步扩大中国—东盟自由贸易区和中国—东盟博览会的影响，在第七届中国—东盟博览会期间举办中国—东盟自由贸易区建设成就展，具有重要意义。

一是通过展示中国—东盟自由贸易区建设进程，全面反映中国与东盟各国在中国—东盟自由贸易区建设过程中的合作交往历程以及在政治、经济、文化、社会等方面取得的巨大成就。

二是通过展示中国—东盟自由贸易区建设给中国与东盟各国带来的新机遇，充分反映中国—东盟自由贸易区建设是一个合作互利共赢的过程，有利于促进中国和东盟各国的经贸往来和多领域合作，有利于双方经济发展和人民生活水平的提高，有利于双方战略伙伴关系的和谐发展，增强各国共创中国—东盟自由贸易区美好未来的信心。

成就展以图片、图表、文字、音频、视频等形式，展示中国—东盟自由贸易区建设成就，体现中国与东盟各国在政治、经济、文化等各领域的合作共赢，体现广西在承办中国—东盟博览会、中国—东盟商务与投资峰会中以及中国—东盟自由贸易区建设中的重要作用。

位于广西民族博物馆的中国—东盟自由贸易区建设成就展入口

Entrance of the CAFTA Achievements Exhibition located at Guangxi Nationality Museum

成就展的展示内容有三个方面：

一是中国—东盟自由贸易区建设内容。包括中国—东盟自由贸易区发展回顾展示；中国—东盟自由贸易区建设成果展示；中国—东盟自由贸易区建设大事记图文展示。

二是中国—东盟博览会、中国—东盟商务与投资峰会成效展示。包括历届中国—东盟博览会开幕式现场模型展示；中国—东盟博览会、中国—东盟商务与投资峰会发展历程图片及影视资料展示；中国—东盟博览会、中国—东盟商务与投资峰会对促进中国—东盟自由贸易区在政治、经贸、多领域合作等方面发展的成果展示。

三是以中国—东盟自由贸易区建设与发展为主题的艺术展。艺术展旨在通过美术、书法、摄影、篆刻等艺术形式，充分展示中国—东盟在文化、艺术领域的交流与发展，为自贸区的建成和取得的成就营造良好的艺术氛围。艺术展的作者来自中国和东盟的艺术家、少年儿童，艺术展的书画、摄影、雕刻等艺术作品主要反映了中国—东盟自由贸易区建设内容和成果，表达中国和东盟各国人民对美好生活的赞美和对中国—东盟自由贸易区良好发展的愿景。

二　中国—东盟自由贸易区建设成就展的筹备

（一）广泛动员，建立强有力组织机构

广西壮族自治区党委、自治区人民政府对本次中国—东盟自由贸易区建设成就展高度重视。自治区党委书记、自治区人大常委会主任郭声琨，自治区主席马飚，自治区党委常委、自治区副主席陈武分别对办好成就展作出指示，成立了由自治区党委宣传部牵头，广西壮族自治区公安厅、文化厅、广电局、外事办，广西国际博览事务局，广西贸促会，广西社科院，自治区文联，广西电视台，广西民族博物馆，南宁市政府等单位共同组成筹备机构，设立办公室、展览工作组、自贸区成就及两会展示组、艺术展品工作组、宣传工作组、安保工作组和南宁市工作组等七个工作部门。

（二）精心筹备，亮点纷呈

在广西壮族自治区党委宣传部及自治区相关厅局的共同努力下，中国—东盟自由贸易区建设成就展筹备工作从以下三个方面有条不紊地展开。

一是精选图文资料，征集艺术精品，展示中国—东盟自由贸易区辉煌成就。本次中国—东盟自由贸易区建设成就展精选了反映中国—东盟自由贸

中国—东盟自由贸易区建设成就展展厅
Exhibition hall of the CAFTA Achievements Exhibition

易区成就、博览会和商务与投资峰会成效等相关内容的图片900多张，制作视频资料7个。通过自治区文联、书协、美协、摄协及相关单位，征集了书法、美术、摄影、篆刻等艺术作品共455件，共有330位中国和东盟国家书画艺术家参与创作，其中书法作品95件、美术作品87件、篆刻作品149件、摄影作品76件、少年儿童作品47件、陶瓷作品1件。

二是运用现代展示手段，呈现亮点，确保隆重、大气。在展览形象设计方面，本次中国—东盟自由贸易区建设成就展充分运用现代科技手段，力求达到美观、大气、新颖、具有时代感的效果。展览设计与布展工作高效而有序地开展，2010年8月上旬启动成就展筹备工作，8月中旬已经确定展示设计方案，并根据展示内容进行修改和完善，部分展示项目已开始进场设计作业，整体布展施工工作于10月中旬完成。

中国—东盟自由贸易区建设成就展展厅

Exhibition hall of the CAFTA Achievements Exhibition

三是加强宣传，营造氛围。为了更好地宣传中国—东盟自由贸易区建设成就展以及中国—东盟自由贸易区的美好前景，成就展筹备机构制定了宣传方案和观众组织、现场文艺演出等相关工作细案，选定了成就展宣传口号。2010年7月26日，在国务院新闻办举行的中国—东盟经贸关系进展暨第七届中国—东盟博览会、商务与投资峰会新闻发布会上，正式发布了举办成就展的新闻。9月8日，又在广西举行了中国—东盟自由贸易区建设成就展新闻发布会，向大众介绍了成就展的重要意义和主要展览内容，通报了成就展筹备最新进展，对成就展进行了全面推介。

2010年9月8日，中国—东盟自由贸易区建设成就展新闻发布会在广西举行

The press conference of the CAFTA Achievements Exhibition held in Guangxi on September 8, 2010

（三）中国—东盟自由贸易区建设成就展书法长卷赠送仪式

2010年10月11日上午，在中国—东盟博览会、中国—东盟商务与投资峰会指挥中心举行了中国—东盟自由贸易区建设成就展书法长卷赠送仪式，广西文联代表长卷创作书法家向中国—东盟博览会秘书处赠送了以中国和东盟10国领导人寄语博览会为内容的书法长卷。

书法长卷是专门为中国—东盟自由贸易区建设成就展创作的。该卷以中国和东盟国家领导人关于中国—东盟博览会寄语为书写内容。中国国家主席胡锦涛对博览会的寄语书于长卷的首要位置，东盟国家领导人依次是：文莱苏丹哈桑纳尔，柬埔寨首相洪森，印尼总统苏西洛，老挝时任总理波松，马来西亚时任总理巴达维，缅甸时任总理登盛，菲律宾时任总统阿罗约，新加坡总理李显龙，泰国时任总理素拉育和越南总理阮晋勇等。

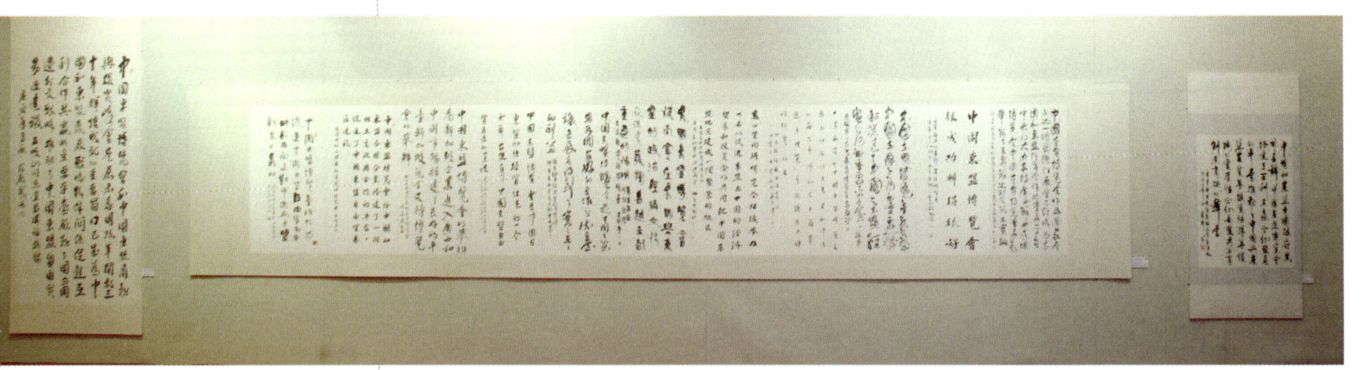

书法长卷
Long calligraphy scroll

该卷总长9米，宽1.8米。书体汇集了行草隶篆不同类别。风格庄重舒展，豪放凝重，又不失灵巧娟秀。卷容华美，气势宏大，给人以强烈的视觉冲击力。字里行间倾注了书法家们对博览会的满腔热忱。

这个长卷由广西知名书法家集体创作完成。广西书法家协会副主席、书法家韦克义，书法家刘炳清、王精、林建勋、刘德宏、刘炳玉、黄大业、陈小冰、甘文峰、彭洋、冯华春等11人参加了集体创作。

艺术无国界，笔端传真情。在中国—东盟自由贸易区如期建成的今天，书法作为中国传统的艺术形式，在中国与东盟的交流合作中发挥着重要的作用。

三　中国—东盟自由贸易区建设成就展开馆仪式

2010年10月18日下午，在装扮一新的广西民族博物馆，中国—东盟自由贸易区建设成就展开馆仪式隆重举行。广西壮族自治区党委常委、自治区副主席陈武宣布开馆。中国商务部贸发局副局长贾国勇、印尼工商会馆中国委员会副秘书长施瑞场在仪式上致辞。泰国等东盟国家驻南宁外交使节、广西壮族自治区人大常委会副主任吴恒、自治区政协副主席蒋培兰，以及中国和东盟各国代表共500多人参加开馆仪式。开馆仪式由中国—东盟博览会秘书处秘书长、广西国际博览事务局局长郑军健主持。

开馆仪式上，与会的各国嘉宾共同拉动红绸，红色幕布缓缓打开，寓意中国—东盟自由贸易区如期建成，中国与东盟共同谱写中国—东盟自由贸易区建设新篇章。随着恢弘激昂的音乐响起，五彩斑斓的花瓣与气球从天而降，两侧环梯上的300位小朋友摇动手中的鲜花，礼仪人员展开一幅领导及嘉宾对自贸区的寄语长卷，对所有嘉宾表示热烈欢迎。

2010年10月18日，中国—东盟自由贸易区建设成就展开馆仪式在南宁举行

The opening ceremony of the CAFTA Achievements Exhibition held in Nanning on October 18, 2010

贾国忠在致辞中说，中国和东盟国家经过十年的共同努力，建成了惠及19亿人口的中国—东盟自由贸易区。中国—东盟自由贸易区建设启动以来，双方合作不断加深，给双方企业和人民带来了实实在在的好处，达到了共赢的效果。第七届中国—东盟博览会适逢中国—东盟自由贸易区如期建成的第一年，中国—东盟自由贸易区建设成就展作为本届博览会的一个重要组成部分，将通过回顾中国—东盟自由贸易区建设历程，展示中国—东盟自由贸易区建设成就，展望中国—东盟自由贸易区美好前景。

第七届中国—东盟博览会主题国印度尼西亚代表印尼工商会馆中国委员会副秘书长施锦场致辞说，中国—东盟自由贸易区建设成就展集中展示了中国—东盟自由贸易区建设的成果，主动反映中国与东盟互利共赢，进一步增强了大家共建中国—东盟自由贸易区的决心。而由中国和东盟10国共办的中国—东盟博览会，则为企业享受自贸区商机提供了较好的平台。他表示，2010年是自贸区建成的第一年，博览会内容更丰富，更有特色，更富商机。印尼工商会馆中国委员会作为博览会支持协会商，将一如既往地支持办好博览会，在第七届博览会上，印尼工商会馆中国委员会将有幸结交更多的朋友，更加深入地开展合作，让我们携手并进，共同搭建合作平台，共享自贸区商机，共同创造自贸区更加美好的明天！

随后，广西壮族自治区党委常委、自治区副主席陈武宣布：“中国—东盟自由贸易区建设成就展开馆！”掀起了整个开馆仪式的高潮。

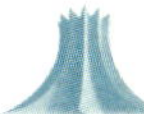

四　中国—东盟自由贸易区建设成就展盛况

中国—东盟自由贸易区建设成就展由中国—东盟自由贸易区成就展区，中国—东盟博览会、中国—东盟商务与投资峰会成就展区和艺术展区组成，以时间发展为主线，以图片、图表、文字、音视频等形式呈现，全面反映中国与东盟各国在中国—东盟自由贸易区的建设过程以及在政治、经济、文化、社会等方面取得的巨大成就，给广大观众对中国—东盟自由贸易区和博览会留下了深刻印象。中国—东盟自由贸易区建设历程的历史图片和视频，历届博览会的“开幕现场”微缩模型，“魅力之城”印章篆刻，以及风格各异的中国和东盟各国艺术家创作的书画作品……这些元素构成了精彩纷呈的中国—东盟自由贸易区建设成就展。

（一）辉煌成就生动展现

在中国—东盟自由贸易区成就展区，中国—东盟自由贸易区建设历程和辉煌成就得以充分而生动地展示。

中国—东盟自由贸易区建设历程部分回顾了中国—东盟自由贸易区建设的大事。从1991年中国与东盟开始对话合作，到2010年1月1日中国—东盟自由贸易区如期建成，各阶段主要事件逐一展现。中国—东盟自由贸易区建设的10年是辉煌的不平凡的10年。为突出展示中国—东盟自由贸易区建设的辉煌历程，成就展第一部分即以图文的形式，大事记的手法，直观地展示中国与东盟从开始建立友好关系，到提出建设中国—东盟自由贸易区的设想，到双方签署《中国—东盟全面经济合作框架协议》，确定建设中国—东盟自由贸易区；从中国—东盟自由贸易区建设进程正式启动，到“早期收获计划”的实施；从双方确定举办以中国—东盟自由贸易区为宗旨的中国—东盟博览会，到博览会成为中国与东盟友好交流、经贸促进和多领域合作的重要平台，成为中国—东盟自由贸易区建设的“助推器”；从中国—东盟自由贸易区《货物贸易协议》、《服务贸易协议》和《投资协议》的相继签署，到中国—东盟自由贸易区如期建成的历史重要事件，展示了中国—东盟双方在共同建设中国—东盟自由贸易区中达成的重要共识，取得的显著成果；反映了中国与东盟各国积极参与中国—东盟自由贸易区建设，以及共建中国—东盟自由贸易区，共享硕果，共同繁荣的信心和决心。

中国—东盟自由贸易区建设成就部分主要展示中国—东盟自由贸易区深化双方战略伙伴关系、务实推动双方的经贸合作以及拓展加深双方多领域合作、催生并巩固了众多的合作机制等方面取得的成就，包括在中国—东盟自由贸易区逐步实施降税的背景下，双方在货物贸易、服务贸易、双向投资以及农业、信息通讯、人力资源开发、湄公河开发、交通、能源、文化和旅游、公共卫生、环保等十一个重点领域广泛合作的成果，充分反映中国与东盟携手合作、互利共赢的大好局面。

中国—东盟自由贸易区建设成就展场景

Exhibition hall of the CAFTA Achievements Exhibition

（二）凸显中国—东盟博览会和中国—东盟商务与投资峰会推动作用

中国—东盟博览会和中国—东盟商务与投资峰会在中国—东盟自由贸易区建设进程中发挥了巨大作用。成就展对此给予了全面展示。

中国—东盟博览会和中国—东盟商务与投资峰会展区通过历届国家领导人和部长级贵宾出席图片，博览会开幕式模型，“魅力之城”展示，历届博览会经贸成效数据以及商务与投资峰会、各主题论坛和高规格专业论坛等精彩内容，充分展示了自2004年首届中国—东盟博览会和中国—东盟商务与投资峰会举办以来，对深化区域合作、推动中国—东盟自由贸易区建设，促进中国与东盟商企合作，以及推动中国与其他国家和地区友好交流、多领域合作发挥的巨大作用。

中国—东盟博览会开幕式是中国和东盟各国政要出席的一个重大仪式。隆重大气的仪式富于文化内涵，新颖形象地体现博览会“友谊、合作、发展、繁荣”的主题，彰显博览会10+1>11的精神。开幕式展现中国和东盟国家友好交往源远流长的历史和日益深化合作的现实，是双方战略伙伴关系深入发展的象征，预示中国—东盟自由贸易区前景辉煌。开幕式已成为中国—东盟博览会与众不同、独具魅力的品牌。“两会”展区匠心独运地把七届博览会的开幕式场景制作成微缩模型，再现经典瞬间。第一届“共启友谊之门”、“共注合作之水”、“绽放繁荣之花”、“敲响发展之钟”，第二届“聚流成河”，第三届“珠联璧合”，第四届“同舟共进、扬帆远航”，第五届“金桥飞架，五载同心”，第六届“合作化危为机，信心照亮航程”，到第七届的“水润花开，共享硕果”，这些场景再现给许多观众留下了深刻的印象。每届开幕式新意迭出，以“凝聚不散，包容不骄，公平不倚，克难不懈”的“水”为元素贯穿始终，各具鲜明特点，又一脉相承，生动形象地把中国—东盟合作的历史、现实、未来、内涵及寓意，以及博览会的作用和意义展现出来，充满创新精神和文化内涵，受到各国领导人和社会各界的高度赞誉，给观众留下的美好记忆。

展览还展示了历届博览会11国“魅力之城”的59枚印章。古朴的篆体，

第六届中国—东盟博览会开幕式场景微缩模型
The miniature model of the opening ceremony of the 6th CAEXPO

配上精美的雕刻，凸显了中国与东盟携手合作的精神。本届博览会中国“魅力之城”钦州的印章也在这一展区展示。

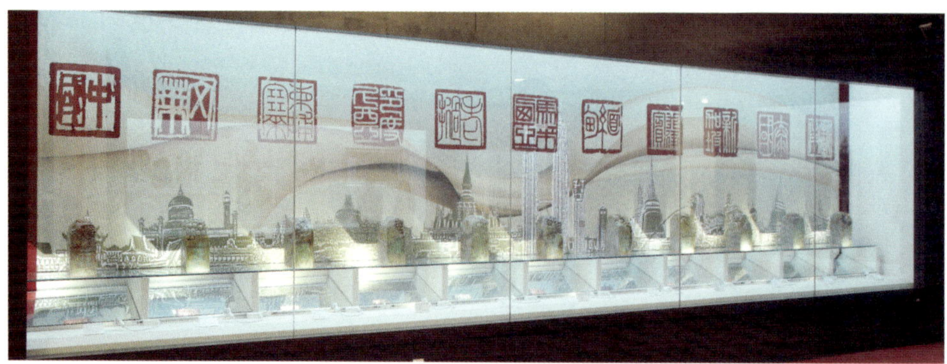

十一国印章
Seals of country name of China and the 10 ASEAN countries

（三）艺术展现合作成果

艺术展区是成就展特殊而又重要的组成部分。艺术展区通过艺术的形式展示了中国与东盟的交流与合作，营造浓厚的文化氛围。

11国艺术家热情参与，描绘了中国—东盟自由贸易区辉煌前景。艺术展作品内容多以中国—东盟自由贸易区建设进程和成就为题材。中国和东盟10国领导人寄语博览会为内容的书法长卷是其间的最大亮点，展示了博览会对中国—东盟自由贸易区建设的独特贡献以及中国—东盟自由贸易区的美好未来。6位知名画家共同创作的中国画长卷《繁花似锦》,以中国和东盟国家具有代表性的花卉绿植为描写对象，展示了一派花团锦簇、欣欣向荣的景象，寓意中国和东盟各国共同繁荣的辉煌前景。

多国艺术家共同参与，艺术展体现了广泛的国际性。展示的作品由中国和东盟艺术家专门为成就展创作完成，东盟10国均有艺术家参与创作。参加创作的东盟国家艺术家共有66位，占全部艺术家的近三成。

形式各样的艺术作品，艺术地彰显了中国—东盟自由贸易区在各领域的繁荣成就。艺术展区共展出400多件作品，包括书法、美术、摄影、篆刻和少儿作品等。书法作品以诗、词及对联形式，反映中国—东盟自由贸易区建设的历史沿革、大事记或国家领导人重要讲话等内容。美术作品重点描绘中国—东盟友谊、合作、发展的画卷，以及中国和东盟10国的历史、人文和地域风情等。摄影作品从不同角度反映中国—东盟自由贸易区建设的进程和取得的成就，反映中国、东盟10国的自然人文景观和发展新面貌。印章雕刻作品体现合作、诚信、永恒的精神。少儿画展则寓意中国—东盟友好合作与发展世代承传，展望中国—东盟自由贸易区建设与发展的美好未来。

五　中国—东盟自由贸易区建设成就展得到各方高度评价

社会各界对中国—东盟自由贸易区建设成就展高度关注，成就展开放期间，前往博物馆参观的人流络绎不绝。据不完全统计，参观人数达十多万人。许多单位和学校都自发地组织人员到现场观摩，亲眼目睹中国—东盟自由贸易区建设成就，感受中国—东盟自由贸易区带来的变化。

中国—东盟自由贸易区建设成就展受到了社会各界的广泛赞誉。中央政治局委员、中宣部部长刘云山看了成就展，评价说很好。马来西亚贸工部副部长贾谷·东加·沙甘说，成就展办得很好，可以使人们清楚地了解到中国—东盟自由贸易区及博览会一步步成长的历程。前来参观的很多高校学生纷纷表示，成就展让他们更深刻地了解到自贸区建设的各阶段的历程和自贸区建设取得的各项成就，让他们对中国—东盟自由贸易区的美好前景充满了信心，更加激励他们努力学习，做服务广西、服务中国—东盟自由贸易区的有用人才。

第五章

5 创新展览大平台 传导自贸新商机

——第七届中国一东盟博览会展览和洽谈活动

2010年，全球经济形势仍复杂多变，世界经济复苏的基础仍然非常脆弱。然而，从1月1日起，中国一东盟自由贸易区全面建成，中国与东盟90%以上的商品已实施零关税。在此带动下，双方经贸合作呈现快速增长态势。

因此，中国和东盟各国企业对第七届中国一东盟博览会寄予更高的厚望。为满足各国企业在自由贸易区建成后的新需求，第七届中国一东盟博览会采取一系列新措施，提升服务，进一步提高实效。

——展览内容创新。新增服务贸易专题，重点展示金融服务、物流服务、教育交流服务。

——专业化创新。继续举办农业展、金融展，增设珠宝首饰展、木材与木制品展。设立东盟品牌展区、食品展区和家具展区，提高东盟展品的行业集中度，突出展示东盟品牌企业。加强与东盟商协会、行业协会和企业的合作，加大采购商邀请力度，强化商贸配对和投资促进服务。

——服务创新。强化以客户为中心的服务理念，贯彻ISO9000质量管理体系，提高服务的专业化、标准化、机制化、个性化，为宾客提供全方位便捷、规范、安全、高效的服务。

第七届中国一东盟博览会商品贸易成交总额17.12亿美元，比上届增长3.5%，签约国际合作项目投资额66.9亿美元，比上届增长3%，签约国内合作项目投资额674.46亿元，比上届增长9%。经贸成效进一步提高。

Innovative CAEXPO for More CAFTA Opportunities
—Exhibition and Business Talks of the 7th CAEXPO

The year 2010 witnessed the volatile and difficult world in terms of economy. But since the full establishment of the CAFTA on January 1, more than 90% of the commodities of China and ASEAN have been exempted from tariffs, which has brought the fast growth in the bilateral economic and trade cooperation.

As a result, enterprises of China and ASEAN countries placed higher expectation on the 7th CAEXPO than ever. To meet the demands brought by the CAFTA, the 7th CAEXPO has adopted a series of new measures to improve the services and effectiveness.

—Innovation in exhibits: The Pavilion of Trade in Services was added, to highlight financial service, logistic service, and education exchange service.

—Innovation in specialization: The agricultural and financial exhibitions were resumed, Jewelry Show, CAEXPO Timber and Wood Products Exhibition were added. Special exhibition areas were arranged to showcase ASEAN brand galleria, foodstuff, and furniture, to highlight ASEAN brand names. Efforts were made in strengthening cooperation with chambers of commerce and industrial associations of the ASEAN countries to intensify the invitation and to promote the business matching and investment.

—Innovation in services. The customer-centered concept was strengthened, and the ISO 9000 quality control system was put into practice to provide more professional and quality services to meet the demand of the guests, to ensure the services are easily-accessible, standard, safe and high-efficient.

The total trade volume of the 7th CAEXPO reached US$1.712 billion, a growth of 3.5% over the last CAEXPO; the total volume of international contracts concluded stood at US$6.69 billion, a rise of 3% over the previous session; the figure for domestic contracts concluded was RMB 67.446 billion, 9% higher than the last, which all showed a better outcome in economic and trade terms.

CHAPTER FIVE

一 第七届中国—东盟博览会展览活动特点

第七届中国—东盟博览会作为中国—东盟自由贸易区建成后举办的新一届盛会，充分反映中国—东盟自贸区建设成果，体现中国与东盟互利合作和共办共赢。第七届博览会有商品贸易、投资合作、服务贸易、先进技术、"魅力之城"等5个专题，参展企业2200家，共设展位4600个，比上届增长15%。其中，中国内地及港澳台地区使用展位3379个，外国企业使用展位1221个，其中东盟10国使用展位1178个。印尼、老挝、马来西亚、缅甸、泰国、越南等六个东盟国家包馆。

本届博览会展览活动具有以下特点：

1. 组展呈现"三个提高"，展位供不应求。

——东盟各国参展规模及专业化进一步提高。东盟国家使用展位数1178个，创历届新高。印尼、老挝、马来西亚、缅甸、泰国、越南等六国包馆。其中，印尼组织150家企业参展参会，创历史新高。博览会的东盟展位数在中国国内展会的东盟展位数中居于前列，博览会已经成为东盟等外国企业开拓中国市场的重要渠道。东盟10国均组织本国品牌企业参展，东盟品牌展区成为本届亮点。东盟各国还在本国展区内按行业布展，突出展示农产品食品、木材家具、轻工工艺、珠宝等行业产品，有效提高了本届博览会的专业化水平。

——国内企业重复参展率进一步提高。国内各省市各行业申请展位数4000个，已超过国内规划展位数约43%，展位供不应求。各行业的重复参展率逐步提高。其中，食品加工、包装机械、工程机械、国际合作展区的重复参展率分别达到40%、52%、82%、90%。重复参展率是反映展会对企业吸引力的重要标志，这充分证明博览会的市场认知度不断提升。

第七届博览会围绕中国与东盟合作的重点行业，加快培育博览会的品牌专业展。本届博览会继续举办农业展，新增珠宝展，全面展示东盟国家的宝

第七届中国—东盟博览会盛况

The grand occasion of the 7th CAEXPO

石资源和中国玉石、珍珠、贵金属和设计首饰等优势。会期之后还举办了中国—东盟博览会木材及木制品展，成为西南地区最大的木业专业展。

——区域外国家和地区参展积极性进一步提高。第七届博览会加大对区域外国家和地区的招商招展力度，区域外国家和地区参展踊跃。日本、法国、澳大利亚等国企业均踊跃参展。其中日本预定展位较上年增长了137.5%。

2. 采购商邀请力度加大，会期商贸配对活动加强针对性。采购商是决定展会成效、吸引参展商的重要因素。第七届中国—东盟博览会通过多种渠道邀请更多的专业采购商参会。除东盟国家的采购团组外，法国、加拿大、德国、法国、澳大利亚和日本等区域外国家，上海、青岛、宁波、广东、河北、江苏、福建、厦门等国内省市，以及中国电力企业联合会、中国国际经济技术交流中心、中华供销总社、中国土畜进出口商会等境内外近60家机构都组织采购团组参会。

第七届博览会加强对采购商的服务。不仅通过博览会官方网站、中国—东盟商务数据库，做好贸易配对、投资政策及环境咨询等日常商贸服务，而且在会期继续举办参展商讲坛、采购说明会等一系列商贸对接活动。商贸配对活动覆盖100%的采购团组，还为每一个国家专门成立工作小组，为所有参加博览会的采购团组安排全陪翻译和工作人员。

3. 投资促进活动更加丰富。投资合作是中国与东盟合作的重要领域。第七届中国—东盟博览会在做好货物贸易的基础上，扩大博览会在投资促进方面的作用，加强了与东盟投资促进机构的合作，加大投资项目的征集、推介、对接力度。会期举办东盟及中国重点省市投资环境推介会、投融资项目对接会、企业股权（债权）投融资交易会、项目签约等一系列投资促进活动。

二　商品贸易专题

商品贸易专题设在南宁国际会展中心二层及分会场。

东盟商品主要展示：品牌展品、食品农产品、家具家居、工艺品及珠宝饰品、日用消费品、服务业产品。

中国商品主要展示：工程机械及运输车辆、电力与新能源设备、食品加工与包装机械、建筑材料、电子电器、珠宝首饰、农产品和食品。

4号展厅是泰国的独立商品展区，共130个展位，参展企业121家，这是泰国连续第四次包用独立展厅参展。本展厅主要展示泰国的优势和特色商品，包括农产品、食品、轻工工艺品、珠宝、时尚用品、美容产品、日用化工产品等。参展的知名企业有：泰国皇太后大学、莫拉可有限公司、PSN国际集团公司、泰国国家石油（大众）有限公司、双莲有限公司等。

5号展厅是马来西亚的独立商品展区，共169个展位，参展企业96家。这是马来西亚连续第五次包用独立展厅参展。本展厅主要展示马来西亚的优势

商品贸易专题中国商品展区
Chinese Commodity Section in the CAEXPO Pavilion of Commodity Trade

和特色商品，包括：食品饮料、家具、服务贸易产品、汽车、日用消费品等。参展的知名企业有：爱乐凤公司、阿默西尔实业公司、丽薇芙肌肤护理有限公司、视界有限、义香有限公司、马来西亚迈威吸尘器有限公司、东方食品工业有限公司、译拉食品有限公司等。

6号展厅是越南的独立商品展区，共192个展位，参展企业124家。这是越南连续第五次包用独立展厅参展。本展厅主要展示越南的优势和特色商品，如食品、木制品、手工艺品等。参展的知名企业有：平仙日用品生产公司、边和威拿咖啡合资公司等。

7号展厅是机械设备（食品加工和包装机械）展区，使用展位226个，参展企业121家。参展企业大部分是历届博览会多次重复参展的企业。中国食品和包装机械工业协会连续六届组织本行业有实力的企业和名牌产品参展。主要展品有：饮料加工机械、肉类加工屠宰设备、面点加工机械、干燥机械、过滤净化机械、贴标机、颗粒粉末及塑料包装机、真空包装机等。参展的知名企业包括：科诺华麦修斯电子技术（北京）有限公司、嘉音包装机械（深圳）有限公司、泉州远东环保设备有限公司、广州利慧包装有限公司、深圳海川食品科技有限公司、汕头大自然包装机械厂有限公司、上海炬钢机械有限公司、梧州市正一机械厂公司等。

机械设备展区
Machinery and Equipment Section

8号、9号展厅是建筑材料与设备展区，共使用展位335个，参展企业169家。本展厅展示在建材和设备方面有优势、产品适合东盟市场的中国建材企业。展示的商品包括：建筑陶瓷、新型化学建材、门窗幕墙、卫生洁具、木业机械等。参展的知名企业有连续六届参展的南南铝业、广东广铝集团、广

建筑材料与设备展区
Building Materials & Equipment Section

州市安泰化学、平果亚洲铝业有限公司、中宇建材集团有限公司、嘉汉板业（广西）发展有限公司等。

10号展厅是电子电器展区，由深圳市包馆，共使用展位158个，参展企业100家。本展厅集中展示与东盟市场有互补性、需求量较大的电子电器类产品。主要展品包括：通讯及通信设备、软件及IT服务、厨房电器、制冷设备、音像视听及数码产品等，参展的知名企业有：高新奇、普天宜通、顺恒利、火王、中科诺奋达、东原、万业隆、邦贝尔、赢合等。

电子电器展区
Electronics & Electrical Appliances Section

11号展厅是电子电器与新能源展区，共使用展位202个，参展企业119家。本展厅集中展示与东盟市场有互补性、需求量较大的电子电器类产品。主要展品包括：通讯及通信设备、软件及IT服务、厨房电器、制冷设备、音像视听及数码产品等。参展的知名企业有北京纽曼电子、江苏春兰空调、远大空调、阿里巴巴、万和、万家乐、福建南孚电池、新华电池等。

电子电器与新能源展区
Electronics & Electrical Appliances and New Energies Section

12号展厅是新能源设备展区，共使用展位240个，参展企业140家。本展厅集中了中国在电力与新能源设备领域的重要生产基地和骨干企业，对中国电力工程勘探、设计，电网建设，技术成果，电力设备进行了全面展示。展品主要有发电设备、输配电设备、变电设备、电线电缆、电气自动化设备、仪器仪表、电力保护设备，以及新能源装备。参展企业有：南方电网、大唐集团、宁波风神风电、中国星月集团、杭申控股集团有限公司、河南环宇电源集团等。

13号展厅是文莱、柬埔寨、菲律宾、新加坡4个东盟国家商品展区。4国共使用展位187个，参展企业126家。

文莱在本展厅使用商品展位30个，参展商品包括清真食品、饮品、电信产品等。文莱工业和初级资源部、文莱斯市中华总商会、文莱中国友好协会等12家机构参展。

柬埔寨在本展厅使用商品展位80个，参展商品包括家具、珠宝、手工艺品、农产品、食品等。参展企业53家。参展企业有老汉兴酒业集团有限公

东盟国家商品展区文莱展区
Brunei Pavilion in ASEAN Commodity Section

司、吴哥啤酒、加华银行等。

菲律宾在本展厅使用商品展位45个，参展商品包括农产品、食品等。参展企业28家。参展机构有蓝美仁公司、斯特凡诺制鞋公司等。

新加坡在本展厅使用商品展位32个，参展商品包括食品、饮料、服务业、商协会形象等。有新加坡工商联合总会、丰隆亚洲有限公司、康元饼干厂（新加坡）私人有限公司、亚太酿酒、星辰银行（中国）有限公司等20家企业参展。

14A号展厅是缅甸的商品展区，共84个展位，参展企业74家。本展厅主要展示缅甸的优势和特色商品。包括：珠宝玉器、食品农产品、手工艺品、中药产品等。参展机构有：缅甸联邦工商会、缅甸林木产品商协会、缅甸豆类商协会、缅甸渔业协会、缅甸工业联合会、缅甸农产品食品加工出口协会等。

14B号展厅是老挝的独立商品展区。这是老挝连续第二次包用独立展厅集中展示本国商品。本展区共使用展位87个，参展企业44家。本展厅主要展示老挝的优势和特色商品，包括：木材家具、手工艺品、珠宝、食品等。参展机构及企业有：老挝国家工商会、达沙旺木制仿古家具制造有限公司、老挝—印中集团、面诺克咖啡等。

15号展厅是印度尼西亚的独立商品展区，共使用122个展位，参展企业74家。印度尼西亚是本届博览会的主题国，这是印度尼西亚连续第四次包用独立展厅参展。本展厅主要展示印尼的优势和特色商品。包括：家具、手工艺品、农产品、纺织、珠宝、食品、旅游等。参展机构有印度尼西亚贸易部出口促进局、印度尼西亚投资协调署等。

16号展厅是珠宝首饰展区，共使用展位168个，参展机构65家。珠宝首饰展是本届博览会增设的展区，旨在充分利用2010年中国—东盟自贸区全面建成的契机，结合目前中国—东盟自贸区19亿人口的庞大消费市场及90%产品零关

珠宝首饰展区
Jewelry Show

税的优势（彩色宝石、钻石、玉石、珍珠进口关税为零），借助中国—东盟自贸区各成员的优惠商贸政策，发挥中国珠宝产业卓越的加工设计能力与东盟国家丰富的彩宝玉石及原材料资源等有利条件，为促进中国与东盟各国珠宝玉石产业的发展、加强中国与东盟各国珠宝产业交流与合作搭建平台。

参展企业有：上海的老庙黄金、香港的慧福珠宝、浙江的山下湖珍珠、龙湖珍珠、辽宁的玉圣阁、中国珠宝进出口公司、山东昌乐中国宝石城、深圳威妮华、新疆的玉锦兰、广西的至尊珠宝、大福珠宝、永明宫珍珠等知名品牌。

室外展场是工程机械和运输设备展区。展示面积10000平方米，参展企业78家。连续参展企业占80%以上，其中连续六届博览会参展企业占31%。本展区主要展品有：建筑施工机械、农用运输车、重型汽车、皮卡等。知名企业有：柳工、厦工、山东临工、美国寿力、长城汽车、北汽福田等。

工程机械和运输设备展区
Engineering Machinery & Vehicles Section

此外还举行了农业展。农业是中国—东盟自由贸易区建设的先行者，2004年开始中国与东盟600种农产品削减并取消关税。据统计，中国进口东盟国家产品的关税平均已经降到了5.8%， 700多种农资、农产品及食品更是率先降税，绝大部分商品已经实现零关税，中国从东盟各国的进口量实现了500%的增长。2010年，中国—东盟自由贸易区已顺利建成，农业领域自由贸易优势将更加明显，东盟已成为中国第四大贸易伙伴。同时，随着中国—东盟农产品零关税的逐步实施，自贸区的建成，不仅给双方带来巨大的市场和出口平台，还将促进了中国农产品贸易市场的多元化和农业现代化建设。

第七届中国—东盟博览会农业展开展仪式于2010年10月20日在广西展览馆举行。广西壮族自治区党委副书记陈际瓦、自治区副主席陈章良为农业馆开展。整个展馆分为A、B、C3个区域，一层前厅A区主要是花果苗木、茶叶及食品等；一层后面B区球厅，主要展示大陆及台湾各类包装食品；二层C区是农药、化肥等农用生产资料，集中展示各类食品及农产品。整个农业展使用展位达600个，参展企业370家。

本届博览会农业展与上届相比，在展览及效果上有了明显提升。一是参展企业质量有明显提高。有香港五丰集团、椰树集团、山西汾酒集团、台湾金门酒厂实业股份有限公司、重庆有友实业有限公司、史丹利化肥等。特装比例达到35%，高于上届的10%。日本食品、马来西亚特色咖喱、新西兰优质乳制品等成为一大亮点。二是港澳台和境外企业参展积极。台湾岛内企业首次大规模参展，参展企业共有58家，展位数达102个，展位规模相较2009

第七届中国—东盟博览会农业展开展仪式
Opening ceremony of the 7th CAEXPO Agriculture Exhibition

农业展展区
Exhibition hall of the 7th CAEXPO Agriculture Exhibition

年增长了50%；香港五丰集团组织旗下上海、四川、江西、广西等分公司参展；马来西亚、越南和日本、新西兰等企业积极参展，新西兰乳业集团通过本次农业展找到了南宁、崇左、桂林等地的代理商。三是中国国内企业参展踊跃，北方省份参展增长显著，各地农业特色鲜明。江西、天津、山西、陕西、海南企业统一特装，整体展示；新疆、宁夏、内蒙、青海、甘肃等北方省市参展踊跃，不仅企业数量增多，并且重复参展企业增多，如内蒙古乳香飘乳业、青海青台万达生物等均为重复参展企业。四是精心安排一系列围绕农业合作的商贸促进活动。与广西侨办共同举办“茶文化广西茗珍品尝”活动；与广西林业厅共同举办中国—东盟花卉产业座谈会等，海峡两岸花卉企业参加；策划了名优企业推广、花艺表演、茶叶企业推广等活动，促进了农产品、食品领域供需双方的交流互动，得到企业积极参与和高度评价。五是经贸成效好。本届农业展商品成交9544.7万美元，同比增长70.5%。

三　服务贸易专题

服务贸易专题设在南宁国际会展中心2号展厅，是本届博览会新增设的专题，旨在配合中国—东盟自贸区《服务贸易协议》的签订实施。本专题主要展示中国和东盟金融服务、物流服务和文化教育服务。共使用展位160个，参展单位共49家。

金融服务展区。本展区充分发挥金融机构在抵御风险、促进投资贸易便利化中的作用，加强中国与东盟金融合作。在中国人民银行、中国银监会、中国证监会、中国保监会的支持下，本展区集中了一批实力雄厚的中国和东盟国家金融机构参展，主要有中国进出口银行、广西北部湾银行、华夏银行、中国建设银行、中国农业银行、中国工商银行、柳州银行、广西农村信用合作社、中国邮政储蓄银行、中国信用保险公司、中国银行等。重点展示各类金融管理机构的金融政策、主要职能、服务理念、信息资讯等内容，以及各类金融机构为企业所提供的金融服务产品。包括信用贷款、国际结算、企业理财、资产管理、证券发行、投/融资、金融信息服务及技术等。

金融服务展区
Financial Services Section

物流展区
Logistics Section

物流服务展区。本展区重点展示仓储、运输和物流园区开发与合作等服务内容，参展单位主要有东盟—川桂商贸物流中心，该项目计划建设用地3000亩，规划总建筑面积约300万平方米，计划投资86亿元人民币，是广西统筹推进的重大项目。该项目是集商贸、物流、加工为一体的现代商贸物流项目，定位为：大商贸、大市场、大物流，构建中国—东盟商贸、物流平台。项目建成后具有商品展示、批发零售、电子商务、仓储物流、配送、包装、加工和信息处理的功能，以及商务办公、休闲、娱乐等配套服务功能。项目由广西四川商会会长单位广西桂嘉汇集团投资开发。此外，其他参展单位还有上海、浙江、福建等省市的物流体系、物流园区和物流服务企业。

教育服务展区。本展示区重点展示国际教育合作、职业培训、留学咨询等服务内容，参展单位涵盖了国内、东盟国家和美国、法国的高等院校和教育机构，主要有泰国川登喜皇家大学、印尼雅加达国立大学、泰国孔敬大学、越南河内经营与工艺大学、法国克莱蒙费朗第一大学、越南河内国家大学、越南顺化医药大学、美国西俄勒冈大学等。

四 投资合作专题

投资合作专题包括1号展厅的国际经济合作展区和会期一系列投资促进活动。

（一）国际经济合作展区

1号展厅是投资合作专题的国际经济合作展区，以促进中国企业“走出去”到东盟国家开展投资和国际经济合作为特色，使用展位面积1535平方米，折合170个展位，24家企业参展。本展区在前六届博览会的基础上更加突出展示中国企业在对外承包工程和各行业投资合作领域中的整体实力和核心竞争力，进一步突出宣传“走出去”的成果。本展区由连续多届组展的中国对外承包工程商会继续组织了阵容强大的企业参展，涉及机械、电子、冶金工程、路桥建设、水电等行业，知名企业有中国机械工业集团、中国铝业、中国通用技术集团、中国葛洲坝集团、中国路桥工程公司、北京建工

国际经济合作展区
International Economic Cooperation Section

集团、中国水利电力对外公司、斯道拉恩索集团等。中国“走出去”比较活跃的省区市如上海、天津、辽宁、安徽、河南、云南、贵州、广西等也组织了实力雄厚的企业参展。本展厅集中了中国实力雄厚的“走出去”企业和省市，体现了中国与东盟国际经济合作的成果和广阔前景。

（二）投资促进活动

本届博览会期间，共举办各类推介会、研讨会、政策宣讲会46场。其中东盟10国主办或参与主办的会议11场，中国国家部委及有关商协会举办10场，国内有关省市举办7场，中国港台地区以及法国、德国等其他国家举办4场，其他14场。本届投资推介会主题更广泛、内容更丰富、合作更深入、安排更紧凑。各主办单位精心组织的专场推介活动成为本届博览会投资促进活动的靓丽风景线。

在东盟国家主办的11场会议中有9场由各国经贸主管部门主办，数量居历届之最，主办单位也由以往的商协会主办向贸易、投资、工业等国家经贸主管部门主办转变。印尼作为第七届中国—东盟博览会主题国，专门成立了由贸易部、文化旅游部、投资署共同组成的主题国联合工作组，组织了庞大的代表团参加博览会，举办系列主题国活动和印尼国家推介会。

在7场中国国内省区市推介会中，宁夏回族自治区人民政府已经连续7届均举办投资说明会，湖南省、河北省、安徽省、陕西省和哈尔滨市政府等也连续几年前来办会推介本省商机。

国际方面，联合国采购说明会首次在本届博览会上亮相。德国技术合作公司在继2007年、2009年先后两次在博览会举办专题研讨会后，本届博览会又继续举办区域经济合作专题会议进行推介。法国马恩河谷省继在博览会上

联合国采购说明会
UN Procurement Presentation

多次举办专题会议后，本届博览会又继续举办专题会议进行推介。

（三）签约仪式

2010年10月20日上午，第七届中国—东盟博览会国际经济技术合作项目签约仪式在南宁举行。柬埔寨国务兼商业大臣占蒲拉西、文莱工业和初级资源部长叶海亚、老挝工贸部长南·维亚吉、印尼贸易部副部长赫斯蒂·殷塔·克雷斯娜丽尼、马来西亚工贸部副部长贾谷·东加·沙甘等东盟国家代表，东盟秘书处代表苏柏什，文莱驻华大使张慈祥，中国对外承包商会秘书长于晓虹，广西壮族自治区领导莫永清、梁胜利以及部分省市的代表出席了签约仪式。

本次大会签约仪式共签订国际经济合作项目76个，总投资额32.98亿美元。其中中国企业对东盟国家投资项目12个，总投资4.32亿美元；中国利用外资项目64个，总投资28.66亿美元。项目涉及工业制造、基础设施、交通能源、农业及农产品加工、旅游开发、商贸物流、软件与信息服务等产业。

签约项目中，与东盟国家的合作项目30个，总投资额11.53亿美元。其中，中国对东盟国家投资项目12个，总投资4.32亿美元；东盟国家对中国投资项目18个，总投资7.21亿美元。港澳台项目29个，总投资14.02亿美元，全部为对国内各省区市投资项目。欧美项目11个，总投资5.48亿美元。其他国家和地区项目6个，总投资1.95亿美元。

在签约项目的产业分布上，第一产业项目6个，总投资3.3亿美元；第二产业项目51个，总投资21.58亿美元；第三产业项目19个，总投资8.1亿美

2010年10月20日，第七届中国—东盟博览会国际经济技术合作项目签约仪式在南宁举行

The contract signing ceremony of international economic and technical cooperation projects of the 7th CAEXPO held in Nanning on October 20, 2010

元。项目双向投资涉及的国家和地区有：印度尼西亚、缅甸、文莱、越南、泰国、柬埔寨、新加坡、马来西亚和美国、英国、法国、加拿大、日本等国家以及香港、澳门、台湾地区。

参加本次大会签约的还有来自中国的广东、江西、吉林、湖南、广西等省区以及中直单位的企业。

本次国际经济技术合作签约项目的特点是：香港对外投资势头强劲，以22个项目、总投资11.2亿美元成为连续七届中国—东盟博览会最大的对外投资来源地区。商贸物流项目和旅游开发项目成为投资热点。国际项目专场共签订商贸物流和旅游开发项目15个，签约金额6.23亿美元，占本专场第三产业项目签约金额的77%，较第六届翻了一番多。软件与信息服务业项目填补了第六届的空白。

10月20日上午，第七届中国—东盟博览会国内经济技术合作项目签约仪式在南宁举行。重庆市副市长刘学普，广西壮族自治区领导莫永清、杨道喜等出席了签约仪式。

本次大会签约的国内经济合作项目96个，总投资492.74亿元人民币。其中，第一产业项目1个，总投资8000万元；第二产业项目74个，总投资354.81亿元；第三产业项目21个，总投资137.13亿元。

参加签约的企业分别来自北京、山东、江苏、上海、浙江、福建、广东、深圳、河南、湖南、四川、重庆、河北、安徽、江西、广西等 16 个省、市、自治区和中央直属企业。签约项目涉及工业制造、基础设施、交通能源、农业及农产品加工、商贸物流仓储、旅游开发等行业。

本次国内经济技术合作签约项目有以下特点：商贸物流和旅游开发是投资热点，项目签约金额118.13亿元，占第三产业项目签约金额的86%；制造业项目依然是本届博览会签约项目的主角，其中微电机、数字通讯、LED光电、数码消费电子等新技术、新材料、新产品生产项目在制造业项目中的比例已超过20%。

五　先进技术专题

农业先进适用技术暨高新技术展区设在南宁国际会展中心3号展厅，由中国科技部主办。本展区分为“农村先进适用技术”和“高新技术”两个板块，本展区根据东盟国家的实际需求与合作前景，结合中国在农业和高新技术方面的优秀成果，以服务东盟，服务农村，服务企业，改善民生为宗旨，集中选取了中国有关部委和各地方政府推荐的363家企业、411个农村先进适用技术及高新技术项目参加展示。

本展馆设计以流畅的弧线为主导，以科技蓝为主色调，运用点、线、面结合，地面与立面相互呼应，并辅以声、光、电等高科技手段，营造了一个气势磅礴，张合有度，色彩鲜明，极具科技感及现代感的展馆形象。前言及农村先进适用技术板块整体造型犹如展翅飞翔的航空母舰，装载着累累果实，礼遇四方来宾，并寓意农村先进生产技术日新月异，飞速发展的美好前景。这个板块从实施“农业科技成果转化资金专项”和“星火计划”取得的成果中选取了305个优秀项目进行展示，涉及农业种植养殖、农产品深加

农业先进适用技术暨高新技术展区
Agricultural Applicable and Advanced Technology in the Pavilion of Agricultural Advanced & Applicable Technologies

工、现代农业装备、农业生物肥料和农村民生科技等领域。

高新技术板块造型由四个原子及火炬构成，并以自然界生态植物造型为抽象概念，喻意高新技术的发展应以节能、低碳、环保为准绳，可持续发展，完美地融入国家火炬计划的概念。高新技术板块从实施“火炬计划”和建设“高新技术开发区”取得的成果中精选了106个项目进行展示，涉及节能环保技术、机电一体化技术和高新材料技术等领域。

本展区展示的特色项目有：

1. 育种成套设备。中国农业部规划设计研究院研发生产的育种成套设备，包括种子风选机、种子清选机、种子分选机、种子包衣机、刷种机等系列机械，具有技术成熟，操作方便、适用性强等多项优点，可用于水稻、玉米、棉花、牧草等多种农作物的育种，能大大降低育种劳动强度和生产成本，提高种苗成活率和工作效率。

2. 空气能热泵热水器。中国广东佛山市顺德区轩科电器有限公司研发生产的空气能热泵热水器及机组系列产品具有节能环保、安全可靠等优点，技术及性能达到了国际领先水平，可满足家用和商用生活热水供应的需要，产品出口东南亚、西欧、中东、台湾等多个国家和地区。

3. CCD 智能色选机。中国安徽合肥泰禾光电科技有限公司运用目前世界色选行业内最尖端科技——CCD智能色选技术研发生产的CCD 智能色选机，改变了我国分选技术落后的现状，大大提高了我国同类产品在国际国内市场上的竞争力。设备达到国际先进水平，获得了多项国际、国内的专利和认证。目前CCD智能色选机已经运用于粮食加工、工业生产、资源回收利用等领域。

六 “魅力之城”专题

“魅力之城”专题设在2号展厅。“魅力之城”是每届博览会的亮点，由各主办国选择本国具有代表性的城市作为“魅力之城”，综合展示其在贸易、投资、科技文化、旅游等方面的发展和商机。“魅力之城”使中国和东盟合作由国家层面延伸到城市层面，进一步深化中国与东盟的友好关系。

（一）“魅力之城”展区

为体现本届博览会“自贸区与新机遇”的主题，本届博览会“魅力之城”各国主要选择在自贸区建设中具有巨大商机的城市参展，展示面积1588平方米。

“魅力之城”展区
Pavilion of Cities of Charm

本届博览会“魅力之城”专题展内容丰富，创意不断。11个“魅力之城”展区造型新颖，风情各异，都按照各自国家和城市经济、历史、民俗文化等特点设计建造。中国钦州展馆的帆船造型充满活力，主题国印尼梭罗展馆精美的木雕和艳丽的蜡染等传统手工艺品让人称赞，文莱斯里巴加湾展馆的民俗表演让人回味，柬埔寨磅湛省展馆的古代门楼原汁原味，老挝甘蒙展馆的设计别有洞天，马来西亚吉隆坡展馆的现代感令人心驰神往，缅甸曼德

勒展馆充满历史文化气息，菲律宾三宝颜展馆展示了独特的旅游风光，新加坡展馆的生命之树含义深远，泰国清莱展馆古色古香的木船格外显眼，越南大叻展馆的松林瀑布清新脱俗。

11个“魅力之城”的简要内容如下（按展位实际排列顺序，即从1号展厅方向往3号展厅方向介绍）：

1. 马来西亚吉隆坡。吉隆坡坐落于美丽的雪兰莪州，位于马来西亚半岛中央偏西海岸，是马来西亚的首都和最大城市，是马来西亚政治、经济、金融、商业和文化中心，也是全国交通和电信枢纽，是东南亚一座五彩缤纷的著名都市，城市座右铭为“进步与繁荣”。该展区展示了马来西亚旅游业的勃勃生机。本届马来西亚“魅力之城”展示面积108平方米，与上届持平。

马来西亚吉隆坡
Kuala Lumpur of Malaysia

2. 缅甸曼德勒。曼德勒是曼德勒省的省会，位于缅甸中部偏北的内陆，是几个古代王朝曾经建都的地方，是著名的故都、缅甸的第二大城市和中部地区的经济、文化和交通中心。因背靠曼德勒山而得名，曼德勒的巴利语名称为“罗陀那崩尼插都”，意为“多宝之城”，又因缅甸历史上著名古都阿瓦在其近郊，故被称为“瓦城”。曼德勒被列为联合国世界文化遗产。该展区展示了曼德勒的历史文化以及这座城市在中国—东盟自贸区建成背景下的新商机。本届缅甸“魅力之城”展示面积108平方米。

缅甸曼德勒
Mandalay of Myanmar

3. 新加坡新加坡城。新加坡位于东南亚的心脏，是贸易和商业的主要枢纽，具有高度发达的市场经济体系。该展区展示了新加坡城市化与环境保护及其知名品牌、产品和服务等。本届新加坡“魅力之城”展区面积200平方米，与上届持平。

新加坡新加坡城
Singapore City of Singapore

4. 老挝甘蒙。甘蒙是老挝省级行政区，主要城市为“他曲”。甘蒙位于老挝中部，地理位置重要。有全国最主要矿区南巴屯锡矿，以及目前老挝最大的水力发电站南吞2号。该地区岩溶地貌分布广泛，风景美丽，有珍贵野生动物，为旅游胜地。该展区展示了甘蒙的自然风光及连接老挝与泰国的湄公河友谊大桥，此桥的通车将为加强自贸区的商品贸易流通提供便利。本届老挝“魅力之城”展示面积为108平方米。

老挝甘蒙
Khammouan of Laos

5. 越南大叻。大叻位于越南南部，是越南林同省省会，以空气清新，湖泊、瀑布、松林众多闻名。大叻四季如春，年均温度在摄氏十七度上下，

越南大叻
Dalat of Vietnam

是越南少有的高原度假胜地，被誉为“常春城”和“小巴黎”，是越南一个受欢迎的旅游目的地。该展区展示大叻城市魅力及旅游资源。本届越南“魅力之城”展示面积为108平方米，与上届持平。

6. 印度尼西亚梭罗。梭罗也被称为苏腊卡尔塔，现在仍是梭罗王室的家乡，以两个宫殿——梭罗皇宫和旺古尼嘉兰皇宫引以为豪，是印尼文化中心之一，是一个处处可见舞蹈、音乐和哇扬戏的地方。印尼是本届中国—东盟博览会主题国。印尼政府对出任主题国非常重视，精心准备，搭建了展示印尼深厚文化底蕴和巨大经济潜力“魅力之城”展区。中方对印尼出任主题国予以高度重视和特别礼遇安排，中国和印尼领导人共同出席印尼国家馆的开馆仪式。本届印尼“魅力之城”展示面积270平方米，比上届增长50%。

印度尼西亚梭罗
Solo City of Indonesia

7. 柬埔寨磅湛。磅湛省位于柬埔寨东南部，湄公河纵贯中部，地势平坦，是柬埔寨人口最多、面积最大的农业大省，同时也是重要的贸易集散地

柬埔寨磅湛
Kampong Cham of Cambodia

和水陆交通中心。该展区展示磅湛省丰富的资源和魅力的风光。本届柬埔寨“魅力之城”展示面积为216平方米，与上届持平。

8．中国钦州。钦州地处中国华南经济圈、西南经济圈与东盟经济圈的结合部，陆地面积1.08万平方公里，海岸线长562.6公里，总人口371万，是一座具有1400多年历史的古城，自古以来就是“海上丝绸之路”通往东南亚、南亚各国的重要港口，又是一座散发着蓬勃生机的北部湾新兴港口工业城市。钦州拥有海陆空立体交通网络，既是西南地区最便捷的出海通道，又是中国与东盟便捷、高效的国际大通道。随着中国—东盟自由贸易区建成，广西北部湾经济区开放开发上升为国家战略，作为中国—东盟自由贸易区建设的前沿，钦州成为客商关注的热点和投资的重点。钦州正以“建大港、兴产业、造新城”为三大发展引擎，加快建设成为北部湾临海核心工业区，面向中国—东盟的区域性国际航运中心和物流中心，具有岭南风格、滨海风光、东南亚风情的宜商宜居城市。钦州港在三年内将建成年吞吐能力超亿吨，集装箱吞吐量突破100万标准箱北部湾集装箱干线港，目前集装箱吞吐量已在北部湾港口中跃居第一位。钦州正在实施“千百亿产业崛起工程”，力争引进一批能够代表先进制造业的项目，以石化、造纸、电子、粮油、能源、冶金、现代物流等为重点形成临港产业集群，积极培育新能源、海洋产业等战略性新兴产业。近年来，钦州市先后荣获“中国优秀旅游城市”、“中国吸引华商投资之

中国钦州
Qinzhou of China

潜力城市”等荣誉称号，被确定为全国流通领域现代物流示范城市、中国第二批加工贸易梯度转移重点承接地，成为中国目前31个重点承接地中唯一的沿海城市。

广西钦州保税港区于2008年5月29日获国务院批准设立，是中国距离东盟国家最近的保税港区，在与东盟各国港口合作方面具有广阔前景。其功能定位为面向中国东盟合作的自由贸易港、国际航运中心、物流中心和出口加工基地，广西北部湾经济区开放开发的核心平台。中国—东盟自由贸易区建成后，钦州保税港区将凭借其完善的港口设施、发达的集疏运体系、便捷的通关手续，为中国的货物出口东盟及东盟产品进入中国市场提供便利，将成为中国—东盟自由贸易区和泛北部湾区域经济合作的一个重要平台。

该展区充分展示钦州在中国—东盟自由贸易区建设中的巨大商机和城市特色。本届中国“魅力之城”使用面积270平方米，与上届持平。

文莱斯里巴加湾
Bandar Seri Begawan of Brunei

9. 文莱斯里巴加湾。斯里巴加湾濒临文莱河，邻近文莱湾，是文莱的政治、经济、文化中心。因在水上建城，有“东方威尼斯”之称。该展区集中展示文莱的旅游资源、民俗民风、文化特色等。本届文莱“魅力之城”展示面积108平方米，与上届持平。

10. 泰国清莱。清莱府位于清莱盆地中心，是泰国最北的府城，东北部和北部与缅甸、老挝为邻，距首都曼谷市约785公里，是重要的通关与贸易中心。该展区展示清莱港口环

泰国清莱
Chiang Rai of Thailand

菲律宾三宝颜
Zamboanga of the Philippines

境、经济发展和地理位置及旅游、风土人情等。本届泰国“魅力之城”展示面积200平方米，与上届持平。

11. 菲律宾三宝颜。三宝颜位于棉兰老岛之西，临巴西兰海峡，是棉兰老岛的西部港口，南三宝颜省直辖市。是摩洛人的黄铜和紫铜制品中心，也是贝壳集散地，重要的渔业基地，为菲律宾的国际转运港，香港—马尼拉—澳大利亚航线必经之地，泛菲公路的南方终点。该展区展示三宝颜市经济社会发展成就及独特的旅游风光。本届菲律宾“魅力之城”展示面积108平方米，与上届持平。

（二）“魅力之城”活动精彩纷呈

本届博览会“魅力之城”专题活动更加丰富多彩，更加深入务实。

2010年10月21日晚，“魅力中国·钦州之夜”活动在南宁举行。第七届博览会11国“魅力之城”——中国广西钦州、文莱斯里巴加湾、柬埔寨磅湛、印尼梭罗、老挝甘蒙、马来西亚吉隆坡、缅甸曼德勒、菲律宾三宝颜、新加坡新加坡城、泰国清莱和越南大叻的代表们欢聚一堂，正式缔结为“友

2010年10月21日，“魅力中国·钦州之夜”活动在南宁举行
“Charming China, Night of Qinzhou” held in Nanning on October 21, 2010

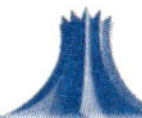

谊之城”。

本届博览会期间，各城市之间还开展了投资促进活动。中国“魅力之城”钦州市领导拜访了马来西亚国际贸易与工业部副部长，共同探讨推动马来西亚（钦州）产业园合作向前发展。马来西亚积极响应，在钦州召开马来西亚（钦州）产业园推介会，共同推动产业园合作向前发展。马来西亚工业发展局率大批马来西亚企业代表到钦州进行实地考察，详细评估钦州市经济发展特别是合作建设产业园的相关条件，进一步探讨产业园的布局空间、发展定位、发展模式等。两国官员和客商聚首谋划参照苏州工业园在钦州打造马来西亚（钦州）产业园。

“魅力之城”专题务实地推进了各城市的投资合作。仅以中国“魅力之城”钦州为例，来自东盟各国及韩国、香港、澳门的企业家，国内知名央企、民企、外企共500多名客商组团参加了钦州商机专场推介会暨项目签约仪式，签约项目30个，总投资110.7亿元。

本届博览会“魅力之城”专题别出心裁，给11个“魅力之城”展馆准备了各自的纪念章，同时也给游客们准备了城市“护照”，让人流连忘返。钦州的白海豚，印尼的苏腊卡尔塔，马来西亚的双子塔等11国“魅力之城”有代表性的吉祥物或建筑都被刻成印章，荟萃在小巧而精致的护照本里。在“魅力之城”展区，游客不用出境、奔波，就可借博览会“护照”将这些极具东南亚及中国特色的物品“带回家”。印于扉页上的“中国—东盟博览会让自贸区明天更美好！”及“10+1>11”的字句则一下子拉近了中国和东盟10国的距离。

“魅力之城”护照
Passport of CAEXPO Cities of Charm

本届博览会“魅力之城”专题获得各方好评。印尼副总统布迪约诺在印尼馆开馆仪式上的致辞中，热情洋溢地推介印尼“魅力之城”梭罗：“梭罗确实能表现印尼形象，宣传印尼贸易。在梭罗这个城市里，有各种各样的民族，有很多非常勤奋的手工艺制造商，他们来自不同省份，有着自己的宗教和文化背景，能聚在一起做生意，这就是印尼健康民族发展的象征，也能代表中国—东盟博览会的团结合作精神。”

中国“魅力之城”钦州市市委书记张晓钦说，中国—东盟自贸区的建设，改变了钦州的区位条件，钦州从一个相对封闭、边远的城市，变成了对外开放的前沿城市。本届博览会成为中国“魅力之城”，为钦州提供了一个极好的平台。

来自马来西亚的参展商陈振隆说：“走进‘魅力之城’展厅，就好像是来到了中国和东盟11个国家的11座城市，很漂亮，很有吸引力。”

刚游完上海世博会的刘杰说，此次在自己家乡举办的中国—东盟博览会上，拿着博览会的护照，过足“盖章瘾”，让他感到非常自豪。这让他有种如临东盟10国一样，一两个小时就游遍中国和东盟的11座“魅力城市”，多年后都会珍惜那种观展的感觉。

马来西亚驻广州总领事馆旅游市场部副领事赛努斐绩告诉记者，很多南宁市民来到马来西亚“魅力之城”馆，都会问很多的问题，问得很专业很仔细，说明这个专题展非常有用，我们可以借助这个平台来展示马来西亚的文化以及生机勃勃的旅游业。

文莱国家旅游局官员Salinah说，中国是文莱旅游的第二大市场，大概每个月有2000名中国游客到文莱旅游。这与每届博览会“魅力之城”的精心展示有着密切的联系。“魅力之城”的展示，增加了中国游客对文莱的了解。

10月24日上午，在第七届中国—东盟博览会即将圆满闭幕之际，中国—东盟博览会秘书处举行新闻发布会，正式对外宣布：第八届中国—东盟博览会中国“魅力之城”确定为海南省国际旅游岛。

发布会上专门举办了第八届博览会中国“魅力之城”移交仪式，进行了首次在博览会亮相的“魅力之城”印章交接仪式。第七届博览会“魅力之城”钦州市副市长李杏把“魅力之城”印章传递给第八届博览会“魅力之城”代表、海南省边境经济贸易协调办公室副主任姬国辉。“魅力之城”印章交接仪式，表达了在自贸区建成的机遇下，中国与东盟城市之间友好交流、互利共赢的共同愿望，预示着中国—东盟博览会“魅力之城”的传承与发展。

七　商贸促进活动

第七届博览会通过组织采购团巡馆、商贸对接等更具针对性的活动，制作采购商和投资商标志、徽章等方式，促进了企业间的互动，贸易配对取得良好成效，客商满意度普遍提高。会期举办了三场大型贸易对接会，东盟国家和国内各省区市采购团与参展企业进行了对接，采购企业总数达到了376家。会期将东盟各国采购团的采购对接活动集中举办，吸引了众多国内参展企业积极参与。各采购团和参展企业均对此次采购对接活动表示满意。本届博览会还首次邀请联合国机构举办采购说明会，联合国项目事务厅、联合国采购司、联合国世界粮食计划署、联合国儿童基金会驻华代表处、联合国开发计划署驻华代表处等5家机构参与采购演讲。国内外参展企业对成为联合国采购的供应商表现出极大兴趣，与联合国采购官员展开了热烈的现场洽谈。

本届博览会首次举办中国—东盟行业合作工作会议，促进行业贸易对接。会期举行了两场东盟主要参展行业的工作会议——中国—东盟博览会食品与农产品商协会工作会议和中国—东盟博览会木材与木制品商协会工作会

第七届中国—东盟博览会贸易对接会
Trade Matching Program of the 7th CAEXPO

议。双方相关行业商协会及重要企业代表共同商讨以博览会为平台，进一步开展行业合作，并在条件成熟后酝酿新的专业展。

会期还举行了中国—东盟博览会投资合作工作会议，东盟各国投资促进部门和东盟秘书处参加了会议。与会各方共同商讨通过博览会平台，加强本国投资促进部门、地方政府和产业园区间合作，重点做好中国企业“走出去”和东盟国家投引资项目的对接。东盟方对第七届博览会继续加强开展投资合作的工作表示高度赞赏。

本届博览会通过一系列商贸促进活动，促进中国和东盟重点合作领域和重点行业的合作。由中国与越南举办的“中国凭祥—越南同登跨境经济合作区建设工作商讨会”围绕跨境经济合作区的定位、范围、功能、管理体制、运行模式等进行了深入探讨，双方还在会上签署了《中越凭祥—同登跨境经济合作区工作商讨会会议纪要》，取得了务实成果。中国—东盟基础设施合作高峰论坛从工程技术和标准、项目融资、风险管理等操作层面对新形势下加强中国—东盟基础设施合作进行交流，达成重要共识。第二届中国—东盟工程项目合作与发展论坛旨在构建桂—港—东盟地区科技社团之间的常态交流模式，促进中国与东盟区域的科技社团间的交流合作。中国—东盟自由贸易区政策与实务研讨会则以大陆台商为主要对象，为促进大陆台商了解自贸区政策、紧抓自贸区机遇，扩大对自贸区投资进行的第四次宣讲会。2010年中国—东盟物联网（RFID）产业论坛、装备制造业共享中国—东盟自贸区发展新机遇高峰论坛、中国—东盟家纺贸易合作会议等则在专业合作领域进行了广泛探讨，增强了共识，深化了合作。中国—东盟自贸区建成后，除贸易便利化外，推动实现自贸区内投资便利化是重要内容，本届博览会上举办的3场有关投融资主题的会议也格外引人关注。投资中国—企业股权（债权）投融资交易会开幕式及融资培训会、中国—东盟博览会投融资项目对接会、投资中国—企业股权（债权）投融资交易会项目路演等会议重点讨论了在自贸区建成的背景下，如何抓住中国—东盟自贸区投资逐步实现自由化所带来的机遇，实现投资的互利共赢。

八　第七届中国—东盟博览会公众开放日

2010年10月24日是第七届中国—东盟博览会公众开放日。这场一年一度的盛宴，以丰富多彩的活动、琳琅满目的商品、东盟美食、各国风情等特色，不仅吸引了众多南宁市民前往观展，也吸引了许多远道而来的客人。

1. 赏异国风情。“魅力之城”展区里，东盟国家的民族风情表演，吸引了大量观众。在这里，中国和东盟10国“魅力之城”通过现场歌舞表演、图片、画册、电视等形式，向观众展示了本地的旅游风光、文化遗产和各领域的发展商机，有参观者认为此乃“逛一馆，游遍十一国”。

在泰国专题展区，有观众亲身体验泰式按摩，驻足欣赏惟妙惟肖的纸伞

公众开放日
Public open day

绘画。在文莱斯里巴加湾展区，来自文莱的演员在极富民族特色的音乐声中跳起了热情奔放的舞蹈。

2. 购各国商品。在公众开放日，各国特色商品受到了观众的青睐。东盟商品展区内，咖啡飘香，各种精制的珠宝首饰分外耀眼，红木制品雕龙画凤，栩栩如生。泰国的榴莲糕又香又甜。在印尼展馆，用桃核、竹子、石片制成的灯具，用贝壳制成的碗碟，精美又实用。不少市民刚进馆，购物袋已经沉甸甸的了。

农业展展区上奇特的农产品
Agricultural products on display

3. 农业展人气旺。在农业展上，台湾风味小吃吸引了众多“食客”。香港的鸡仔饼、佛手果、八珍醋姜等食品也成为抢手货。广西雅长兰科植物国家级自然保护区的展位，展出了数十盆珍稀植物——铁皮石斛。这种石斛是现有石斛属植物中经济价值最高的种类，受到了观众的喜爱。在农业展上展出的海南黄花梨、檀香、柚木、罗汉松、红豆杉等名贵树种，也有很高的人气。1005公斤重的“茶王”、珍贵兰花、方形西瓜等新奇农产品更让参观者大开眼界。

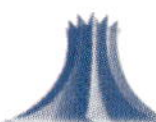

九　首届中国—东盟博览会木材与木制品展

2010年11月19—22日，由中国—东盟博览会秘书处和中国木材与木制品流通协会承办的首届中国—东盟博览会木材与木制品展在南宁国际会展中心举行。这是博览会首个与主展时间错开的独立专业展。

本次展会设置了中国商品和东盟及国外商品两大展区，共有中国和东盟5个国家约400家企业参展，展品包括实木家具、竹藤家具，板式家具，木制工艺品、木材、林木加工机械、木制建材用品、木质别墅、室外园艺景观等。东盟国家展馆面积达2900平方米，展位100多个。博览会合作伙伴——越南贸易促进局出口促进中心、老挝国家工商会等相关单位均组织了大批本国企业参展，东盟国家的一些知名木材经营企业如越南德禄寿有限公司，老挝Somsakith Furniture Factory等重点展示了东南亚高质量的木材、实木、红木家具和独具特色的木制工艺品。中国国内参展企业200多家，其中包括嘉汉板业、太启集团有限公司、深圳海百纳实业有限公司、青岛千川木工设备有限公司等国内知名企业。

展会期间还举办了一系列专业论坛与活动，传递了最新行业信息和动态，发布实施木材行业的一些重要标准等，取得良好成效。

首届中国—东盟博览会木材与木制品展上展出的实木家具
Solid wood furniture displayed at the 1st CAEXPO Timber & Wood Products Exhibition

第六章

深化对话交流 扩大合作领域
——第七届中国—东盟博览会高层论坛

随着中国—东盟经贸合作的快速发展，双边对海关、质检、交通等相关领域的服务配套提出了新需求。同时，经贸合作与人文领域的交流结合在一起推进，更能深化双边全面持久的合作，形成经济社会发展的持续推动力。

因此，每届博览会都围绕多个领域，举办一系列高层会议和交流活动，为双方十一大重点领域合作提供务实平台。

第七届中国—东盟博览会以“自贸区与新机遇”为重点主题，紧扣自贸区建成，围绕金融、能源、电力、医学、减贫、海事、司法合作等领域，举办了一系列高规格会议、论坛和交流活动。

各场会议和活动规格高，均有中国和东盟国家部长级官员、国家直属企业负责人、国际知名专家学者出席，就深入开展各领域的交流合作达成了很多共识，取得务实成果。

例如，第二届中国—东盟金融合作与发展领袖论坛通过了《论坛共识》，论坛首次增设的中国—东盟银行家圆桌会议形成了《中国—东盟银行家圆桌会议倡议》。

中国—印度尼西亚能源论坛围绕加强石油天然气、可再生能源、电力和煤炭等方面互利合作的内容进行了深入讨论，签署了《印尼巴厘岛塞露坎巴湾电厂股东合资协议书》等多项合作协议。

其他各场交流活动也取得了丰硕成果，进一步拓宽和丰富了中国—东盟合作的“南宁渠道”。

Deepening Dialogues and Exchanges & Expanding Cooperation Fields

—High-end Forums of the 7th CAEXPO

With the rapid development of China-ASEAN economic and trade cooperation, both sides have raised higher demands in terms of supporting services such as customs, quality inspection, transport and other related fields. At the same time, the promotion of both economic and cultural exchanges can play a bigger role in deepening the long lasting cooperation by providing a sustainable driving force behind the social and economic development.

Therefore, each session of the CAEXPO holds a series of high-end conferences and exchange activities centering on a variety of fields, to provide a pragmatic platform for cooperation in the top 11 priority fields between the two sides.

With "CAFTA & New Opportunities"as its theme, the 7th CAEXPO staged a series of high profile conferences, forums and workshops, centering on the bilateral cooperation in finance, energy, electric power, medicine, poverty relief, maritime affairs and justice, in the context of the establishment of the CAFTA.

The events have attracted ministers or officials of the equivalent ranking of China and the ASEAN countries, heads of Chinese central state-owned companies, internationally renowned scholars and researchers, reaching consensus and pragmatic outcomes in a variety of fields for exchange and cooperation.

For instance, the 2nd China-ASEAN Summit Forum on Financial Cooperation and Development adopted the *Consensus of the Forum*; the newly added China-ASEAN Bankers Round Table Conference reached the *Proposal of the China-ASEAN Bankers Round Table Conference.*

The Indonesia-China Energy Forum had in-depth discussion on the cooperation in natural gas and petroleum, renewable energy, electric power and coal, concluding an agreement on shareholding of electric power plant in Bali of Indonesia and others.

Other events held concurrently have also achieved satisfying results, widening and enriching the "Nanning Channel" in the China-ASEAN cooperation.

CHAPTER SIX

一 第四届中国—印度尼西亚能源论坛

由中华人民共和国国家能源局和印度尼西亚共和国能源和矿产资源部共同主办、广西壮族自治区人民政府承办的第四届中国—印度尼西亚能源论坛，于2010年10月19日在广西南宁举行。中国国家发展改革委副主任、国家能源局局长张国宝，印度尼西亚国企部部长穆斯塔法·阿布巴卡尔出席开幕式并致辞。来自中国、印尼两国政府及相关能源企业代表在论坛上以中国—东盟自贸区建成背景下“中国与印尼两国的能源合作”为主题，就石油天然气、新能源、电力煤炭等方面合作进行了深入探讨，并签署多项合作协议。

中国国家能源局副局长钱智民、总工程师吴贵辉，广西壮族自治区主席马飚、自治区副主席林念修，中国南方电网公司董事长赵建国，中电控股有限公司（中国区）总裁柯愈明，印尼国家电力公司总经理Dahlan Iskan，印尼巴厘通用能源公司总经理Andre Raharja，以及两国政府和相关能源企业共200多位代表出席论坛。

2010年10月19日，第四届中国—印度尼西亚能源论坛在广西南宁举行

On October 19, 2010, the 4th Indonesia-China Energy Forum held in Nanning, Guangxi

张国宝在致辞时表示，中国和印尼同为亚洲重要国家，有着传统的友谊和贸易来往。建交60年来，两国关系取得长足进展，双边关系提升到一个新的历史高度。中国和印尼都是人口众多、地域辽阔的发展中大国，共同面临发展经济、改善民生的任务，双方合作空间广阔，近年来双方在经贸领域的交流与合作日益增多，为巩固两国战略伙伴关系奠定了坚实基础。近年来中国与印尼能源合作不断深化和务实，两国积极探索基础设施投资、设备购买与能源贸易相结合等新的合作方式，在油气、电力、煤炭等领域的互利合作取得了新的成果，能源合作呈现良好的态势。印尼是中国第二大煤炭进口国，中国愿意加大与印尼在能源领域的互惠合作，并为应对能源安全和气候变化、可持续发展作出新的贡献。

张国宝还为两国能源合作提出四点建议。一是拓宽能源合作领域。大力拓展在水电、风能、太阳能、生物质能、地热能等可再生能源领域的互利合作；二是深化能源投资合作。中方欢迎印尼能源企业到中国投资，同时也鼓励有实力的中国企业到印尼投资，积极参与电力、煤炭、油气等项目建设；三是扩大双边能源贸易。进一步拓宽能源贸易渠道，提高能源贸易水平；四是深化和扩大双方在能源和其他资源领域合作力度。两国相关政府部门可以通过对话磋商和沟通协调，完善机制，为两国企业创造良好的合作环境，使能源资源合作成为两国合作的亮点。

穆斯塔法·阿布巴卡尔在致辞时说，举办中国—印度尼西亚能源论坛对加强印尼与中国合作，尤其是能源和矿产资源合作具有十分重要的战略意义。印尼和中国能源互补性强，近年来双方在能源领域的合作得到提高。印尼政府正在能源领域推行改革，从能源供应方管理改为需求方管理，加强对新能源领域和矿产储备勘探的投资，提高能源利用效率，推行能源节约和多元化。中国经济发展迅速，吸引了其他国家与中国建立合作关系。印尼看到了两国在油气、煤炭、电力、可再生能源等领域的合作成就，希望通过中国—印度尼西亚能源论坛以及其他平台进一步加强和深化能源领域双边合作。

论坛开幕前，广西壮族自治区主席马飚与国家发改委副主任、国家能源局局长张国宝进行了会谈。马飚对国家发改委、国家能源局长期以来给予广西发展特别是能源发展的大力支持表示感谢。长期以来，国家发改委、国家能源局高度重视和支持广西能源发展，在重要规划编制、重大项目核准、中央资金支持方面为广西提供了巨大帮助，加快了广西能源建设，为广西经济发展提供了坚强的能源保障。当前广西努力将电力产业打造成14个千亿元产业之一，同时大力发展可再生能源，希望国家发改委、国家能源局一如既往大力支持广西加快能源建设。张国宝对第七届中国—东盟博览会和第七届中国—东盟商务与投资峰会的召开表示祝贺，对广西为第四届中国—印度尼西亚能源论坛的顺利召开所做的工作表示感谢。张国宝表示近年来广西高度重视能源结构调整，大力发展可再生能源，取得了良好成效。新一轮西部大开发的标志性工程防城港核电站工程也已经开工建设，令人鼓舞。国家发改委、国家能源局将继续支持广西能源建设，同时希望广西在发展清洁能源方面取得更大的成绩。

论坛上，中国和印尼两国政府和企业的代表进行了主旨发言。中国国电集团就绿色能源作了《让绿色电力照亮绿色经济》的专题报告，中国华电集团就中印尼双方能源合作作了《务实进取 再创辉煌 加快中印尼能源领域合作》的主旨发言，中海油集团就油气方面作了《合作、支持、促进油气事业发展》的介绍。双方还就石油天然气、新能源和电力煤炭等领域相关领域进行了分组讨论和交流，共同探讨了中国—东盟自贸区建成背景下中国与印尼两国的能源合作，达成广泛共识。

两国相关企业还签署了多项合作协议和合作备忘录。中国华电集团与印尼巴厘通用能源公司签订了“印尼巴厘岛塞露坎巴湾电厂股东合资协议书”，中国百色市万维投资有限公司与印尼土地资源矿业有限公司签订了“合作开采矿山、锰产品深加工的备忘录”，中国衡阳鸿菱石油管材有限责任公司与印尼Dhiva公司签订了“合资公司组建协议”，中国广西投资集团公司与印尼达尼多煤炭集团就双方煤炭战略合作达成了初步协议，相关企业也达成了多项合作意向。论坛取得了丰硕成果。

第四届中国—印度尼西亚能源论坛在中国—东盟自由贸易区正式全面启动背景下召开，是深化中国—东盟合作的具体体现，将进一步巩固友谊与合作，推动中国、印尼两国乃至整个中国—东盟自由贸易区能源合作，造福于两国人民。

二　第二届中国—东盟金融合作与发展领袖论坛

2010年10月20日，由广西壮族自治区人民政府、中国人民银行、中国银行业监督管理委员会、中国证券监督管理委员会、中国保险监督管理委员会（以下简称“一行三会”）共同主办，广西壮族自治区人民政府承办的第二届中国—东盟金融合作与发展领袖论坛在广西南宁成功举行。

第二届中国—东盟金融合作与发展领袖论坛旨在巩固第一届中国—东盟金融合作与发展领袖论坛成果，务实推进第一届举办期间所达成《中国—东盟金融合作与发展领袖共同宣言》的实施，拓展中国与东盟金融合作平台，充分发挥中国—东盟博览会与广西在中国与东盟合作中的重要作用，为区域内经济的持续、健康、快速发展提供强有力的金融支持。

论坛以“深化合作机制，构建中国—东盟自由贸易区金融互利共赢发展新格局”为主题，分设“区域经济一体化下银行业的‘走出去’战略”、“中国—东盟自由贸易区建成后区域性银行业机构的跨越式发展之道”、“中国—东盟自由贸易区内中小企业的融资和上市策略”及“中国—东盟自由贸易区建成后保险业的发展机遇”等四大议题进行研讨，吸引了来自中国

2010年10月20日，第二届中国—东盟金融合作与发展领袖论坛在广西南宁举行

On October 20, 2010, the 2nd China-ASEAN Summit Forum on Financial Cooperation and Development held in Nanning, Guangxi

"一行三会"及东盟国家金融主管部门高官、国际金融机构相关代表、中国及欧美等地区商业金融机构首脑、金融界知名专家学者约400人参加，其中包括总部或总行级领导37人、境内金融机构87家、境外机构（含港、澳地区机构）21家。

本届论坛呈现五个亮点：

1. 品牌效应初步显现。第一届中国—东盟金融合作与发展领袖论坛的成功举办，使金融论坛的品牌效应初步显现，中国与东盟合作的"南宁渠道"得到进一步拓展，主要体现在四个方面：一是举办第二届金融论坛，继续将金融合作作为博览会的重点合作与交往领域。论坛得到广西壮族自治区人民政府和"一行三会"的高度重视和大力支持，除继续出任论坛主办单位外，广西壮族自治区党委书记、自治区人大常委会主任郭声琨出席论坛开幕式并致辞，中国人民银行行长助理李东荣，中国证监会主席助理朱从玖，中国银监会代表、广西银监局局长苏保祥出席论坛并发表主旨演讲，广西壮族自治区党委常委、自治区副主席陈武主持开幕式。二是第一届中国—东盟金融合作与发展领袖论坛的参会单位和嘉宾均对论坛的举办给予积极肯定和支持，柬埔寨加华银行、中国进出口银行、中国银行、交通银行、北京银行、天津银行、德勤华永会计师事务所等多家2009年的参会单位2010年再次莅临。三是金融论坛辐射面进一步扩大，参加本届金融论坛的东盟国家由上届的3个增至6个，分别为印尼、柬埔寨、老挝、缅甸、泰国、越南。此外，澳门金融管理局、中国农业银行、深圳证券交易所、中国工商银行河内分行、加拿大西联汇款公司、拉维基亚集团公司、苏拉国际合伙人有限公司、美国红岸投资公司等多家国内外知名金融机构首次参会。四是论坛筹备期间，部分国内金融机构表示了与论坛组委会合作办会的意向，如中国风险投资研究院、天津国际融资服务有限公司等均表达欲与论坛合作，共同举办风险投资对接会等活动的意愿。

2. 丰富充实办会资源，办会思路进一步明晰。中国—东盟金融合作与发展领袖论坛遵循办会规律，拓宽办会思路，充分发挥博览会的平台作用，由依靠"一行三会"影响力办会逐步转向由专业机构办会，不断扩充办会资源。本届论坛联手中国银行业协会，共同举办中国—东盟银行家圆桌会议，受到广泛关注，并取得圆满成功。该会议得到东南亚国家联盟银行业协会的积极回应，老挝开发银行行长兼老挝银行业协会主席奔达·答拉位、越南工商银行代表阮氏妹还分别在会议上发言。会议紧扣时代主题，就"推动合作交流，加强中国—东盟自由贸易区金融平台建设与完善"、"中国—东盟自由贸易区成立后，银行业协会如何更好地发挥纽带作用"等问题进行深入交

流，探讨共同发起成立中国—东盟银行家联盟的可行性和运行机制，并形成《中国—东盟银行家圆桌会议倡议》，准确定位银行业在中国—东盟自贸区经贸合作、商业交流中应发挥的积极作用，会议取得了良好效果。

3. 形成论坛专业宣传渠道，论坛影响力进一步提升。本届论坛改变传统新闻宣传模式，进一步加大宣传推介力度，除了依靠中国—东盟博览会、中国—东盟商务与投资峰会拥有的大众传媒资源外，还积极主动与《上海证券报》、《金融时报》、《国际金融报》，财新传媒旗下的《中国改革》及《新世纪周刊》，《中国企业家杂志》、《贸易金融杂志》及和讯网等财经界知名媒体合作，打造中国—东盟金融合作与发展领袖论坛专业宣传队伍，建立论坛宣传资源库，形成论坛专业宣传渠道，有效提升了中国—东盟金融合作与发展领袖论坛在业界内的专业度和知名度。

4. 论坛实效性强，得到参会各方高度认可。泰国银行家协会秘书长瓦差・永克提坤专门致函论坛组委会，对论坛予以高度赞扬。他认为，本次论坛内容丰富，信息翔实，取得了巨大成功。他相信，本次论坛将会进一步增强、促进中国与东盟的金融合作，并指引双方合作向纵深发展。各国参会代表对金融论坛给予肯定和赞扬。

本届论坛取得了丰硕成果：

1. 建立中国—东盟银行家圆桌会议机制。论坛通过了《中国—东盟银行家圆桌会议倡议》，并决定将定期举行中国—东盟银行家圆桌会议，充分发挥中国银行业协会与东盟银行业协会的桥梁和纽带作用，进一步加深中国与东盟在金融领域内开展信息交流、资源共享、服务协作等方面的合作，丰富金融论坛的探讨内容，扩大金融论坛的成效和影响力。

2. 达成《第二届中国—东盟金融合作与发展领袖论坛共识》。论坛充分探讨了中国—东盟自由贸易区建成为各国金融业带来的机遇与挑战及相关发展策略，推动区域内金融业磋商与合作机制的建立和完善，进而为区域内经济的持续、健康、快速发展提供强有力的金融支持，并达成《第二届中国—东盟金融合作与发展领袖论坛共识》，传承首届金融论坛《中国—东盟金融合作与发展领袖共同宣言》的精神和宗旨，推动建立中国—东盟自由贸易区互利共赢金融发展的新格局。

3. 深化政银、银银及金融机构间的合作。本届论坛为参会各方提供了开展合作交流的平台，进一步深化政银、银银及金融机构间的合作。加拿大西联汇款公司借参会之机深入考察广西的金融投资环境，寻找合作机会，并与广西壮族自治区金融办、自治区外汇管理局等区内金融主管单位进行深入交流；北京银行计划在南宁开设分行；包商银行积极开展各项活动，主动与到会的东盟金融机构进行非正式会谈；天津银行与广西北部湾银行开展对接活动，寻求发展机会；河内证券交易所与苏拉国际合伙人有限公司通过论坛双方表现出强烈的合作意愿；中国注册会计师协会率出席论坛的18家境内百强会计师事务所代表参加了“中国—东盟自贸区会计服务出口示范基地”揭牌仪式，并表示该协会将继续指导各地开展示范基地建设工作，推荐一批基础比较好、综合能力较高、有发展意愿的会计师事务所提供相关特殊领域、高端需求、高技术难度、高附加值的专业服务。

三　第三届中国—东盟智库战略对话

2010年10月17—18日，由中国社会科学院国际研究学部、中国广西国际博览事务局、中国广西社会科学院、中国广西北部湾发展研究院和东盟智库网络主办，广西社会科学院和广西北部湾发展研究院承办的第三届中国—东盟智库战略对话在广西南宁市举行。

柬埔寨和平与合作学院院长（柬埔寨前副首相兼外交部长）诺罗敦·西里武，广西壮族自治区党委常委、宣传部长沈北海，中国社会科学院国际研究学部主任张蕴岭，广西社会科学院、广西北部湾发展研究院院长吕余生，以及来自柬埔寨、印度尼西亚、马来西亚、新加坡、泰国、越南、美国、中国等国家的专家学者出席本次对话会。

本次对话会议以“加强新形势下的中国—东盟合作”为主题，下设后金融危机：世界局势与中国—东盟合作、东南亚地区经济与政治、中国与东南亚关系、中国—东盟自由贸易区现状与前景、区域合作与中国南宁—新加坡经济走廊建设、文化交流合作与壮老泰（包括岱、侬、掸、印度泰人）族群

2010年10月17—18日，第三届中国—东盟智库战略对话在广西南宁举行

On October 17-18, 2010, the 3rd China-ASEAN Think Tanks Strategic Dialogue held in Nanning, Guangxi

参加第三届中国—东盟智库战略对话的各国专家学者
Scholars and experts at the 3rd China-ASEAN Think Tanks Strategic Dialogue

文化比较等6个议题。这次会议的层次高，议题设置科学，既有现实意义又有较高的前瞻性；会议提出了“南宁—新加坡经济走廊建设”，为中国与东盟的全面合作提供了全新的有重大价值的思路。

沈北海在致辞中指出：中国与东盟双方拥有广泛切实的共同利益。中国—东盟自由贸易区如期建成，标志着中国与东盟战略伙伴关系已经站在一个新的高度。面对复杂多变的国际形势，中国与东盟的合作需要在原来的基础上有新的思维。广西扩大开放合作需要有新的智慧和新的举措。

中国社会科学院国际研究学部主任张蕴岭教授在致辞中认为，中国与东盟关系发展中出现的经济、政治、安全等问题都需要双方加强对话、进行协商和进行开诚布公的讨论，以促进中国与东盟未来的发展。

广西社会科学院院长、广西北部湾发展研究院院长吕余生研究员在致辞中提出四点建议：第一，把每年一次的中国—东盟智库战略对话形成常态对话机制，以智库的共识去推动和影响政府间的共识；第二，整合中国—东盟智库资源，形成合作共赢机制，使务虚合作变成务实合作；第三，联合各国智库对一些重大战略问题进行前瞻性研究，为政府提供决策咨询；第四，努力推动广西北部湾经济区智库中心和中国—东盟研究交流基地建设，打造中国—东盟智库合作基地与平台。

本次对话会议取得了圆满成功，取得了丰硕成果。智库交流作为中国—东盟人文交流的重要组成部分，是双方携手合作、寻求共赢的重要载体，对于增进相互沟通与了解至关重要。会议期间，中国和东盟国家的专家学者们紧紧围绕“加强新形势下的中国—东盟合作”这个主题，就各方面的内容和领域，包括经济、政治、安全、文化等交换了意见、提出了建设性对策和建议，为更好地推动中国—东盟自由贸易区的发展，并最终建立共同体作出了很大的贡献。会议认为，当前，中国与东盟合作的当务之急是要逐步实现人员、货物以及其他生产要素的自由流动，在这个过程中，南宁—新加坡经济走廊的建设可以发挥重要的作用。

四 第四届中国—东盟社会发展与减贫论坛

2010年7月13—15日，第四届中国—东盟社会发展与减贫论坛在广西桂林举行。本次论坛由中国国务院扶贫办、广西壮族自治区人民政府主办，中国国际扶贫中心、广西壮族自治区扶贫办、广西桂林市人民政府、广西国际博览事务局承办，联合国开发计划署、中国国际经济技术交流中心、广西外资扶贫项目管理中心支持。

本次论坛以“自由贸易与减贫”为主题，探讨中国—东盟自由贸易区给各国减贫带来的机遇和挑战。来自文莱、柬埔寨、印度尼西亚、老挝、马来西亚、缅甸、菲律宾、新加坡、泰国和越南等东盟10国社会发展与减贫部门负责人、该领域的知名专家学者、著名企业家、NGO代表以及国际组织的代表140人与会。

论坛开幕式由中国国务院扶贫办副主任郑文凯主持，广西壮族自治区人民政府副主席梁胜利、柬埔寨经济财政部助理秘书长Sunly Thearith、东盟秘书处副秘书长Dato's Misran Karmain、联合国开发计划署代理代表Silva Morimoto、桂林市市长李志刚等分别致辞；中国国务院扶贫办副主任郑文

2010年7月13—15日，第四届中国—东盟社会发展与减贫论坛在广西桂林举行

On July 13-15, 2010, the 4th China-ASEAN Social Development and Poverty Reduction Forum held in Guilin, Guangxi

凯、联合国驻马来西亚系统协调员Kamal Malhotra、中国商务部国际司参赞张克宁分别以“贸易自由化背景下的中国减贫”、“贸易自由化、经济增长和发展战略：亚洲成功经验的实证与示范”、“推进贸易投资自由化，实现发展减贫目标”为题作了主旨发言；东盟10个国家代表围绕论坛主题进行国别演讲，分别介绍各自国家的社会发展与减贫战略，贸易自由化的措施、相关发展战略和项目的背景、目标、操作模式与前景展望等。会后，还举办了欢迎晚宴。

本次论坛的平行会议分别以“贸易自由化、减贫进程及其影响”和“中国与东盟国家间的贸易与贫困”两个主题展开讨论。东盟秘书处副秘书长Dato’s Misran Karmain、中国商务部国际贸易经济合作研究院亚非研究部研究员、主任徐长文，英国Sussex大学教授分别做了“自由贸易、减贫战略与国际合作”，“自贸区促进中国与东盟经贸和扶贫事业发展”和“贸易、增长与贫困的地理版图：通用原则与中国实证”的主题发言。

论坛闭幕式由广西壮族自治区扶贫办主任吴宇雄主持，中国国务院扶贫办党组成员、国际合作和社会扶贫司司长张磊作了会议总结。会议期间，全体与会代表在桂林进行了实地参观考察。

本次论坛主题为“自由贸易与减贫”，旨在深入分析和评估中国—东盟自由贸易区建成对中国及东盟各国的影响，尤其是自贸区给贫困群体带来的影响，交流各国在贸易自由化和经济议题过程中推动本国社会发展与减贫进程的成功经验、挑战及应对措施，提出在自贸区时代不断推进区域内减贫与社会发展合作的政策建议，进一步推动中国与东盟各国在减贫领域的交流与合作。出席论坛的代表们一致认为，减贫是中国和东盟国家发展进程中面临的挑战之一，为共同应对挑战，加强中国与东盟国家间减贫交流和合作显得尤为重要。通过论坛这个平台进行交流和讨论，促进了各国对贸易与减贫关系的认识，为及时采取针对性的措施提供了依据和参考。

本届论坛取得了多方面成果，进一步扩大了共识、促进了交流、增进了友谊，主要成效有以下几个方面：

1. 通过国别演讲和提问解答，充分交流分享了各国在减贫领域的经验与做法。如中国国务院扶贫办副主任郑文凯在主旨发言中指出，中国减贫成就来自于经济社会的全面发展，同时也得益于有针对性的减贫措施。尤其是进入新世纪以来，中国推出一系列惠农政策和专项减贫措施。其中，有两项重要减贫措施与贸易发展联系密切，使贫困人口深受其益：一是大力实施产业化扶贫，开辟贫困地区产品进入市场的有效途径；二是全面加强义务教育、职业技能培训，拓展贫困农户劳动力进入市场的广阔空间。

2. 论坛平行会议围绕“自由贸易与减贫”展开研讨，深入分析了贸易与减贫之间的关系和作用机制，阐述了中国—东盟国家间贸易对各国减贫影响的实证研究结果，对如何发展自由贸易和有效促进减贫提出了很多建议。

3. 各方重视、准备充分，保障了减贫论坛的会议水平和成效。东盟10个国家和东盟秘书处都派出较高级别代表团出席论坛，中国国务院扶贫办、外交部、商务部、农业部、海关总署、国务院发展研究中心等8个部委和单位、9个国际机构和驻华使馆、13个省（区、市）扶贫办、13家科研院校派出代表参加会议；参会代表均认真准备发言材料，并在会前对会议材料进行了收集和整理，编印了《主题研究报告》和《论文集》；研讨与实地考察相结合，更深入地了解在融入自由贸易进程中广西产业扶贫的思路与做法；会议主办方精心组织，科学安排，保证了论坛组织严密有序、会议内容丰富、宣传氛围浓厚、接待服务周到，受到与会各方的一致好评。

4. 媒体关注、社会反响强烈。本届减贫论坛受到众多国内新闻媒体的关注，《人民日报》、《中国日报》、中国国际广播电台、新华社广西分社、广西电视台、《广西日报》、广西人民广播电台、广西《金色通道》杂志社、桂林电视台、《桂林日报》、桂林市广播电台等新闻媒体对论坛进行了宣传报道，在国内外引起了强烈反响。

五　首届中国—东盟红十字论坛

2010年10月11—12日，由中国红十字会总会和广西壮族自治区人民政府联合主办、广西壮族自治区红十字会承办的首届中国—东盟红十字论坛在广西南宁举行。广西壮族自治区副主席、广西红十字会会长李康出席论坛开幕式并致辞。来自中国红十字会总会、红十字国际委员会、红十字会与红新月会国际联合会和印度尼西亚、老挝、马来西亚、泰国、越南、蒙古等国红十字会，国内各省（自治区、直辖市）行业、新疆生产建设兵团红十字会，香港、澳门红十字会及台湾红十字组织的120名代表参加了本次论坛。论坛由中国红十字会总会副会长郝林娜主持，与会嘉宾对“气候变化下的灾害风险管理”问题进行了热烈而卓有成效的探讨。

李康在致辞中说，广西与东盟国家山水相连、文化相通，红十字运动源远流长，合作成果丰硕。特别是近年来，广西与东盟红十字组织以“发扬人道、博爱、奉献的红十字精神，保护人的生命和健康，促进人类和平进步事业”为宗旨，积极致力于改善最易受损人群的境况，在抗击异常气候条件下的地震、海啸、雪灾和洪水灾害等历次行动中，真诚相待，相互配合；同时在防病治病、社区服务、人文关怀以及抗击世界金融危机等方面加强交流，密切协作，取得明显效果。本次中国—东盟红十字论坛是在中国—东盟自由贸易区正式建成第一年举办的，论坛以气候变化下的灾害风险管理为主题，中外嘉宾共同面对新形势、应对新挑战，探讨红十字事业发展的新问题。这对加强东盟各国在人道领域的交流与合作，进一步增进了解，加深友谊，凝聚共识，形成合力，更加广泛地动员人道力量保护人的生命、改善人民福祉、促进地区和谐稳定将起到积极的作用。

中国红十字会党组书记、常务副会长王伟，中国民政部减灾处副处长肖鑫，广西红十字会专职副会长方南亭分别在论坛上作主旨发言。王伟在发言中以印度洋海啸、汶川地震、玉树地震等灾害救援为例介绍了中国红十字

2010年10月11—12日，首届中国—东盟红十字论坛在广西南宁举行
On October 11—12, 2010, the 1st China-ASEAN Red Cross Forum held in Nanning, Guangxi

会在救灾备灾、应急救援、救护培训等方面取得的成绩和经验，并提出了“创新筹资机制、加强备灾体系、提高救援专业化水平、培养社区志愿者参与灾害预警及救灾组织管理、加强新闻宣传提高公信力、加强志愿者队伍建设”等六项提高灾害管理水平的意见。肖鑫在发言中介绍了中国减灾体制，以及灾害应急响应、灾害信息发布、救灾应急物资储备、灾情预警会商和信息共享、重大灾害抢险救灾联动、灾害应急社会动员、国际合作交流等七大减灾机制建设情况，以及中国政府在适应气候变化中所做的工作。方南亭以在广西实施的社区为本备灾项目为例，介绍了广西红十字会近年来应对灾害变化所做的努力及取得的经验：在气候变暖的背景下，广西主要的极端天气气候事件发生的频率明显增多，强度明显增大，导致干旱、洪涝灾害频发，从2002年起实施的社区备灾项目指导灾害多发地区居民进行社区易受损性能力评估分析、鼓励指导社区群众了解备灾知识，学习现场应急救护、自救互救、应急避险知识，掌握备灾措施，制定本社区和家庭备灾应急方案，开展各种形式防灾避险演练，修建减灾工程等，有效地减少了灾害损失和人员伤亡，发言得到了国际红十字组织的高度关注。

红十字国际委员会东亚地区代表处主任蒂埃里·梅拉先生，红十字会与红新月会国际联合会地区项目协调员华美菱女士，以及越南、印度尼西亚红十字会的代表也分别在论坛上发言。

与会成员共同探讨了气候变化下的灾害风险管理策略，交流各国红十字会应对自然灾害的经验，借鉴各国红十字会在降低灾害风险方面所做的研究、所取得的经验，对更好地应对气候变化所带来的挑战具有十分重要的作用；对加强中国红十字会与东盟各国红十字会或红新月会在人道领域的交流

与合作，进一步增进相互了解，加深友谊，凝聚共识，形成合力，更加广泛地动员人道力量，起到了积极的作用。

论坛形成了《中国—东盟红十字论坛共识》：承认本地区红十字与红新月在灾害管理方面面临着共同的挑战；认识到适应气候变化及降低灾害风险的重要性；考虑到有必要加强在救灾及降低灾害风险的协调；感谢中国红十字会发起并组织此次论坛，并借此机会加强战略伙伴关系以推动2020战略的执行；同时强调：有必要推动本地区红十字/红新月运动伙伴之间在救灾及降低灾害风险方面的紧密合作与协调；加强国家红会之间的经验与知识分享，尤其在以社区为本的减灾、对气候变化的适应和志愿者发展方面；将重建家庭联系融入救灾工作，提高地区内国家红会重建家庭联系网络的工作能力，并加强协调；倡导传播红十字与红新月运动基本原则，在地区内承认并宣传国际救灾法。

论坛举办期间恰逢广西红十字会建会100周年，广西红十字会于2010年10月11日上午举办了建会100周年纪念大会，全国政协副主席、中国红十字会名誉副会长李金华，广西壮族自治区党委书记、自治区人大常委会主任、广西红十字会名誉会长郭声琨出席了纪念大会并作重要讲话，红十字国际委员会、红十字会与红新月会国际联合会、东盟各国和蒙古国红十字组织的领导，各省（市、区）、香港、澳门特别行政区红十字会及台湾红十字组织代表，广西历任红十字会会长、老红十字会工作者、红十字先进集体和个人参加了纪念大会。大会总结了广西红十字百年光荣历史和辉煌成就，展望广西红十字事业发展的美好未来。

六　中国—东盟电力合作与发展论坛暨中国—东盟电力经贸合作洽谈会

2010年10月20—21日，由中国电力企业联合会和中国国际贸易促进委员会电力行业委员与中国—东盟博览会秘书处共同主办的中国—东盟电力合作与发展论坛暨中国—东盟电力经贸合作洽谈会在广西南宁召开，会议主题为“中国—东盟经济一体化背景下的电力经贸合作共赢”。

会议采取主题报告、经贸洽谈、参观展览等形式，邀请东盟各国特别是老挝、越南等电力和经贸主管政府部门代表以及中国电力行业的投资机构、运营机构、电力设备供应商、贸易公司、电力施工建设、总承包单位、电力商务领域有关金融、投资、法律、咨询等机构100多位代表参加会议。代表们充分交流，共同探讨了中国与东盟国家电力企业投资与合作的机遇和挑战。

中国电力企业联合会专职顾问、中国国际贸易促进委员会电力行业委员会会长谢振华在会议上发表了主题报告。广西壮族自治区副主席杨道喜出席会议并致辞，中国驻老挝大使馆经济商务参赞张玉成、中国—东盟商务理事会秘书长许宁宁也应邀出席并讲话。

会议作为探讨中国—东盟自由贸易区运行下中国电力行业与东盟国家进行投资与贸易合作的平台，取得了良好效果，受到与会代表的好评。

2010年10月20—21日，中国—东盟电力合作与发展论坛暨中国—东盟电力经贸合作洽谈会在广西南宁召开

On October 20-21, 2010, China-ASEAN Power Cooperation and Development Forum & China-ASEAN Power Economic and Trade Cooperation Fair held in Nanning, Guangxi

七　中国—东盟海事磋商机制第六次会议

2010年10月20—21日，由中国海事局主办、广西海事局承办的中国—东盟海事磋商机制第六次会议在广西南宁举行。广西壮族自治区副主席杨道喜、广西壮族自治区政协副主席蒋培兰出席了会议。中国交通运输部副部长徐祖远向大会发来贺信。来自中国、泰国、柬埔寨、新加坡、越南、马来西亚、缅甸、印度尼西亚、文莱、老挝等国海事主管当局和东盟秘书处40多名代表参加了会议。

中国—东盟海事磋商机制建立始于2003年10月在缅甸仰光举行的中国和东盟“10+1”交通部长会议，是中国与东盟确立睦邻伙伴关系的结果。中国—东盟海事磋商机制的目标是在平等、互相尊重、互惠互利的基础上，各方同意遵循有关法律、法规、规则，在海事领域积极开展合作和交流，就有关问题共同协商，交流信息和经验，加强中国和东盟地区在海事领域的友好关系和合作。中国—东盟海事磋商机制第一次会议于2005年12月在广州召开，迄今为止已召开了五次会议。建立6年来，在中国和东盟各国海事机构的共同努力下，始终以确保水上航行安全、促进海洋环境保护为己任，围绕国际海事界及地区间双方共同关注的热点、难点问题进行了广泛而深入的探讨。

中国—东盟海事磋商机制会议议题涵盖了当前海上航行安全、海洋环境保护的热点、难点问题，如，海员素质的提高（包括船员培训、教育、发证），溢油应急反应体系的建立与完善，海上搜寻救助，IMO公约、规则（包括2006海事劳工公约等）的实施，海事管理技术（包括AIS、LRIT、VTS等）的发展与应用，马六甲海峡船舶航行安全与防止船舶污染等。该机制已成为中国—东盟海上合作的重要平台，为促进中国—东盟海上合作、加强中国—东盟良好的海上合作关系发挥了重要作用。通过定期召开会议，中国和东盟在交通运输领域的合作不断深化，在加快交通基础设施衔接，促进交通运输便利化，支持建设中国—东盟自由贸易区，协调经济社会持续发展

2010年10月20—21日，中国—东盟海事磋商机制第六次会议在广西南宁举行

On October 20-21, 2010, the 6th China-ASEAN Conference of Maritime Consultative Mechanisms held in Nanning, Guangxi

等领域均取得了显著的成就。

作为第七届中国—东盟博览会的9个高层次论坛之一，中国—东盟海事磋商机制第六次会议代表就海上航运安全、船员素质、溢油应急、环境保护等问题进行协商与会谈，并对中国—东盟海事磋商机制谅解备忘录相关后续工作进行了完善。

广西壮族自治区副主席杨道喜在致辞中表示，中国—东盟海事磋商机制第六次会议在广西北部湾经济区核心城市南宁举办，具有重要意义。随着2010年中国—东盟自贸区的建成运营，“南新经济走廊”建设顺利推进，中国—东盟合作进入全面深入发展的新阶段，2010年上半年中国与东盟双边贸易额比2009年同期增长54.7%，东盟已成为中国的第四大贸易伙伴，来往于中国与东盟各国港口的商船数量不断增多，加强中国与东盟各国在海事领域的合作与交流，保证航运安全、船舶保安和防止船舶污染海洋成为各国经济发展的迫切需要。因此，中国—东盟海事磋商机制会议作为中国和东盟各国在海上安全、海上保安和海洋环境保护领域交换信息、分享经验和加强合作的重要平台，为促进和加强中国—东盟良好的海上合作关系发挥了重要作用。

中国海事局常务副局长陈爱平在会上宣读了中国交通运输部副部长徐祖远的贺信，徐祖远在致辞中说，本次会议将对中国—东盟海事磋商机制谅解备忘录相关后续工作进行完善，为2010年11月文莱召开的中国—东盟交通运输部长会议上正式签署做好准备。他指出，为落实2009年10月第十二次中国与东盟领导人会议上中国和东盟领导人就构筑互联互通的区域基础设施网络达成的共识，中国政府正在推进《中国—东盟交通合作战略规划》，启动战略规划优先项目的实施，交通运输便利化将得到进一步发展，交通运输对经济发展“助推器”功能将更加凸显。他强调，中方愿意在交通运输各领域与

东盟各国开展进一步合作，促进船舶更安全，水域更清洁，运输更便捷。他认为，通过双方的共同努力，一定能够实现中国—东盟各国共同繁荣、共同发展、共同富强、共创美好未来的远大目标。

本次会议回顾了2010年4月在马来西亚召开的第19届海事交通工作会议相关情况，完成了中国—东盟海事磋商机制谅解备忘录工作，为11月在文莱召开的中国—东盟交通运输部长会议上正式签署做好准备。来自文莱、柬埔寨、中国、印度尼西亚、马来西亚、缅甸、新加坡和越南的代表在会上做了演讲发言。

会议形成共识，中国政府积极推进《中国—东盟交通合作战略规划》，启动战略规划优先项目的实施，交通运输便利化将得到进一步发展，交通运输对经济发展"助推器"功能将更加凸显，中国和东盟在交通运输领域的合作正在不断深化。广西是中国唯一与东盟既有陆地接壤，又有海上通道的省区，是中国面向东盟的重要门户和前沿地带，是西南地区最便捷的出海大通道。中国交通运输部海事局正在积极努力，进一步推动通往广西北部湾经济区以及连接东盟的南下通道交通运输便利化。

八 第二届中国—东盟国际口腔医学交流与合作论坛

2010年10月28—31日，由中华人民共和国卫生部、广西壮族自治区人民政府主办，广西医科大学附属口腔医院承办的第二届中国—东盟国际口腔医学交流与合作论坛在广西南宁沃顿国际大酒店成功举行。

10月29日上午10时，第二届中国—东盟国际口腔医学交流与合作论坛在广西南宁沃顿国际大酒店多功能厅隆重开幕。老挝人民民主共和国卫生部部长本梅·达拉洛（H.E. Dr.Ponmek Dalaloy）、广西壮族自治区人民政府主席马飚、自治区副主席李康、自治区政协副主席李彬、中国工程院院士邱蔚六以及来自中国、文莱、柬埔寨、印度尼西亚、老挝、马来西亚、缅甸、菲律宾、新加坡、泰国、越南等东盟十国政府卫生官员、口腔医学会会长等中外嘉宾200多人出席开幕式。

开幕式由广西壮族自治区副主席李康主持。自治区主席马飚、老挝人民

第二届中国—东盟国际口腔医学交流与合作论坛上专家合影
Experts and scholars at the 2nd China-ASEAN Forum on Dentistry

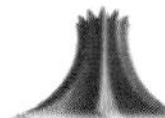

民主共和国卫生部部长本梅·达拉洛、中国卫生部疾控局副局长孔灵芝，柬埔寨王国卫生部副秘书长、柬埔寨卫生部口腔委员会主席赫姆·钦，菲律宾共和国卫生部部长助理保利恩·让·尤比尔等先后致辞。

马飚在论坛致辞时说，随着中国—东盟自由贸易区如期建成和连续7届中国—东盟博览会在南宁成功举办，广西成为中国与东盟各国的经济、政治、文化等交流合作的平台和“桥头堡”。他说，广西将继续扩大和深化与东盟国家的互利合作，为促进中国与东盟卫生事业和经济社会的发展进步作出积极贡献。

老挝人民民主共和国卫生部部长本梅·达拉洛致辞称，中国—东盟国际口腔医学论坛是一个良好的平台，老挝十分珍惜这样的机会与中国及东盟各国共同探讨口腔医学乃至更广领域中的发展战略与合作事宜。作为东盟的一个新成员国，老挝与其他国家能够从老成员国和中国在口腔卫生教育、学术交流、职业培训和物美价廉的临床医疗设备的贸易方面取得的进步与经验中获益。

中国卫生部疾控局副局长孔灵芝在论坛致辞表示，中国卫生部非常重视口腔医疗卫生事业的发展，重视与其他国家的交流与合作。希望东盟各国、海内外口腔医学界专家能以中国—东盟口腔医学交流与合作论坛为平台，积极探索和推动中国与东盟国家之间医学领域合作机制建设，不断丰富和拓展中国与东盟全面合作关系。

菲律宾共和国卫生部部长助理保利恩·让·尤比尔称，菲律宾人民当前的口腔卫生状况仍需大力改善，口腔疾病发生率高居92%，而调查显示高达77%即近三分之二的人民享受不到口腔医疗或从未去看过牙医。口腔卫生设备及物品的供应也是农村地区的一大难题。她希望随着科学技术的进步，通过各国的共同努力，通过保障适当而低廉的卫生服务来帮助许多人获得更高标准的全面健康，让各国人民都实现获得高质量口腔卫生服务的权益。

在论坛上，各国代表以“促进中国—东盟口腔领域全面合作，共享双赢”为主题，围绕“中国—东盟自贸区背景下，中国及东盟各国口腔医学发展面临机遇与挑战”、“中国及东盟各国口腔医学教育交流与合作的状况与展望”、“中国及东盟各国口腔公共健康教育的经验交流”三个议题进行探讨，就中国与东盟各国在口腔医学教育、口腔医疗信息以及各国之间的交流与合作进行陈述与展望。

在论坛开幕式前，广西壮族自治区主席马飚会见了与会的东盟各国主要嘉宾。自治区副主席李康、自治区政协副主席李彬、中国卫生部疾控局副局长孔灵芝、自治区政府秘书长王跃飞等参加会见。

中国—东盟国际口腔医学交流与合作论坛每两年举办一次，中国广西壮族自治区南宁市为论坛永久举办地。本论坛宗旨在于搭建中国与东盟各国口腔医学交流与合作的平台，大力推动与促进中国与东盟国家在口腔医学教育、口腔医疗、口腔医疗器械设备商务与贸易等方面的交流与合作，促进各国口腔医学界之间的相互了解，增进友谊，进一步推动中国与东盟面向和平与繁荣的战略合作伙伴关系。

通过举办两届中国—东盟国际口腔医学交流与合作论坛等活动，一方面推动了东盟各国医疗卫生事业的交流与合作，促进了中国—东盟口腔医学的发展；另一方面打开了中国和东盟科研、教育交流的大门，推动中国—东盟博览会向更广泛的领域和更高的层次发展。老挝国家卫生部长本梅·达拉洛对论坛的作用给予高度评价，认为这是一个崭新时代的开启，它会给东盟成员国和中国在口腔卫生教育、学术交流、职业培训和临床医疗设备贸易创造更多合作机会，取得更多成果。

本次论坛最突出的亮点是突破了政府机构交流的层面，增加了学术交流的内容。不仅就中国和东盟各国口腔医学教育交与合作的状况与展望，以及各国口腔公共健康教育的经验进行了探讨和交流，还邀请了来自美国、澳大利亚、荷兰、日本、以色列等19个国家口腔医学专家带来最前沿的口腔学术演讲，并为有学习需求的中外嘉宾开设了技术学习班，突出了论坛专业、务实、创新的特色。

九　“加强国际司法交流与合作，促进区域经济发展与繁荣”研讨会

2010年10月29—31日，由广西壮族自治区高级人民法院、广西法官协会举办的”加强国际司法交流与合作，促进区域经济发展与繁荣“研讨会在广西南宁举行。来自阿富汗、澳大利亚、柬埔寨、印度尼西亚、老挝、萨摩亚、塞舌尔、斯里兰卡、越南以及亚洲开发银行等国家和国际组织的首席大法官、大法官和其他司法官员就“加强国际司法交流与合作，促进区域经济发展与繁荣”的主题进行深入探讨，达成共识。研讨会的成功举办，有效促进了广西与亚太地区各国的交流合作和中国—东盟自由贸易区的建设发展。

广西壮族自治区党委书记、自治区人大常委会主任郭声琨在研讨会期间会见了与会外宾代表，自治区党委常委、秘书长余远辉参加会见。自治区党委书记郭声琨在会见与会外宾代表时，简要介绍了广西经济社会发展情况和发展优势。他表示，改革开放以来，广西的面貌发生了历史性变化，法制建设也取得了重大进步。在这一历史进程中，司法机关积极发挥职能作用，有力地促进了社会和谐稳定，保障了社会公平正义。希望以举办此次研讨会为契机，进一步加强司法交流与合作，共同分享司法工作有益经验，不断增进大家的友谊。

广西壮族自治区主席马飚，中国最高人民法院副院长奚晓明，广西壮族自治区党委常委、政法委书记温卡华等广西领导，阿富汗最高法院首席大法官阿布杜尔·萨拉姆·阿齐米、老挝最高人民法院院长坎米·赛亚冯、塞舌尔最高法院首席大法官弗莱德里克·艾贡达-楠德等分别出席了开幕式、闭幕式并致辞。广西壮族自治区高级人民法院院长罗殿龙主持开幕式。

广西壮族自治区人大常委会副主任吴恒，自治区政协副主席蒋培兰，自治区副主席、公安厅厅长梁胜利、自治区检察院检察长张少康，柬埔寨最高法院大法官金·萨塔维、斯里兰卡最高法院大法官苏瑞西·钦安德拉、越南

2010年10月29—30日，“加强国际司法交流与合作，促进区域经济发展与繁荣”研讨会在广西南宁举行

Seminar on Strengthening International Judicial Exchanges and Cooperation, Promoting Regional Economic Development and Prosperity held in Nanning, Guangxi on October 29-30, 2010

最高人民法院副院长蒋维亮等大法官出席研讨会。

马飚在开幕式上致辞说，进一步深化双边和多边司法交流与合作，对于增加各国司法间的认识和了解，解决各国间在经贸往来中出现的司法问题、困难，共同研究应对机遇合作与交流中的新问题等方面具有重要的作用。他表示，本次研讨会有利于与会各方相互学习借鉴司法制度方面的宝贵经验，有利于推动司法改革，更好地促进和维护司法公正。

阿富汗最高法院首席大法官阿布杜尔·萨拉姆·阿齐米在开幕式上致辞说，我衷心地感谢主办方邀请我来到中国这个美丽的国家，参加如此重要的会议。我谨代表我的祖国和我的同事，并以我自己的名义，表达对此次邀请的感谢。研讨会使我深刻了解了中国司法体系建设取得的进展和成功的经验，效果非常好。

奚晓明在开幕式上致辞说，随着世界经济全球化的发展和中国—东盟自由贸易区的建成，在加强双边或多边经贸往来的同时，积极开展区域司法合作已成为亚太国家和地区的共同需要与选择。区域经济一体化和自由贸易区的建成迫切需要各国司法界进一步加强交流合作，增进对各方法律的了解，协力应对各种挑战，为实现区域经济的共同发展提供强有力的法律支持和法制保障。他强调，要通过法官之间的交流，不断增进各国法律文化间的相互理解，增进友谊，深化合作，为实现本地区的和谐与繁荣作出积极的贡献。

老挝最高人民法院院长坎米·赛亚冯在开幕会上致辞说，这次司法交流对我们意味深长，老挝从中受益匪浅。我非常赞赏中国在加强国际司法交流

与合作，促进区域经济发展与繁荣方面发挥着重要的领军作用。我坚信今天的研讨会将进一步增强我们之间的司法合作，分享彼此的司法理念，借鉴经验，为维护东盟及亚太地区各国的经济共同发展提供强有力的司法保障。

温卡华在闭幕会上致辞说，研讨会为中国广西与东盟及亚太国家和地区提供良好的司法交流平台，也是与会各方真诚寻求合作的具体体现，给广西司法界提供了难得的学习机会，开阔了我们司法交流与合作的视野。大家这次相聚的时间虽然短暂，但是我们共同结下的友谊是长存的。我们有充分的理由相信：司法对于区域经济社会的健康发展，将发挥越来越大的促进和保障作用，本区域司法各领域的交流合作，将提升到一个新的更高的水平。

塞舌尔最高法院首席大法官弗莱德里克·艾贡达-楠德在闭幕会上致辞说，在经济全球化与区域经济一体化的背景下，法治规律和司法规律的共同性，以及不同国家司法文化的差异性等因素都决定了必须加强亚太地区的司法交流与合作。这将有利于在亚太地区内构建统一的市场经济环境；有利于区域内各国节约司法资源，降低经济发展的市场成本；有利于建立起科学的区域经济管理模式；能够为区域经济系统的良性可持续发展提供实现机制，对促进亚太地区区域经济发展具有十分重要的意义。

广西壮族自治区高级人民法院院长罗殿龙表示，举办这次研讨会，旨在增进中国与亚太国家和地区司法界的相互了解。研讨会的宗旨表达了大家对司法合作在区域经济发展中所发挥的重要作用的关注，也表达了中国与亚太国家和地区司法界扩大交流合作的强烈期盼。研讨会的举办，将进一步发展和增进广西与东盟各国及其他亚太国家和地区的友好互信，有利于进一步加强各国法官的司法交流，提高广西法院和法官的开放程度和能力。

第七章

飞歌传情 共话友谊
——第七届中国—东盟博览会文化交流活动

亚洲是人类文明的重要发祥地之一，它是多元文化的摇篮、多样文化的沃土和多彩文化的家园。在历史的长河中，亚洲东方的中国和东盟各国人民创造了各具特色、精彩纷呈的文化。

中国与东盟地缘相近，人文相通。近年来，双方在文化领域的交流合作不断推进，增进了友谊，增加了互信。

2005年，中国和东盟签署了《文化合作谅解备忘录》，标志着中国与东盟各成员国之间的文化交流与合作进入了新的发展时期。每届中国—东盟博览会的举办，为双方加强文化交流、增进友好关系提供了务实的平台。

中国—东盟博览会举办几年来，举办了一系列丰富多彩的文化交流活动。包括：博览会开幕晚会暨南宁国际民歌艺术节晚会“大地飞歌”、“风情东南亚”晚会、中国—东盟建立对话关系15周年纪念峰会文艺晚会、中国—东盟汽车拉力赛、中国—东盟青年艺术品创作大赛、中国—东盟博览会高尔夫名人赛和网球联谊活动……

第七届中国—东盟博览会文化交流活动除往届南宁国际民歌艺术节等内容外，还有中越友谊手印墙揭幕仪式、中国—东盟媒体汽车拉力赛、2010年国际田联世界半程马拉松锦标赛、中国东盟与茶文化——2010广西茗珍品尝活动等新内容，内容更加丰富，更加精彩纷呈。

Songs for Friendship

—The Cultural Exchange Events of the 7th CAEXPO

Asia is one of the most important birthplaces of human civilization, a cradle of a variety of cultures. In the long history, China and the ASEAN countries, which are all located in the east part of Asia, have created unique and distinctive cultures of their own.

With near and close geographical and cultural links, China and ASEAN have promoted the cooperation in cultural sectors, enhancing the friendship and mutual trust.

In 2005, China and ASEAN concluded the *Memorandum of Understanding on Cultural Cooperation*, marking a new stage for China and the ASEAN countries in their cooperation of cultural exchanges. The annual CAEXPO has provided a pragmatic platform for both sides in this connection.

Since the convening of the CAEXPO in 2004, a host of diverse and colorful cultural events have been held, including Flying Songs over Vast Lands — the opening gala of CAEXPO & the Nanning International Arts Festival of Folk Songs, "Charming Southeast Asia" Evening, Gala of the Commemorative Summit Marking the 15th Anniversary of the ASEAN- China Dialogue Relations, China-ASEAN Auto Rally, China-ASEAN Youth Artwork Creativity Competition, CAEXPO Golf Celebrities Invitational and tennis activities.

Apart from the traditional programs, the 7th CAEXPO has added other new contents, including the inaugural ceremony of China-Vietnam Friendship Handprint Wall, China-ASEAN Media Auto Rally, 2010 IAAF World Half Marathon Championships, China-ASEAN Tea Cultures—2010 Guangxi Precious Tea Appreciation, diversifying the event.

CHAPTER SEVEN

一 “2010·大地飞歌”南宁国际民歌艺术节暨第七届中国—东盟博览会开幕晚会系列文化活动

（一）“2010·大地飞歌”南宁国际民歌艺术节暨第七届中国—东盟博览会开幕晚会

2010年10月20日晚20：30，“2010·大地飞歌”南宁国际民歌艺术节暨第七届中国—东盟博览会开幕晚会在广西体育中心华丽唱响。

出席晚会的有郭声琨、马飚、马铁山等广西壮族自治区领导，广西壮族自治区党委常委、南宁市委书记车荣福致辞并宣布开幕，南宁市市长黄方方主持开幕仪式。东盟各国代表团，中央国家机关有关部门负责同志，各省（区、市）代表团，出席“两会一节”的部分代表、重要客商、参展商观看演出。来自世界18个国家的艺术家和偶像明星汇聚一堂，在富有广西民族特色的绚丽舞台上，为八方来客献上了一场视觉与听觉的艺术盛宴。

本台晚会由曾担任2006年、2007年“大地飞歌”晚会舞蹈总监的国家级导演姜钢任总导演，晚会以“我与民歌共成长”为主线，围绕一个主题——民歌，两个原则——传承和创新，三个兼顾——国际性、地区性、民族性，四个坚持——大腕云集、流光溢彩、漫天焰火、万众欢腾的理念，分别由“红歌永流传”、“青春备忘录”、“五洲快乐风”、“民歌中华情”四大板块组成。每个板块通过精心策划制作，让观众一起品味不同时代的民歌文化情结。“红歌永流传”以传唱多年的红色经典歌曲为主，经过全新包装呈现流行风格，与全场观众们一起感受经典历史的辉煌；“青春备忘录”上，从第一代校园歌曲开始，直到今天的校园歌曲，每一代原创歌手都登台亮相，与观众们一起回味青春的美好岁月；“五洲快乐风”展现从东盟、亚洲到世界各国的民歌风采，与时代歌潮一起成长走向世界；“民歌中华情”展现的都是中国经典的民歌，但这些歌曲经过重新编配，展现出完全不同以往的风格，让观众们与中华传统民歌一起成长、继往开来。

本台晚会首次移师广西体育中心，新的场地给大地飞歌晚会的舞台创意和表现带来了创新的机会。独特的创意舞台搭建灵感来自广西壮乡屋檐，广西的民族建筑多建在山上或坡上，屋檐林立，富有层次感。把这样的概念引入舞台，既可以看到乡村民族建筑的传统美，同时也加入时尚元素，让时尚与传统完美融合，充分体现出它的时代美。2010年的舞台巨大，占了整个体育场的三分之一，整体是一个山坡形状，基础部分就有二三十米，加上机械部分，会达到三四十米，可以说是前所未有、气势如虹。舞台上有许多可以任意移动和变换的立体组合，打破以往舞台空间只有地面的形式，而向空中延伸，从而构成明和暗、大和小、局部和整体的对比，随着场景的变化开合，呈现多层次性和变化性，让观众身临其境。

晚会大规模运用高科技手段，利用彩砖、高空威亚、数码灯等全新的舞美元素，尤其是高空威亚首次在民歌节舞台上登场采用，营造了大纵深、立体化、天马行空般的视觉空间，达到宜静宜动的舞台效果。同时，多媒体数码灯的大量运用，制造出神奇的视觉效果，给民歌节舞台营造出空透迷人的梦幻感，实现大空间的舞台造景与色彩的变换。

2010 年 10 月 20 日，“2010 · 大地飞歌”南宁国际民歌艺术节暨第七届中国—东盟博览会开幕晚会在广西南宁举行

Nanning International Arts Festival of Folk Songs & Inauguration of the 7th CAEXPO held in Nanning, Guangxi on October 20, 2010

晚会明星大腕云集，星光璀璨。晚会邀请的明星有：俄罗斯跨界歌唱家维塔斯；内地歌手孙楠、柏文、老狼、吕薇、姚贝娜；港台歌手陶喆、潘玮柏、齐豫、叶加修、王梦麟、南方二重唱；广西籍歌手严当当、陈春燕、弦子、胡夏，以及本土乐队焦点乐队、哈嘹组合等；外国演员除了东南亚各国的演员外还邀请了《蓝色多瑙河》的原唱——维也纳合唱团。

本台晚会以景引人、以情感人、以歌动人，迷幻浪漫的璀璨灯光，活力四射的舞姿，五彩缤纷的焰火，热情涌动的人群，组成流光溢彩的金秋夜景，成为又一次精彩绝伦的音乐盛宴。

（二）2010年南宁国际民歌艺术节“绿城歌台” 广场文化活动

2010年10月21—23日，南宁国际民歌艺术节“绿城歌台”广场文化活动在南宁市六县六城区的广场、社区、学校、企业等地演出，共设置14个歌台，来自5大洲19个国家19个团体将近200名外国艺术家参加了演出。歌台节目内容丰富多彩，既有特色浓郁的本土节目，也有充满异域风情的表演，深受广大群众的欢迎，观众达20多万人次。

2010年“绿城歌台”的节目注重内容和形式的多样化，并结合时代的特点着力展示世界各国的民族文化和民族风情。据统计，除了壮、汉、苗、瑶等国内几十个民族的歌舞表演外，许多国家的艺术家都带来了本民族优秀的传统歌曲和舞蹈等节目。此外，在节目上还增加了多个富有民族特色的互动节目，演员或抛出美丽的绣球，或抛出寓意深深的“渡河公”，传达美好的愿望，场面热烈、欢庆、祥和。

本次活动注重传承民族优秀文化遗产，彰显民族文化魅力。在“绿城

绿城歌台
Mini-shows in downtown Nanning

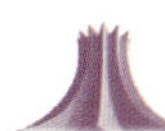

歌台”的舞台上，出现了南宁市宾阳县的游彩架、马山县的会鼓舞蹈、武鸣的《三月三》，江南区的《傩舞》，邕宁区的《嘹罗山歌》等非物质文化遗产，彰显了其深厚的文化内涵和民族魅力，对弘扬和传承优秀的非物质文化遗产也起到了积极的促进作用。

（三）“美在广西”广西青年歌手演唱会

2010年10月21日晚，由南宁国际民歌艺术节组委会、广西文化厅共同主办，南宁市文化新闻出版局承办的“美在广西”广西青年歌手演唱会，作为2010南宁国际民歌艺术节活动内容之一，在南宁人民会堂举行。

“美在广西”广西青年歌手演唱会上歌手表演三重唱

Trio performed at the Guangxi Youth Singers' Concert “Beauty in Guangxi”

晚会共有14首曲目，采用大乐队现场伴奏的方式，选取不同风格的曲目，以民族、美声、通俗、原生态等不同唱法，以独唱、二重唱、三重唱、小组唱、合唱等形式表现。来自自治区歌舞团、广西艺术学院、南宁市艺术剧院的青年歌唱演员集体亮相，陈春燕、廖鸿飞、危瑛、袁泉、何梦苓、舒春秀等广西乐坛新秀为观众带来了一场高雅愉悦的视听盛宴。

二　中越友谊手印墙揭幕仪式

2010年10月20日上午，雄伟的广西体育中心彩旗招展，鼓乐喧天，中越友谊手印墙揭幕仪式隆重举行。越南外交部副部长裴青山，广西壮族自治区党委副书记陈际瓦，自治区党委常委、南宁市委书记车荣福，越南驻广西总领事阮英勇和广西壮族自治区外事办公室、共青团广西区委等区直部门及南宁市领导共20多人出席活动。陈际瓦、裴青山共同为中越友谊手印墙揭幕，车荣福主持揭幕仪式，来自中国和越南的500多名青年见证了这一重要时刻。

在揭幕仪式上，广西壮族自治区党委副书记陈际瓦发表了讲话。陈际瓦说，8月在广西举行的中越青年大联欢是两国历史上第一次大规模的青年交流活动，意义重大、影响深远，为发展中越两国全面战略合作伙伴关系和两国世代友好事业书写了精彩华丽的新篇章。中越青年手印墙手印收集是中越青年大联欢活动的项目之一，旨在为中越青年大联欢活动留下永久纪念，以此激励两国青少年铭记使命，永做两国世代友好接班人。

2010年10月20日，中越友谊手印墙揭幕仪式在广西南宁举行

The inaugural ceremony of China-Vietnam Friendship Handprint Wall held in Nanning, Guangxi on October 20, 2010

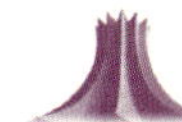

陈际瓦强调，青年是中越友好关系的未来。我们将充分利用广西在对越交往中独特地缘优势、人文优势，利用好中越友谊手印墙、中越青年友谊林等中越青年大联欢活动成果，充分发挥青年朝气蓬勃的特点和桥梁纽带作用，努力为增进两国人民的友谊和感情，实现“中越两国人民永做好邻居、好朋友、好同志、好伙伴”的总目标作出积极贡献。

中越友谊手印墙是2010年8月中越青年大联欢活动期间，由中共中央政治局委员、中央书记处书记、中组部部长李源潮和越共中央政治局委员、中央书记处书记、中组部部长胡德越亲自启动建设的，是中越两国青年交往史上具有里程碑意义的中越青年大联欢活动的重要项目之一。这个以青春和友谊为主题的手印墙，共收集了包括中越两国领导人、中越各界青年代表在内的5600多个手印，体现了纪念性、代表性和永久性统一。中越友谊手印墙的建成，是中越两国领导人和青年的珍贵记忆，是中越两国心手相牵、携手并进、永续辉煌的历史印记，对于进一步坚定两国青年继承中越传统友谊的信心和决心，激励两国青少年铭记使命，推动中越友好世代相传有着重要意义。

三　2010南宁·东南亚国际旅游美食节

2010年10月16—24日，由广西壮族自治区商务厅、南宁市人民政府主办，南宁市商务局、旅游局、江南区政府、南宁餐饮行业协会、南宁市礼之本广告策划有限公司共同承办的2010南宁·东南亚国际旅游美食节在南宁市隆重举行。南宁市领导黄方方、谢寿堂、胡建华、吕洁、李志勇、袁曼虹以及自治区有关部门领导出席了开幕式。中国烹饪协会副会长刘秀军在开幕式上宣读了中国烹饪协会给2010南宁·东南亚国际旅游美食节的贺信，南宁市市长黄方方致辞并宣布2010南宁·东南亚国际旅游美食节开幕。

2010南宁·东南亚国际旅游美食节荟萃中外美食，活动精彩纷呈。美食节设中国—东南亚美食、中华美食、本土民族特色美食等三大展区，共201个展位，汇聚了100多种不同风味的美食与小吃。本市参展的餐饮名店30多家，国外和市外参展商参展比例超过30%。美食节主要活动内容有：本土美食“马蹄糕王”品尝会、2010邕城名菜名点小吃评选活动、2010邕城传统包粽子百人趣味竞技赛、南宁市首届涂鸦大赛、邕州老街街舞大赛、壮乡及东南亚传统民族文化展演、百姓小舞台、广西旅游节庆文化推荐展、邕州老街画廊文化展等。

美食节开幕式当天，11米长、6米宽的双色“马蹄糕王”引爆美食盛宴。这块堪称世界上最大的双色马蹄糕寓意着东盟10国与中国的友谊长长久久，同时也预祝2010南宁·东南亚国际旅游美食节举办成功；“坐着轻轨看南宁”现场绘画秀等众多文化节目共同为美食节添光增彩。美食节期间，数十场活动高潮迭起：美食才艺大比拼让数千观众亲眼见证了数十件名菜、名点、名小吃的诞生过程；面塑、糖艺、冰雕、菜肴围边设计等首次在美食节上亮相；百人包粽子大赛吸引了区内120名选手参与；东南亚风情演出，群众文艺演出、江南区百姓小舞台文艺演出等，让旅游美食节融入深厚的文化底蕴和丰富的本土民族风情；美食节摄影比赛吸引了众多摄影爱好者；首届

2010南宁·东南亚国际旅游美食节上厨师展示厨技

Chefs displayed their cooking skills at the 2010 Nanning-Southeast Asia International Tourism and Food Festival

街舞大赛则向观众呈献无限活力与激情……精彩的节庆，时尚的趣味活动，吸引了大量游客前来并参与其中。

本届美食节呈现出活动内容最丰富、形式最多样、规格档次更高、本土特色更浓、国际性更强、文化娱乐互动元素更多等特点，让广大市民在充分品味天下美食的同时，进一步感受邕城民俗，领略地方文化风采。据统计，美食节举办期间，共迎来参展人数36万人次，比上届增长33.3%，总销售额超过1800万元，吸引了各国客商现场参观。

四　第七届中国—东盟国际高尔夫名人邀请赛、国际精英邀请赛及“网球之友”联谊活动

2010年10月21日，第七届中国—东盟国际高尔夫名人邀请赛在南宁青秀山国际高尔夫球会举行。随着老挝副总理阿桑·劳里开出的第一个彩球，广西壮族自治区党委常委、自治区副主席陈武宣布本次比赛正式开杆。

柬埔寨国务兼商业大臣占蒲拉西，老挝外交部副部长本格·桑宋萨，柬埔寨首相府部长、财经部国务秘书乌拉本，老挝国家旅游局副局长苏卡申·普提山，中国全国人大常委会委员、广西法学会会长彭祖意，中国驻泰国原大使张九桓等参加本次邀请赛。中国—东盟博览会秘书处秘书长郑军健在开杆仪式上致辞，仪式由中国—东盟博览会秘书处副秘书长李文杰主持。

10月22日，第七届中国—东盟高尔夫国际精英邀请赛在南宁嘉和城高尔夫球会开幕。中国—东盟博览会秘书处副秘书长李文杰、广西投资集团董事长管跃庆、广西投资集团总经理冯柳江、中国—东盟博览会合作伙伴代表以及部分业余、半职业高尔夫球选手等80人参加此次邀请赛。

2010年10月21日，第七届中国—东盟国际高尔夫名人邀请赛在广西南宁举行

The 7th CAEXPO Golf Masters' Invitational held in Nanning, Guangxi on October 21, 2010

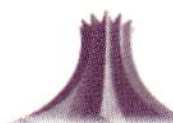

本届精英赛首次尝试以职业赛事规则进行比赛，在开球前由中国高尔夫球协会国家二级裁判宣读了赛事规则。经过高水平的较量，最终优秀选手以低于标准杆3杆的优异成绩获得了总杆冠军，其他选手也取得了优秀的成绩。

10月21日下午，第七届中国—东盟博览会“网球之友”联谊活动在广西体育局江南训练基地新网球馆举行开球仪式。广西壮族自治区党委原副书记、广西网球协会名誉主席丁廷模出席仪式并宣布开球，中国—东盟博览会秘书处副秘书长李文杰在仪式上致辞。

本届博览会“网球之友”联谊活动由广西体育局、广西国际博览事务局共同举办。

每届中国—东盟博览会期间举办的“网球之友”健身联谊活动，以球为媒，以球会友，为各国参展参会人员提供了良好的健身、休闲、会友方式和场所，成为博览会期间的重要体育交流活动。

五　2010中国—东盟国际汽车拉力赛暨中国—东盟媒体汽车拉力赛

2010年10月1日，由国家体育总局、广西壮族自治区人民政府、东盟秘书处共同主办，中国汽车运动联合会与广西壮族自治区体育局共同承办的2010中国—东盟国际汽车拉力赛暨中国—东盟媒体汽车拉力赛从广西南宁发车。广西壮族自治区党委常委、宣传部长沈北海出席发车仪式，自治区副主席李康、中国国家体育总局汽车摩托车管理中心副主任詹郭君、东盟秘书处市场一体化司司长苏巴什·保斯·皮莱分别在仪式上致辞。

由27辆车、129名来自中国、越南、泰国、老挝、柬埔寨、马来西亚、新加坡的参赛车手、国内外媒体记者和工作人员组成的车队，经过17天6000公里的行程，途经越南、老挝、柬埔寨、泰国4个国家，于10月19日从凭祥友谊关入关顺利回国，安全、圆满地完成了拉力赛的各项任务。

本届拉力赛在传承往届赛事“共融、共享、共创”的宗旨，以实现“和谐之旅、友谊之旅、合作之旅、欢乐之旅”为目标的基础上，通过精心策划，积极开创办赛新思路，在以下几个方面进行了创新。

1. 新主题。本届拉力赛新定主题为“激情拉力，集结友谊”，寓意拉力赛是一项以汽车运动为载体，促进中国和东盟各国人民之间友谊的体育赛事。围绕着“共融、共享、共创”的宗旨，拉力赛始终坚持为中国—东盟博览会、中国—东盟自由贸易区、泛北部湾经济合作服务，承担促进广西经济建设，增进中国与东盟各领域友好交流与合作的历史使命。经过前三届赛事的实践和成果积累，赛事已然成为中国与东盟地区具有广泛影响力的以汽车运动为平台的体育外交活动。

2. 新赛事。为响应东盟秘书处举办中国—东盟媒体汽车拉力赛的提议，组委会决定将首届中国—东盟媒体汽车拉力赛与2010中国—东盟国际汽车拉力赛合并举办。本次中国—东盟媒体汽车拉力赛邀请国内外媒体12家，

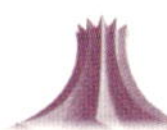

2010年10月1日，2010中国—东盟国际汽车拉力赛暨中国—东盟媒体汽车拉力赛发车仪式在广西南宁举行

The launching ceremony of the 2010 China-ASEAN International Auto Rally & the China-ASEAN Media Auto Rally held in Nanning, Guangxi on October 1, 2010

共计记者21名参赛。其中，国外媒体有越南《工商报》、泰国《东盟经济时报》、老挝《万象时报》、柬埔寨《华商日报》等。

3. 新赛制。为增加赛事的专业性与趣味性，本届拉力赛创新赛制，设置了四段集结赛、越南场地趣味赛以及泰国卡丁车场地赛。

4. 新活动。2010年4月下旬，2010中国—东盟国际汽车拉力赛在北京举行新闻发布会。国家体育总局、广西壮族自治区人民政府领导出席了发布会。发布会得到了中央电视台、广西电视台等区内外主流媒体的广泛报道。

2010年8—9月，组委会举办了2010中国—东盟国际汽车拉力赛暨中国—东盟媒体汽车拉力赛形象大使选拔赛。经过激烈的角逐，冠、亚军作为本届赛事的形象大使随队出赛并参与各项交流活动，给拉力赛增添了新亮点。

5. 新高度。2010年是中国与越南建交60周年、中国与泰国建交35周年，拉力赛首次提出主题国概念，设置泰国和越南为赛事的主题国，在两国举行了拜会、联谊酒会、参观著名文化历史景点等内容丰富的交流及赛事活动。

车队所到之处，都受到热烈欢迎。在泰国曼谷，车队指挥部拜会了我国驻泰国大使馆，并与泰中友好协会、泰国广西总会共同举办了联谊酒会，泰国前总理、泰中友好协会会长功·塔帕朗西先生出席酒会并发表讲话。本次酒会因此成为拉力赛历史上级别最高的大型外事活动。此外，出席联谊酒会的还有来自泰国国家体育局局长卡诺帕、泰国国家旅游协会副主席素提逢、中国驻泰国大使馆文化参赞秦裕森、泰国皇家汽车协会秘书长马鲁萨特、泰国广西总会会长封祖超等。

在素可泰和芭堤雅，车队受到当地政府的热烈欢迎，省长和市长在酒店迎接车队并接见车队代表，特别是在素可泰，泰方破例安排车队在著名的素可泰皇朝历史公园（平时只作为迎接国宾级领导的活动场所）缓行，并把发车仪式安排在公园内，意义尤为重大。

此外，中国驻外使馆官员及途经各国政府相关部门领导人均应邀出席拉力赛境外活动，在活动致辞和采访中对拉力赛4年来在文化、体育、经济和对外交往方面取得的丰硕成果予以充分肯定，希望赛事今后越办越好。

2010中国—东盟国际汽车拉力赛在各方面成果都超过了预期，铺就了一条中国与东盟以及东盟各国之间睦邻友好、合作共赢的通畅渠道，为广西树立良好国际形象起到积极作用。拉力赛现已成为国家体育总局、中国汽车运动联合会最有影响力的赛事之一。在第五届中国赛车风云榜揭晓会上，中国—东盟国际汽车拉力赛作为国内目前唯一形成传统的跨境赛事，凭借其涵盖竞赛、旅游、汽车文化交流、经贸活动等丰富多彩赛事内容，荣获大会颁发的“最具成长价值赛事”大奖。

六　2010年国际田联世界半程马拉松锦标赛

2010年国际田联世界半程马拉松锦标赛于2010年10月16日上午在南宁鸣枪开赛，这是此项世界级路跑赛事首次在中国举办。

国际田联主席拉明·迪亚克，中国国家体育总局副局长、中国田径协会主席段世杰，广西壮族自治区党委常委、南宁市委书记车荣福分别在开赛仪式上致辞。

比赛分为男、女半程马拉松，男、女10公里以及4公里健康跑，来自世界33个国家和地区的133名国际田联注册运动员报名参赛。埃塞俄比亚、肯尼亚、美国、日本等均派出强大阵容，中国队派出高来源、朱晓琳等六名选手参赛。比赛全程21.0975公里，选取了具有南宁市标志性景点的路段，充分展示南宁市的发展巨变和绿城风采。

经过1个多小时的激烈角逐，肯尼亚的选手基普拉加特第一个冲过终点，以1小时8分24秒的成绩，摘取女子组冠军。肯尼亚的选手科普洛普以1小时07秒的成绩获男子组冠军。

第五届南宁国际半程马拉松比赛暨28届南宁解放日长跑活动也于同日举行。比赛吸引了中国国内各省区市和日本、加拿大、芬兰、美国等国家的15000多位专业队员及长跑爱好者参加。

七　中国东盟与茶文化——2010广西茗珍品尝活动

2010年10月20日，由广西壮族自治区侨务办公室和广西海外交流协会主办、广西东盟经济与文化研究中心协办的“中国东盟与茶文化——2010广西茗珍品尝活动”在南宁举行。来自美国、英国、加拿大、日本、新加坡、马来西亚、泰国、菲律宾、文莱、印度尼西亚、柬埔寨、香港、澳门等20多个国家和地区的海外重点侨商代表、国内侨商会代表以及广西企业代表150多人聚集邕城，一起研究探讨广西茶业产业市场的现状和发展趋势，共谋广西茶叶新商机，同享八桂茗香盛宴。

活动以“细品八桂茗香、话语国际合作”为主题，旨在充分运用中国—东盟博览会平台和中国—东盟自由贸易区建成的优惠政策，发挥侨务资源优势，通过国内外媒体的宣传，让世界了解广西的茶业产业情况和传播历史悠久的中国茶文化，促进经贸和文化合作与交流，推动广西茶叶产业的健康发展。

广西壮族自治区侨务办公室主任、广西海外交流协会会长冯祖华，广西壮族自治区侨务办公室副主任钟志英、林容蓉，广西壮族自治区侨务办公室

2010 年 10 月 20 日，中国东盟与茶文化——2010 广西茗珍品尝活动在广西南宁举行

China-ASEAN Tea Cultures & 2010 Guangxi Precious Tea Appreciation held in Nanning, Guangxi on October 20, 2010

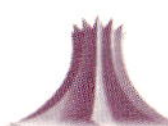

纪检组长班美月、副巡视员陈宁出席活动。此次活动由广西壮族自治区侨务办公室副主任林容蓉主持。

广西壮族自治区侨务办公室主任、广西海外交流协会会长冯祖华表示，中国—东盟自由贸易区正式建成后，广西市场无疑成为东盟国家拓展国内市场的最主要目标。自治区侨办作为海外华商的娘家，将帮助他们整合广西的有利资源，牵线搭桥，为他们寻找合适的商机，实现互惠互利，合作共赢。这次活动就是个很好的例子，希望借此机会，将本次活动做成品牌，做成名片，推向世界。

主办单位特别邀请了马来西亚茶商公会、吉隆坡茶艺协会以及广西著名的茶叶专家、广西绿色食品办公室主任黄正恩等国内外茶叶专家现场讲演。黄正恩对广西茶叶生产的历史、茶叶的加工工艺、茶叶品位、口味特点、功能等广西茶业进化史和发展趋势作了精彩的讲解，让各位与会人士对广西茶叶产业有了全新的认识。广西梧州、柳州、百色、贵港、钦州等市县的广西茶叶知名厂商代表推介各自的知名品牌，并开展独具中国特色的茶文化、茶艺表演，深受与会客商欢迎。会后，主办单位组织商家代表、侨商、海内外媒体记者参观中国—东盟博览会农业展茶叶展区进行互动交流和采访报道等丰富多彩的活动。

海外华商代表纷纷表示，通过这次活动，第一次了解到家乡原来还有这么好的茶叶，却一直“养在深闺人未识”，希望以后多举办这样的活动，把广西的茶叶和其他物产好好向海外宣传推介。与会的各位华商代表都对广西茶叶产业的发展寄予厚望，期望加强与广西茶商的合作交流，共谋发展，实现互利共赢。

第八章

全心服务 专业细致
——第七届中国—东盟博览会服务支撑体系

从国际国内会展业发展的规律看，一个展会的整体效果如何，要看统筹协调机制是否高效，服务支撑体系是否完善。这也是展会健康持续发展的重要保障。

第七届中国—东盟博览会统筹协调工作机制更加高效、应变能力进一步提高。南宁市加大基础设施建设力度，积极推进人居环境建设，营造服务第七届中国—东盟博览会优良环境。

本届博览会展览现场管理更加科学，为客商营造良好展览洽谈环境。海关、检验检疫、公安边防部门采取便利化措施，展品和人员通关快捷便利高效。接待服务创新工作方法，加强管理，注重细节，既节约办会又提高了服务质量。证件工作安全有序，流程顺畅，便捷高效。会期继续开通南宁往返东盟10国首都或主要城市的临时直航包机，服务更加个性化，上座率进一步提高。食品安全监管和医疗卫生服务更加细致，保障有力。志愿者服务在信息化管理、培训、激励机制、整体形象、规范管理等方面创新，服务更加周到。新闻宣传和营销推介力度更大，亮点纷呈，影响扩大。创新安全保卫模式，实现科技安保、人文安保、规范安保。

第七届中国—东盟博览会指挥体系和服务支撑体系更加成熟，更加完善，各项工作更加常态化、机制化，为中国—东盟博览会长效发展奠定了更坚实的基础。

Considerate and Professional Services

—The 7th CAEXPO Supporting Service System

Judging from the past experience and development laws of domestic and international convention and exhibition industry, the overall quality of an exhibition and convention is determined by the efficiency of coordination system and quality of supporting services, which will play an important role in sustaining the industry.

The command and coordination mechanism of the 7th CAEXPO is more efficient and more competent in response abilities. The host city Nanning made efforts in improving the infrastructure, and living environment, creating a good atmosphere for the event.

The 7th CAEXPO saw more scientific on-site administration and management, and better environment for exhibition and business talks. Competent government agencies such as Customs, quarantine and quality inspection, public security, border control all adopted measures to facilitate the Customs clearance and formalities for exhibits and visitors. New methods were used in reception, management was reinforced and details were heeded to reduce costs and ensure high quality of the services.

The pass-issuing was carried out in a safe and orderly way, providing a smooth and efficient service for event participants. Direct chartered flights between Nanning and major ASEAN cities were arranged to provide more business-friendly services, achieving a high seating rates. More efforts were made in food safety and medical & health services to ensure a more forceful and considerate guarantee system. Innovative measures were adopted in the management of volunteers, including their e-managing, training, encouraging policies and overall image, to provide more considerate services. The efforts of publicity and marketing were reinforced to well sharpen the brand of the CAEXPO. Innovation was also made in security measures to achieve scientific, cultural, human-oriented and regulated security services.

The 7th CAEXPO saw a more mature and sophisticated commanding and support system. With all works and functions more systemized and regularized, it has provided a more solid foundation for the long term development of the CAEXPO.

CHAPTER EIGHT

一 统筹协调

第七届中国—东盟博览会、中国—东盟商务与投资峰会是中国—东盟自由贸易区如期全面建成后举办的新一届盛会，对统筹协调的要求更高。国务院办公厅、商务部、外交部、中国贸促会等有关部委领导加强对统筹协调工作的领导，靠前指挥，派出工作组到南宁指导工作。中国—东盟博览会、中国—东盟商务与投资峰会广西指挥中心加强对会期活动的组织协调，确保了领导人活动安排、主题国活动、开幕式、中外领导人巡视展馆等重要活动的安全、有序、顺畅。

（一）统筹协调工作机制更加完善，应变能力进一步提高

经过几年的探索，中国—东盟博览会、中国—东盟商务与投资峰会广西指挥中心建立了比较成熟的工作机制和模式，在筹备时间短、各项工作任务重且调整变化大的情况下，工作人员应对得法，处置得当，应急反应快。

为做好会期活动统筹工作，指挥中心统筹协调部提前编制活动总表，做了多套方案。即使在会期活动变化大、变化快的情况下，也能确保会期各项活动的顺利进行。在实际操作过程中，整个活动统筹工作强度大，协调面广，指挥中心统筹协调部精心策划会期重要活动安排，并协调相关部门做好相关工作。活动总表在短短3天内完成了修改、报审及印刷，并提前两天发放到指挥中心各部门，高效率高质量的工作，确保各项活动的顺畅。此外，指挥中心各工作部应变能力进一步提高，各类工作方案均能按职责分工与相关安保、宣传、接待等部门顺利沟通对接，说明指挥中心工作机制运行有效，办会的常规套路已运转成熟。

（二）文秘工作更加规范，联合值班职责更加明晰

本届中国—东盟博览会、商务与投资峰会广西指挥中心的文件、会议更加集中，在2010年10月5—18日短短13天之内形成高峰。文秘工作高速运

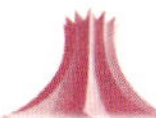

转，短期内高效率地处理了1660多份文件，文件收到即办即送，做到流转实时记录，去向清晰；文件印发基本实现当日签发当日印送；会议通知做到快速、准确、不误事；会务工作细致周到、高效有序，会议室安排衔接顺畅；会议记录纪要准确及时，基本做到当天会议当天完成纪要，确保了指挥中心领导指令快速传达；档案管理、资料收集归档工作有序进行，各项工作秩序良好。

联合值班室与现场管理职能的分工更加科学，联合值班室更好地兼顾到会展中心现场，又集中精力做好指挥中心工作，实现了会期内指挥中心文电流转、拟稿会稿、文件印制、用印、会议通知和服务一切顺畅。

（三）信息简报更加高效，促进了各部门间协调配合

自2010年9月指挥中心集中办公以来，共编制《指挥中心工作快报》8期，21000多字，及时刊登了郭声琨、马飚、陈武等广西壮族自治区领导对办好博览会的重要指示，通报了各工作部工作信息，起到了信息的上通下达的作用。《工作手册》进行全面改版，使其更符合集中办公工作需要和实际，并在10月之前发放完毕，节省了筹备工作时间，提高了工作效率；《贵宾手册》按时按质编印完成并及时发放。指挥中心还发送各类工作短信75条，合计9万多次，比上届增长50%。

此外，在法律事务、机动车辆管理、办公设备管理、供水、供电、电话、网络、卫生、食堂等各项工作正常有序，服务质量进一步提高。

第七届中国—东盟博览会、商务与投资峰会广西指挥中心多次召开会议，统筹部署“两会”事宜

The Guangxi Commanding Center of the 7th CAEXPO and the CABIS held theme meetings to make arrangements for the two events

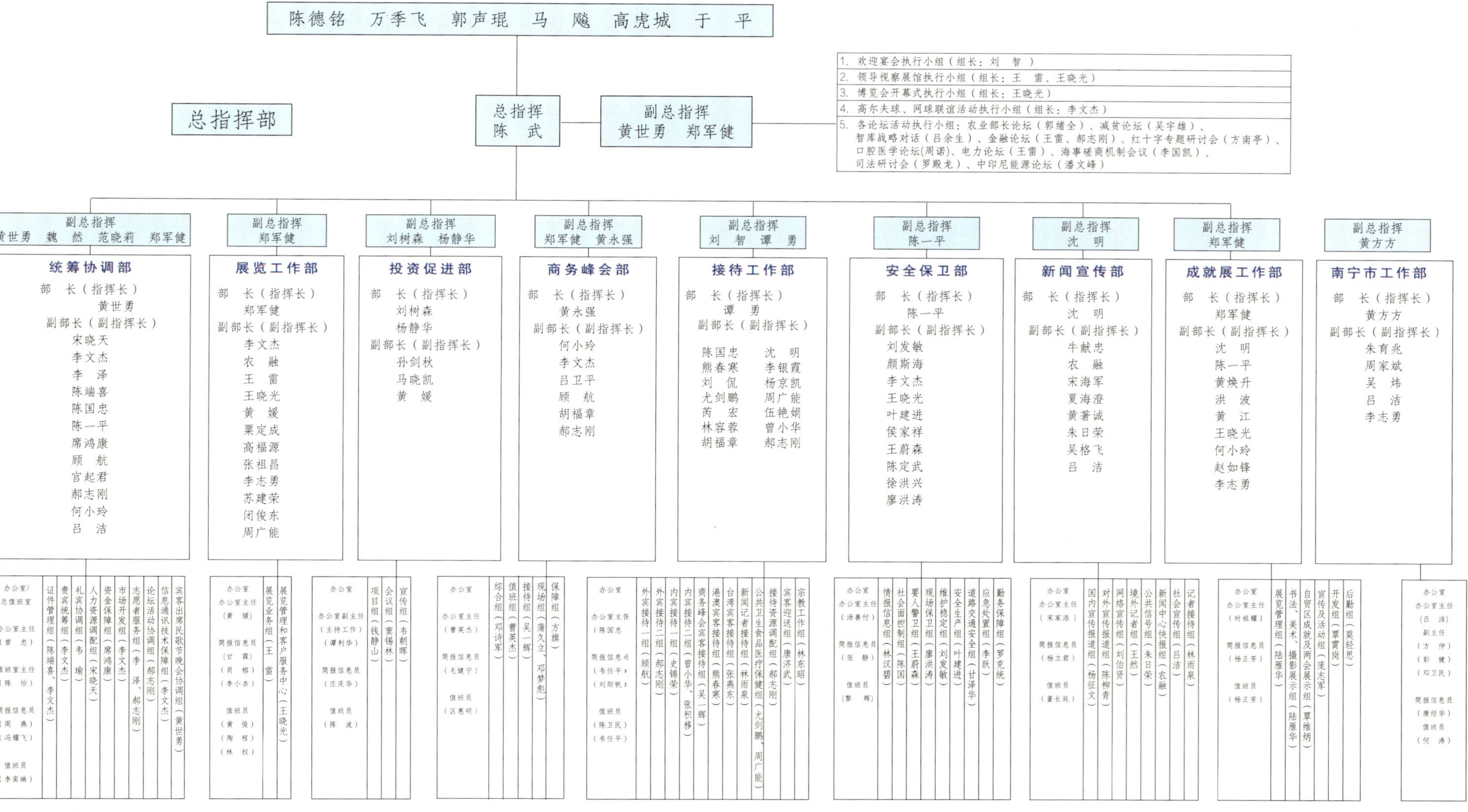
第七届中国—东盟博览会、中国—东盟商务与投资峰会广西指挥中心
陈德铭　万季飞　郭声琨　马　飚　高虎城　于　平
总指挥部
总指挥
陈　武
副总指挥
黄世勇　郑军健
1. 欢迎宴会执行小组（组长：刘　智）
2. 领导视察展馆执行小组（组长：王　雷、王晓光）
3. 博览会开幕式执行小组（组长：王晓光）
4. 高尔夫球、网球联谊活动执行小组（组长：李文杰）
5. 各论坛活动执行小组：农业部长论坛（郭绪全）、减贫论坛（吴宇雄）、智库战略对话（吕余生）、金融论坛（王雷、郝志刚）、红十字专题研讨会（方南亭）、口腔医学论坛(周诺)、电力论坛（王雷）、海事磋商机制会议（李国凯）、司法研讨会（罗殿龙）、中印尼能源论坛（潘文峰）
副总指挥
黄世勇　魏　然　范晓莉　郑军健
统筹协调部
部　长（指挥长）
黄世勇
副部长（副指挥长）
宋晓天
李文杰
李　泽
陈端喜
陈国忠
陈一平
席鸿康
顾　航
宫起君
郝志刚
何小玲
吕　洁
证件管理组（陈端喜、李文杰）
贵宾统筹组（李文杰）
礼宾协调组（韦　瑜）
人力资源调配组（宋晓天）
资金保障组（席鸿康）
市场开发组（李文杰）
志愿者服务组（李　泽、郝志刚）
论坛活动协调组（郝志刚）
信息通讯技术保障组（李文杰）
宾客出席民歌节晚会协调组（黄世勇）
副总指挥
郑军健
展览工作部
部　长（指挥长）
郑军健
副部长（副指挥长）
李文杰
农　融
王　雷
王晓光
黄　媛
粟定成
高福源
张祖昌
李志勇
苏建荣
闭俊东
周广能
展览业务组（王　雷）
展览管理和客户服务中心（王晓光）
副总指挥
刘树森　杨静华
投资促进部
部　长（指挥长）
刘树森
杨静华
副部长（副指挥长）
孙剑秋
马晓凯
黄　媛
项目组（钱静山）
会议组（覃锡林）
宣传组（韦朝晖）
副总指挥
郑军健　黄永强
商务峰会部
部　长（指挥长）
黄永强
副部长（副指挥长）
何小玲
李文杰
吕卫平
顾　航
胡福章
郝志刚
综合组（邓诗军）
值班组（曹英杰）
接待组（吴一辉）
现场组（蒲久立、邓梦彪）
保障组（方旗）
副总指挥
刘　智　谭　勇
接待工作部
部　长（指挥长）
谭　勇
副部长（副指挥长）
陈国忠　沈　明
熊春寒　李银霞
刘　侃　杨京凯
尤剑鹏　周广能
芮　宏　伍艳娟
林容蓉　曾小华
胡福章　郝志刚
外宾接待一组（顾航）
外宾接待二组（郝志刚）
内宾接待一组（史锦荣）
内宾接待二组（曾小华、张积移）
商务峰会宾客接待组（吴一辉）
港澳宾客接待组（熊春寒）
台湾宾客接待组（张燕东）
新闻记者接待组（林雨泉）
公共卫生食品医疗保健组（尤剑鹏、周广能）
接待资源调配组（郝志刚）
宾客迎送组（唐济武）
宗教工作组（林东昭）
副总指挥
陈一平
安全保卫部
部　长（指挥长）
陈一平
副部长（副指挥长）
刘发敏
颜斯海
李文杰
王晓光
叶建进
侯家祥
王蔚森
陈定武
徐洪兴
廖洪涛
情报信息组（林汉碧）
社会面控制组（陈国）
要人警卫组（王蔚森）
现场保卫组（廖洪涛）
维护稳定组（刘发敏）
安全生产组（叶建进）
道路交通安全组（甘泽华）
应急处置组（李跃）
勤务保障组（罗克统）
副总指挥
沈　明
新闻宣传部
部　长（指挥长）
沈　明
副部长（副指挥长）
牛献忠
农　融
宋海军
夏海澄
黄著诚
朱日荣
吴格飞
吕　洁
国内宣传报道组（杨征文）
对外宣传报道组（陈柳青）
网络宣传组（刘伯贤）
境外记者组（王然）
公共信号组（朱日荣）
新闻中心快报组（农融）
社会宣传组（吕洁）
记者接待组（林雨泉）
副总指挥
郑军健
成就展工作部
部　长（指挥长）
郑军健
副部长（副指挥长）
沈　明
陈一平
黄焕升
洪　波
黄　江
王晓光
何小玲
赵如锋
李志勇
展览管理组（陆雁华）
书法、美术、摄影展示组（陆雁华）
自贸区成就及两会展示组（覃维炳）
宣传及活动组（庞志军）
开发组（覃青岗）
后勤组（黄轻思）
副总指挥
黄方方
南宁市工作部
部　长（指挥长）
黄方方
副部长（副指挥长）
朱育兆
周家斌
吴　炜
吕　洁
李志勇

二 基础设施

2010年，南宁市委、市政府积极围绕开展“四个主题年”和“五场攻坚战”的中心工作，做好基础设施建设工作，全力服务第七届中国—东盟博览会。

（一）紧扣科学发展、加快发展、率先发展、和谐发展主题，积极推进人居环境建设取得新发展，营造服务第七届中国—东盟博览会优良环境

“中国绿城”建设成果不断深化。南宁市进一步改善和提高城市人居环境，“中国绿城”建设成果不断深化，较为成功的做法和创新点如下：尊重自然、保护自然，顺应固有规律，利用诸多自然生态环境要素来持久改善人居环境的“中国水城”建设；按市级、城区级、街道（乡镇）级和小区（村庄）级四级配置的公共服务设施梯次体系；高度重视住房保障工作；大力开展城市交通出行环境建设；不断深化“林在城中、城在林中”的生态环境建设；较高的可再生能源使用比例；注重城市水环境治理，加强污水处理设施和配套管网建设，实现县县建有污水处理厂；强化污水处理厂运行管理，充分发挥污水处理厂的处理能力等。

城市无障碍建设取得突破性进展。南宁市积极推进城市道路、广场、园林和公共建筑、住宅小区无障碍设施建设和改造完善工作。其中，市政道路、城市广场、过街音响装置、公园绿地、市直管中小学校、市民政直属福利机构等6个无障碍设施改造完善工程列入2010年第二批城建计划，各项改造完善工程已基本完成。

城镇污水、生活垃圾处理设施建设项目稳步推进，县城污水、生活垃圾集中处理实现零的突破。截至2010年12月31日，南宁市污水垃圾项目共完成投资7.52亿元。江南污水处理厂二期工程和埌东污水处理厂三期工程已于2010年12月30日通水试运行，市区污水处理能力从44万立方米/天提高到78万立方米/天，市区污水集中处理率达到85%以上，顺利实现科学发展三年计

南宁市容
Cityscape of Nanning, the host city of the 7th CAEXPO

划目标；市辖六县污水处理厂已全部建成，实现污水集中处理。马山县生活垃圾卫生填埋场已建成并已填埋垃圾，横县、上林县、隆安县生活垃圾卫生填埋场库区及主要配套工程已基本建成，具备可填埋垃圾的条件。除上林县外，其余5县全部实现生活垃圾无害化处理。

建筑节能领域取得新进展。申报南宁市可再生能源建筑应用城市示范的项目（预计2011年竣工）达到26项，应用面积250万平方米，可再生能源建筑应用取得了良好的示范效果。

（二）深入开展“项目建设年”、“服务企业年”活动，积极配合推进“五场攻坚战”重点项目建设，全力服务第七届中国—东盟博览会

城建项目建设继续加强。分三批实施城建计划，共14类，计划总投资1185.66亿元，2010年计划总投资331.38亿元，实际完成投资256.08亿元，占年度计划总投资的77.28%。

重点项目稳步推进。五象新区攻坚战安排城建计划项目60项，年度计划总投资61.03亿元，实际完成总投资49.99亿元，完成率81.91%。东盟商务区及凤岭新区安排城建计划项目22项，年度计划总投资9.84亿元，实际完成总投资6.46亿元，完成率65.65%。城市交通路网项目安排城建计划144项，年度计划总投资60.16亿元，实际完成总投资44.79亿元，完成率74.45%。“中国水城”建设项目安排水环境及内涝整治23项，年度计划总投资23.35亿元，实际完成总投资26.36亿元，完成率112.93%。交通基础设施攻坚战（城市交通基础设施类）有16个项目，各项目计划总投资72.73亿元。2010年计划投资29.15亿元，本年度累计完成投资25.62亿元，占年度计划总投资的87.86%；各项目累计完成投资38.51亿元，占计划总投资的52.95%。

公用行业建设、运行情况良好。供、排水固定资产完成投资7.41亿元，同比增长64.56%。其中污水完成固定资产投资6.39亿元，同比上升146.99%。完成售水量28673万立方米（不含南湖补水），自来水出厂水质综合合格率达到100%；自来水管网水质综合合格率达到99.97%；自来水管网压力合格率达到100%；预计完成污水处理量1.45亿立方米，同比增长7.5%。全年完成燃气项目投资7000万元；敷设市政干管29.03公里，历年累计建设374.92公里。

（三）南宁·中国—东盟国际商务区各国商务联络部（办事处）办公楼移交使用

为了打造一个具有东南亚风情和特色的、永不落幕的中国—东盟博览会，更好地服务中国—东盟博览会，南宁·中国—东盟国际商务区设立东盟各国商务联络部（办事处），旨在推动中国与东盟各国以及日本、韩国和中国港澳地区的经贸往来，拓展合作领域，为双方的合作和交流建立一个新的平台。这既是服务世界、服务东盟、服务广西的客观需要，也是南宁市加快建设区域性国际城市和广西“首善之区”的重大举措。

东盟各国商务联络部（办事处）位于南宁凤岭南片区、中国—东盟国际商务区基地园区内，规划用地每个国家基地园区60亩，其中对应国家的商务联络部（办事处）用地各为6亩。中国—东盟国际商务区地理位置优越，环境优美，公共设施齐全，于2010年9月建设完成。

2010年10月20日上午，南宁·中国—东盟国际商务区各国商务联络部（办事处）办公楼移交使用仪式在南宁·中国—东盟国际商务区桂雅路隆重举行。仪式由南宁市人民政府主办，南宁市“三街一区”建设管理办公室、南宁市住房保障和房产管理局、南宁市外事侨务办公室承办。广西壮族自治

2010年10月20日，南宁·中国—东盟国际商务区各国商务联络部（办事处）办公楼移交使用仪式在广西南宁举行

On October 20, 2010, the handover ceremony of Commercial Liaison Office buildings in China-ASEAN International Business District was held in Nanning, Guangxi

区党委副书记陈际瓦、自治区副主席梁胜利以及南宁市四家班子领导出席仪式。参加仪式的还有柬埔寨王国国务兼商业大臣占蒲拉西、文莱工业和初级资源部部长叶海亚、缅甸商务部贸易司司长Mr.Khin Muang Lay、菲律宾贸易工业部副部长克里斯托伯等东盟各国政府代表，东盟国家驻南宁总领事馆官员，各国联络部（办事处）基地园区建设单位负责人以及南宁市有关部门和单位领导。

南宁市市长黄方方致辞时说，中国—东盟国际商务区作为中国与东盟合作的重要平台，经过多年的精心打造，取得了丰硕的成果。今天建成移交的各国商务联络部（办事处）办公楼，是继2009年10月南宁领事馆区一期工程移交之后，南宁市加快完善中国—东盟国际商务区的服务功能，着力建设区域性国际城市的重点工程，成为双方友好合作的新象征。它的启用，将为中国与东盟在经贸等领域的合作提供更加优质、高效、便捷的服务，推动南宁市进一步扩大对外开放步伐，吸引更多的国家和企业到南宁投资发展。

柬埔寨王国国务大臣兼商业部长占蒲拉西代表参加仪式的东盟国家政府作了发言。

最后，陈际瓦在热烈的礼炮声中分别将各国商务联络部（办事处）金钥匙移交给各国商务部代表。这标志着中国与东盟各国商务交流又构筑了新平台，为打造永不落幕的中国—东盟博览会提供有力的保障，对中国—东盟友好合作具有重要意义。

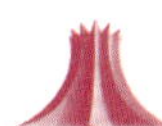

三　展览现场管理和配套服务

（一）现场服务

第七届中国—东盟博览会现场服务继续以“重商、服务、透明、有序、实效”为原则，强化以客户为中心的服务理念，贯彻ISO9000质量管理体系，提高服务的专业化、标准化、机制化、个性化，努力为各位宾客提供全方位便捷、规范、安全、高效的服务。

1. 各项服务优中选优，降低服务成本，提高服务质量。通过公开招标，本届博览会主会场核选出南宁国际会议展览公司为主场搭建商，广西外运公司和广西中邮物流公司为物流运输商，充分发挥了地方企业的地缘优势和有利条件，减少服务环节，降低服务成本，提高了服务效率。

2. 现场餐饮品种多样、卫生安全、供应充足。现场7家餐饮企业提供中西式快餐、清真餐、米粉和咖啡饮品的供应，每日供餐数量不少于1万份，

咨询服务
Information service

供应及时、数量充足、价格合理。其中，肯德基实行全天供餐服务，现场餐饮服务首次实现了用餐无时限的突破。

3. 境外展品通关便利、监管到位。继续对东盟国家参展商实行定额代缴的税款政策，既保证了参展商的积极性，又为秘书处节省了办展成本。广西出入境检验检疫局和南宁海关对博览会通关展品采取了十项便利措施，同时加强现场查验和巡查的工作力度。

4. 齐心协力抓管理，展览现场秩序井然。加强联合执法组现场巡查及展品进馆检查，展览秩序明显改善，得到客商广泛好评。

5. 人员和展品进出馆管理安全便利、高效畅通。安保工作继续坚持安全和便利相结合的原则，启用了大型活动安全保卫工作机制，加强安全检查和公共安全管理，加大治安管理力度，形成多重安全防护网，各种案件发生得到有效控制。公众开放日人流量控制适度，闭馆后夜间撤展秩序井然。首次划定了团组大巴上落点，设置了VIP通道，为车辆和人员进出展馆提供了便利。

6. 展馆环境整洁，保洁工作有口皆碑。各项保洁工作明确标准，做到保洁质量与成本控制并重，获得了展览业和参会各界人士的一致好评。

（二）通关服务

1. 海关。

南宁海关把认真做好第七届中国—东盟博览会监管服务工作列入关区全年重点工作，并将其作为海关支持西部大开发和广西北部湾经济区建设重点内容部署落实。在总结前六届博览会监管服务工作经验的基础上，创新思路，强化措施，健全机制，努力为参展参会人员、展品提供优质便捷的服务，切实保障博览会的顺利举办。

海关服务
Customs service

（1）组织领导到位，强化统筹协调和决策执行。建立强有力的工作机构，成立以关长为组长的支持服务中国—东盟博览会领导小组，抽调业务骨干在南宁口岸

设立驻会监管工作组，在南宁、桂林空港和凭祥、东兴等边境口岸设立现场监管小组，强化机关、现场海关两级联络员制度，确保组织领导到位；提高监管服务意识，将该项工作列入全年工作计划和重要督办事项，提升关区上下对该项工作的责任心和紧迫感；制定完善的工作方案，结合历届工作经验查漏补缺，完善监管服务工作方案和应急预案，统筹安排、周密部署各项工作，并强化对现场工作的指导，确保领导小组决策和工作方案有效贯彻落实。

（2）落实监管到位，确保既管得住又通得快。严格执行《南宁海关对中国—东盟博览会进口展品监管实施细则》的各项规定，规范展品监管作业程序；不断优化监管模式增强实际监管掌控力，对货运渠道进境展品实行口岸快速转关、展馆集中监管、海关核准出库进馆，对参展商随身携带进境展品实行口岸申报验放、驻点核对入馆的监管模式，确保海关对进出展馆展品的全过程监管；加强对展会期间展馆的巡查以及价格调研，推进信息化管理，运用自主研发的“中国—东盟博览会展览品海关管理子系统”，有效实现进境展品审批、申报、查验、放行、进出仓等监管全过程的计算机信息化管理，进一步提升监管服务水平。

（3）有效服务到位，打造文明高效海关形象。继续落实《南宁海关服务中国—东盟博览会十项长期便利措施》，积极支持推动地方办出特色创出品牌，不断扩大博览会的影响力；通过在博览会监管现场开展“创先争优”等活动，加大对博览局、物流单位工作人员的培训指导力度，积极营造良好的服务环境，对入境参展代表团实施“贴身式、跟进式”服务，积极做好海关法规宣传，开通博览会通关咨询电话，提前发放《通关指南》和《申报单》，积极为参展人员提供政策和业务咨询，及时处理进出境人员及展品通关疑难问题，确保参会人员、展品的快速通关，树立了良好的海关形象，得到主办方及各国代表团的一致好评。

（4）内外协调到位，打造海关与地方双赢局面。加强对国家相关政策和地方经济发展态势的跟踪研究，会同地方政府就展会发展和海关监管面临的问题积极向国务院反映，协调解决存在的问题并争取政策支持；主动走访和联系自治区政府及博览局等有关部门，通报海关监管服务博览会的新思路、新措施，就展品提前申报、留购产品估价、展品集中监管、保证金征收、加强馆区管理等事项积极研究并达成共识；密切与口岸联检部门的协作沟通，并与深圳、广州、上海等6个区外海关建立了展品转关联系配合机制和应急处置机制，齐心协力共同做好支持和服务工作，确保境外参展物资能快捷顺利转关。

本届展会期间，南宁海关共受理申报的进境展品253票、总重163.4吨、货值92.8万美元；监管进出境航班116架次、进境人员30623人次，出境人员33245人次，给予印尼副总统布迪约诺、老挝副总理阿桑·劳里、越南副总理张永仲等东盟国家领导人以通关礼遇39人次。南宁海关以优质高效的服务，始终确保博览会进出境人员、货物、物品的便捷有序通关，得到各级领导的充分肯定和社会各界的一致赞誉。

2. 检验检疫。

在服务第七届中国—东盟博览会中，广西出入境检验检疫局既做好出入境检验检疫服务，促进快捷通关，又做好疫情疫病防范，严防疫病疫情和有害生物传入，确保出入境人员及货物的安全、健康、卫生，出色地完成了任务。

在服务本届中国—东盟博览会工作中，广西出入境检验检疫局积极向国家质检总局汇报服务工作情况，继续争取国家质检总局在政策上的支持和指导，得到了国家质检总局的高度重视。2010年10月19—20日，国家质检总局局长支树平率领总局食品安全局、国际合作司、动植检司有关负责人出席了博览会和商务与投资峰会开幕式，视察了博览会现场办公室、检测中心大楼和广西局机关，通过视频系统了解防城港、东兴口岸检验检疫机构服务博览会的情况，充分肯定了广西检验检疫部门在服务博览会所作的努力，要求广西出入境检验检疫局紧紧抓住中国—东盟自由贸易区建成运行，广西北部湾开放开发建设，以及广西作为中国连接东盟国家桥头堡的作用越来越凸显的大好发展机遇，牢记光荣使命，提升自身能力，努力做好疫病疫情防控、质量提升、队伍建设、精神文明建设等各项工作，尤其是在服务中国—东盟自由贸易区方面，要力争把握新动向，出台新举措，取得新成效，促进新发展。

检验检疫
Quality and quarantine inspection

广西出入境检验检疫局重点做好以下工作：

一是加强组织领导，规范工作程序。广西出入境检验检疫局和凭祥、防城港、东兴、桂林、北海等5个口岸分支局均成立专门领导小组和相关工作组，要求全局各单位充分认识服务博览会工作的重要性，及时将工作重点调整到服务博览会工作上，举全局之力服务好本届博览会。设立博览会检验检疫现场办公室，抽调精干人员，配备先进检测设备，在会展现场为参展商提供优质、高效的把关服务。修订《中国—东盟博览会出入境检验检疫指南》，编制完善《广西检验检疫服务中国—东盟博览会工作手册》，建立一整套服务国际会展工作管理文件和体系，做到检验检疫服务博览会思想到位、组织到位、人员到位、部署到位。

二是出台优惠政策，提供优质服务。在国家质检总局的支持下，出台服务博览会优惠政策措施，如在各主要口岸开通参展物品和参会人员检验检疫专用通道，实行24小时值班制度；对入境参展物品实行“口岸查验、展出地集中检验检疫监管”，提供提前预报检，优先检验检疫，优先出证，优先通关；落实好在入境参展的部分动植物及其产品检疫审批、未获“3C”认证产品展后销售、免收展品的检验检疫费用、在广西区外入境参展物快速通关等多项优惠政策。

三是加强检验检疫监管，防止疫情疫病传入。认真总结前六届博览会参展物检验检疫监管的成功经验，进一步完善查验措施，优化查验手段，简化检验环节，在为本届博览会东盟各国入境参展商品、出入境参会人员提供优质服务同时，把好祖国的南大门，严防国外疫病疫情和不合格商品入境。博览会期间，共查验来自东盟10国、澳大利亚、日本、韩国及中国台湾等国家和地区涉及食品、木制品、家具、化妆品、机电设备、陶瓷、日用品等展品254批，总值36.78万美元。从入境参展物及木质包装内检出检疫性有害生物双棘长蠹6头，其他有害生物黑双棘长蠹5头；检出来自无任何审批手续的禁止输入偶蹄动物及其产品牛头皮4件、天然牛角12件；在一批参展大米中检出含有大量杂草籽及仓储害虫，以上均按规定实施退运或销毁处理。共查验入出境飞机93架次，查验入出境人员7652人次，截留禁止旅客携带入境动植物产品12批次24.4公斤，未发生口岸突发公共卫生事件。

四是实施快速检测，提高检测效率和准确性。坚持以食品安全监管为重点，进一步完善参展食品检验检疫操作规程，重点监控大宗食品和易发生安全问题的食品。针对参展食品主要来源东盟国家和地区，种类繁多、质量门槛低等特点，在确保参展食品质量安全的前提下，采取切实措施提高检测技术、提高检测效率、提高检测准确性，提升检验检疫监管水平，为博览会参展物品质量安全提供强有力的技术保障。在现场办公室配备细菌快速检测仪，加强对二氧化硫、甲醇、有机磷类农药残留、甲醛、菌落总数等主要指标的现场快速检测，检测时间从过去的3—5天缩短至1个小时内。对食品微生物、添加剂、重金属等项目，第一时间送往技术中心实验室检验，确保48小时内出检验结果。从参展客商的反馈情况看，本届博览会参展物品检测实现了安全、准确、快速，取得了良好的社会效果。

五是加强密切合作，提高通关速度。加强与地方政府及博览局、海关、外运等有关部门的协调与合作，改进检验检疫查验和通关模式；在会展现场与海关实现“联合办公、共同查验、一站式服务”作业模式，在人员出入境口岸实现与海关“一机两屏”查验，加快展品和携带物品验放速度；主动收集博览会参展物品、入境人员的相关信息并实行信息互通，资源共享。

六是开通服务博览会专门网站，提供信息便利化服务。在专门网站上中英文双语公布我国有关检验检疫政策、实用办事指南、重要信息等，方便境内外客商及有关人士查询；提供实时、滚动的检验检疫动态信息及疫病、疫情警示网上通报；开通网上报检、打印、查询、动植物及其产品入境检疫网上审批等功能；建立检验检疫服务信箱，随时解答参会人员和参展商的问题。

七是加强宣传报道，树立国门卫士形象。在服务博览会期间，广西检验检疫局进一步提高新闻宣传意识，加强信息宣传力度，积极配合新闻媒体做好宣传工作。通过有关网站和新闻媒体，及时将本届博览会出入境检验检疫工作中的亮点、大众关注的食品安全问题、检验检疫先进设备及先进检测技术、服务博览会好的经验和相关法律法规政策向各国参展商、广大进出口企业、社会各界进行介绍和宣传，让社会各界更加知悉、理解与配合检验检疫工作。

3. 人员通关服务。

2010年，广西公安边防认真总结前六届中国—东盟博览会边防检查工作的成功经验和不足，采取有针对性的措施，积极抓好各项工作落实，有力保障了第七届博览会的成功举办。

（1）着眼服务提高素质。从适应中国—东盟博览会服务需要的角度出发，立足本职，贴近实战，进一步充实和调整素质培训的计划和目标，组织开展有关东盟国家风土人情、涉外礼仪、执勤外语等内容的培训。以防范不法人员蓄意扰乱口岸秩序等为重点，严密各项措施的落实，在演练中提高实战技能，不断提高服务博览会的针对性和有效性。总队依托桂林边防检查站设立出入境证件研究中心，有针对性地加强对东盟国家证照资料的收集研究，为博览会的成功举办提供素质保障。

（2）优化现场通关环境。加强与有关单位的协调沟通，切实掌握东盟国家与会代表、交通运输工具的入出境动态，及时组织开展好勤务工作，不断提高工作效率和服务水平。在南宁、桂林、友谊关、东兴等重点口岸设置

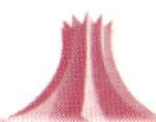

“两会一节”专用通道，集中所有检查员进驻执勤一线，实行全员上勤，并选派业务精、外语好的检查员，专门担负对各国领导人、重要外宾的出入境勤务工作。专门制作东盟各国文字的边检提示，在执勤现场大屏幕播放，在验证台上放置卡通形象的问候卡。同时，编写东盟各国文字的出入境卡片样式，交由机组指导旅客填写，确保与会嘉宾快捷顺畅通关。

（3）提供优质高效服务。认真研究论证不同与会嘉宾对口岸通关的需求，成功推出了一系列便民利民措施：

开通“24小时边检服务热线”，专门组成由英、越、泰语会话能力强的检查员成立现场服务小组，为与会嘉宾提供相关咨询和通关服务；优化优先通道、移动通道、便利通道、临时通道等服务模式，积极为各国政要、外交人员以及老、弱、病、残、幼、孕等需要救助的旅客提供优质高效服务；陆地口岸边检站根据参展商的入出境请求，发挥涉外职能作用，加强与越方口岸管理部门联系协商，延长通关时间，方便人员和参展货物入出境；海港、内河港口岸边检站与船方或船舶代理公司建立联系机制，实行24小时预约报检，随时接受船方或代理公司的办理通关手续申请。

第七届中国—东盟博览会筹备和举办期间，广西公安边防总队圆满完成与会东盟各国30个专（包）机、8个代表团和7000多人次的出入境边防检查任务，为博览会的成功举办创造了良好的口岸通关环境。

（三）接待服务

广西壮族自治区党委、政府对第七届中国—东盟博览会、商务与投资峰会接待工作高度重视，博览会、商务与投资峰会广西指挥中心多次召开工作会议进行了专门部署，并成立指挥中心接待工作部，经过各有关单位的共同努力，圆满完成了本届博览会的接待工作。

1. 建立健全接待工作机制，统筹安排各项工作。

指挥中心接待工作部从全局和政治的高度，充分认识进一步做好博览会、商务与投资峰会接待工作的重要性。坚持有利筹办、简化礼仪、务实节俭、杜绝浪费、尊重宗教和民族习惯的原则，围绕实现建设节约型会议的目标，狠抓落实，切实提高接待保障能力和服务水平。指挥中心接待工作部负责博览会、商务与投资峰会宾客的接待工作。工作部下设办公室及外宾接待一组、外宾接待二组、内宾接待一组、内宾接待二组、商务峰会宾客接待组、港澳宾客接待组、台湾宾客接待组、新闻记者接待组、公共卫生食品医疗保健组、接待资源调配组、宾客迎送组、宗教工作组，共13个内设机构。接待工作部坚持以人为本的原则，精心组织，周密安排，科学管理，优质服务，确保宾客乘兴而来，满意而归。

第一，接待宾馆方面。第七届接待宾客的数量将比上届更多。为了进一步提升接待宾馆的服务质量，接待工作部对南宁市宾馆接待能力进行了调查，并组织协调相关职能部门对博览会、商务与投资峰会接待宾馆的资质进行重新核定，并授予博览会、商务与投资峰会指定接待宾馆牌匾，确保宾馆接待服务质量。坚持“先外后内、先上后下，确保重点、兼顾一般，相对集中、就近安排”的宾馆分配原则，落实接待宾馆，确定100多家宾馆作为博览会、商务与投资峰会宾客接待场所。此外，会期为稳定酒店客房价格，自治区人民政府对南宁市宾馆客房房价实行了最高限价临时干预措施。

第二，征调车辆方面。为实现优质服务、厉行节约的目标，在征调车辆方面采取如下措施：一是采取“先征调后分配”的方式，既便于征调车辆的管理，也减少不必要的浪费。二是对服务博览会、商务与投资峰会的接待用车加油进行了改革，取消往届凭油票加油的做法，改为指派专门工作人员核对车牌号，并由专门工作人员、司机、加油员三人，同时在专用登记本上签名确认的做法。加强油料管理，节约经费开支。

第三，宾客接待方面。进一步完善对口接待工作机制，明确160个宾客接待单位及其负责人、联络员及联系方式，完善了贵宾信息平台，做好信息跟踪，收到反馈，及时汇总。会期，各对口宾客接待单位为接待对象提供了优质服务。

第四，专场活动方面。接待工作部办公室与展览部及各场活动的主办、承办及接待单位协调，团结协助、密切配合，制定了机场迎送、宾馆预订、会场预订以及接待用车安排等相关方案，各工作组也相应做好各组工作方案和应急预案，会期圆满完成了各专场活动的接待任务。

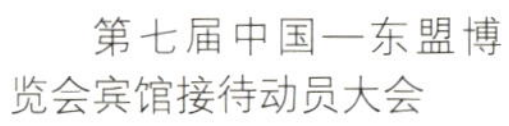
第七届中国—东盟博览会宾馆接待动员大会

Mobilization Meeting of Reception Departments and Hotels for the 7th CAEXPO

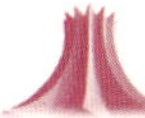

2. 创新接待工作方式，在节俭的前提下提高接待服务质量。

本届博览会、商务与投资峰会在接待宾客方面，重视接待资源的合理安排，厉行节约，努力创办“节约型”博览会。对于涉及多场活动的人员，如一些部级宾客同时参加博览会、商务与投资峰会、论坛等活动，在餐饮、住宿、用车、宴会等方面，明确了接待对象的归口问题，做到既不由于重复交叉接待而浪费接待资源，也不因为遗漏接待而有失礼仪。努力改进工作作风，严格执行各项规章制度，严肃工作纪律、制度约束和强化工作督查。

本届“两会”十分重视食品安全工作。自治区食品安全协调委员会各成员单位综合监督、组织协调“两会”活动期间从“田头”到“餐桌”各环节的食品安全保障工作，确保宾客和群众的饮食安全；派驻食品安全监督员进驻各接待宾馆、饭店，加强食品安全、公共场所和饮用水卫生监督保障工作；加强各重要专题活动场所的食品安全工作。

宗教工作组将到有穆斯林宾客入住的宾馆、饭店指导做好宗教礼仪和餐饮卫生等方面的服务工作，重点检查指导南宁市清真寺做好清真快餐、接待穆斯林宾客的准备工作。

在接待宾客车辆的分配上，指挥中心接待工作部认真调查研究，做好详细的用车计划，严格按规定配车，车随人走，避免资源浪费。同时，预留好充足的机动车辆，避免发生疏漏。并积极主动与交通运输厅、高管局、交警部门、石油公司等取得联系，提前做好“两会”征调车辆免费过桥过路、车辆安检、高速公路免费通行、石油储备等工作。对征调司机进行教育培训，确保车辆行驶顺畅、服装整洁统一、服务一流，树立广西接待新形象。

宾客接待是宾客接待工作的重中之重。指挥中心接待工作部在往届博览会的基础上，对宾客接待单位重新进行筛选，进一步明确、调整、补充了“两会”宾客接待单位共160个，比上届增加了相当数量的备选单位，机动单位数量充足，需要则选，不需要也不浪费。真正做到了精心组织，科学管理，使对口接待工作更具有灵活性和可操作性。

（四）证件服务

第七届中国—东盟博览会证件工作围绕“人到证到”的工作目标，采取各项措施，理顺办证程序，坚强技术保障，提高证件质量，充足设备及人员，保障各项应急，按照“安全有序、便捷高效”的要求组织开展。会期共制作发放人员证件129189张，与上届相比增长11.53%。

本届博览会证件工作采取以下措施，取得良好成果：

1. 分工明确，流程理顺。结合参会人员的地域分布和各项办证需求的特点，证件组从受理端分设区内小组、国内小组、境外小组、贵宾小组、车证小组、标贴小组，分块负责，工作任务、流程直观明了、脉络清晰。同时，与各部门同仁配合合作，采取并联式的集中办证方式，理顺各环节的流程，大大提高了办证的效率。

2. 铺设面宽，工作效率高。证件组总计组织投入839人，动用280台电脑和打印设备，会期完成了相当于400个标准展位的临时搭建任务，在指挥中心一楼设立预办证中心，在会展中心搭建占地1600平方米、配备80个办证终端的现场办证大厅，在锦华大酒店、南宁饭店等11家境外客商集中的宾馆设立办证点。分期、分步快速消化近13万的办证洪峰。

3. 设备专业，技术保障。采用先进技术，确保主分会场办证数据和门禁验证系统同步更新使用，全球眼现场监控，保障展会现场安全。制证公司充分利用自身成熟经验，投入专业的制证设备，确保在第一时间内以最快速度制出证、理好证。各参会单位称赞办证效率“一年比一年高”。

4. 准备充分，经受考验。由于本届博览会珠宝展展位需求增加，现场办证大厅地点可能会有所变动。针对出现的新情况，证件组多次到场馆实地踏勘，克服重重困难，制定多套的现场办证大厅建设方案，经多次勘查研究，最终确定以会展中心16号馆继续作为现场办证大厅，有针对性地提出了现场办证搭建工作的解决方案，为现场办证工作打下坚实的基础。

5. 培训到位，微笑服务。证件组与广西民族大学合作，定向招募110名优秀实习人员参与证件管理工作，邀请中国移动广西分公司的专业培训师对参与证件工作的人员进行微笑服务培训，包括商务礼仪、客户沟通、仪容仪表等培训内容，全方位为参会人员提供最优质的办证服务。据电话回访调查，超过95%的被调查者满意本届博览会的证件工作，90%以上的被调查者认为工作人员服务态度很好。

同时，证件组对外承诺提供微笑服务，在证件申办、受理、发放各环节全面推行“首问责任制”、“限时办结制”和“责任追究制”三项制度，明确办证各环节、各岗位的责任要求和服务规范，实现办证服务的标准化、规范化。

6. 有的放矢，办证高效。预制证阶段，证件组按照“先区内，后区外”的原则，实行“一个口子对外”专人负责追踪服务，通过短信平台、电话等多种渠道催报信息，工作人员主动服务，积极联络各单位证件管理员，实时通报各办证环节需要注意的事项，并且实行分时间段预约发证。同时，制证中心设立双办证通道。主通道负责正常的大批量证件制作；辅助通道作为应急、绿色办证通道使用，有力地化解办证高峰。

现场办证大厅设置合理的办证通道，提高现场办证能力和办证速度，保证资料符合要求的客商在受理后5分钟内（平均）可拿到证件，同时完善现场办证咨询、查询、证件遗失补办等服务。为解决境外客商办证晚的问题，在东盟各国客商集中的11家宾馆设立境外客商办证服务点，提供“一站式”现场办证服务。从10月17日至10月23日，共现场办理证件近2万张，客商对便利的办证服务非常满意。

7. 服务个性化，确保重点。证件组专门设置贵宾证件小组，指定专人负责省部级领导的证件工作， 确保领导能及时凭证参加活动。针对车证工作“车证少，需求大”的特点，车证小组与安保部门提前充分沟通联系，结合接待工作部及相关部门提供的接待和参会要求，提前部署，简化流程，抓住环节，采取定人、定车号的措施，确保满足重要领导和贵宾的参会用证需求。

办证服务
Pass-issuing service

（五）直航包机

第七届中国—东盟博览会继续开通南宁往返文莱斯里巴加湾、柬埔寨金边、印尼雅加达、老挝万象、马来西亚吉隆坡、缅甸仰光、菲律宾马尼拉、泰国曼谷、新加坡新加坡城、越南胡志明等东盟10国首都或主要城市的临时直航包机，共安全运送博览会参会参展商1856人次，平均上座率达64%，比上届博览会提高10%。

2010年，“领导重视，决策正确，组织科学，目标明确”成为本届博览会包机工作顺利执行的重要保证，取得了如下成果：

1. 优化政府采购模式。2009年，临时直航包机首次采用政府采购并自行组织的形式开展，取得了良好效果。2010年第七届中国—东盟博览会期间，创新包机执行工作形式，委托专业招标公司采取竞争性谈判及单一来源相结合的模式，完成了采购任务，达到了减低费用成本的预期目的。

2. 优化包机信息发布确认流程。新流程进一步确保沟通渠道顺畅，使东盟方能通过新途径更准确及时了解包机动态、反馈建议、及时安排制定合理参会行程。

3. 制定个性化包机信息。坚持以客商为中心，不断改善各项服务质量。包机执行专业性强，为方便销售代理和客商更好理解包机专业术语，在总结往年经验基础上，针对东盟各国不同情况，按国别制定包机信息，分期分批分国家公布包机航线时刻及价格，与上届相比，时间提前了近一个月。

4. 应急工作主动到位。包机工作专业性强、涉及面广，不可控因素相当多，指挥中心及时与航空及相关主管部门联系协调，确保包机各航线航权申请。同时，积极制定应急预案，保障全部包机安全、顺利飞行。

（六）食品安全

国家食品药品监督管理局对第七届中国—东盟博览会食品安全工作高度重视，在设备和技术上给予大力支持，提高了第七届中国—东盟博览会餐饮食品安全保障的科技水平，为实现餐饮食品安全保障万无一失的目标提供了坚实的技术保障。

为确保第七届中国—东盟博览会食品安全，广西壮族自治区食品药品监督管理局突出“三个重点”，即重点人群、重点接待宾馆饭店、重点场馆；严抓“三项措施”，即制定详细方案、开展实施前准备及评估、严格实施保障；严把“三个环节”，即食品对口配送环节，检验检测环节，加工制作环节；做到“三个确保”，即确保出席活动的国家首脑、重要外宾以及重要活动的食品安全万无一失；确保接待宾馆不发生食物中毒事故；确保全区餐饮服务单位不发生重大食品安全事故，为出席博览会的中外嘉宾提供了良好的安全饮食氛围。

博览会期间，自治区食品药品监督管理局对开幕式、民歌节、国宴、自治区欢迎宴会、南宁市欢迎宴会、专机用餐、各论坛和两场高尔夫球赛茶点等进行了重点保障。在南宁市共保障餐饮食品安全约68305人次，其中宴会31个，5190人次；全程监管对口配送到南宁会展中心、展览馆、华南城等活动场馆的快餐38776份以及高尔夫球赛贵宾145人的用餐；监督销毁超时未食用盒饭225份；监督荔园等七家重点宾馆检测蔬菜农药残留9507公斤，销毁

不合格蔬菜225公斤。具体做法如下：

1. 周密部署，扎实推进工作开展。广西食品药品监督管理局先后制定《第七届中国—东盟博览会中国—东盟商务与投资峰会餐饮服务食品安全保障工作方案》、《应急预案》、工作进度表等，召开博览会、商务与投资峰会食品安全保障工作视频会议，对工作进行动员部署和专项培训。

2. 认真督查，落实制度保障。督查各重点接待宾馆饭店严格实行食品原（辅）料采购索证索票制度、进货验收制度和登记备案制度、食用报告等制度，确保原料的质量安全。

3. 严格检查，保证食品质量。对指挥中心送检的酒、矿泉水、饮料、茶叶等进行检验，对重点宾馆饭店的食用油、酱油、白酒、葡萄酒和饮料等5个品种21批次进行抽检，产品全部合格并封存备用。

4. 建立机制，做好应急处置。博览会期间，食品药品监督管理部门以全程监督和重点监督相结合，紧紧围绕防止食物中毒和食品污染，制定和落实各项防范措施，推行食品安全监管员、卫生专业人员和农残检测员“三员”驻点制度，加强原料使用前检测，对进入重点接待宾馆饭店的蔬菜、水果实行对每个品种、每批次全部进行农药残留快速检测；加强对菜单及加工、供应方式等进行审查，对加工现场进行全程监督；对冷菜制作、备餐及供餐时间、食品中心温度、食品留样等关键环节进行动态监控；对加工过程不符合要求的，及时制止并提出整改意见；对临时或擅自改变供应的品种、加工工艺、供餐方式或供餐时间等的，重新审核，符合要求后方可供餐，不留食品安全隐患。

同时，食品药品监督管理部门与卫生、农业部门建立有效的信息沟通机制，相互通报工作动态；进驻重点宾馆饭店的食品安全监管员每天实行“零报告制度”，确保指挥应急响应及时准确到位。

（七）医疗卫生服务

根据中国—东盟博览会、商务与投资峰会指挥中心的总体部署，博览会、商务与投资峰会公共卫生食品医疗保健工作领导小组按照职责分工，统一思想，全力以赴，做好博览会、商务与投资峰会公共卫生食品医疗保健服务工作。

1. 加强领导，完善机制。成立了由广西卫生厅、广西食品药品监督管理局等8个部门组成的博览会、商务与投资峰会公共卫生食品医疗保健工作领导小组，由卫生厅与食品药品监督管理局各1名分管领导任组长，下设医疗保健小组、食品安全小组、医疗救治小组、疾病控制小组、后勤保障小组与维护稳定小组6个工作小组。领导小组多次召集有关厅局和直属医疗卫生机构召开会议专题研究部署工作，制定下发《2010年第七届中国—东盟博览会和中国—东盟商务与投资峰会公共卫生食品医疗保健工作实施方案》，明确任务，完善部门协作机制，从服务于博览会的大局出发，团结协作，认真履行各自职责，确保把各项措施落实到位，努力把博览会、商务与投资峰会的医疗保健和公共卫生食品安全工作做好。

2. 强化培训，提高队伍服务能力。一是加强“两会”重点接待宾馆饭店餐饮服务管理人员的培训。自治区食品药品监督管理局对23家“两会”重点宾馆饭店及展馆快餐定点供应商的相关人员进行餐饮服务食品安全知识培训，增强了餐饮服务管理人员的责任意识、守法意识和防范意识；二是做好服务人员现场应急救治培训。广西卫生厅对博览会期间参与重点接待宾馆共223名服务员进行了徒手心肺复苏培训，对直接参与博览会医疗保健工作的7家区直保健基地的95名医务人员和救护车司机进行了干部保健工作制度、急救设备的使用操作、徒手心肺复苏、有害气体中毒、骨折、气管异物、食物中毒的现场急救，突发传染病的处理及上报流程等方面的培训，并模拟突发意外、中毒及群死群伤情况下应急处理进行了考核；三是提高服务人员的综合服务能力。南宁市卫生部门对服务医疗单位负责人、医务人员、部分服务行业人员及青年志愿者共7500多人进行了相关知识培训，同时开展食源性疾病等11个相关专题的业务培训班，累计培训专业人员300多人，服务行业人员5500多人，使各类工作人员熟练掌握各种急救应对措施，为顺利完成医疗保健工作提供有力保障。

3. 落实医疗保障措施，满足嘉宾保健需求。会期共派出驻点医疗保健组14组、大型活动医疗组6组开展相关服务工作，并为6场重要大型宴会提供医疗保健服务。会议期间，共为340余人次开展医疗保健工作，主要是上呼吸道感染、胃肠型感冒、皮肤过敏和外伤等。南宁市共派出166个现场应急医疗保障组、309名医护人员和136辆（次）救护车，连续28天（次）对日流量超5万人（博览会、美食节、轻工展）、2场（次）现场容量超过3万人（民歌节开幕式）、12场（次）现场容量超过3千人的大型活动现场实施了现场医疗保障，特别是在南宁市体育中心设立专门的现场救治点。据不完全统计，各类活动现场类计应急处置上呼吸道感染、胃肠疾病、软组织挫伤、中暑和外伤等各种伤病演员、嘉宾、工作人员和群众1600多人次，圆满完成博览会、商务与投资峰会医疗卫生保障任务。

4. 做好公共场所卫生监管工作。派出疾控专业工作人员47人次、车辆35辆次，对荔园山庄、西园饭店等11家自治区重点接待单位开展环境卫生

质量、公共用具、二级供水卫生质量等公共环境监测工作，监测覆盖率达100%；对11个重点接待单位的会议室、餐厅、停车场、客房、垃圾堆、民工住区及周围外墙2—3米绿化带等进行应急消毒和灭害处理，并采集食品样品316份进行食品卫生项目检测。经过规范、彻底消杀后，所有接待场所的室内空气和环境安全，室内、室外病媒生物密度均符合中国—东盟博览会会展接待要求。

检查餐厅卫生情况
Restaurant food safty inspection

南宁市卫生局共出动执法人员2098人次、车辆298辆次，对辖区范围内的经营性公共场所进行了1120家次、生活饮用水经营单位116家次监督检查。会期出动卫生监督员208人次、车辆23辆次，对市属接待国内外嘉宾的宾馆饭店的客房、会议厅（室）等公共场所开展监督监测，对有重点接待任务的14家宾馆二次供水水质进行监督监测。会期，各重点宾馆和大型活动场所均未报告传染病疫情，全区未出现重大突发公共卫生事件。

（八）志愿者服务

第七届中国—东盟博览会、商务与投资峰会共招募680名城市志愿者和1320名专业志愿者。会期，志愿者主要服务于会展中心各场馆、新闻中心、办证现场、场馆门禁等40多个岗位，从事礼仪接待、文秘翻译、咨询接待、会场布置、现场办证、后勤保障、应急支援等方面工作。

本届中国—东盟博览会志愿者工作呈现以下亮点：

1. 加强信息化管理，普及博览会知识，首次采用“中国—东盟博览会志愿者网上招募选拔系统”。为提升志愿者各项工作的信息化水平，进一步优化流程、完善服务，在本届博览会志愿者工作中首次采用“中国—东盟博览会志愿者在线招募选拔系统”，该系统在接受学生在线报名的同时对学生进行初步考核，可对学生进行有效筛选，并通过学生报名收集个人有效信息，为后期办理志愿者证件提供极大便利。

2. 志愿者培训更系统，服务能力更强。一是集中培训，培训除了介绍本届博览会的概况和礼仪知识外，主办方还特别邀请参与北京奥运会、上海世博会志愿者培训工作的专家对博览会志愿者进行系统的培训，开展了志愿服务理念教育、团队意识教育等。二是成果检验，通过模拟场景服务、礼仪知识问答、应急处理演练等形式对志愿者进行成果检验，加深志愿者对所学知识的理解。三是岗前培训，用人单位组织志愿者到服务地点，志愿者们轮流扮演志愿者和服务对象两个角色，开展志愿服务实战演练工作。通过多次培训及演练，志愿者服务博览会的水平得到了提高。

3. 创新激励约束机制，首次引进徽章文化激励志愿者。为不断激发广大志愿者的服务热情，志愿者工作组借鉴北京奥运会和上海世博会志愿者的成功经验，引用志愿者徽章文化，专门设计了一套志愿者徽章，用时尚的徽章对志愿者每天的服务进行评价、认可和鼓励。这套徽章共分为两组11枚，方形的一组包括“一起加油”、“坚持不懈”、“我服务 我快乐”等内容，提醒志愿者在奉献中保持乐观的心态；圆形的一组为本届志愿者服装的图案，上面分别有1—3颗星，代表志愿者的等级，将根据志愿者服务表现颁发带有“星”的徽章，以此激励每一个在岗的志愿者，始终如一地做好每一项服务。星级徽章由高校带队老师，志愿者用人单位及博览会志愿者工作组发放，每天对志愿者进行评定，对表现优秀的志愿者发徽章进行奖励。对于城市志愿者，共青团广西区委设立“青年志愿者创先争优岗”和“共青团员先进示范岗”，以榜样的力量激励青年志愿者在志愿服务的奉献中创先进争优秀，同时向社会各界展示城市志愿者积极向上的精神风貌。

4. 志愿者整体形象有新突破。本届博览会志愿者的服装、装备突破以往的单一设计，加强创新，将中国—东盟自贸区建成这一喜事融合到志愿者的整体形象设计当中，更为凸显文化内涵，渲染中国—东盟自贸区建成的喜庆气氛，提升志愿者的自豪感。一是在志愿者服装设计方面加入印章元素。为庆祝自贸区建成，突出中国—东盟合作主题，将七届博览会开幕式主题词由名人刻成印章是本届博览会的一大亮点，印章同时又是诚信、合作的象征。此次将印章元素融入志愿者服装设计中，在精选服装布料的基础上融入更丰富、更有内涵的象征性元素，寓意志愿者在服务过程中将中国与东盟国家之间的文化、情谊不断传递和延续。二是志愿者读本首次设计成“口袋装”的样式。为增强志愿者读本的使用性、便携性、实用性，借鉴北京奥运会志愿者工作手册设计形式，首次采用“口袋装”，文字内容更为浓缩、精简，设计风格更为活泼、时尚，充分体现了志愿者年轻积极的精神面貌。口袋装的志愿者读本更加方便了志愿者随时随地翻阅查询各种实用信息，体现了人性化的设计理念，有助于提升志愿者的服务水平和服务质量。

志愿者展示徽章
Volunteers displayed their badges

5. 加强志愿者管理，首次给馆内志愿者加贴标贴。为进一步提高会场管理、监督力度，规范志愿者服务队伍，提升志愿者整体形象，作为允许进入会展中心展馆内的首要标志，首次在进入会展中心服务的志愿者证件上加贴“会展中心馆内志愿者”标贴，这一做法可有效控制志愿者进入会展中心人数、进一步规范志愿者行为，更有利于对志愿者的监督及管理。

四 新闻宣传

第七届中国—东盟博览会、第七届中国—东盟商务与投资峰会、第十二届南宁国际民歌艺术节（以下简称“两会一节”）新闻宣传工作按照指挥中心的部署，协调各方面的力量，周密策划，精心组织，有序推进，宣传主题突出，内容丰富，特色鲜明，预热阶段深度报道创意频出，会期宣传高潮迭起，社会各界反响良好，得到了与会领导和参会嘉宾高度赞誉，为“两会一节”的成功举办营造了良好的舆论氛围，达到了宣传推介广西、扩大“两会一节”影响，促进中国与东盟经济、文化交流与合作的目的。

广西壮族自治区领导郭声琨、马飚、沈北海、陈武高度重视“两会一节”宣传工作，分别提出明确要求并作了部署。自治区党委宣传部把“两会一节”宣传当作一项重要任务列入年度工作计划，并牵头成立了“两会一节”指挥中心新闻宣传部，确定了“两会一节”宣传方案。新闻宣传部在努力争取中宣部和中央主要新闻媒体对“两会一节”宣传报道的重视和支持的同时，组织协调中外媒体围绕中国和东盟友好合作、中国—东盟自贸区顺利建成的主题，聚焦“两会一节”的举办，充分发挥各类媒体的优势，全方位、多角度展开宣传报道，全面提升“两会一节”的影响力。

（一）前期宣传起步早，形式多，做足声势

2010年8月中旬开始，中央驻桂和自治区主要新闻媒体分阶段、有步骤地对“两会一节”筹备工作亮点等进行宣传报道，并每周至少播发两篇。《光明日报》的深度报道《新起点 新机遇 新使命——写在第七届中国—东盟博览会举行之际》，被全国各大媒体转载；中新社的专题报道被印尼《千岛日报》、菲律宾《商报》、柬埔寨《华商日报》、泰国《星暹日报》刊用，在海外形成了大面积的覆盖；《广西日报》推出“两会一节”博览会特刊 28个版，刊发《自贸区前程似锦 博览会任重道远》、《博览会是广西经济发展助推器》、《博览会投促效益显著》等一批重点报道。广西电视台

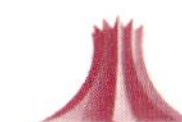

制作播放宣传专题片，每天在重要时段播出。《广西新闻》与《新闻在线》《资讯晚报》等栏目坚持每天播出一至二条“两会一节”相关新闻稿件。

以中国—东盟自贸区如期建成为契机，开展了第七届中国—东盟博览会主题口号征集、中国—东盟博览会合作媒体广西行、中国—东盟媒体汽车拉力赛、第七届中国—东盟博览会携手共进30天、中国—东盟自由贸易区建设成就展等一系列活动。《广西日报》、广西人民广播电台、广西电视台、广西新闻网等区直媒体相继开设专刊专栏，组织策划了“自贸区系列宣传、创新及亮点系列、筹备动态系列、重点贵宾和企业专访系列、专业性宣传系列、博览会论坛宣传系列”等宣传报道活动。广西新闻网征集市民、高校学生、网民以主持人的身份报道第七届中国—东盟博览会、商务与投资峰会；通过广西手机报推出《“两会一节”服务手册》，关注逛展寻“宝”、购票、交通出行、民歌节、安全外贸等便民资讯；推出“辣评民歌节”栏目倾听读者声音等，均获得了积极反响。

（二）会期新闻发稿量大，报道集中，高潮迭起

据统计，共有境内外199家媒体、1458名记者参会采访报道“两会一节”。其中，中央媒体122人，中央驻桂媒体159人、行业媒体67人、外省媒体52人、广西媒体911人、港澳媒体31人、台湾媒体10人、东盟国家媒体88人、其他外国媒体18人。人数比2009年媒体报名人数增加，特别是外国媒体记者比2009年增加较多，台湾媒体首次参与报道。参加采访报道的媒体和记者数量多，规模大，众多新闻媒体开展广泛深入的报道，有力地扩大了“两会一节”的知名度和影响力。

截止到10月24日，参与采访的中央媒体、广西媒体、网络媒体、港澳台媒体、外国媒体共发稿9900多篇（条、幅），对“两会一节”的各项活动进

国内外媒体聚焦“两会”
Media at the events from home and abroad

行了充分报道。其中，中央媒体发稿1300多篇，区内媒体发稿4000多篇，网络媒体3900多篇，港澳台媒体120多篇，外国媒体发稿600多篇。此外，各种网上相关链接85万余条，新闻页面9460篇。主要有以下几个特点：

1. 现场直播时间长，影响面广。

主要媒体组织的现场直播，把“两会一节”的盛况及时向广大观（听）众传播，形成了强大的宣传声势。中央人民广播电台，中央电视台新闻频道、第四频道，同时对第七届中国—东盟博览会开幕式和中国—东盟商务与投资峰会开幕式进行直播。中国国际广播电台用英语、中文分别对博览会、峰会的开幕式进行了现场直播。广西人民广播电台联合中央人民广播电台、中国国际广播电台、广东人民广播电台对博览会、峰会开幕式等重要活动进行了现场直播；广西人民广播电台“北部湾之声”还联合越南之声、越南广宁省广播电视台在会展中心设立透明直播室，共同直播博览会开幕式。广西电视台对博览会、峰会开幕式，以及印尼副总统布迪约诺与中国企业CEO圆桌对话会等三场重要活动进行现场直播。

“两会一节”期间，人民网、新华网、中国网络电视台、中国网、国际在线、中国广播网、中国新闻网、新浪网、广西新闻网、中国—东盟博览会官方网站等10家网站对博览会开幕式、峰会开幕式、东盟国家领导人与企业家圆桌对话会、中国—东盟商会领袖论坛、中国—东盟经贸与物流论坛、“大地飞歌·2010”第12届南宁国际民歌艺术节暨第七届中国—东盟博览会开幕晚会、“两会一节”闭幕新闻发布会等七场重要活动，以图文、视频等方式对会议进行了网络直播。

2. 中央媒体及境外主流媒体报道力度大，质量高。

人民日报：共刊发相关稿件及照片37篇（幅），并出版了一期博览会特刊。在特刊上，刊发了《自贸区新起点　博览会新机遇——写在第七届中国—东盟博览会即将举办之际》等重点稿件。

新华社：通过文字、摄影、音视频等对“两会一节”进行全方位立体报道，共发稿1035篇。其中对内稿件881篇，对外稿件112篇，重点栏目稿件32篇。《开局良好 成就瞩目——中国—东盟自贸区建成“元年”观察》、《“共同利益”是加固中国—东盟战略合作的基石》等一批针对性强的、对内及对外重点报道，凸显了中国—东盟合作共赢的大局。同时，在2010年第42期《瞭望》推出了《精彩中国—东盟博览会，辉煌中国—东盟自贸区》专题。此外，还播发对外英文稿件25篇，英文重点栏目5篇，其中有10篇稿件被CNC英文台作为重点稿件采用。

中央电视台：派出了30人的报道团队参加了本届博览会和峰会的宣传报

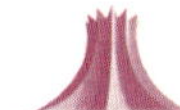

道工作。中央电视台第一频道、第二频道、第四频道和第九频道的各新闻栏目共发稿50篇，其中在中央电视台《新闻联播》节目中发稿3篇，单篇播出了《第七届中国—东盟博览会、中国—东盟商务与投资峰会在广西南宁隆重开幕》和《贾庆林会见出席第七届中国—东盟博览会的东盟国家领导人》的消息，以及《中国—东盟博览会参展商超过往届》、《第七届中国—东盟博览会闭幕》的消息，社会反响良好。

港澳台媒体：共发稿近200条消息（文章），约10万字和50幅图片，电视报道的时长约4个小时，海内外近50家媒体转载1100次，扩大了“两会一节”在海外的影响。香港凤凰卫视两名记者全程采访，采访了泰国商务部长、新加坡商务代表、广西壮族自治区主席马飚等。香港亚洲电视一行8人的制作组前来广西采访，制作两集共12分钟的“两会一节”专题报道。台湾7家媒体共10人来广西采访。“两会一节”期间，《香港文汇报》、《香港商报》、《澳门日报》刊出专版宣传，约2万字30幅图片，有力地扩大了对“两会一节”的宣传，取得了良好的效果。

外国媒体：印尼、菲律宾、泰国、文莱、越南等东盟国家以及日本、希腊等国家、地区的84家主流媒体共106名外国记者参加“两会一节”宣传报道，在头版头条或重要版面刊登、发表“两会一节”相关新闻报道600多篇。

3. 网台互动，立体传播，多语种直通东盟。

中国国际广播电台：派出了23人的采访团队，用越南语、菲律宾语、泰国语、老挝语、印尼语、柬埔寨语等东盟10国语言和中文、英语播发“两会一节”新闻，并在北美、老挝、柬埔寨等国家和地区落地播出。

媒体云集“两会”
Gathering of media

中国新闻社：累计发出对外文字和图片通稿100余篇（幅）。对外通稿被东盟各国、美国、澳大利亚以及港澳台地区的媒体广泛采用。其中，《“南宁渠道”推动中国—东盟自贸区建设》等重点稿件同时被多家外报头版头篇或内版头篇全文采用，在海外产生了重大影响。

国际在线：推出英语、越南语、马来语、印尼语、泰国语、老挝语、菲律宾语、缅甸语等8个语种的专题报道，全面报道博览会和商务与投资峰会的盛况。

广西人民广播电台：“北部湾之声”联合越南之声、越南广宁省广播电视台在会展中心设立透明直播室，共同直播博览会开幕式，并连线新加坡新传媒电台、泰国国家广播电台、柬埔寨国家电台，报道博览会、商务与投资峰会盛况。

（三）社会宣传形成合力，营造出喜庆、隆重、热烈氛围

为做好2010年“两会一节”的社会宣传工作，以整洁优美、和谐文明、充满生机的城市形象和热烈、喜庆的社会宣传氛围迎接“两会一节”的召开，在精品线路全段（机场出站口—机场高速路—壮锦大道—白沙大道—葫芦鼎大桥—青山路—滨江路—荔园山庄—竹溪大道—会展中心；南宁大桥—平乐大道—五象大道—体育中心；民族大道全段）、主要道路以及广西展览馆、广西民族博物馆、市人大会堂、会展中心、民族广场、火车站等节庆主要活动场所周边、主要接待场所周边和窗口单位周边采用布置小品造型，设置宣传广告、宣传标语等多种形式开展氛围营造工作。据不完全统计，2010年“两会一节”期间，南宁市共组织设置小品造型84组（其中改造造型67组，新设计安装的造型17组），完成机场高速路、白沙大道、竹溪大道、民族大道、南宁大桥桥体广告宣传画面28块（14座），完成白沙岔路口、机场出入口、三岸收费站旁平面广告宣传画面5块，完成青竹立交桥隔音墙宣传画面208块，完成民族大道、竹溪大道、白沙大道、青山路、滨江路、东葛路、新民路、越秀路、滨湖路、长湖路等路段设置POP旗1400杆，建设完成南宁大桥至广西体育中心4500 米、面积约22500平方米的平面广告牌，设置空飘气球36个、气拱门4个、标语横幅38条，协调12家单位在LED电子显示屏播放宣传标语。组织重要路段的阅报栏电子显示屏、楼宇电视安排滚动播放“两会一节”的宣传片和宣传标语，每天约1000条（次）；组织南宁市高大建筑物、沿街商店开放霓虹灯、轮廓灯、彩灯等；在南宁市三星级以上宾馆酒店播放“两会一节”宣传片和摆放宣传资料等；组织摆放鲜花300万盆，鲜花造型景观70多处。

（四）宣传推介亮点纷呈，提升了博览会品牌影响力

在博览会宣传推介方面，继2009年成功实施“大事有我”、“借事造势”基础上，进一步执行更为积极的“我造大势”的工作思路，提升了博览会品牌影响力。

1. 主动造势，策划先行，为中国—东盟自贸区和博览会营造了良好舆论氛围和较高关注度。与央视等媒体策划自贸区半年系列宣传，组织中国—东盟媒体记者拉力赛、新增中国—东盟博览会主题口号和诗词楹联征集活动、东盟媒体广西行活动和“魅力之城”新闻发布会，推动国务院新闻办继续举办第七届新闻发布会，将中国—东盟自由贸易区政策宣传台卡、资料和中国—东盟博览会的宣传品摆入了全国商务、海关、检验检疫系统的对外服务窗口，首次组织东盟媒体广西行活动，首次为“魅力之城”组织新闻发布会，进一步扩大了博览会的影响力。

2. 社会宣传工作紧扣博览会的新特点和自贸区如期建成的新形势，把本届博览会的特色宣传、亮点宣传和自贸区宣传紧密结合。宣传写作和报道会前、会中、会后持续不断，在数量和质量方面继续取得新突破；专门策划了自贸区成就系列宣传，达到了宣传自贸区和博览会的双重目的；新闻吹风会和新闻发布会成系列，形成持续新闻高潮；突出宣传新增加的成就展、服务贸易展、珠宝展；《快报》实现了会前、会中和会后三阶段出齐的目标，内容丰富，图文并茂，时效性强，形成了博览会宣传的又一个主阵地。

3. 市场营销力度大，推介效果好。本届博览会增加了与重点国家媒体的合作，突出了在主题国印尼的推介，首次在新加坡电视播发中国—东盟博览会招商广告，首次在合作媒体组织整版推介。博览会秘书处先后与东盟10国31家媒体和国内20家行业媒体签订合作协议，在报纸、杂志、网络（部分）等媒体上，以广告、软文、新闻、专访等形式发布第七届中国—东盟博览会相关信息；同时配合广西代表团出访东盟和东盟国家领导人访问中国等大事，开展博览会的宣传推介。经统计，本届博览会在东盟国家共发布广告218次，软文和新闻355篇次，整版专刊2次；在国内行业媒体共发布招商招展广告62次，软文和新闻94篇次，起到了很好的推介效果。

五 安全保卫

2010年的第七届中国—东盟博览会、中国—东盟商务与投资峰会是中国—东盟自由贸易区建成后举办的新一届盛会，规格高、规模大、活动多、时间长。在党中央、国务院领导同志的关怀下，在广西壮族自治区党委、政府和公安部以及自治区“两会”指挥中心、自治区“两会”安全保卫工作领导小组的领导下，全区公安机关和全体公安民警、武警官兵及各增援力量继续发挥团结协作、全力以赴、连续作战、无私奉献的精神，突出重点，周密部署，精心组织，整体作战，狠抓各项安保措施落实，确保了“两会一节”各项重要会议、活动的安全顺利进行，达到了自治区党委、政府和公安部提出的“绝对安全、万无一失”的工作要求，实现了“五个不发生”的工作总目标，圆满地完成了各项安全保卫任务。

（一）强化领导，靠前指挥，推动安保工作高效统一协调运转

公安部和广西壮族自治区党委、政府对“两会一节”安全保卫工作高度重视。广西壮族自治区党委召开常委会议对2010年“两会一节”筹备工作进行研究，对安保工作迅速作出部署。自治区党委书记、自治区人大常委会主任郭声琨，自治区主席马飚分别对安保工作作出重要指示，为“两会一节”安保工作指明了方向。自治区领导温卡华、陈武、梁胜利等多次亲临安保一线，率先垂范，亲自挂帅，亲自研究、亲自动员部署、亲临现场督导和指挥，把大量精力投入到安保工作中，以集体的智慧和魄力确保安保工作扎实有序推进。2010年10月13日，自治区公安厅召开全区公安机关“两会一节”安保工作电视电话会议，对安保工作再动员部署。公安部派出工作组到广西指挥、协调、指导安保工作。公安部继续批复同意广西公安机关在南宁机场、凭祥口岸、东兴口岸设立临时签证办公室，为境外人员办理临时落地签证。同时，各级领导还在政策、装备和经费方面给予大力支持。

（二）建立健全安保工作机构，精心规划安保工作方案

广西壮族自治区成立“两会”安保工作领导小组，自治区党委常委、政法委书记温卡华为组长，自治区副主席、公安厅厅长梁胜利为副组长，自治区有关部门主要领导为成员，设维护稳定和安全保卫工作指挥部。同时，在“两会”广西指挥中心成立安全保卫部，自治区公安厅副厅长陈一平为指挥中心副总指挥兼安保部部长（指挥长），自治区综治办、自治区公安厅、自治区国家安全厅、广西国际博览事务局、自治区安监局、南宁市公安局、武警广西总队、武警广西边防总队、武警广西消防总队、警卫局等有关部门负责人为副部长（副指挥长），确保安全保卫工作指挥调度的统一高效。针对2010年“两会一节”活动需求，精心制定调整安全保卫工作总体方案和各项分方案、预案。按照“细之又细、实而又实”的要求，经过反复的论证，不断修改和完善，做到每一项工作、每一场活动、每一个环节、每一个岗位都有明确的规定，并具有很强的可操作性。据统计，仅南宁市公安局就制定安保方案和应急预案120个。

（三）全警参与，举全区之力，做好“两会一节”各项安保工作

2010年“两会一节”新启用广西体育中心作为民歌节晚会场地，增设华南城、广西民族博物馆两个展览场馆，还新增珠宝贵重物品展，展馆、展位和参展商为历届最多，加上受广州亚运会的安保工作抽调警力的影响，所需警力明显缺口，凸显“两会一节”安保工作任务的艰巨性。安保部门继续提出“举全区安保之力”，确保“两会一节”安全顺利举行。全区各级公安机关行动迅速，全警动员、全力以赴，全力做好“两会一节”各项安保工作。南宁市公安局作为2010年“两会一节”安保工作的主力军，全市民警一律停止休假，警力除部分留守值班外，可用警力全部投入安保工作中。为缓解警力和装备不足，安保部协调武警官兵、广西警官高等专科学校、广西警官学校、广西政法管理干部学院学员，公安厅机关民警以及崇左、贵港、钦州、防城港、来宾市公安机关民警支援“两会一节”安保工作，从全区抽调警犬30头协助做好防爆安检工作；同时，动员社会安保力量协助安保部门开展工作。据统计，2010年“两会一节”全区直接参战的警力达1.3万人，投入安保力量25万多人次，为历年之最。

（四）突出重点，严密部署，圆满完成“两会一节”安保工作任务

协调南宁海事部门对邕江水域实行管制，南宁市公安局派出警用巡逻艇加强巡逻。启动环桂环邕治安检查卡点，在进邕的各个交通要道、路口设立卡点，24小时对进城的车辆进行安全检查，对可疑人员依法盘查，防止违禁

集中部署安保工作
Safety and security work arrangement

物品和犯罪分子流入南宁。协调部署空中警戒工作，将先进的警用直升机投入安保工作，在空中监控、空中指挥、线路警卫等方面发挥了突出的作用，南宁也成为使用自有警用直升机直接投入重大国际活动安保实战工作的城市。全区各地公安机关增派警力加强了面上治安巡逻防范，维护社会面上治安秩序，确保各重点要害部门、要害部位的安全。在“两会一节”期间，组织开展万人大巡防，组织开展对重点人员、不确定群体的监控和各类矛盾纠纷的调处排查，全面加强街面、繁华场所的巡逻防范和单位、住宅小区的看家护院工作，确保社会面治安得以有效控制。

（五）创新安保模式，实现科技安保、人文安保、规范安保

2010年“两会一节”安全保卫工作大胆创新，积极推行科技安保、人文安保、规范安保理念，创新推出便利措施，既方便了来宾和群众，又确保安全，赢得了各方面普遍好评，整个安保工作取得了新的突破。一是大力推行科技安保，有效提高安保工作的效率和水平。充分发挥视频监控系统作用，实现在直观状态下的点对点指挥。应用卫星视频设备，实现远程指挥和实时调度。首次动用直升机参与安保，使用排爆机器人以及远距离探测仪等将一批先进设备应用到安保工作中，极大提高了安保工作效率和安全系数，确保安全。二是大力推进人文安保，较好地兼顾了安全与便利。实行“无缝转场”，既确保了活动安全，又方便与会人员。科学设定行车路线，加强交通指挥，使用卫星定位导航系统，动态监控和科学调度，方便广大与会人员和群众出行。对一般交通违章，以批评教育为主，不作实际处罚。开通穿梭

巴士、的士，方便与会人员。与工商、城管、食品安全监督、质量监督等部门联合执法，有效维护展馆良好秩序。三是创新安保警务方式，安保工作措施进一步规范。严格按规范要求，按方案实施各项安保工作。以块为主，即以场馆、现场、线路为整块，将该块的安保任务分包给某个建制单位负责，进一步明确责任分工，将职责落实到具体单位和个人。实行记者安检前移，对记者及所携器材采取事先安检后派警员专车送入场，方便记者。规范培训和演练，确保参战人员按规范要求上岗执勤。“两会一节”期间，安保民警坚持理性、平和、文明、规范执法，恪尽职守、认真负责，文明有礼、热情服务，展示了一流的思想作风、一流的实战技能、一流的执法水平，实现了安保执法“零差错、零失误、零投诉”的工作目标。特别是在安检执勤过程中，安保民警做到文明、细致、周到、热情，在坚持安检标准不降低的前提下，兼顾好人性化服务，做到保证安全与尊重人格、尊重隐私的和谐统一，实现了“被检人员满意、场馆绝对安全”的效果，向国内外展现了广西公安民警文明、专业、敬业的良好形象。

第九章

深化合作创佳绩 互利共赢显成效

——第七届中国—东盟博览会的重要成果

经贸成效是反映展会是否成功的重要标志之一。

第七届中国—东盟博览会根据中国—东盟自由贸易区建成后的新需求，发挥共办特色和优势，高度集中了中国和东盟10国的企业、商品、项目、资金等信息，加大贸易配对和投资促进力度，把自贸区的贸易投资便利化从政府层面推进到企业层面，让企业更好地享受自贸区商机。本届博览会贸易成交额、签约国际国内合作项目投资额均比上届进一步提高，经贸成效显著。

各国政要对本届博览会予以高度评价，认为博览会一届比一届办得出色，希望能够更好地借助中国—东盟博览会的平台，不断深化和拓展合作，也坚信中国—东盟博览会的成功举办必将推动东盟10国与中国在经贸、旅游、文化、投资等方面的合作取得更大的发展。

各国商协会负责人和企业家认为，本届博览会促进了中国与东盟的行业对接，为广大客商搭建了一个广阔而有效的合作和沟通平台。

各国嘉宾对通过博览会加强与广西在各领域的合作更加充满信心，认为广西发展潜力巨大，前景十分美好。

2010年，中国—东盟博览会再次获得会展业界颁发的多项大奖，体现了博览会在会展业界得到了充分肯定，品牌影响力不断扩大。

Mutual Benefits from Deepened Cooperation
—Achievements of the 7th CAEXPO

The economic and trade outcome is one of the most important indicators of the success of the event.

The 7th CAEXPO has well used its unique co–sponsoring mechanism and advantages to meet the new demands of enterprises of China and ASEAN, upon the establishment of the CAFTA. It has provided a large quantity of enterprises, commodities, projects, capitals and promoted business matching, as well as advanced the trade and investment facilitation from governments to enterprises, helping them to gain more benefits brought by the CAFTA. The trade volume, and the contracts of international and domestic projects concluded at the 7th CAEXPO were higher than that of last CAEXPO, achieving a remarkable outcome.

Political and government leaders of China and ASEAN all sang high praises of the 7th CAEXPO, believing the event was more successful than the previous one, and more opportunities and cooperation could be made available through the CAEXPO, which will play an important role in further promoting the bilateral cooperation in economy and trade, tourism, culture, and investment.

Heads of chambers of commerce and businessmen of China and ASEAN believed that the 7th CAEXPO has promoted the matching of industries of both sides and provided a large and effective platform for cooperation and communication among business communities.

Guests and visitors of China and the ASEAN countries showed their confidence in the role of the CAEXPO in boosting their cooperation in all fields of Guangxi, which was of great potential in their eyes.

In 2010, the CAEXPO was again honored with a number of awards by the convention and exhibition industry of China, marking that the CAEXPO brand has gained wide recognition in the industry.

CHAPTER NINE

一　经贸合作再上新台阶

第七届中国—东盟博览会紧扣中国—东盟自贸区建成后的新需求，增加了新内容，通过新举措，把中国—东盟自贸区一系列贸易和投资便利化传导给企业，成效显著，商品贸易成交额、签订国际国内经济合作项目总投资额再创新高。

（一）商品贸易成交额再创新高

贸易成交额创历届新高。本届中国—东盟博览会实现商品贸易成交额达到17.12亿美元，比上届增长3.5%，成交总额为历届最高。按交易类别分，出口额14.28亿美元，比上届增加1.57亿美元，增长12.3%，占成交总额的比重为83.5%，比上届提高6.6个百分点；进口额0.01亿美元，比上届下降96.2%，占成交总额的比重为0.07%；商品出口额增长明显，占据成交总额主导地位。按交易方式分，商品交易合同金额为8.02亿美元，比上届增长1.5倍，占成交总额的比重为46.9%，比上届提高27.6个百分点；意向金额9.09亿美元，比上届下降31.9%，占成交总额的53.1%，比上届下降27.6个百分点。本届博览会合同金额大幅增加，比重明显提升。

第七届中国—东盟博览会商品贸易出口、进口、国内贸易比重

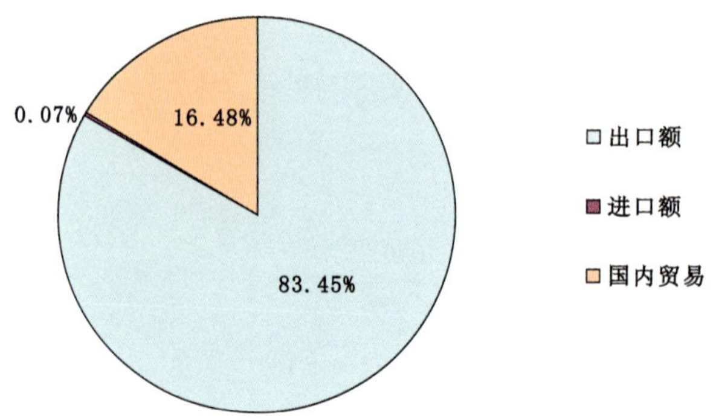

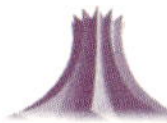

第七届、第六届中国—东盟博览会商品成交情况对比表

	第七届（亿美元）	第六届（亿美元）	第七届比第六届增减（%）
成交总金额	17.12	16.54	3.5
出口额	14.28	12.72	12.3
进口额	0.01	0.34	−96.2
国内贸易	2.82	3.49	−19.1
合同金额	8.02	3.19	151.8
意向金额	9.09	13.35	−31.9
境外企业合计	7.27	2.82	157.7
合同金额	6.51	0.79	719.2
意向金额	0.76	2.03	−62.5
广西企业成交金额	1.65	5.17	−68.1
出口额	0.73	3.44	−78.8
进口额	0.00	0.00	
国内贸易	0.92	1.73	−47.0
合同金额	0.53	0.93	−42.9
意向金额	1.12	4.25	−73.7

轻工工艺类商品成交额位居榜首。第七届中国—东盟博览会轻工工艺类商品成交额由上届排第六位跃升为第一位，达4.58亿美元，占成交总额的26.7%。成交额排在第二至第五位的商品分别是：电子电器类4.32亿美元，占25.3%，与上届相比仍然保持第二位；机械设备类1.57亿美元，占9.2%，由上届第一位退居第三位；食品类1.55亿美元，占9.0%，从上届第五位上升到第四位；农产品类1.04亿美元，占6.1%，由上届的第八位上升到第五位；汽车及配件类0.98亿美元，占5.7%，由上届的第三位退居第六位。

第七届中国—东盟博览会各类商品成交情况表

商品种类	累计成交金额（亿美元）	所占比重（%）	排位
轻工工艺类	4.58	26.7	1
电子电器类	4.32	25.3	2
机械设备类	1.57	9.2	3
食品类	1.55	9.0	4
农产品类	1.04	6.1	5
汽车及配件类	0.98	5.7	6
建筑材料类	0.85	5.0	7
五金化工及矿产品类	0.42	2.5	8
珠宝和玉器	0.34	2.0	9
农业生产资料类	0.08	0.5	10
其他商品	1.38	8.1	
合计	17.12	100.00	

国内企业商品贸易成交情况。本届博览会国内企业商品贸易成交总额9.80亿美元。其中，国内企业与境外企业成交额6.93亿美元，占70.7%；与东盟各国企业成交额6.04亿美元，占成交总额的61.6%。其中与新加坡成交额为1.96亿美元，占与东盟各国企业成交总额的32.5%，排在首位；与马来西亚成交额1.43亿美元，占23.7%，排在第二位；与越南成交额1.26亿美元，占20.9%，排在第三位；与印度尼西亚成交额0.47亿美元，占7.8%，排在第四位。国内企业与港澳台企业成交额0.21亿美元，占2.1%。国内企业与境内企业成交额2.66亿美元，占国内企业成交总额的27.1%。

第七届中国—东盟博览会国内企业与各国或地区商品贸易成交情况表

国别（地区）	成交金额（万美元）	累计比重（%）
总计	97955	100.0
国内企业与境外企业成交额	69289	70.7
东盟国家	60374	61.6
文莱	1102	1.1
印度尼西亚	4725	4.8
马来西亚	14298	14.6
菲律宾	828	0.8
新加坡	19601	20.0
泰国	3667	3.7
越南	12602	12.9
老挝	606	0.6
缅甸	1347	1.4
柬埔寨	1599	1.6
其他国家	8914	9.1
国内企业与港澳台企业成交额	2074	2.1
国内企业与境内企业成交额	26593	27.1

广西企业成交合同金额比重明显上升。本届博览会广西企业商品贸易成交额16472.2万美元，占本届博览会成交总额的9.6%，在国内参展单位中排第三位。按交易类别分，广西企业商品出口额7292.46万美元，占成交总额的比重为44.3%；进口额24万美元；国内贸易9155.74万美元，占成交总额的比重为55.6%。按交易方式分，合同金额5288.61万美元，占成交额的比重32.1%；意向金额11183.59万美元，占成交额的比重67.9%。从与境内境外企业成交情况看，广西企业与境外企业成交7491.01万美元，占成交总额的比重为45.0%。其中与东盟国家成交3025.98万美元，占成交总额的比重18.2%。文莱成为本届博览会广西最大贸易伙伴，成交额最多，达1000万美元；其次是泰国（641万美元）；第三位是越南（430.56万美元）。广西企业与境内企业成交额9142.38美元，占成交总额的比重为54.9%，广西企业与港澳台企业成交额9.08万美元，占成交总额的0.1%。

广东、福建、山西、浙江、江苏等省市成交额较多。除广西外，本届博览会各省市企业成交额合计5.76亿美元，比上届下降32.5%，占本届博览会成交总额的33.6%，占境内企业成交总额的58.7%。广东企业成交额最多，达3.31亿美元，占境内企业成交总额的33.8%；中直单位2.41亿美元，占境内企业成交总额的24.6%；福建、山西、浙江和江苏成交额分别为0.34亿、0.30亿、0.30亿和0.20亿美元，分别占境内企业成交总额的3.5%、3.1%、3.1%和2.1%。

第七届中国—东盟博览会各省市区商品贸易情况表

地区	成交总额（万美元）	所占比重（%）
合 计	98125.38	100
广西	16472.20	16.79
广东	33133.71	33.77
福建	3447.98	3.51
山西	3042.67	3.10
浙江	3040.36	3.10
江苏	2011.10	2.05
安徽	1888.92	1.93
江西	1711.49	1.74
天津	1574.32	1.60
山东	1515.75	1.54
北京	844.48	0.86
重庆	672.12	0.68
河北	659.20	0.67
上海	590.80	0.60
青海	503.21	0.51
宁夏	451.70	0.46
湖南	398.33	0.41
湖北	318.78	0.32
贵州	314.81	0.32
河南	287.04	0.29
四川	271.80	0.28
内蒙古	256.00	0.26
辽宁	176.45	0.18
云南	172.80	0.18
黑龙江	112.69	0.11
海南	50.13	0.05
甘肃	40.15	0.04
吉林	26.25	0.03
陕西	25.49	0.03
新疆	14.73	0.02
西藏	0.05	0.00
中直单位	24099.88	24.56

（二）投资合作再上新台阶

借中国—东盟自贸区如期建成的强劲东风，本届中国—东盟博览会投资合作项目签约再创上新台阶，共签订国际经济技术合作项目135个，总投资66.9亿美元，较上届增长3%；共签订国内经济技术合作项目156个，总投资674.46亿元人民币，较上届增长9%。本届博览会投资合作有以下特点：

一是中国东盟合作质量明显提升。本届博览会上，中国与东盟签约的投资合作项目数量多，合作领域广，合作质量不断提升。本届博览会中国与东盟签约的投资合作项目共57个，总投资25.13亿美元，分别占国际合作项目的42.2%和37.6%，其中中国对东盟国家的投资项目36个，投资总额15.02亿美元，东盟国家对中国的投资项目21个，投资总额10.11亿美元。合作领域包括农业、制造业、商贸物流、旅游开发、矿产开采及加工、交通能源设施建设等。

二是重大项目多、投资数额大成为一大特色。本届博览会签约的国际合作项目，总投资额达1亿美元以上有25个，单个项目平均投资额达4801万美元，比上届的4735万美元有所提高；国内合作项目投资额5亿元人民币以上的有46个，单个项目平均投资额达4.32亿元，较上届的3.03亿元增长43%。

三是新技术、新能源、新材料项目明显增多。本届博览会投资合作签约项目中，第二产业的项目数和投资总额仍占第一位，制造业继续唱主角。但是与往届不同的是，新技术、新能源、新材料等技术含量高、发展潜力大的战略性新兴产业项目明显增多，主要包括LED光电、数码电子产品、太阳能的利用、生物质能发电、精细化工、生物医药等。从本届博览会投资合作签约项目中可以看到，中外各国经贸投资活动，进一步顺应世界经济发展趋势和加快经济发展方式转变、加快结构调整的要求。

四是商贸物流项目成为一大亮点。中国—东盟自贸区建成后，中国与东

第七届中国—东盟博览会上举行的商品推介会

Commodity promotion conferences at the 7th CAEXPO

盟90%的产品贸易实现零关税，通关便利化水平进一步提高，双方贸易量物流量将持续增加，商贸物流业自然能从中获得更多的商机。因此，商贸物流业成为国内外客商的投资热点。本届博览会投资合作签约项目中，商贸物流合作项目多，投资金额大，成为一大亮点。其中国际合作的商贸物流项目19个，总投资额5.85亿美元，分别占国际合作项目总数的14.1%和8.8%；国内合作的商贸物流项目15个，总投资额89.13亿元，分别占国内合作项目总数的9.6%和13.2%。

五是广西对外资的吸引力进一步增强。中国—东盟自贸区建设启动以来，尤其是随着每年一届的中国—东盟博览会在南宁举办，广西成为中国与东盟经贸交流与合作的前沿和窗口，在国际国内区域合作中的战略地位和作用日益显现，发展前景广阔，商机无限，成为越来越多国内外客商的投资热土。本届博览会投资合作签约项目中，广西签订利用外资项目84个，总投资44.26亿美元，分别比上届增长42.3%和17.1%；国内21个省区市和中央直属企业对广西的投资合作项目146个，投资总额671亿元人民币，比上届增长10.8%。

二　各界评价

作为中国—东盟自由贸易区建成后的新一届盛会，第七届中国—东盟博览会顺势而为，展览内容更加丰富，更加贴近中国—东盟自由贸易区的发展需求，展览形式更加专业，更加准确地传导中国—东盟自由贸易区的商机，受到各国政要、共办方官员、商协会和国际组织负责人，以及中外嘉宾和广大客商的一致好评。广西作为博览会永久举办地，广大中外嘉宾和广大客商纷纷表达了与广西加深了解、加强合作的强烈愿望。

（一）中国—东盟博览会：共赢的时代　合作的平台

各国政要和广大客商对本届博览会给予了积极的评价，一致认为博览会一届比一届办得出色，希望能够更好地借助中国—东盟博览会的平台，不断深化和拓展合作，也坚信中国—东盟博览会的成功举办必将推动东盟10国与中国在经贸、旅游、文化、投资等方面的合作取得更大的发展。

各国政要充分肯定了博览会在深化中国—东盟友谊，推动自贸区建设和促进双方经贸发展等方面起到了积极的作用。

中共中央政治局常委、全国政协主席贾庆林说，中国—东盟博览会、中国—东盟商务与投资峰会已成为中国同东盟国家对话、交流、合作的有效平台。

印尼副总统布迪约诺说，在自贸区建成之际举办的第七届博览会具有特殊的意义，它不仅为双方商家企业展示产品、宣传形象、结识新伙伴提供了便利，创造了商机，而且也将推动东盟与中国在竞争日益激烈的全球市场中进一步加强经济合作，最终实现共赢。

老挝副总理阿桑·劳里说，中国—东盟博览会和商务与投资峰会的举办十分成功，内容丰富，形式多样，值得我们很好考察和学习借鉴。

中国商务部国际贸易谈判代表兼副部长高虎城表示，中国—东盟博览会作为中国—东盟自贸区建设的“助推器”，对推动中国—东盟自贸区建设，推动双方经贸合作，起到了不可替代的作用。

文莱工业和初级资源部部长叶海亚表示，每次参加博览会都能感受新发展、新动向。2010年文莱的清真食品首次在博览会上展出，将进一步促进友好合作。

印尼贸易部部长冯慧兰在评价博览会时说，中国—东盟博览会至今已成功举办六届，搭建了中国和东盟经贸和多领域合作的平台，取得丰硕成果，成功推进了自贸区的建成。中国—东盟博览会不仅找到了一个举办地，而且为中国—东盟大家庭找到了一个家。

缅甸商务部部长吴丁乃登说，参加过中国几个城市的展览会，南宁是最好的。缅甸参展商积极性很高。

菲律宾贸工部副部长克里斯托伯说，对于东盟成员国来说，中国—东盟博览会不仅是促进东盟与中国贸易和投资的重要平台，也是东盟成员国之间交流合作的重要平台。

各国共办方官员、商协会会长和国际机构负责人对博览会的品牌影响力和平台作用给予了高度评价。

中国商务部合作司处长陈文林说，加拿大首次组团对接东盟，充分说明中国—东盟博览会品牌影响力快速提升，市场认知度不断增强，给世界各国企业带来了越来越多的商机。

东盟秘书处负责人兰安琪女士表示，中国—东盟博览会外国展位数连年提高，目前外国展位数在中国国内展位中居于前列，博览会已经成为东盟等外国企业开拓中国市场的重要渠道。

缅甸商务部贸易司副司长丁·特温高兴地提到，中国—东盟博览会举办以来，缅甸与中国之间的市场不断扩大，中国投资商通过博览会平台，有机会了解缅甸的情况。可以说，博览会吸引了更多的外资进入缅甸。

马来西亚驻广州商务领事沈国安说，博览会秘书处安排的中国“走出去”企业与马来西亚贸工部副部长贾谷·东加·沙甘面对面会谈等高端对接活动成效显著，希望2011年继续举办此类的对接活动。

印尼中华总商会总主席纪辉琦说，印尼中华总商会多次组团到南宁参加中国—东盟博览会，深切感受到博览会一年办得比一年好。

广东家纺协会常务副秘书长萧健承说，中国—东盟博览会是一个很好的窗口和展示平台，作为一个行业商会组织，希望加强商会与商会之间的对接，以使中国与东盟的合作进一步扩大。

文莱—中国友好协会秘书长陈家福说，博览会年年都有新主题，我们也可以得到很多资讯和服务。中国—东盟博览会这个平台是目前唯一一个东盟

第七届中国—东盟博览会盛况

Grand occasion of the 7th CAEXPO

和中国合作的大平台。有了这个平台，就可以把企业做得更大，同时也可以促进别的国家和东盟国家以及中国的交流。这个平台很便利，让企业以后有更大的发展空间。

中外嘉宾和客商普遍认为中国—东盟博览会为广大客商搭建了一个广阔而有效的合作和沟通平台。

南宁永凯实业集团有限公司董事局主席赖可宾说，中国—东盟博览会汇集了来自东盟各国的客商和熟悉东盟各国政策法规的专家，通过和他们的交流，能了解东盟各国的人文历史、政策法规和投资环境，防范“走出去”可能遇到的各种风险，加快企业走进东盟的进程。

越南边和威拿咖啡股份有限公司范光武说，这七届来，博览会的展位数量越来越多，展位设计越来越漂亮，主办方的服务工作越来越细致，最重要的是，博览会在东盟国家的影响力越来越大，几乎每个东盟国家都知道中国—东盟博览会。

新加坡丰隆亚洲有限公司总裁张冬贵表示，通过中国—东盟博览会和中国—东盟自贸区这两个平台，从制造、贸易、旅游、管理技术、城市规划、环保节能等方面，不止是东盟受益，中国也受益。

第三次参会的法国马恩河谷省议会副省长罗汉·加尼尔高兴地说，中国—东盟博览会总是让人感到非常震惊，也让人印象深刻。

（二）广西以开放的姿态对接东盟市场

越南副总理张永仲谈到广西时说，广西和越南山连山、水连水，又是同志加兄弟，近年来，广西经济增速越来越高，经济总量越来越大，发展质量越来越好。希望广西继续加大在越南的投资，越南各省将和广西加强沟通和互访，进一步推动双方在各领域进行全方位的交流与合作。

老挝副总理阿桑·劳里表示，随着中国—东盟博览会连年在广西举办，老挝与广西的交往日益密切，交流与合作不断深化。老挝将一如既往地支持广西承办中国—东盟博览会和商务与投资峰会。希望广西政府组织更多的本地企业到老挝考察投资，组织更多的游客到老挝观光旅游。

菲律宾贸易与工业部副部长艾德里安·克里斯托伯说，菲律宾与广西有着很强的互补性，尤其体现在农业方面。希望广西派出更多的代表团到菲律宾考察投资，双方进一步探讨扩大合作。

柬埔寨国务兼商业大臣占蒲拉西表示，广西发展潜力巨大，前景十分美好，柬埔寨永远支持广西承办好中国—东盟博览会，也希望广西加大力度促进广西企业到柬埔寨投资。

菲律宾宿务省省长格温多琳·加西亚说，很高兴再次来到广西访问。在一年当中两次来到这里，充分证明广西是宿务省最重要的友好省区之一。相信依托现有良好基础，两省区交流与合作一定能够取得更大的成绩。宿务十分愿意在教育、港口建设领域与广西商讨具体合作，热切希望宿务到南宁的直航航班尽快开通，进一步加强两地人民的交往，深化传统友谊与交流合作。

印尼中华总商会总主席纪辉琦说，多次来到广西，深切感受到广西的巨大变化，广西近年来通过承办中国—东盟博览会，不断深化与印尼等东盟国家的交流与合作，双方都在合作中受益匪浅。

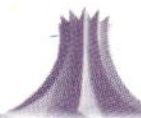

三　中国—东盟博览会再获殊荣

中国—东盟博览会举办以来，知名度在会展业界日益提高，影响力进一步扩大，2010年，中国—东盟博览会又获得中国会展业几项大奖。

2010年5月9日，在第八届中国会展节事财富论坛上，中国—东盟博览会被评为“2009—2010年度中国会展产业金手指奖·十大影响力展览会”，中国—东盟博览会秘书处秘书长、广西国际博览事务局局长郑军健被评为“2009—2010年度中国会展产业金手指奖·十大新闻人物”。

2010年8月20日，中国—东盟博览会在2010中国会展行业年会·世博会主题展策划与中国会展业发展论坛上被评为“新世纪十年·中国会展杰出典

2010 年，中国—东盟博览会获得的中国会展业部分大奖奖牌
The CAEXPO wins major awards of Convention & Exhibition Industry in China in 2010

范奖”和“新世纪十年·中国十大品牌展会”，中国—东盟博览会秘书处秘书长、广西国际博览事务局局长郑军健被评为“新世纪十年影响中国会展业60人”

2010年10月31日，中国—东盟博览会在第六届中国节庆产业年会暨2010中国节庆产业金手指奖颁奖盛典上荣获“十大经贸博览类节庆最具魅力品牌奖”，中国—东盟博览会秘书处秘书长、广西国际博览事务局局长郑军健荣获2010年中国节庆产业金手指奖年度“十大新闻人物”奖。

2010年12月11日，在首届中国会展业年会暨北京国际会展产业高峰论坛上，中国—东盟博览会再获殊荣，被评为“2010年中国十佳展览会”。

2010年12月29日，中国—东盟博览会在第八届中国会展业论坛年会·颁奖盛典上荣获“2010年度中国十大国际影响力展会”；中国—东盟博览会秘书处秘书长、广西国际博览事务局局长郑军健荣获“2010年度中国会展业杰出人物”奖。

2005年来，中国—东盟博览会每年都获得会展业权威机构颁发的多个奖项。

2005年7月10日，在首届中国国际会展文化节暨2005年中国会展年会上，时任中国—东盟博览会秘书长、广西国际博览事务局局长张晓钦荣获“2004中国会展十大新闻人物”奖。

2005年12月16日，在2005年中国会展业(高峰)论坛大会上，中国—东盟博览会及举办地和会址连获殊荣。经过大会评选，中国—东盟博览会被评为2005年度中国十大知名品牌展会，排名仅次于广交会，列第二位；博览会举办地——南宁被评为2005年度中国优秀会展城市；博览会会址——南宁国际会展中心被评为2005年度中国十大优秀会展中心；博览会常设机构——广西国际博览事务局获得2005年度中国会展业特别贡献奖。

2007年1月12日，在上海举行的第三届中国会展业高峰论坛大会暨“中国会展之星”2006年度评选颁奖盛典上，中国—东盟博览会被评为“2006年度中国十大最具影响力政府主导型展会”；南宁国际会展中心被评为“2006年度中国最佳会展中心”；时任中国—东盟博览会秘书长、广西国际博览事务局局长张晓钦荣获“2006年度中国会展十大新闻人物”奖。

2007年4月1日，在第四届中国会展节事财富论坛暨2006年度中国会展产业年度评选颁奖盛典上，中国—东盟博览会被评为2006年度中国会展业最具影响力会展25强，时任中国—东盟博览会秘书处秘书长、广西国际博览事务局局长张晓钦荣获“2006年度中国会展业十大新闻人物”奖。

2008年1月4日，在上海召开的第四届中国会展业高峰论坛大会暨2007年

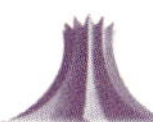

度“中国会展之星”颁奖盛典上，中国—东盟博览会被评为2007年中国十大最具影响力国家级品牌展会，继续保持较高的行业地位。

2008年1月12日，在首次举办的中国行业品牌展会“金手指奖(TOP3)”颁奖典礼上，中国—东盟博览会被评为最具影响力品牌展会。

2009年3月28日，中国—东盟博览会在第六届中国会展节事财富论坛上被评为“2008年度十大会展”，中国—东盟博览会秘书处秘书长、广西国际博览事务局局长郑军健被评为“中国会展产业十大新闻人物”。

2009年5月27日，在上海举行的第六届“中国会展之星”颁奖盛典上，中国—东盟博览会再获殊荣，被评为2008年中国最具影响力政府主导型展会，中国—东盟博览会秘书处秘书长、广西国际博览事务局局长郑军健被评为“中国会展之星年度人物”。

2009年9月27日，在2009全国节庆会展工作会议暨中国会展（节庆）创新发展论坛暨庆祝建国60周年——中国节庆会展（评选）颁奖盛典上，中国—东盟博览会荣获建国60周年・中国最具影响力的品牌展会暨政府主导型展会百强，中国—东盟博览会秘书处秘书长、广西国际博览事务局局长郑军健被评为“建国60周年・中国会展风云人物”。

2009年9月28日，在上海举行的“建国60周年・60个会展品牌・中国会展60人评选活动”中，中国—东盟博览会被评为“建国60周年，60个会展品牌”，中国—东盟博览会秘书处秘书长、广西国际博览事务局局长郑军健荣获“中国会展业60人”奖。

2009年12月27日，在第七届中国会展高峰论坛上，中国—东盟博览会被评为2009年度中国十大国家级品牌展会；中国—东盟博览会秘书处秘书长、广西国际博览事务局局长郑军健荣获“2009年度会展十大新闻人物”奖。

从2004年首届博览会成功举办以来，在7年的成长过程中，博览会荣获了15个（次）业内顶级大奖，充分体现了博览会的影响力和行业地位，这是对博览会作出的成绩的肯定，同时也是对博览会今后发展的激励。中国—东盟博览会将再接再厉，开拓创新，更好地发挥平台的作用，为服务中国—东盟友好合作作出更大贡献。

第十章

10 万千商机 惠泽企业

——第七届中国—东盟博览会企业案例

中国—东盟博览会是互利共赢的大平台，它为企业开拓中国—东盟自由贸易区市场提供了战略高地和巨大商机。

从本届博览会看，新加坡丰隆亚洲有限公司成为中国—东盟博览会首席战略合作伙伴，中国移动广西公司、中国有色矿业集团、广西投资集团、广西农垦集团等成为博览会战略合作伙伴，这些企业通过博览会平台开拓了市场，获取商机，成效显著。

主要体现在以下方面：

——第一时间获取权威信息。博览会战略合作伙伴第一时间在更高层面上了解中国和东盟10国宏观政策信息，帮助企业决策。

——高端公关，展示自身实力。博览会战略合作伙伴优先与业内著名专家、企业CEO以及中国和东盟39家商协会领袖建立良好沟通网络，优先获得中国—东盟博览会秘书处提供的经贸、人文等合作信息渠道，借助中国—东盟博览会多领域资源，获得贸易、投资、旅游、教育、文化等多领域合作商机。

——媒体聚焦。博览会战略合作伙伴优先受到中外媒体的重点关注，高效提升其品牌在业内的知名度和国际形象。优先获得高端推介机会，直接面向中国—东盟博览会高质量的潜在客户现场推介，优先获得稀缺紧俏的黄金广告位，宣传效果倍增速显。

新加坡丰隆亚洲有限公司总裁张冬贵表示，通过成为中国—东盟博览会的首席战略合作伙伴，增加了品牌知名度，增加了投资的机遇。

More Opportunities for More Enterprises
—Trade Deal Cases of the 7th CAEXPO

China–ASEAN Expo is a large platform for mutual benefit and win–win result, which provides huge opportunities and strategic highland for businesses to gain access to the tremendous market brought by the CAFTA.

At the 7th CAEXPO, Hong Leong Asia Ltd. of Singapore became the CAEXPO Chief Strategic Partner, while other companies including China Mobile (Guangxi), China Nonferrous Metal Mining (Group) Co., Ltd, Guangxi Investment Group, and Guangxi State Farms became the CAEXPO Strategic Partners, which all found business opportunities and achieved satisfying outcomes.

The benefits can be identified as follows:

— Timely available authentic information: The CAEXPO Strategic Partners can get access to the macro policies and information regarding China and ASEAN, which will be helpful in decision making.

— Present company images at high end level. The CAEXPO Strategic Partners have formed good connections with industrial experts, CEOs of enterprises, and heads of the 39 CAEXPO Supporting Chambers of Commerce of China and ASEAN, to get information of economic, trade and culture through the CAEXPO Secretariat, for more opportunities of cooperation in trade, investment, tourism, education, and culture.

— Attention of media: The CAEXPO Strategic Partners can receive more attention from media to highlight their brands and company images. They can also get access to high end promotion opportunities targeting quality potential customers at the CAEXPO, and the gold product placements for advertisement to maximize publicity.

Mr. Teo Tong Kooi, President of Hong Leong Asia Ltd. of Singapore, said that by being the Chief Strategic Partner of the CAEXPO, the company has raised the recognition of the brand, and also gained more opportunities for investment.

一　企业开拓中国—东盟自由贸易区大市场的重要平台

第七届中国—东盟博览会在中国—东盟自由贸易区全面建成之际举办，吸引了各国众多企业参展参会，成为各国企业开拓中国—东盟自由贸易区大市场的重要平台。世界五百强企业之一的新加坡丰隆亚洲有限公司，就是通过这个平台获得良好成效的典型案例之一。

（一）新加坡丰隆亚洲有限公司基本情况

丰隆亚洲有限公司是一家在新加坡上市公司，隶属新加坡丰隆集团。新加坡丰隆集团的业务包括房地产、酒店、金融服务和制造营销业等，而丰隆亚洲是专注制造及营销业务。丰隆亚洲20世纪90年代起在中国进行投资，现已成为中国和东南亚地区最大的制造商之一，在中国投资的业务包括：河南新飞电器有限公司、广西玉柴机器股份有限公司和利士工业包装。此外，在新加坡、印尼及马来西亚，丰隆亚洲集团的建材业务是当地的最大生产及供应商之一。

新加坡丰隆亚洲有限公司展位

Exhibition booth of Hong Leong Asia Ltd. of Singapore

丰隆在中国的第一个制造业投资就是在广西。广西玉柴机器股份有限公司（简称“玉柴”）是中国玉柴国际有限公司的子公司，而玉柴国际是丰隆亚洲集团成员之一。 玉柴国际于1994年在纽约股票交易所上市。自丰隆亚洲投资入股玉柴，玉柴已发展为中国最大的柴油发动机生产企业，产能从3万台发展到目前的超过60万台柴油发动机。根据中国汽车工业协会数据统计，过去几年玉柴发动机的销量在行业内排名第一。玉柴目前在全国各地均有投资，而产品也出口到东南亚和世界各地。

自1994年投资入股河南新飞电器有限公司（新飞电器）以来，目前丰隆亚洲持股90%。在16年内，新飞电器快速增长，年产能由1994年的30万台冰箱扩展至超过800万台冰箱（柜）。新飞电器的经营业绩也迅速提升，平均每年以15%的速度递增，在中国已是第二大冰箱及冷柜制造商。据中国标准化研究院和清华大学中国企业研究中心最新提供的2010年度中国顾客满意度调查显示，新飞位居冰箱类产品前两位，其中性价比和产品可靠性两项关键指标则位居第一位。

利士工业包装制造各种塑料包装产品以提供于工业包装与消费包装市场。其在中国拥有3家厂房，即天津、上海及东莞，供应于国际跨国企业和国内大型企业。利士在业界享有广泛美誉。此外，利士在马来西亚和印度尼西亚也设有生产基地。

此外，丰隆亚洲集团的建材业务在新加坡和马来西亚享有市场领先地位。其业务范围广泛——生产及销售各种建材产品，包括搅拌混凝土、水泥预制件产品、水泥、钢铁、碎石产品等。丰隆亚洲集团的建材业务可以为客户提供一站式及便利的服务。

新加坡丰隆集团旗下的千禧国敦酒店集团（Millennium & Copthorne Hotels）于1996年在英国伦敦上市，目前在全球18个国家拥有或经营管理超过120家国际三星级、四星级和五星级酒店，是在中国以外亚洲最大的控股酒店集团。丰隆集团在20世纪60年代开始涉足金融服务业。目前，丰隆金融已成为新加坡最大的金融公司，全岛共有28家分支机构。

多年来，丰隆亚洲秉承回馈社会的企业使命，积极履行社会责任，累计支持、赞助中国体育、教育、慈善等公益事业1亿多元。2010年9月，新飞电器还再度携手中国足协，成为中国之队主要赞助商，从而成为继中超之后，第一家同时赞助国内两大顶级足球赛事的企业。新飞电器除了提供奖学金赞助贫困学生，也是赛扶（中国）的赞助商，为社会培养高层次复合型人才和扩大大学生在国内知名大企业的就业机会作出贡献。

（二）新加坡丰隆亚洲有限公司牵手中国—东盟博览会

2010年10月13日，第七届中国—东盟博览会首席战略合作伙伴签约仪式暨新闻发布会在南宁举行，广西壮族自治区主席马飚，自治区党委常委、自治区副主席陈武等领导出席发布会，与新加坡丰隆亚洲有限公司总裁张冬贵共同见证签约仪式，丰隆亚洲有限公司成为首个与博览会结成首席战略合作伙伴的东盟企业。

丰隆亚洲有限公司牵手中国—东盟博览会对公司发展有何意义？为何选择中国—东盟博览会？

在新闻发布会上，丰隆亚洲有限公司总裁张冬贵说，丰隆亚洲荣膺第七届中国—东盟博览会首席战略合作伙伴，可谓是登上了中国—东盟商界最高级别的沟通、交流、发展平台之一，通过博览会这一平台，将进一步扩大丰隆亚洲的业务影响力，进一步拓展中国和东南亚市场，将有更多的机会享受到投资贸易便利化带来的无限商机。

张冬贵说，伴随2010年中国—东盟自由贸易区的建成，将拥有19亿人口、接近6万亿美元GDP、4.5万亿美元贸易总额。中国—东盟自由贸易区是发展中国家组成的最大的自由贸易区。中国—东盟博览会以中国—东盟自贸区为依托。中国—东盟自贸区建设的成果为博览会持续发展提供了内在的市场动力。同时，博览会为企业分享自贸区建设成果，进一步开拓市场，提供了难得的好平台。而中国与东盟10国则是丰隆亚洲的主要业务所在区域，因此，丰隆亚洲携手中国—东盟博览会，将促进丰隆亚洲的业务发展，扩大市场覆盖面。

张冬贵强调，中国—东盟自由贸易区是中国与其他经济体最早建立、进展最快、效果最好的自贸区，是重要的国际贸易通道、能源走廊和经济纽带，已成为全球经济体系中重要的新兴力量，发展前景十分广阔。继中国—东盟自由贸易区启动后，中国加快构建广西北部湾经济区的步伐，并致力于打造“南新铁路”、打造南宁—新加坡经济通道，未来泛亚铁路东线将形成南北贯通交通物流走廊，加快区域经济一体化进程。丰隆亚洲将抓住中国—东盟自贸区建成以及泛北部湾经济区构建的机遇，加大在中国的投资，积极开拓中国和东南亚市场，特别是借助中国—东盟博览会平台，继续深化经贸合作，促进区域经济朝着更大规模、更高质量、更可持续的方向发展。

二 企业充分展示形象，提升品牌影响力，全面开拓自贸区市场

2010年10月19日下午，第七届中国—东盟博览会在南宁隆重开幕。中国与东盟国家领导人、部长出席开幕式。新加坡高级贸易代表团团长、丰隆亚洲总裁张冬贵以特邀贵宾身份出席了第七届中国—东盟博览会开幕式，丰隆亚洲成为开幕式一大新闻亮点，新华网、人民网、新浪、搜狐、网易、中国经济网等媒体纷纷报道丰隆亚洲成为博览会战略伙伴的重大意义，宣传了丰隆亚洲有限公司通过博览会开拓中国—东盟自由贸易区市场的重要举措。

10月19日上午，第七届中国—东盟博览会开幕在即，新加坡贸工部兼新闻通讯艺术部政务次长陈振泉在新加坡高级贸易代表团团长、丰隆亚洲总裁张冬贵的陪同下参观了博览会国际会展中心的丰隆亚洲展馆，张冬贵向陈振泉介绍了丰隆亚洲在中国投资的核心业务：中部的河南新飞电器、西南的广西玉柴机器和沿海的上海、天津、东莞利士工业包装。此外丰隆亚洲的建材业务在新加坡、印尼、马来西亚已发展成为当地最大的生产及供应商之一；并向陈振泉重点介绍了新飞电器的对开门大容积风冷高端冰箱等高品质、高技术新产品。陈振泉对丰隆亚洲在中国的快速发展表示满意。

10月13日下午，广西壮族自治区主席马飚在南宁会见新加坡丰隆亚洲有限公司总裁张冬贵，对丰隆亚洲成为中国—东盟博览会首席战略合作伙伴表示祝贺，这是中国—东盟博览会举办六届以来，国外企业第一次成为首席战略合作伙伴，必将起到很好的带动和示范作用，进一步推进广西与东盟的交流合作。当前，广西正在加快实施18个重点产业调整和振兴规划，衷心希望与丰隆亚洲在先进制造业等领域进一步加强交流合作，将全力支持丰隆亚洲在广西寻找合作、扩大投资。

张冬贵对广西壮族自治区政府给予丰隆亚洲的关心和支持表示感谢。他说，丰隆亚洲对能够成为中国—东盟博览会首席战略合作伙伴感到十分荣幸。这是对丰隆亚洲的认可，也是一个新的平台。丰隆亚洲将认真履行首席战略合作伙伴的职责，进一步推动东盟与中国的经贸交流合作，进一步加强与广西的合作。

广西壮族自治区党委常委、自治区副主席陈武一同参与会见。

10月20日，第七届中国—东盟博览会展览活动开始。丰隆亚洲以其强大的团队、豪华的阵容盛装亮相此次博览会，为博览会增辉添色，成为南宁国际博览中心的一大亮点。在会展中心一楼特装的以枣红色巨型战舰造型的丰隆亚洲展台，矗立在162平方米的硕大区间，丰隆亚洲及旗下的新飞、玉柴、利士、建材四大企业的标识、企业及文化理念介绍的展板依次排列，展现出丰隆亚洲集团跨行业、多领域、国际化的大企业形象。而位于二楼新加坡商品馆展区内靓丽多彩的新飞冰箱、冷柜、酒柜、空调及利士包装等产品，则成为引人注目的风景线，展现出丰隆亚洲作为亚洲制造业巨头的非凡实力，吸引了越来越多的合作者。

张冬贵对丰隆亚洲通过博览会平台在中国市场取得更好的成绩充满信心。他认为，已经成为家电制造领域和柴油机制造领域、包装建材领域龙头企业的丰隆亚洲一定会在泛北部湾大区域整合提升的大舞台上、在中国制造唱响全球的大背景下，使企业在“4R”、“QPP”等跨文化先进管理理念的指导中，加强战略规划和布局、提高管理和服务能力，为中国和东盟19亿人民提供更为优质的产品和服务。

三　中国—东盟博览会惠泽众多企业

通过第七届中国—东盟博览会，众多企业展示了企业形象，提升了品牌影响力，开拓了中国—东盟自贸区市场，取得了良好成效。

（一）中国移动广西公司：为打造中国—东盟信息交流中心作贡献

中国移动广西公司连续六年成为中国—东盟博览会战略合作伙伴，2010年被授予博览会“首席荣誉战略合作伙伴”称号。公司助力广西打造中国—东盟开放合作的物流基地、商贸基地、加工制造基地和信息交流中心，积极服务北部湾基础通信设施建设、港口信息化、通信服务贸易、农村信息化等广西经济社会发展各项事业，积极促进和引领物联网与TD—SCDMA的产业融合发展和业务创新，倡导更为领先、便捷、高效的移动新生活。

第七届中国—东盟博览会期间，中国移动广西公司积极部署，铸造精品网络，全面保障通信顺畅。公司结合往年保障经验，并根据第七届博览会活动规模制定了相应的应急通信保障方案，成立了应急通信保障组织机构，并构建起区、市、县三级应急通信保障小组，确保盛会的通信网络畅通无阻。

中国移动广西公司服务中国—东盟博览会

China Mobile (Guangxi) provides services for the 7th CAEXPO

除传统话音业务外，公司重点保障数据业务和WLAN无线业务畅通，全面展示具备我国自主知识产权的TD—SCDMA制式的G3业务，以“最先进的技术、最精彩的业务、最专业的服务”为博览会增添一份精彩。

在优质的通信网络基础上，公司精益求精，对会展中心、体育中心等主要场所和四星级以上酒店进行地毯式的网络强化测试，并对各活动场馆周边30个基站进行优化扩容。共出动应急通信车7辆，对覆盖活动区域的基站话务进行24小时严密监控，保证活动区域内通信无阻。针对各种突发通信事件，公司形成了系统的应急保障系统，建立并完善了多套自然灾害、突发事件类应急预案，并不定期在内部开展实战演练，保障盛会期间的通信畅通。

（二）中国有色矿业集团有限公司：携手博览会，共谱合作新华章

中国有色矿业集团有限公司通过中国—东盟博览会，积极开拓东盟市场，成效显著。目前，中国有色矿业集团有限公司在东盟的8个国家拥有投资项目，东盟是其重要的海外市场之一。中国有色矿业集团有限公司在泰国投资建设有色金属资源再生利用项目——泰中铅锑合金厂是泰国最大的铅生产企业，其产品占泰国市场份额的30%以上；正在建设的缅甸达贡山镍矿项目总投资8.22亿美元，是中缅矿业领域最大的合作项目；正在投资开发的老挝帕克松铝土矿项目进展良好；公司承建的越南生权铜矿及大龙冶炼厂结束了越南不产铜的历史。

“随着中国—东盟自贸区全面建成，中国有色矿业集团将通过中国—东盟博览会这一充满机遇的平台，进一步展示企业实力与形象，在中国与东盟

中国有色矿业集团有限公司展位
Exhibition booth of China Nonferrous Metal Mining (Group) Co., Ltd

的合作中获得更多的机会、发挥更大的作用。”中国有色矿业集团有限公司总经理罗涛在谈及与中国—东盟博览会进行战略合作时表示，中国有色矿业集团有限公司以前瞻眼光与博览会合作，给予了博览会战略性支持，同时也通过博览会这一平台进一步扩大了在东盟国家的影响力。双方将强强联合，携手为推动双边经贸合作作出应有的贡献。

区域经济一体化与经济全球化，已经成为当今世界经济发展的两大趋势。罗涛认为，中国加入WTO，有力地推动了中国参与经济全球化的进程。中国—东盟自贸区是比WTO程度更深、进程更快的开放，成员国已相互取消90%以上的关税和非关税壁垒，消除绝大多数服务部门的市场准入限制，实现投资自由化。同时，自贸区又是双向、互利的开放。中国—东盟自贸区拥有19亿人口，接近6万亿美元的经济总量，是世界人口最多的自贸区，市场合作前景广阔。

（三）广西投资集团：拓展与东盟的能源资源合作

乘中国—东盟自由贸易区建成的东风，广西投资集团不断深化与东盟国家的合作。在第七届中国—东盟博览会上，广西投资集团与东盟客商就能源资源的深度开发与利用深入洽谈，加快推进相关项目。同时，寻找新的商机，携手合作，共谋发展，成效显著。

作为中国—东盟博览会长期合作伙伴，广西投资集团非常注重利用中国东盟博览会这个平台与东盟国家开展经贸交流与合作，并取得积极成效。早在2004年第一届中国—东盟博览会上，集团下属的鹿寨化肥公司便与马来西

广西投资集团展位
Exhibition booth of Guangxi Investment Group

亚、泰国、越南等客户签署产品出口意向协议，协议总额达3460万元。以此为契机，鹿寨化肥公司此后几年对东盟的出口业务不断扩大。2008年，在第五届中国—东盟博览会上，广西投资集团与越南安圆集团签订《越南高平铝土矿投资合作备忘录》。经过中越双方的持续努力，项目前期工作获得重大进展，项目于2010年12月底开工，预计18个月建成投产。建成后产品主要供应集团下属电解铝企业，以进一步提高集团原料自给能力，促进广西铝工业的发展。

通过中国—东盟博览会，广西投资集团适时实施“走出去”战略，结识了大批东盟客商，建立了互信互访机制，了解东盟国家的投资环境，拓展了更多的合作商机。2010年8月，该集团与印尼第四大煤炭生产商达尼多煤炭集团公司签订了《煤炭战略合作框架协议》，就煤炭贸易、广西北海煤炭配送中心和印尼煤矿投资合作达成了共识；与印尼华泰能源公司签订了《关于合作开发印尼煤矿项目意向协议》，就印尼煤矿项目的开发、生产及销售进行全面合作。项目建成以后，将有效缓解广西电煤供应紧张的局面。

2010年9月上旬，广西壮族自治区主席马飚率团出访越南期间，广西投资集团与越南安圆集团签署了《越南宁顺省安风风电场项目合作框架协议》，项目装机容量18万千瓦，总投资2 5亿元。东盟地区正在成为广西投资集团对外投资的重要区域，该集团在东盟国家的产业布局和构建能源战略基地的步伐在不断加快。

（四）广西农垦：“走出去”的排头兵

连续7届担任中国—东盟博览会战略合作伙伴的广西农垦集团，在第七届博览会上共签订国际国内投资合作项目46个，签约金额167.8亿元人民币。其中对外投资项目9个，总投资额1.62亿美元，再次成为广西企业向东盟“走出去”的排头兵。

广西农垦承建了国家级重点项目——中国—印尼经济合作区。在第七届博览会上，广西农垦又签订了4个与中国—印尼经贸合作区相关合作项目。一是由在全球制鞋业中位于前五名的台湾隆典实业有限公司投资的制鞋基地项目，项目总投资5000万美元，占地面积约28.86公顷。项目建成后，将年产运动鞋120万双。二是隆平高科印度尼西亚有限公司种子培育加工基地项目，建设水稻种子培育加工基地及仓储，总投资额100万美元。三是中印经贸合作区标准厂房建设项目。项目业主为隆平高科印尼东太阳能公司，主要经营日光照明设备、节能灯具。东太阳能公司拟建设中国—印尼经贸合作区准厂房3000平方米，总投资额100万美元。四是中国—印尼经贸合作区惠贾

广西农垦集团展位
Exhibition booth of Guangxi State Farms

工业公司建材加工项目。拟购买中国—印尼经贸合作区内1.84公顷土地，用于建设铝型材加工工厂，产能1万平方米/年，总投资额100万美元。此外，广西农垦还与柬埔寨丰发有限公司签订了木薯淀粉、燃料乙醇木薯产业项目。双方拟在柬埔寨王国马德望省合作投资建设木薯产业加工项目。初步计划合作项目建设规模为年产30万吨木薯淀粉、年产30万吨燃料乙醇，项目总投资估算约1.5亿美元。

四　企业家对中国—东盟博览会平台给予充分肯定和赞誉

丰隆亚洲有限公司总裁张冬贵表示，通过成为中国—东盟博览会的首席战略合作伙伴，增加了品牌知名度，增加了投资的机遇。

他说："作为中国—东盟博览会首席战略合作伙伴，我们很高兴地看到中国与东盟之间投资和贸易都在增加，尤其是今年的博览会，越做越大，我们的投资信心也随着加大。"

通过博览会，丰隆亚洲有限公司与其他企业一样，更加看好中国—东盟自贸区建成后投资的前景。

张冬贵说，现在不仅是新加坡，全世界的跨国企业都到中国来了。我们的强势就是语言方面，我们比其他跨国公司对中国的本土文化更了解。所以我们这次通过成为中国—东盟博览会的首席战略合作伙伴，增加我们的品牌知名度。当然我们是寻找投资项目，有些中小型企业主动来找我们，我相信这是很好的机遇。我们希望通过中国—东盟博览会这个平台，增加我们投资的机遇。

对于博览会在促进中国与东盟合作方面的作用，张冬贵给予高度评价。他说，通过中国—东盟博览会和中国—东盟自贸区，从制造、贸易、旅游、管理技术、城市规划、环保节能等方面，不止是东盟受益，中国也受益。东盟很多国家没有高技术，以往是从欧美国家进口，现在是从中国出口到东盟国家，比如说玉柴机械，目前在越南、马来西亚、泰国的销量每年都在增加，这是品牌知名度的问题。中国出口到东盟的产品，一步步在提高，一定会促进双方贸易和制造业等领域更多的交流合作。

中国移动广西公司总经理顾雄说，中国移动广西公司通过中国—东盟博览会平台，业务取得了快速发展。中国移动广西公司的移动通信网络信号已覆盖广西所有城市、乡镇、行政村，目前客户总数突破2100万户，是广西区域通信行业的主导运营商和协助政府推进广西经济社会信息化发展的主力

军，在广西百强企业排名中连续多年名列前茅。

中国有色矿业集团有限公司总经理罗涛表示，博览会是我国十大最具影响力的国家级品牌展会之一，是中国与东盟交流合作的重要平台，也是中国企业开拓东盟市场、实现国际化经营便捷、有效的经贸平台。中国有色矿业集团希望通过加深与博览会的合作，更好地借助博览会的平台，积极参与东盟国家有色金属资源开发和工程项目建设，为东盟国家经济发展作出更大的贡献。他说："中国有色矿业集团将通过与博览会的战略合作，进一步拓展在东盟的投资。"

广西投资集团董事长管跃庆认为，中国—东盟博览会在推动中国企业开拓东盟市场起到了很好的经贸平台作用，主要体现在四个方面：一是展示中国企业的优势产品，开拓东盟产品市场。二是展示国内急需的东盟国家商品，特别是资源性产品和原材料。三是提升中国企业知名度和影响力，扩大招商引资。四是为中国企业"走出去"穿针引线。

广西农垦局副局长杨海空说，中国—东盟自贸区的如期建成，使得博览会这个平台的作用得到了更好发挥。广西农垦通过博览会，充分自身优势，不断加强与东盟国家经贸合作，加快实施"走出去"战略，取得了积极成效。

第十一章

自贸区新起点 博览会新机遇
——中国—东盟博览会服务中国—东盟自由贸易区展望

中国—东盟博览会已成功举办七届，搭建了中国—东盟友好交流、经贸促进和多领域合作的重要平台，成为中国—东盟自由贸易区具有广泛影响力的国际盛会，为中国与东盟、发展中国家与发展中国家共同发展树立了典范。

随着2010年中国—东盟自由贸易区如期全面建成，中国—东盟经贸合作站在了新的历史起点上，中国—东盟博览会也迎来新的发展机遇。

首先，中国—东盟自贸区建成后的中国—东盟博览会取得了新的突破。其次，中国—东盟自贸区建设符合中国—东盟当前和长远利益，受到中国和东盟双方重视，信心更强，决心更大，作为中国—东盟自贸区平台的博览会前景更为光明。第三，中国—东盟自贸区的升级与活力带来了中国—东盟博览会竞争能力的增强。

展望未来，中国—东盟博览会要紧扣新形势，继往开来，围绕服务中国—东盟自由贸易区建设，坚持创新，进一步完善合作发展新模式；完善机制，推动全方位合作；扩大实效，服务举办地经济发展；持续推动自贸区建设，深化中国—东盟经贸合作。

New Starting Point for CAFTA, New Opportunities for CAEXPO

—Prospects on CAEXPO Serving CAFTA

The CAEXPO, which has been successfully held for 7 consecutive years, has provided an important platform for the friendly exchanges, trade promotion, and cooperation in various fields between China and ASEAN. It has become the most influential international trade event within the CAFTA, setting up a good example for the common development of developing countries.

With the establishment of the CAFTA in 2010 as scheduled, the economic and trade cooperation between China and ASEAN stands at a new starting point, and the CAEXPO is also facing new opportunities for development.

First, the CAEXPO after the establishment of the CAFTA has made new breakthrough. Second, the CAFTA is in the common interests of China and ASEAN, and will bring a bright future for both sides. Third, the upgrading and vitality of the CAFTA will reinforce the competitiveness of the CAEXPO.

Looking ahead, the CAEXPO will keep close watch on the new situation and make innovation in cooperation and development models, with an aim to better serve the CAFTA. What's more, the event will improve the mechanism to advance overall bilateral cooperation; expand the pragmatic effect, and boost the local economic development of the host province, so as to continuously push forward the building of the CAFTA and deepen the economic and trade cooperation between China and ASEAN.

CHAPTER ELEVEN

一　中国—东盟博览会发挥了中国—东盟自由贸易区"助推器"作用

中国—东盟博览会作为中国和东盟各国及东盟秘书处共同主办的国际盛会，秉承"促进中国—东盟自由贸易区建设、共享合作与发展机遇"的宗旨，走过了七年的发展历程。经过七年的探索，博览会形成了集政治、外交、经贸、人文为一体，与东盟全方位开展合作的新模式，搭建了中国—东盟友好交流、经贸促进和多领域合作的重要平台，成为中国—东盟自由贸易区具有广泛影响力的国际盛会，为中国与东盟、发展中国家与发展中国家共同发展树立了典范。

（一）搭建了友好交流的平台，以政治外交影响力带动了经贸等多领域合作

七届中国—东盟博览会有38位中国和东盟国家领导人、1300多位部长级贵宾出席。会期举行多场双方领导人、部长、地方负责人之间的会谈，以及政界商界高端对话，增进了政治互信，也推动了商家的务实合作，带动了文化、教育等多领域的交流活动。

特别是博览会建立了主题国机制，每届中国—东盟博览会轮流由一个东盟国家担任主题国。由主题国领导人率团出席当届中国—东盟博览会，会期举办一系列高层次、精彩、富有商机的主题国活动，促进了友好合作，体现了互利共赢。主题国系列活动包括：

——博览会开幕式由主题国领导人代表东盟方致辞，由主题国部长级官员主持。

——主题国领导人出席主题国开馆仪式。

——主题国领导人出席同期举办的中国—东盟商务与投资峰会并演讲。

——举行政界商界高端对话，促进友好交流，推动商界合作。

——主题国专场推介会将强力推介主题国独特的贸易投资环境、优势和

2010年10月21日，第七届中国—东盟博览会主题国印度尼西亚举办国家推介会

The Promotion Conference of Indonesia, Country of Honor of the 7th CAEXPO, held on October 21, 2010

商机，中国和其他国家和地区的名优企业将参会、洽谈和签约。

——主题国精心推出独具特色的文艺演出，促进文化交流。

——各国媒体云集，宣传主题国风采，助主题国企业塑造品牌、扩大影响。

从2007年起，文莱、柬埔寨、老挝、印尼先后出任了第四、第五、第六、第七届博览会的主题国，举办了一系列主题国活动，促进了中国—东盟友好合作。

（二）搭建了经贸促进的平台，发挥了中国—东盟自贸区建设“助推器”的作用，以经贸合作成果促进政治互信和友好交流

中国—东盟博览会是中国—东盟自贸区的直接产物，无论是宗旨、定位，还是内容、形式等宏观和细微之处，都体现了中国—东盟自贸区的元素，突出博览会是为中国—东盟自贸区服务的特点，使中国—东盟自贸区更深入人心。

从宗旨和定位来看，中国—东盟博览会以“促进中国—东盟自由贸易区建设，共享合作与发展机遇”为宗旨，紧紧围绕《中国—东盟全面经济合作框架协议》，以及中国—东盟自贸区建设实际进程，以双向互利为基本原则，以中国—东盟自贸区内的经贸合作为重点，同时面向全球商界开放，既突出了博览会的主旨，又体现了博览会的开放性。

从内容看，每届博览会围绕中国—东盟自贸区建设进程以及中国和东盟国家的经济发展水平、资源禀赋、产业结构、行业特点而设置展览内容，以中国—东盟自贸区内的合作为重点。在商品贸易方面，博览会紧扣自贸区《货物贸易协议》，展示降税商品和零关税商品。在展品类别上，以中国与

第七届中国—东盟博览会机械设备展区
The 7th CAEXPO Machinery & Equipment Section

东盟互有需求，交易量大的商品为主，如机械设备、电子电器、建筑材料等。举办更具实效的贸易配对活动，提高了双方商品贸易水平。在投资合作方面，博览会专门设立投资合作专题，组织具有雄厚实力"走出去"的中国企业参展，展示国际工程承包、劳务合作、资源开发等内容，举办一系列投资促进活动，增进了企业的了解和交流，促进了投资合作。在服务贸易方面，博览会结合自贸区《服务贸易协议》的实施，设置服务贸易专题，展示金融、物流、教育等内容，并围绕旅游、物流、金融、法律、海关等服务领域，开展了一系列交流活动，促进了服务领域的合作。

从博览会的开幕式看，它充分体现了中国—东盟博览会在中国—东盟自贸区建设中发挥的重要作用。例如，博览会开幕式是中国和东盟各国政要出席的一个重大仪式。开幕式展现中国和东盟国家友好交往源远流长的历史和日益深化合作的现实，是双方战略伙伴关系深入发展的象征，预示中国—东盟自贸区前景辉煌。每届开幕式以"水"为元素贯穿始终，生动形象地把中国—东盟合作的历史、现实、未来，以及博览会的作用和意义展现出来，充满创新精神和文化内涵，受到各国领导人和社会各界的高度赞誉。

从博览会的文化创新看，博览会作为唯一以中国—东盟自由贸易区为主题的展会，不仅在展览内容、活动设计上紧扣自贸区建设，而且在展会的文化内涵上进行挖掘、创造，通过博览会反映自贸区的成就和美好前景。例如，在第七届博览会期间举办了中国—东盟自由贸易区建设成就展，全方位地展示了中国—东盟自贸区的历程、成就和美好前景。独具特色的是成就展

设有书画摄影展，中国和东盟国家330位书画艺术家（其中东盟国家艺术家66位，占20%）以及少年儿童以自贸区及中国与东盟友好合作为题材，创作了一批书法、美术、摄影、篆刻等作品，艺术地反映了自贸区合作共赢的主题，也很好地反映了中国与东盟在文化等领域合作的成就，得到了中央政治局委员、中宣部部长刘云山，马来西亚贸工部副部长拿督贾谷·东加·沙甘等政要的高度评价。

中国—东盟自由贸易区建设成就展展出的美术作品
Fine artworks displayed at the CAFTA Achievements Exhibition

综上所述，中国—东盟博览会高度集中了11国的企业、商品、项目、资金等方面的信息，将中国—东盟自贸区的投资贸易便利化从政府层面推进到了企业层面，成为自贸区建设的“助推器”。七届博览会共有26.54万名客商参会，贸易成交额98.83亿美元，签约国际合作项目投资额417.52亿美元，签约国内合作项目投资额4027.92亿元，取得了良好的经贸成效。

一个典型的例子就是，中国广西的东风柳州汽车有限公司将中国—东盟博览会作为开辟东盟各国市场的捷径，已经连续七届通过中国—东盟博览会的平台，展示产品，提高了产品知名度，开拓了东盟市场。2010年1—11月，东风柳汽生产的200辆“风行菱智”汽车销到缅甸，600多辆商用车在越南、菲律宾、印尼、缅甸4国热卖，总销售额达2000多万美元。东风柳汽出口模式已呈现多样化。过去，主要单一依靠整车出口，2010年7月，风行车CKD工厂在缅甸建成投产，标志着东风柳汽从中国—东盟博览会“走出去”到东盟投资迈出了新的步伐。

中国—东盟博览会的举办，促进了中国—东盟经贸合作。2004年，首届中国—东盟博览会举办。中国和东盟双边贸易额提前一年实现了1000亿美元的目标。2007年，双边贸易额提前三年实现2000亿美元的目标。博览会体现了自贸区的双赢效果，推动中国—东盟战略伙伴关系提升到一个更高的水平。

东风柳州汽车有限公司展区
Exhibition area of Dongfeng Liuzhou Motor Co., Ltd

（三）搭建了多领域合作的平台，为中国—东盟自贸区建设和双方在经贸、人文等领域的合作提供机制保障

随着中国—东盟经贸合作的快速发展，双边对海关、检验检疫、金融、港口、物流等相关领域的服务配套提出了新需求，对经贸领域如何与文化、教育、体育等人文领域的交流更紧密结合也有了更高要求。博览会根据这一形势需要，7年来共举办了180多个高层次会议和论坛及相关活动，邀请各国各领域的政府官员、企业家、专家学者参会进行对话交流，研究解决上述领域相关问题的办法和机制，形成了相关领域的一系列合作机制，为经贸、人文等多领域的交流合作提供了机制保障。

例如，博览会围绕中国和东盟十一大重点合作领域（农业、信息产业、人力资源开发、相互投资、湄公河流域开发合作、交通、能源、文化、旅游和公共卫生、环保），每届确定一个重点主题，举办主题论坛和相关活动，推动务实合作。第四届博览会的重点主题是“港口合作”，会期中国交通部主办了中国—东盟港口发展与合作论坛。第五届博览会的重点主题是“信息通信合作”，会期中国工业和信息化部主办了第三次中国—东盟电信周及相关论坛。第六届博览会的重点主题是“海关与商界合作”，会期中国海关总署主办了中国—东盟海关与商界合作论坛。第七届博览会的重点主题是“自贸区与新机遇”，会期中国有关部委举办了能源、金融等一系列高层论坛。

通过每届博览会期间举办一系列会议、论坛和活动，在博览会框架下聚集了越来越多的中国—东盟合作机制。包括：（1）交流培训机制，如中国—东盟妇女培训中心、中国—东盟青少年培养基地、中国—东盟自贸区会计服务出口示范基地等；（2）合作促进机制，如中国—东盟青年企业家协

2010年10月20日，首届中国—东盟银行家圆桌会议在广西南宁举行
The 1st China-ASEAN Bankers' Round Table Meeting held in Nanning, Guangxi on October 20, 2010

会、中国—东盟农资商会等；（3）对话磋商机制，如中国—东盟质检部长磋商合作机制等。通过以上机制，形成了中国—东盟合作的“南宁渠道”。

博览会还设立“魅力之城”专题，每届每个国家选派一个城市担任“魅力之城”，展示城市形象和发展商机，促进城市合作。每届博览会期间还举办南宁国际民歌艺术节等一系列文化体育交流活动，增进中国与东盟各国友好往来。

中国商务部国际贸易谈判代表兼副部长高虎城2010年7月在国务院新闻办公室举行的中国—东盟经贸关系进展暨第七届中国—东盟博览会、第七届中国—东盟商务与投资峰会新闻发布会上表示，中国—东盟博览会作为中国—东盟自贸区建设的“助推器”，对推动中国—东盟自贸区建设，推动双方经贸合作，起到了不可替代的作用。

二　中国—东盟自贸区新起点，中国—东盟博览会新机遇

2010年，中国—东盟自贸区如期全面建成。中国—东盟自贸区从此站在了新的历史起点上，中国—东盟博览会也迎来发展的新机遇。这种新机遇，突出表现为以下三个方面。

首先，中国—东盟自贸区建成后的中国—东盟博览会取得了新的突破。中国—东盟博览会以促进中国—东盟自贸区建设为宗旨，中国—东盟自贸区建成以后，博览会如何跟上发展的变化，取得新的突破，成了人们普遍关注的问题。2010年10月19—24日，第七届中国—东盟博览会在南宁成功举办，同期举办第七届中国—东盟商务与投资峰会，中共中央政治局常委、全国政协主席贾庆林出席开幕式。作为中国—东盟自贸区建成后的新一届盛会，第

第七届中国—东盟博览会签约现场
The contract signing ceremonies of the 7th CAEXPO

七届中国—东盟博览会以“自贸区与新机遇”为主题，在延续了往届嘉宾规格高、展位逐年增多的特色的同时，紧扣中国—东盟自贸区建设进程设置展览内容，传导中国—东盟自贸区商机，在多个领域取得了实效，“助推器”作用显得更加突出。第七届中国—东盟博览会经贸成效再创新高，交易总额达到17.12亿美元；签署国际经济合作项目135个，总投资额66.9亿美元；签署国内经济合作项目156个，总投资674.46亿元。第七届博览会深化了中国与东盟合作，巩固了中国—东盟自贸区成果，增强了11国继续共同推进中国—东盟自贸区建设的信心。

第七届中国—东盟博览会进一步推动了中国—东盟务实合作。第七届中国—东盟博览会是中国—东盟自贸区建成后的第一届博览会。本届博览会除保持原有的高规格和共办特色外，还紧扣中国—东盟自贸区建成的新需求，根据《货物贸易协议》、《服务贸易协议》和《投资协议》签订实施的新形势，在已有货物贸易、投资合作内容的基础上，增加了新的内容，如：服务贸易专题、珠宝首饰展、中国—东盟自贸区建设成就展等。通过这些新举措，务实推进中国与东盟友好合作，把中国—东盟自贸区一系列贸易和投资便利化政策快速传导给企业，取得了显著的成效，体现了博览会直接为中国—东盟自贸区服务、是中国—东盟自贸区“助推器”的特点。

特别值得一提的是，第七届中国—东盟博览会期间还举办了中国—东盟自贸区建设成就展，集中展示中国—东盟自贸区建设的成果和美好前景，反映中国与东盟互利共赢，进一步增强了中国和东盟10国共建中国—东盟自贸区的决心。

第七届中国—东盟博览会的成功举办，用鲜活的事实，证明了中国—东盟自贸区建成后，博览会的使命非但没有结束，反而增添了新的使命与责任，为中国—东盟自贸区建成后博览会的发展方向提供了直接可操作的样板。

其次，中国—东盟自贸区建设符合中国—东盟当前和长远利益，受到中国和东盟双方重视，信心更强，决定更大，作为自贸区平台的博览会前景更为光明。

实践证明，中国—东盟自贸区是互利互惠的，符合双方当前和长远利益。就中国方面而言，为继续发挥自贸区建设在带动我国对外经济发展中的重要作用，《中华人民共和国国民经济和社会发展第十二个五年规划纲要》明确指出：“加快实施自由贸易区战略，进一步加强与主要贸易伙伴的经济联系，深化同新兴市场国家和发展中国家的务实合作。利用亚太经合组织等各类国际区域和次区域合作机制，加强与其他国家和地区的区域合作。”在加快实施自贸区战略的引导和推动下，中国—东盟区域合作进程将会进一步

第七届中国—东盟博览会东盟商品展区
The 7th CAEXPO ASEAN Commodity Section

加快。目前，中国和东盟之间90%以上的货物实现了零关税，下一步将重点提高服务贸易的相互开放水平，同时要做好《中国—东盟投资协议》的实施工作，保障和促进双向投资合作进一步发展。显然，加快实施自贸区战略，积极推进自贸区建设将会为中国—东盟博览会提供更广阔的发展空间。

从东盟方面看，中国—东盟自贸区的建成促进了东盟各国向中国出口的快速增长。仅2010年1月至第七届博览会举办的10月，文莱、缅甸、印尼、马来西亚等东盟国家与中国的贸易额增幅均达到了50%以上。其中，对中国出口增幅最大的国家是文莱，达184.3%，紧随其后的依次是缅甸54%，印尼53.7%，马来西亚50%。中国—东盟自贸区建成后的实践发展成果，消除了少部分东盟国家部分行业担心中国—东盟自贸区建成会对本国产业造成冲击的疑虑，进一步坚定了东盟各国继续共同建设中国—东盟自贸区的信心。信心使东盟国家将和中国共同努力，推动中国—东盟自贸区各个协议的执行，将中国—东盟自贸区的政策传递给企业商家，让本区域所有人都能够从自贸区中获益。这就必然使中国—东盟自贸区获得可持续发展的活力。

其三，中国—东盟自贸区的升级与活力带来了中国—东盟博览会竞争能力的增强。中国—东盟自贸区建成后，自贸区各种政策的实施，使贸易投资更为便利化，中国—东盟区域融合进一步加深，经贸合作硕果更为突出。这就为中国创造了良好的机遇进一步融入东盟市场，也使东盟国家能够在中国这一大市场中占据更重要的位置。

据海关统计数据显示，2010年，中国与东盟双边贸易额达2927.8亿美

元，比上年增长37.5%，高出中国和东盟各国对外贸易平均增幅，超过中国对外贸易平均增幅2.8个百分点。其中，中国对东盟出口1382.1亿美元，增长30.1%；自东盟进口1545.7亿美元，增长44.8%。进出口数据颠覆了此前有人担心的会削弱东盟国家的竞争力疑虑。事实证明，中国—东盟自贸区的建立极大地提升了东盟不少国家的国际竞争力，如2010年公布的全球竞争力指数排名中，印尼从此前的54位上升到第44位，大幅度前移了10位。

中国—东盟博览会是直接为自贸区建设服务的。随着中国—东盟双方贸易规模进一步扩大，投资合作更加活跃，服务贸易开放领域进一步拓宽，中国—东盟博览会的平台传导作用将获得更大的发展空间，博览会的工作更具体，任务更重，在中国—东盟实现互利共赢和自贸区建设中发挥更大作用的机遇会更好。

三　中国—东盟博览会服务中国—东盟自由贸易区展望

随着中国—东盟自贸区已如期全面建成，中国与东盟双方资金、资源、技术和人才等生产要素的流动效率显著提高，双方经贸合作快速增长。中国国务院总理温家宝2010年10月在河内出席第十三次中国与东盟领导人会议期间，提出双边贸易额到2015年达到5000亿美元，并扩大中国对东盟投资。在实现这一目标的过程中，中国—东盟博览会的责任更大，任务更重，对中国—东盟博览会承办工作的新要求更高。

展望未来，中国—东盟博览会要紧扣新形势，完善机制，不断创新，更好地服务中国—东盟自由贸易区建设和发展。

（一）坚持创新，进一步完善合作发展新模式

中国—东盟博览会要继续发挥好平台作用，提升吸引力、影响力，在服务中国—东盟友好合作上更有作为，发挥更大作用，必须通过创新，建立完善集政治、外交、经贸、人文为一体的新的独特合作模式，形成特色。

坚持创新是中国—东盟博览会取得显著成效和不断发展的关键。今后，

第七届中国—东盟博览会上举行的中国—东盟基础设施合作高峰论坛

The China-ASEAN Infrastructure Cooperation Forum held during the 7th CAEXPO

博览会要紧抓中国—东盟自贸区建成和“十二五”规划实施的新机遇，树立创新精神、科学精神、拼搏精神、协作精神，从更高战略层面进一步完善合作发展新模式，做好博览会持续发展工作，增强吸引力、影响力、竞争力，使博览会常办常新，取得实效。

在实践过程中博览会摸索出以政治外交带动经贸以及多领域合作，以经贸和多领域合作促进政治互信、友好交流、政商互动，与东盟全面开放合作的新模式，形成了博览会独特的优势，是其他展会所不具备的。七年的实践证明，这种模式既符合展会发展的规律，也非常符合中国—东盟自贸区发展的需要以及广西经济发展的需要。

完善这种模式也是应对当前国际国内挑战、竞争形势的需要。一方面，美国等西方国家加大了对东盟合作的力度，使中国与东盟的政治互信、经贸合作形势更为复杂；另一方面，国内不少省市通过展会等形式加大开拓东盟市场的力度，在某些方面分散了办好博览会的资源。在这种情况下，既要充满信心，发挥好对东盟合作早发优势，又要保持清醒头脑，不断发展和完善博览会模式的优势和特色，进一步完善各种工作机制，确保博览会在竞争中保持吸引力、生命力，带动经济社会发展。

（二）完善机制，推动全方位合作

中国—东盟博览会是举办地广西在不具备各种基本条件和办会经验情况下举办的，许多工作是在应急状态下实施的。随着形势的发展，博览会必须积累经验，摸索规律，完善工作机制。

中国—东盟博览会承载着政治、外交、经济等多重使命，肩负着带动举办地对外开放、加快发展的重任，而且无先例可循，没有现成的路子可走，承办工作任务尤为艰巨。近年来，国内外会展业发展迅速，展会林立，博览会作为一个年轻的展会，面临着巨大的竞争和挑战。要完成这一任务非常不易，不能因循守旧，必须坚持科学精神，提高工作的机制化、专业化程序，必须突出特色，在办会机制、内容、形式上大胆创新，形成自身独特的优势。

一是进一步完善高规格办会机制，在邀请中国和东盟各国政要出席工作上争取进一步机制化、常态化，提高效率，在邀请部长、国际组织首脑、商协会领袖、世界知名企业家等出席工作上也形成配套的工作机制，体现博览会合作共赢的特色，提升博览会知名度和影响力。以中国—东盟博览会为载体，为政商交流互动搭建平台，让更多各国政要推动经贸活动，与各国企业商家开展交流合作，引导广大企业商家及时把握中国和东盟各国政府有关经济政策及产业发展方向，增进企业商家对中国—东盟自贸区、对中国和广西发展规划、投资环境和投资机会的了解，拓展各国企业间合作的空间，形成政商互动的工作机制，从而把国家层面的共识推进到企业、地方实施层面。

二是使博览会的内容和形式更符合中国—东盟自贸区建设需要，把各国的合作需求变成实践，把中国—东盟自贸区商机传导给各国企业，形成更有竞争力的生存和发展优势。博览会紧扣《货物贸易协议》、《服务贸易协议》和《投资协议》，不断创新展会内容和形式，满足企业开拓自贸区大市场的需求。

有计划扩大博览会规模，把南宁国际会展中心作为第一展区，继续使用广西展览馆作为第二展区举办农业展，新增南宁华南城展览中心作为第三展区举办轻工展，形成“一会三馆”的新格局，更好地满足企业参展需求。同时举办更多的专业展，为双方企业合作创造更多商机。

举办农业展的广西展览馆

Guangxi Exhibition Hall, venue of the 7th CAEXPO Agriculture Exhibition

不断丰富和优化展览内容，让企业更好地享受自贸区商机。在展览内容上兼顾各方需求，引导东盟国家包馆参展，分别集中展示各自特色。在不同国家的展馆中，逐步突出本国重点行业，将重点参展行业集中展示，形成相对独立的展区，提高参展效果。

做大做强投资促进，加强与11国投资促进部门的合作，加强投资项目收集、推介和撮合，建立和完善常态化的投资促进工作机制，突出推动企业“走出去”的特色和优势，积极打造成为“走出去”投资东盟最好的展会。

三是建立合作机制，把各领域的合作常态化、固态化，为经贸以及人文领域交流合作提供保障，发布信息，创造商机。通过举办论坛、会议和相关活动，邀请各国各个领域的政府官员、企业家、专家学者开展对话交流，解决中国—东盟经贸合作快速发展对海关、检验检疫、金融、港口、物流等相关领域的服务配套提出的新问题。

（三）扩大实效，服务举办地经济发展

广西是中国唯一与东盟国家既有陆地接壤又有海上通道的省区，是中国—东盟交流合作的前沿和窗口。博览会要更好地服务中国—东盟自由贸易区，促进区域合作共赢，很重要的一个内容就是服务举办地广西的经济发展。

从前七届中国—东盟博览会举办情况看，博览会将政治外交、经贸促进和多领域合作结合起来，形成与东盟进行全方位、包容性很强的合作发展模式，集中了各种资源和人脉，深化了博览会举办地广西与东盟全面友好合作，为广西发展提供了强有力的支撑。

通过承办博览会，提升了广西在国家战略中的地位，获得了国家政策的倾斜，更多地获得了国家各部委和各省市政府部门的支持和帮助，广西各地基础设施建设和相关产业得到了快速发展，对外开放水平和层次大大提升。通过博览会，广西与各部委的沟通、与各省区市的合作工作更加紧密，更有具体见容。

在新的形势下，博览会将加大整合各种资源的力度，把广西与东盟开放合作的特色进一步扩大、完善和巩固，并不断创新，推动广西与各部委沟通、与其他省区市开展合作的需求由共识走向实践。

——集合国家部委、东盟国家政府部门、商协会和企业、国内各省区市政府、港澳台地区以及中外媒体等各种资源和信息，促进广西与东盟的开放合作更加机制化、常态化。争取更多中国和东盟各国政要与广西地市、部门、企业家交流对话，统筹安排博览会贵宾到各市顺访，实现政企对接与互动，服务广西地市和相关部门对外合作和交流。

——深化平台作用，带动广西各地市的发展。通过博览会平台，深化广西各地市与东盟国家和国内省区市之间交流合作，促成更多类似钦州中马产业园区、广西农垦承建中国—印尼经贸合作区的合作项目，不断扩大广西企业“走出去”规模，提高“走出去”水平，带动广西城市硬件和软件建设，以及社会经济发展。

——发挥博览会文化推动的重要作用，把广西与东盟的合作由经贸领域扩大深化到旅游、教育、文化、体育等更多领域，形成广西与东盟国家经贸与人文相结合的复合型的合作模式，为广西的发展提供更多人力资源，积累更广泛的人脉，促进文化软实力快速提高，为广西全面深化与东盟的经贸合作，把广西建成与东盟合作的新高地创造更加有利的条件。

附 录

第七届中国—东盟博览会组委会中方成员名单

Chinese Members of the 7th CAEXPO Organizing Committee

名誉主任 Honorary Chair	王岐山 Wang Qishan	国务院副总理 Vice Premier of the State Council of China
主 任 Co-chair	陈德铭 Chen Deming	商务部部长 Minister of Commerce of China
副主任 Vice Co-chairs	马 飚 Ma Biao	广西壮族自治区主席 Governor of Guangxi Zhuang Autonomous Region
	毕井泉 Bi Jingquan	国务院副秘书长 Vice Secretary General of the State Council of China
	高虎城 Gao Hucheng	商务部国际贸易谈判代表兼副部长 China International Trade Representative and Vice Minister of Commerce of China
	陈 武 Chen Wu	广西壮族自治区副主席 Vice Governor of Guangxi Zhuang Autonomous Region
秘书长 Secretary General	陈 武（兼） Chen Wu (and)	广西壮族自治区副主席 Vice Governor of Guangxi Zhuang Autonomous Region
委 员 Members	蔡名照 Cai Mingzhao	中宣部副部长 Vice Minister of Publicity Department of the Chinese Communist Party Central Committee
	胡正跃 Hu Zhengyue	外交部部长助理 Assistant Minister of Foreign Affairs of China

张晓强　国家发展和改革委员会副主任
Zhang Xiaoqiang　Vice Commissioner of the National Development and Reform Commission of China

曹健林　科技部副部长
Cao Jianlin　Vice Minister of Science & Technology of China

毕根敬　公安部警卫局副局长
Bi Genjing　Vice Director General of Ministry of Public Security of China

李　勇　财政部副部长
Li Yong　Vice Minister of Finance of China

翁孟勇　交通运输部副部长
Weng Mengyong　Vice Minister of Transport of China

鲁培军　海关总署副署长
Lu Peijun　Vice Commissioner of China Customs

魏传忠　国家质量监督检验检疫总局副局长
Wei Chuanzhong　Vice Minister of the General Administration of Quality Supervision, Inspection and Quarantine of China

祝善忠　国家旅游局副局长
Zhu Shanzhong　Vice Commissioner of China National Tourism Administration

边振甲　国家食品药品监督管理局副局长
Bian Zhenjia　Vice Minister of State Food and Drug Administration

王国庆　国务院新闻办副主任
Wang Guoqing　Vice Director General of the State Council Information Office of China

于　平　中国国际贸易促进委员会副会长
Yu Ping　Vice Chairman of China Council for the Promotion of International Trade (CCPIT)

第七届中国—东盟商务与投资峰会组委会中方成员名单

Chinese Members of the 7th CABIS Organizing Committee

主　任 Chair	万季飞 Wan Jifei	中国国际贸易促进委员会会长 Chairman of China Council for the Promotion of International Trade (CCPIT)
副主任 Vice Co-chairs	陈　武 Chen Wu	广西壮族自治区副主席 Vice Governor of Guangxi Zhuang Autonomous Region
	于　平 Yu Ping	中国国际贸易促进委员会副会长 Vice Chairman of China Council for the Promotion of International Trade (CCPIT)
秘书长 Secretary General	陈　武（兼） Chen Wu (and)	广西壮族自治区副主席 Vice Governor of Guangxi Zhuang Autonomous Region
常务副秘书长 First Vice Secretaries General	黄永强 Huang Yongqiang	广西国际贸易促进委员会会长 Chairman of CCPIT Guangxi Sub-council
副秘书长 Vice Secretaries General	王　俐 Wang Li	中国国际贸易促进委员会国际联络部副部长 Vice Director General of the Department of International Affairs of CCPIT
	何小玲 He Xiaoling	广西国际贸易促进委员会副会长 Vice Chairman of CCPIT Guangxi Sub-council
	吕卫平 Lv Weiping	广西国际贸易促进委员会副会长 Vice Chairman of CCPIT Guangxi Sub-council

第七届中国—东盟博览会主办单位
The 7th CAEXPO Co-sponsors

中华人民共和国商务部
Ministry of Commerce of the People's Republic of China
文莱工业和初级资源部
Ministry of Industry and Primary Resources of Brunei Darussalam
柬埔寨商业部
Ministry of Commerce of the Kingdom of Cambodia
印度尼西亚贸易部
Ministry of Trade of the Republic of Indonesia
老挝工业贸易部
Ministry of Trade and Industry of the Lao People's Democratic Republic
马来西亚国际贸易和工业部
Ministry of International Trade and Industry of Malaysia
缅甸商务部
Ministry of Commerce of the Union of Myanmar
菲律宾贸易和工业部
Department of Trade and Industry of the Republic of Philippines
新加坡贸易和工业部
Ministry of Trade and Industry of the Republic of Singapore
泰国商业部
Ministry of Commerce of the Kingdom of Thailand
越南工业贸易部
Ministry of Industry and Trade of the Socialist Republic of Vietnam
东盟秘书处
The ASEAN Secretariat

第七届中国—东盟博览会支持商协会

中国机电产品进出口商会
中国轻工工艺进出口商会
中国医药保健品进出口商会
中国纺织品进出口商会
中国食品土畜进出口商会
中国五矿化工进出口商会
中国对外承包工程商会
中国食品和包装机械工业协会
中国电力企业联合会
文莱斯市中华总商会
文莱—中国友好协会
柬埔寨总商会
柬埔寨成衣厂商协会
柬埔寨中国商会
柬埔寨中国港澳侨商总会
印尼中华总商会
印尼—中国经济社会与文化合作协会
印尼工商会馆中国委员会
老挝国家工商会
马来西亚中国经济贸易总商会
马来西亚制造商联合会
马中友好协会
马来西亚中华总商会
缅甸联邦工商会
缅甸林木产品商协会
缅甸豆类商协会
缅甸渔业协会
缅甸工业联合会
缅甸农产品食品加工出口协会
菲华商联总会
新加坡工商联合总会
新加坡制造商联合会
新加坡中小型企业商会
新加坡中华总商会
新加坡中国商会
泰国中华总商会
泰国工业院
泰中商务委员会
泰国工商总会
泰中友好协会
越南工商会

第七届中国—东盟博览会、第七届中国—东盟商务与投资峰会活动日程表

专场活动		
活动时间	活动地点	活动名称
10月11日（星期一）		
09:00–12:00	南宁人民会堂	广西红十字会建会100周年纪念大会
13:30–17:30	明园新都酒店5号楼 2楼多功能厅	中国—东盟红十字论坛
10月12日（星期二）		
16:50–18:20	明园酒店5号楼 2楼多功能厅	第七届中国—东盟博览会合作伙伴 签约仪式暨新闻发布会
10月13日（星期三）		
17:00–18:10	明园酒店5号楼 2楼多功能厅	第七届中国—东盟博览会首席战略合作 伙伴签约仪式暨新闻发布会
10月17日（星期日）		
09:00–17:45	明园新都大酒店5号楼 2楼多功能厅	第三届中国—东盟智库战略对话
10月18日（星期一）		
15:30–16:30	广西民族博物馆	中国—东盟自由贸易区建设成就展 开展仪式
10月19日（星期二）		
09:40–10:40	荔园山庄	第四届中国—印尼能源论坛
10:00–11:00	指挥中心A栋6楼会议室	新闻吹风会
上午	南宁国际会展中心	中外贵宾巡馆专场
14:00–14:40	南宁国际会展中心	第七届中国—东盟博览会开幕式

15:20-16:00	广西人民会堂	第七届中国—东盟商务与投资峰会开幕式
18:30-19:30		欢迎宴会
10月20日（星期三）		
08:00-09:00	新都酒店2楼多功能厅	商务早餐会暨中国—东盟企业合作洽谈会
08:30-17:40	沃顿国际大酒店	第二届中国—东盟金融合作与发展领袖论坛
09:00-10:00	广西人民会堂 5楼会议室	东盟国家领导人与中国企业CEO圆桌对话会
09:00-10:00	南宁国际会展中心 101会议室	中国农垦产品质量追溯论坛暨项目签约仪式
09:00-12:00	沃顿国际大酒店2楼 南湖国宴厅1-2号厅	中国—东盟海事磋商机制第六次会议
09:30-11:30	明园饭店5号楼 2楼多功能厅	首届中国—东盟商会领袖论坛
10:00-10:25	广西展览馆	中国—东盟博览会农业展开展仪式
10:00-10:30	会展中心朱槿花厅	第七届中国—东盟博览会经济合作签约仪式（国际）
10:00-11:30	南宁国际会展中心 102会议室	宁夏回族自治区投资说明会
11:28-12:00	华南城	中国—东盟轻工产品展开幕式及巡馆
11:30-12:00	会展中心朱槿花厅	第七届中国—东盟博览会经济合作签约仪式（国内）
10月20日（星期三）		
13:30-17:30	锦华大酒店1楼报告厅	第三届中国—东盟电力合作与发展论坛暨中国—东盟电力经贸合作洽谈会
14:00-16:00	南宁国际会展中心 102会议室	中国—东盟基础设施合作高峰论坛
14:00-17:30	广西人民会堂1楼礼堂	中国—东盟自由贸易区经贸与物流合作论坛
14:30-16:00	会展中心111会议室	装备制造业共享中国—东盟自贸区发展新机遇
15:00-16:00	跨世纪大酒店 5楼多功能厅	陕西商品推介会
15:00-16:30	会展中心105会议室	菲律宾投资机会
15:00-17:00	荔园山庄国际会议中心 1楼小会议厅	中越凭祥—同登跨境经济合作区工作商讨会
15:30-17:00	锦华大酒店贵宾楼 4楼芳华堂	中国湖南—东盟产业合作对接会暨签约仪式
20:30-22:30	广西体育中心	大地飞歌·2010 第12届南宁国际民歌艺术节 暨第七届中国—东盟博览会开幕晚会
10月21日（星期四）		
08:00-13:00	南宁青秀山 国际高尔夫俱乐部	第七届中国—东盟高尔夫国际名人邀请赛

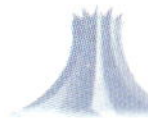

09:00-10:00	会展中心101会议室	印尼国家推介会
09:00-11:30	会展中心102会议室	老挝—中国商业投资论坛
10:00-12:00	南宁沃顿大酒店 3楼3-4号会议厅	“魅力钦州 商机无限”招商推介项目签约仪式
14:00-17:00	会展中心101会议室	柬埔寨投资潜力和商业前景推介会
14:30-16:00	会展中心103会议室	文莱投资研讨会
20:30	南宁市人民大会堂	“美在广西”广西青年歌手演唱会
10月22日（星期五）		
08:00-12:30	南宁嘉和城 温泉高尔夫俱乐部	第七届中国—东盟高尔夫 国际精英邀请赛
14:00-17:00	会展中心102会议室	首届中国—东盟物联网（RFID） 产业论坛
20:30	南宁市人民大会堂	外国艺术家专场演出
10月23日（星期六）		
09:00-17:00	南宁国际会展中心	展览及各类经贸活动
10月24日（星期日）		
09:00-17:00	南宁国际会展中心	博览会公众开放日
09:15-09:45	南宁国际会展中心 111会议室	第八届中国—东盟博览会中国 “魅力之城”新闻发布会
14:00-16:00	荔园山庄国际会议中心 1层小会议厅	博览会高官会议暨第八届博览会国家 专题展区位置抽签仪式
16:30-17:40	南宁荔园山庄国际会议 中心新闻发布厅	第七届博览会、商务与投资峰会 闭幕新闻发布会
10月29日（星期五）		
09:30-17:30	沃顿国际大酒店 3楼北京厅	2010中国—东盟国际口腔医学交流与 合作论坛
待定	南宁国际会展中心	“加强国际司法交流与合作，促进区域 经济发展与繁荣”研讨会
11月30日（星期二）		
待定	待定	中国—东盟农业部长（省长）论坛
会期相关活动		
10月3—18日		2010中国—东盟国际汽车拉力赛暨 中国—东盟媒体汽车拉力赛
10月15日 09:00	广西民族博物馆	第四届中国—东盟青年艺术品创作大赛 获奖作品展开幕仪式
10月18日 12:00	凭祥友谊关广场	2010中国—东盟国际汽车拉力赛暨中 国—东盟媒体汽车拉力赛凯旋颁奖仪式
10月18日 10:18-10:48	南宁市江南区 壮锦大道西侧	广西海吉星农产品国际物流中心 （一期）竣工庆典
10月18日 11:18-11:48	南宁市江南区 壮锦大道西侧	南宁华南城“三路一馆一中心” 启用仪式

10月20日—11月8日	广西民族博物馆	中国—东盟自由贸易区建设成就展
10月20—24日	广西展览馆	中国—东盟博览会农业展
10月20—24日	南宁国际会展中心	中国—东盟博览会珠宝首饰展
10月20—24日	南宁国际会展中心	中国—东盟金融服务展
10月20—24日	南宁国际会展中心	中国—东盟博览会东盟品牌展
10月20—24日	南宁国际会展中心	中国—东盟博览会东盟木材及家具展
10月20—24日	南宁国际会展中心	中国—东盟博览会东盟食品展
10月20—24日	华南城	中国—东盟轻工产品展览会
10月20—24日 19:30-23:30	广西体育局 江南训练基地	第七届CAEXPO“网球之友”联谊活动
10月20日 09:00-11:00	明园酒店5号楼	中国东盟与茶文化——2010广西 茗珍品尝活动
10月20日 11:20-12:00	东盟商务区	南宁·中国—东盟国际商务区各国商务 联络部（办事处）办公楼移交使用仪式
10月20日 16:20-17:00	广西体育中心	中越友谊手印墙揭幕仪式
11月19—22日	南宁国际会展中心	第七届中国—东盟博览会 木材与木制品展

第七届中国—东盟博览会大事记

1月

13—24日

广西壮族自治区党委书记、自治区人大常委会主任郭声琨率领广西代表团访问泰国、新加坡、阿联酋。期间，代表团拜会了泰国总理阿披实、新加坡总理李显龙，与泰国国务部长李天文、商业部部长彭提瓦、新加坡贸工部长林勋强举行了会谈，会见了中国驻泰国大使管木、中国驻新加坡大使张小康、中国驻阿联酋迪拜总领事高有祯，分别访问了阿联酋迪拜世界集团和设立于迪拜的英国合乐中东公司，实地考察了迪拜世界集团旗下公司迪拜环球港务集团建设开发和运营管理的杰拜勒·阿里港口，深入探讨了在各领域进一步加强交流与合作，共同办好第七届中国—东盟博览会、中国—东盟商务与投资峰会等事宜，以应对新的世界经济形势，实现互利共赢的目的。

4月

7日

第七届中国—东盟博览会筹备工作会议在北京召开。商务部党组副书记、商务部副部长高虎城到会讲话并部署工作，广西壮族自治区党委常委、自治区副主席陈武出席会议并致辞。商务部相关司局和全国各省（自治区、直辖市）商务主管部门负责人参加了会议。

9日

第七届中国—东盟博览会高官会议在南宁召开。中国商务部亚洲司司长吕克俭、东盟秘书处高级官员蓬猜及东盟10国高官、中国国际贸易促进委员会与中国—东盟博览会秘书处的官员共聚一堂，研究第七届中国—东盟博览会筹备工作。

27日

第二届中国—东盟金融合作与发展领袖论坛筹备工作协调会议在南宁召开。广西壮族自治区政府副秘书长魏然出席会议并作重要讲话。

5月

6日

在上海举办的第八届中国会展节事财富论坛上，中国—东盟博览会再获殊荣，被评为“2009—2010年度中国会展产业金手指奖·十大影响力展览会”，广西国际博览事务局局长、中国—东盟博览会秘书处秘书长郑军健被评为“2009—2010年度中国会展产业金手指奖·十大新闻人物”。

21日

广西壮族自治区主席马飚在南宁主持召开专题会议，听取第七届中国—东盟博览会、第七届中国—东盟商务与投资峰会、第五届泛北部湾经济合作论坛、中越青年大联欢活动等四项大型活动筹备工作进展情况汇报。

25日—6月2日

广西壮族自治区党委常委、自治区副主席陈武率领广西政府代表团访问文莱、菲律宾与新西兰，宣传推介中国—东盟博览会。期间，代表团先后拜会了文莱王储穆赫塔迪·比拉、文莱工业与初级资源部部长叶海亚、菲律宾贸工部部长杰斯利·拉普斯、菲律宾宿务省省长加西亚及亚洲开发银行第一副行长劳伦斯·格林伍德、奥克兰大区理事会主席迈克·李和新西兰贸易发展局。代表团还参观考察了菲律宾马尼拉港、宿务港和新西兰奥克兰港，与文莱和菲律宾工商企业界进行座谈，会见了文莱国家工商会、文中友好协会、菲律宾华商联合总会等商协会负责人，拜会了我国驻文莱大使闵永年、驻菲律宾大使刘建超，会见了我驻宿务总领事何时敬和奥克兰总领事廖菊华。

7月

1—5日

广西壮族自治区党委书记、自治区人大常委会主任郭声琨率领广西代表团赴台开展经贸文化交流活动，进一步宣传推介中国—东盟博览会，推进桂台企业的交流合作。

13日

第四届中国—东盟社会发展与减贫论坛在广西桂林开幕。国务院扶贫办副主任郑文凯主持开幕式。广西壮族自治区副主席梁胜利、东盟秘书处副秘书长米斯然·卡梅因拿督、柬埔寨财政经济部助理秘书长桑力·提亚里斯、联合国开发计划署代理代表森本秋绘等出席论坛开幕式并分别致辞。

广西壮族自治区党委常委、统战部部长黄道伟到"两会"指挥中心检查指导工作，听取第七届中国—东盟博览会筹备工作及广西与东盟开放合作有关情况的汇报。

26日

中国—东盟经贸关系进展暨第七届中国—东盟博览会和中国—东盟商务与投资峰会新闻发布会在北京举行。商务部副部长高虎城，广西壮族自治区党委常委、自治区副主席陈武，中国国际贸易促进委员会副会长张伟分别介绍中国—东盟经贸关系进展及第七届中国—东盟博览会、第七届中国—东盟商务与投资峰会等方面情况，并答记者问。

8月

18日

在由全国城市会展办公室、全国会展联盟、中国会展经济研究会、《第一会展》杂志联合举办的2010中国会展行业年会·世博会主题展策划与中国会展业发展论坛上，中国—东盟博览会再获会展业大奖，荣获"新世纪十年·中国会展杰出典范奖"和"新世纪十年·中国十大品牌展会"奖。中国—东盟博览会秘书处秘书长郑军健被评为"新世纪十年影响中国会展业60人"。

广西壮族自治区人民政府副秘书长、"两会"指挥中心副总指挥魏然在南宁主持召开中国—东盟自由贸易区建设成就展筹备工作协调会，研究部署相关工作。

26日

广西壮族自治区党委常委、自治区副主席陈武听取广西国际博览事务局关于第七届中国—东盟博览会开幕式筹备工作进展汇报，并对下一阶段重点工作进行了部署。

9月

1—5日

2010中国—东盟博览会合作媒体广西行活动在南宁举行，这是首次东盟10国全部派出媒体专访广西。

2日

广西壮族自治区党委常委、自治区副主席陈武听取广西国际博览事务局关于中国—东盟自贸区建设成就展筹备工作进展汇报，并对下一阶段重点工作进行了部署。

广西壮族自治区人民政府副秘书长黄胜杰率工作组赴京走访中国人民银行办公厅及银监会办公厅，就上述两家单位继续出任第二届金融论坛主办单位等事宜进行了商谈。

6日

第七届中国—东盟博览会、第七届中国—东盟商务与投资峰会广西指挥中心工作会议在南宁召开。广西壮族自治区党委常委、自治区副主席、“两会”指挥中心总指挥陈武出席会议并作重要讲话。会议由自治区人民政府副秘书长、“两会”指挥中心副总指挥魏然主持。会上，各工作部负责人分别汇报了“两会”筹备工作总体进展情况和重大活动初步安排等方面情况。

18日

第七届中国—东盟博览会、第七届中国—东盟商务与投资峰会“携手共进30天”仪式在南宁国际会展中心举行。广西壮族自治区主席马飚宣布活动启动。广西壮族自治区党委常委、自治区副主席陈武在仪式上讲话。柬埔寨王国驻南宁总领事馆总领事英洪，越南社会主义共和国驻南宁总领事馆总领事阮英勇，缅甸联邦驻南宁总领事馆总领事敏隋，泰王国驻南宁总领事馆总领事安特蓬，老挝人民民主共和国驻南宁总领事馆代总领事潘坎·尹他波里，菲律宾共和国驻广州总领事馆、菲律宾贸易投资中心南宁办公室商务领事助理何佳佳等东盟各国驻南宁外交使节，以及广西壮族自治区党委常委、宣传部部长沈北海，自治区党委常委、南宁市委书记车荣福，自治区党委常委、秘书长余远辉，自治区人民政府秘书长王跃飞，企业界代表和服务“两会”的有关部门工作人员参加了仪式。随后，出席启动仪式的领导和嘉宾还参加了少年儿童迎博览会百米书画长卷活动。

20日

中国—东盟博览会、中国—东盟商务与投资峰会中方组委会会议在北京召开。商务部副部长陈健，广西壮族自治区党委常委、自治区副主席陈武，中国贸促会副会长于平，国家质检总局副局长魏传忠，国家食品药品监督管理局副局长边振甲，外交部部长助理胡正跃，以及国务院办公厅、中宣部、国家发改委、科技部、公安部警卫局、财政部、交通运输部、海关总署、国务院新闻办等组委会成员单位代表出席了会议。陈健副部长主持会议并讲话。

27日

中国—东盟博览会、中国—东盟商务与投资峰会广西领导小组在南宁召开2010年第一次会议。广西壮族自治区主席、“两会”广西领导小组组长马飚在会上强调，要抢抓中国—东盟自由贸易区建成的新机遇，继续举全区之力办好“两会”，进一步深化广西与东盟的全面开放合作。“两会”广西领导小组副组长沈北海、车荣福、陈武，广西壮族自治区副主席林念修以及自治区人民政府秘书长王跃飞等出席会议。

10月

11日

由中国红十字会总会、广西壮族自治区人民政府主办，广西壮族自治区红十字会承办的首届中国—东盟红十字论坛在南宁举办。广西壮族自治区副主席、广西红十字会会长李康在论坛开幕式上致辞，中国红十字会总会常务副会长王伟等做了主旨发言。

12日

第七届中国—东盟博览会战略合作伙伴、合作伙伴签约仪式暨新闻发布会在南宁举行。广西壮族自治区党委常委、自治区副主席陈武出席仪式并向企业颁发证书。

13日

第七届中国—东盟博览会首席战略合作伙伴签约仪式暨新闻发布会在南宁举行。新加坡著名企业丰隆亚洲有限公司首次成为博览会首席战略合作伙伴。这是国外企业首次成为中国—东盟博览会首席战略合作伙伴。广西壮族自治区主席马飚出席仪式并颁发证书。广西壮族自治区党委常委、自治区副主席陈武，广西壮族自治区人民政府副秘书长魏然出席了仪式。

15日

第七届中国—东盟博览会、第七届中国—东盟商务与投资峰会志愿者培训上岗志愿者徽章揭幕仪式在广西民族大学举行。广西壮族自治区党委副秘书长黄世勇出席揭幕仪式。

16日

第七届中国—东盟博览会、第七届中国—东盟商务与投资峰会各市工作衔接会议在南宁召开。广西壮族自治区党委常委、自治区副主席陈武对各市参会组织和各市服务“两会”工作进行部署。会议由“两会”指挥中心副总指挥、广西壮族自治区党委副秘书长黄世勇主持。

17日

第三届中国—东盟智库战略对话会议在南宁举行。广西壮族自治区党委常委、宣传部部长沈北海、柬埔寨和平与合作研究院院长（柬埔寨前副总理兼外交部长）诺罗敦·西里武、中国社会科学院国际研究学部主任张蕴岭在开幕式上致辞。

18日

中国—东盟自贸区建设成就展开馆仪式在广西民族博物馆举行。广西壮族自治区党委常委、自治区副主席陈武宣布开馆。商务部贸发局副局长贾国勇在仪式上讲话。广西壮族自治区人大常委会副主任吴恒、自治区政协副主席蒋培兰参加了开馆仪式。

19日

中共中央政治局常委、全国政协主席贾庆林在南宁分别会见了前来出席第七届中国—东盟博览会、中国—东盟商务与投资峰会的印度尼西亚副总统布迪约诺、老挝副总理阿桑·劳里、越南副总理张永仲，并集体会见了柬埔寨、文莱、缅甸、马来西亚、菲律宾、泰国、新加坡等国政府代表团团长和东盟秘书处代表。

参加第七届中国—东盟博览会的中共中央政治局常委、全国政协主席贾庆林，各国政要、国际组织负责人、各代表团领导巡视了博览会展馆。贾庆林主席随行人员及广西壮族自治区领导郭声琨、马飚、马铁山等陪同贾庆林主席巡视展馆。

第七届中国—东盟博览会主题国印度尼西亚馆开馆仪式在南宁国际会展中心隆重举行。印尼副总统布迪约诺，广西壮族自治区主席马飚出席仪式并共同剪彩。印尼贸易部部长冯慧兰，印尼工业部部长希塔亚，印尼国企部部长穆斯塔法·阿布巴卡，广西壮族自治区领导沈北海、陈武、刘新文、蒋济雄等出席开馆仪式。

第七届中国—东盟博览会在南宁国际会展中心隆重开幕。中共中央政治局常委、全国政协主席贾庆林宣布开幕。第七届中国—东盟博览会主题国印度尼西亚副总统布迪约诺、老挝副总理阿桑·劳里、越南副总理张永仲、柬埔寨国务兼商业大臣占蒲拉西等东盟国家领导人出席开幕式。第七届中国—东盟博览会主题国印度尼西亚贸易部部长冯慧兰主持开幕式，广西壮族自治区主席马飚、中国商务部国际贸易谈判代表兼副部长高虎城、印度尼西亚副总统布迪约诺先后致辞。中共中央政治局常委、全国政协主席贾庆林、印度尼西亚副总统布迪约诺、老挝副总理阿桑·劳里、越南副总理张永仲、柬埔寨国务兼商业大臣占蒲拉西、文莱工业和初级资源部部长叶海亚、缅甸商务部部长吴丁乃登、中国商务部国际谈判贸易代表兼副部长高虎城、马来西亚国际贸易和工业部副部长贾谷·东加·沙甘、菲律宾贸易与工业部副部长克里斯托伯、泰国商业部部长助理威拉萨·金那拉、新加坡贸工部兼新闻通讯艺术部政务次长陈振泉、广西壮族自治区党委书记郭声琨、东盟秘书处东盟市场一体化合作司司长苏柏什等嘉宾共同为第七届中国—东盟博览会开幕剪彩。国家质量监督检验检疫总局局长支树平、国家发展与改革委员会副主任张国宝、外交部副部长张志军以及国际组织负责人、世界知名企业家、商协会会长、区域经济研究专家与参展参会客商代表共1300多人参加开幕式。

以"中国—东盟自由贸易区与区域经济合作的展望"为主题的第七届中国—东盟商务与投资峰会开幕式在广西人民会堂举行。中共中央政治局常委、全国政协主席贾庆林，印度尼西亚副总统布迪约诺，老挝副总理阿桑·劳里，越南副总理张永仲，中国商务部国际贸易谈判代表兼副部长高虎城，广西壮族自治区党委书记、自治区人大常委会主任郭声琨，中国外交部副部长张志军，中国国际贸易促进委员会副会长王锦珍，还有东盟各国代表团和商协组织的负责人，中国政府有关部门和各省、市、自治区的负责人，外交使节、国际和区域组织的代表，中国和东盟政界、企业界知名人士以及有关专家学者和媒体记者共1500多人出席开幕式。开幕式由广西壮族自治区主席马飚主持。开幕式上，中共中央政治局常委、全国政协主席贾庆林、印度尼西亚副总统布迪约诺分别发表演讲。同时，中国贸促会副会长王锦珍发表致辞，广西壮族自治区党委书记、自治区人大常委会主任郭声琨致欢迎辞。

中国国家能源局和印尼能源矿产部在南宁联合召开第四届中国—印尼能源论坛。中国国家发改委副主任、国家能源局局长张国宝和印尼国资委主任穆斯塔法·阿布巴卡出席了开幕式并致辞。中国国家能源局副局长钱智民和印尼能矿部代表分别代表两国能源主管部门做主旨发言。

20日

第二届中国—东盟金融合作与发展领袖论坛在南宁隆重召开。广西壮族自治区党委书记、自治区人大常委会主任郭声琨、中国人民银行行长助理李东荣、中国银行业监督管理委员会广西监管局局长苏保祥、中国证券监督管理委员会主席助理朱从玖、印尼国信银行国际股份有限公司主席代表陈廼士、柬埔寨加华银行执行总裁方侨生、老挝开发银行行长奔达·达拉位、缅甸经济银行行长吴耶吞、泰国银行家协会秘书长瓦差·永克提坤、越南河内证券交易所副总裁阮氏煌兰、越南工商银行代表阮氏妹参加了论坛。

第七届中国—东盟博览会农业展在广西展览馆举行开展仪式。广西壮族自治区人大常委会副主任文明致辞，广西壮族自治区党委副书记陈际瓦宣布开幕。广西壮族自治区党委副秘书长黄世勇、中国东盟农资商会会长陈文宝、印度尼西亚中华总商会理事会常务主席陈泳志等出席开展仪式。

第三届中国—东盟电力合作与发展论坛暨中国—东盟电力经贸合作洽谈会在南宁举行。广西壮族自治区副主席杨道喜出席并致辞，中国驻老挝使馆商务参赞张玉成、中国—东盟商务理事会中方常务秘书长徐宁宁到会并发表讲话，中国电力企业联合会第四届理事会党组书记、常务副理事长谢振华作主题报告。广西水利电力建设集团有限公司、西安电力机械厂、中国国电集团公司等电力行业巨头代表受邀参加论坛。

中国—东盟海事磋商机制第六次会议在南宁举行。广西壮族自治区副主席杨道喜、政协副主席蒋培兰出席了会议。中国交通运输部副部长徐祖远向大会发来贺信。来自中国海事局与东盟各国海事主管当局的40多名代表参加了会议。

第二届中国—东盟工程项目合作与发展论坛在南宁国际会展中心开幕。广西壮族自治区党委常委、政法委书记温卡华出席并致辞。来自中国及马来西亚、越南、缅甸等国的工程界知名专家学者、企业代表等100多人出席论坛。

“大地飞歌·2010”第12届南宁国际民歌艺术节暨第七届中国—东盟博览会开幕晚会在广西体育中心举行。广西壮族自治区党委书记、自治区人大常委会主任郭声琨，自治区主席马飚，自治区政协主席马铁山等领导出席了开幕晚会。广西壮族自治区党委常委、南宁市委书记车荣福致开幕辞，并宣布晚会开幕。晚会开幕式由南宁市市长黄方方主持。

21日

第七届中国—东盟国际高尔夫名人邀请赛在南宁青秀山国际高尔夫俱乐部开杆。老挝副总理阿桑·劳里，柬埔寨国务兼商业大臣占蒲拉西，老挝外交部副部长本格·桑宋萨，老挝国家旅游局副局长苏卡申·普提山，全国人大常委会委员、广西法学会会长彭祖意等出席了开球仪式。

22日

中国—东盟博览会秘书处与德国莱比锡国际展览有限公司在南宁签署友好合作备忘录。这是中国—东盟博览会秘书处首次与国外专业团队开展合作。

24日

第七届中国—东盟博览会高官会议暨第八届中国—东盟博览会国家专题展区抽签仪式在广西南宁举行。会议确定第八届中国—东盟博览会将于10月21—26日在南宁举行，设置商品贸易专题、投资合作专题、服务贸易专题、先进技术专题、“魅力之城”等五个专题，重点主题为“环保合作”，主题国为马来

西亚，并抽签确定了第八届博览会11国的国家专题展区位置。会上，颁发了中国—东盟博览会组委会评选出的主题国纪念奖、重大贡献及支持奖、最佳展示奖、最佳参展组织奖、最佳采购商组织奖、最佳投资合作推介奖等奖项。

中国—东盟博览会组委会、中国—东盟商务与投资峰会组委会在南宁召开新闻发布会。中国—东盟博览会组委会副主任兼秘书长、中国—东盟商务与投资峰会组委会副主任兼秘书长、广西壮族自治区党委常委、自治区副主席陈武宣布第七届博览会与商务峰会的基本情况和主要成果并宣布第七届中国—东盟博览会胜利闭幕。会议由中国商务部贸发局副局长贾国勇主持，东盟秘书处代表兰安琪等出席了会议。第七届中国—东盟博览会商品贸易成交总额达到17.12亿美元，比去年增长3.5%。举行了46场投资推介活动，共签订国际经济合作项目135个，总投资额66.9亿美元，比上届增长3%；国内经济合作项目156个，总投资674.46亿元，比上届增长9%。

25日

广西壮族自治区党委书记、自治区人大常委会主任郭声琨主持召开自治区党委常委会扩大会议。会议要求，要进一步增强办好中国—东盟博览会和商务与投资峰会的事业心和责任心，进一步完善和健全办好博览会的有关常态化机制，使2011年的第八届中国—东盟博览会和商务与投资峰会办得更精彩更成功。

29日

中国—东盟博览会·第七届梧州国际宝石节在梧州举行。国家林业局副局长张建龙，中国珠宝玉石首饰协会常务副会长、原地质矿产部副部长陈洲其，中国人民解放军空军原副司令员、中将景学勤，国防大学原教研部主任、少将黄彬，中国扶贫基金会副会长、广州市政协原主席陈开枝，广西壮族自治区党委常委、宣传部长沈北海，自治区人大常委会副主任文明，自治区副主席高雄，自治区政协副主席林国强等领导和嘉宾出席了开幕式。

由中华人民共和国卫生部、广西壮族自治区人民政府主办的第二届中国—东盟国际口腔医学交流与合作论坛在南宁开幕。广西壮族自治区主席马飚、卫生部疾控局副局长孔灵芝、老挝卫生部部长本梅·达拉洛出席开幕式并致辞。自治区副主席李康主持开幕式。自治区政协副主席李彬出席开幕式。自治区政府秘书长王跃飞，中国工程院院士邱蔚六参加了开幕式。

11月

16—23日

广西壮族自治区党委常委、自治区副主席陈武率领广西代表团访问老挝和缅甸，分别拜会了老挝政府总理波松·布帕万、常务副总理宋沙瓦·凌沙瓦及缅甸国家和平与发展委员会第一秘书长丁昂敏乌，就进一步办好中国—东盟博览会，推动广西与老挝、广西与缅甸在各个领域的务实合作，巩固和加强广西与老挝、广西与缅甸的友好合作关系进行了会谈和交流。

19日

以“传承、创新、合作、发展”为主题中国—东盟博览会木材与木制品展在南宁国际会展中心开幕。这是中国—东盟博览会秘书处首次独立举办专业展。

12月

29日

在由全国会展联盟、《第一会展》杂志、全国城市会展管理办公室共同主办的第八届中国会展业高峰论坛大会暨2010年度中国会展行业年度颁奖盛典上，中国—东盟博览会再获会展业大奖，荣获“2010中国十大最具国际影响力展会”奖。广西国际博览事务局局长、中国—东盟博览会秘书处秘书长郑军健被评为“2010年度中国会展业杰出人物”。

第七届中国—东盟博览会重要文件汇编（一）
会议文件

在第七届中国—东盟博览会开幕式上的致辞

印度尼西亚共和国副总统　布迪约诺
（2010年10月19日）

尊敬的贾庆林主席阁下，

各位东盟同事、各位贵宾、各位代表，

女士们、先生们：

非常荣幸能够来到风光如画的中国绿城南宁，出席第七届中国—东盟博览会开幕式。

首先，我想借此机会代表东盟各国来宾，向广西壮族自治区人民政府表示衷心的感谢，感谢贵方给予我们的盛情邀请和热情接待。同时我也要真诚地感谢中华人民共和国政府，感谢你们为在南宁一年一度举办的这次盛会所作出的不懈努力。你们举办的这次盛会，使中国和东盟双方有很好的机会，来庆贺和分享合作与友谊的成果。

东盟与中国是近邻，经贸关系密切，有着众多共同利益。双方共同携手、风雨同行，成功应对当前国际金融危机。在危机时刻，要求我们比以往更进一步加强双方的关系，我们双方发展双边关系最重要的支柱就是中国—东盟自贸区。这一全世界第三大自贸区在今年如期建成，标志着双方的战略合作伙伴关系迈入了新纪元，区域一体化进程也迎来了一个新的里程碑。

经过近20年的时间，中国已经成为东盟各国可以信赖的伙伴，在许多事务上发挥重要作用。作为目前全球第二大和发展速度最快的经济体，中国为东盟创造了很多机遇，同样东盟的繁荣与稳定也有利于中国。只要双方携起手来，就能成为一股推动世界经济发展的强大力量。随着双方的关系进入新阶段，要求我们不仅仅要着眼于贸易和投资方面的联系，我们更要加强双方民众的联系，来保证经济关系平等和可持续发展。

要怎样做才能使我们创造的繁荣成果能够惠及中国和东盟所有民众?

首先，我们必须完善中国—东盟合作体制，我们必须进一步推进投资与服务贸易。

第二，我们必须进一步加强双方的互利合作，解决在经贸发展中的不平衡以及加强能力建设。要保证这些成果的取得，最重要的措施就是要继续支持中国—东盟自贸区的建设。

第三，我们必须通过进一步密切商界、投资者以及其他利益相关方的对话，来加强中国—东盟共同体的建设，中国—东盟博览会就是这一举措的典范。

各位贵宾、女士们、先生们，让我们和谐同行，让我们进一步推进资源互补，加强建设，让我们进一步加强合作来改善我们的伙伴关系。本着一个共同的信念，我们将能够，也一定能够克服前进道路上所遇到的种种困难。正像今年中国—东盟博览会的主题所言，要求我们进一步将自贸区产生的新机遇来进一步落实推进中国—东盟自贸区的建设。

谢谢大家!

在第七届中国—东盟商务与投资峰会开幕式上的演讲

印度尼西亚共和国副总统　布迪约诺

（2010年10月19日）

尊敬的贾庆林主席阁下，

各位尊敬的东盟国家领导人，

各位贵宾、女士们、先生们：

今天，我非常荣幸、非常高兴参加第七届中国—东盟商务与投资峰会。首先，我要代表印度尼西亚代表团的所有成员，诚挚地感谢主办方给予我们的热烈欢迎和热情招待。

各位贵宾、女士们、先生们！

现在，我们已经如期建成了中国—东盟自由贸易区。区域内各个国家都实现了坚实的增长。2009年，印尼经济实现了快速发展，实现了4.5%的增长，今年我们预计增长率将达到6%。2011—2015年我们的增长率将达到7%—8%。东盟是中国投资者最大的投资目的地，自贸区将使东盟对中国的投资更具吸引力。这一自贸区在覆盖的人口方面是世界上最大的自贸区，总人口达19亿。我们中产阶层的数量不断扩展，预计在印度尼西亚，我们2.37亿人口中的13.7%是中产阶层。彼此之间的贸易与投资现在不仅限于原材料和零部件之间的贸易，我们已经建立起了地区的出口市场，我们也将在彼此之间出售更多的制成品和消费产品。

随着经济发展，我们将日益需要建设基础设施，实现可持续的经济发展。印度尼西亚和一些其他的东盟国家以及中国，都制定了国家应对气候变化行动方案，我们将努力降低二氧化碳排放。这不仅是一大挑战，也有助于促进投资，特别是对基础设施的投资。预计2010年印尼投资于基础设施的资金将增长一倍。印尼期待着建设国内一体化的经济体，实现融入世界经济的目标。要实现这一目标我们将升级基础设施，包括道路、桥梁、港口、铁路和发电设施，以及我们所称的软性基础的设施。比如说通讯电子基础设施，我们将推动一系列的公司合作伙伴关系的项目，包括跨越爪哇公路、爪哇铁路的升级。我们的港口将建设1万兆瓦的发电站项目。我们认为此次会议的主题，为中国—东盟自贸区及区域合作的经贸提出了非常明确的前景。

女士们、先生们！

我想简要谈一下印尼政府所采取的改善商务环境的举措。过去几年，我们一直在努力，在这方面取得了显著成果。我们引入了越来越多的投资，商业环境日益改善，商业信心不断上升，在2010年国际评级机构会议把我们的主权债务评级从BB级提升到BB+级，印度尼西亚成为全球最具吸引力的投资地之一。我们的出口也实现复苏，要比金融危机前的更高，去年和今年我们的失业率进一步下降。我们期待着获得更多的商业机遇，我们也欢迎各位前往印度尼西亚，获得更多的投资机遇。

最后，我要预祝第七届中国—东盟商务与投资峰会圆满成功。我认为此次峰会将为印度尼西亚和中国以及其他东盟国家企业间的合作敞开大门。我希望通过此次峰会，中国与东盟10国将能够携手合作，能够提出建设性的举措，改善双方经贸关系，实现互利共赢。我们不应等待观望，现在我们应该采取积极举措，创造财富，为我们的人民带来繁荣。我希望此次峰会的所有参会嘉宾参会愉快，期待此次重要会议圆满成功。

谢谢各位！

在第七届中国—东盟商务与投资峰会开幕式上的致辞

中国国际贸易促进委员会副会长　王锦珍

（2010年10月19日）

尊敬的中国全国政协主席贾庆林阁下，
尊敬的印尼副总统布迪约诺阁下，
尊敬的老挝副总理阿桑·劳里阁下，
尊敬的越南副总理张永仲阁下，
各位领导、嘉宾、女士们、先生们、朋友们：

大家下午好！在中国与东盟经贸合作进入新阶段之际，第七届中国—东盟商务与投资峰会今天正式开幕，中国全国政协主席贾庆林阁下和东盟领导人在百忙中专程前来出席会议，并为中国—东盟新时期的合作发表重要讲话，我们感到非常荣幸。在此，我谨代表中国国际贸易促进委员会、中国—东盟商务与投资峰会组委会，对贾庆林主席等各位领导的莅临表示衷心的感谢！对各位嘉宾的光临表示热烈的欢迎！

今年是中国—东盟自由贸易区正式建成的第一年，本届峰会以“中国—东盟自由贸易区与区域经贸合作的展望”为主题，将围绕自贸区为双方带来的新机遇、新挑战进行交流与探讨。我们高兴地看到，在双方政府的大力支持和企业的共同努力下，中国与东盟之间的经贸联系越来越紧密，合作越来越多，发展越来越好。中国—东盟自贸区对我们来说是新生事物，如何充分发挥其作用，为发展双边经贸合作带来更大的便利，仍是我们面临的挑战，中方有信心与东盟各国共同抓住机遇，应对挑战，为打造一个开放程度更高，相互合作更密切，发展前景更广阔的自由贸易区作出我们的努力。

中国—东盟商务与投资峰会迄今已成功举办了六届，感谢中国和东盟各国有关方面的大力支持。本届峰会将通过东盟国家领导人与中国企业CEO圆桌对话会、商务早餐会暨中国—东盟企业合作洽谈会、中国—东盟商会领袖论坛、区域物流合作专题论坛等一系列活动，继续为双方商界提供商务交流、产品展示、项目合作、信息共享的平台。希望中国与东盟工商界人士广泛交流，务实合作，为实现本地区经济持续发展，互利共赢、共同繁荣的目标而努力。

预祝第七届中国—东盟商务与投资峰会取得圆满成功!

谢谢大家!

第七届中国—东盟博览会重要文件汇编（二）
其他重要文件

在中国—东盟经贸关系进展暨第七届中国—东盟博览会、第七届中国—东盟商务与投资峰会新闻发布会上的讲话

中国—东盟博览会组委会副主任兼秘书长
中国—东盟商务与投资峰会组委会副主任
广西壮族自治区党委常委、自治区副主席
陈　武
（2010年7月26日）

各位记者朋友，
女士们、先生们：

上午好！

在中国和东盟的共同努力下，中国—东盟博览会、中国—东盟商务与投资峰会已成功举办六届，这是中国和东盟10国有关政府部门、商协会和企业共同努力的结果，也离不开社会各界人士特别是新闻界的大力参与。在此，我代表博览会组委会和承办方广西政府向大家表示衷心感谢！

一、第七届中国—东盟博览会、商务与投资峰会在新形势下举办，目前各项筹备工作进展顺利

第七届博览会、商务与投资峰会是中国—东盟自由贸易区如期建成后举办的新一届盛会，具有重要意义。本届博览会、商务与投资峰会将继续搭好平台，深化中国—东盟战略伙伴关系、促进双方经贸合作进一步走向全面深入，服务中国—东盟自由贸易区。中国—东盟自贸区建成半年来，对双方贸易投资的促进作用十分明显。今年上半年双边贸易额达到1365亿美元，同比增长55%，超出同期中国进出口增幅11个百分点。双方累计相互投资总额约694亿美元。上半年广西与东盟贸易额26.3亿美元，同比增长41.6%。进出口规模超过金融危机前同期水平，再创历史新高。这是中国—东盟自贸区建设取得的成果，也是中国—东盟博览会务实推动的结果。

在新形势下，我们紧扣自贸区进程，在展览专题设置、展览内容专业化、展览服务等方面加大创新力度，争取让企业通过博览会、商务与投资峰会，更好地享受自贸区建成后带来的更多商机。

第七届中国—东盟博览会以“自贸区与新机遇”为重点主题，设有商品贸易、投资合作、服务贸易、先进技术和“魅力之城”五大专题。目前国内外企业参展踊跃。据最新统计，国内外预订展位总数达到4522个，超过规划展位数4000个的13%。其中，国内各省各行业预定展位数3219个，已大大超过展位供给数。各行业的重复参展率逐步提高，其中食品加工和包装机械的重复参展率分别为40%和52%，而工程机械及运输车辆的重复参展率更高达82%。重复参展率是反映展会对企业吸引力的重要标志，这充分证明博览会的市场认知度不断提升。

今年东盟国家参展规模继续扩大，东盟10国和东盟秘书处预定展位数1303个，比上届实际展位数多出11.6%。印尼、老挝、马来西亚、缅甸、泰国、越南六个东盟国家包馆。东盟方展位需求已超出预定数120个，展位供不应求。

目前已有10个国家初步确定第七届博览会“魅力之城”，分别是：中国的钦州、文莱的斯里巴加湾、柬埔寨的磅湛省、印尼的梭罗、老挝的甘蒙、马来西亚的吉隆坡、缅甸的曼德勒、新加坡的新加坡城、泰国的清莱和越南的大叻。

二、第七届中国—东盟博览会特色更加鲜明，更加注重实效，进一步发挥中国—东盟自贸区“助推器”的作用

从筹备工作进展来看，第七届中国—东盟博览会有以下特点：

一是共办特色更加突出，进一步深化中国—东盟战略伙伴关系。中国和东盟10国政要、部长级贵宾、国际组织负责人、各国商协会会长、世界知名企业负责人、知名专家学者等将出席第七届博览会，保持高规格。

印尼作为第七届博览会主题国，将在会期举办丰富多彩的主题国活动，包

括国家馆开馆仪式、专场推介会等。

会期将举办中国—东盟自由贸易区成就展，展示中国—东盟自贸区建设取得的成果和美好前景，以及中国—东盟博览会及商务与投资峰会等方面的成效，展览不但内容丰富，而且形式多样，不仅运用现代科技手段，同时也有反映自贸区建设和发展的包括书法、美术和摄影等艺术作品在内的艺术展。

二是经贸促进能力增强，进一步发挥自贸区“助推器”的作用。紧扣自贸区已签署和生效的各个协议，新设服务贸易专题，重点展示金融服务、物流服务、教育服务。继续举办农业展。新增珠宝首饰展，设立东盟品牌展区、食品展区和家具展区，让更多的东盟特色商品进入中国市场，为企业创造更多商机。

由于展览内容针对性更强，中外采购商报名参会很积极。除中国和东盟10国的采购商外，目前已有法国、德国、加拿大、澳大利亚、日本等国家和地区的采购团组报名参会，今年区域外的采购商将更多。

今年我们与东盟10国政府投资促进部门加强合作，在项目收集、推介、对接等方面加大力度，促进相互投资，特别是推动更多的中国企业“走出去”到东盟投资。会期将举办联合国采购说明会、投融资项目对接会、专场贸易配对洽谈会、国内物流园区推介会、广西物流企业采购说明会等。

三是多领域合作进一步扩大，充分体现双方抓住自贸区建成的新机遇，促进全方位、深层次、宽领域合作的共同愿望。

第七届中国—东盟商务与投资峰会将与博览会同期举行。本届商务与投资峰会的主题为“中国—东盟自由贸易区与区域经贸合作的展望”，中国和东盟10国政府官员、著名企业家、专家学者将共同研究探讨自贸区背景和条件下区域经贸合作的重大问题。本届博览会以“自贸区与新机遇”为重点主题，围绕金融、农业、电力、减贫、法律、医学等领域举办多个高层论坛。促进多领域合作。

三、在新形势下，广西将继续举全区之力办好中国—东盟博览会、商务与投资峰会，更好地服务中国—东盟战略伙伴关系，服务中国—东盟自由贸易区

近年来，广西发挥区位优势，通过连续六届成功承办中国—东盟博览会、商务与投资峰会，积极参与中国—东盟自贸区建设，为促进中国—东盟合作作出了贡献，也推动了广西与东盟的开放合作。近年来广西与东盟贸易增幅一直位居全国前列，2003—2009年，广西与东盟贸易额由8.26亿美元增至49.5亿美元，年均增长35%。广西与东盟的相互投资特别是广西对东盟的直接投资也呈快速增长态势。

随着今年1月1日，中国—东盟自由贸易区的如期建成，广西要在服务中国—东盟战略伙伴关系，服务中国—东盟自由贸易区方面发挥更大作用。去年底出台的《国务院关于进一步促进广西经济社会发展的若干意见》，明确广西是"我国面向东盟的重要门户和前沿地带"，强调"继续办好中国—东盟博览会"，支持广西发挥区位优势，扩大以面向东盟为重点的开放合作。

自治区党委、自治区人民政府高度重视与东盟的开放合作。为抢抓中国—东盟自贸区建成的机遇，进一步加强与东盟的开放合作。2009年底，自治区成立了"广西与东盟开放合作领导小组"，成立了领导小组下设的统筹协调办公室，统筹协调与东盟开放合作，督促合作项目的落实。同时，广西出台了《抓住中国—东盟自由贸易区建成机遇加强广西与东盟全面开放合作的工作意见》，对新形势下加强与东盟开放合作作了部署。最近广西还制定出台了十个《广西与东盟全面开放合作专项行动计划》。下一步，我们将认真贯彻《国务院关于进一步促进广西经济社会发展的若干意见》，实施广西与东盟全面开放合作各项行动计划，深化广西与东盟全面开放合作。

我们将在商务部、中国贸促会的指导下，继续承办好中国—东盟博览会、商务与投资峰会，深化共办共赢，提高经贸实效，延伸平台效应，通过完善中国—东盟商务数据库、中国—东盟博览会官方网站，建设中国—东盟虚拟中心等措施，把5天的展会变成365天的综合商务服务，成为永不落幕的博览会，为服务中国—东盟战略伙伴关系，服务中国—东盟自由贸易区作出新的贡献。

女士们、先生们，第七届中国—东盟博览会和商务与投资峰会将是充满机遇、富有商机的盛会，广西作为承办方，将竭诚为各方宾客做好服务。我们也诚挚欢迎国内外新闻界的朋友们多到广西考察，报道盛会。我们期待大家的到来。

谢谢大家！

在第七届中国—东盟博览会、第七届中国—东盟商务与投资峰会闭幕新闻发布会上的讲话

中国—东盟博览会组委会副主任兼秘书长
中国—东盟商务与投资峰会组委会副主任
广西壮族自治区党委常委、自治区副主席
陈　武
（2010年10月24日）

女士们，先生们，
新闻界的朋友们：

下午好！在中国与东盟各国的共同努力下，第七届中国—东盟博览会、中国—东盟商务与投资峰会即将落下帷幕，取得圆满成功。

中共中央政治局常委、全国政协主席贾庆林，印尼副总统布迪约诺、老挝副总理阿桑·劳里，越南副总理张永仲出席本届博览会、商务与投资峰会。中国和东盟国家的商务、能源、金融等部门的部长级官员，国际组织代表、各国商协会会长、世界知名企业家出席盛会。出席本届博览会、商务与投资峰会的部长级贵宾有191人。其中，东盟及其他国家部长级贵宾53人。

今年是中国—东盟自由贸易区建成的第一年，中国和东盟国家领导人、部长级贵宾、国际组织代表、各国商协会会长、世界知名企业家共同出席本次盛会，表明了各方抓住中国—东盟自由贸易区建成的重大机遇，发挥博览会、商务与投资峰会平台作用，加强全面合作，深化互利共赢的共同愿望，增强了各方继续共同推进自贸区建设，深化战略伙伴关系，实现共同发展、共同繁荣的信心和决心。

受组委会委托，下面我介绍本届博览会、商务与投资峰会有关情况。

一、紧扣自贸区建成后的新需求，务实推动中国与东盟合作，成效显著

第七届博览会、商务与投资峰会紧扣自贸区建成后的新需求，除保持原有的高规格和共办特色外，还根据中国—东盟自贸区建成的新需求，增加了新内容。如：博览会新设服务贸易专题，新增珠宝首饰展，举办自贸区建设成就展等。通过这些新举措，把自贸区一系列贸易和投资便利化政策传导给企业，受到企业的欢迎，各方踊跃参展参会。

本届博览会参展企业2200家，各国大企业和品牌企业比上届增多，展位需求量大，供不应求。本届博览会总展位数4600个，比上届增长15%。其中，中国内地及港澳台地区使用展位3379个，外国企业使用展位1221个，其中东盟10国展位1178个，均创历届新高。印尼、老挝、马来西亚、缅甸、泰国、越南等六个东盟国家包馆。东盟10国均组织本国品牌企业参展，东盟品牌展区成为本届亮点。东盟各国还在本国展区内按行业布展，突出展示农产品食品、木材家具、轻工工艺、珠宝等行业产品，有效提高了本届博览会的专业化水平。本届博览会国内外企业重复参展率明显提高。值得注意的是，中国—东盟博览会外国展位数连年提高，目前外国展位数在中国国内展位中居于前列，博览会已经成为东盟等外国企业开拓中国市场的重要渠道。

本届博览会专业观众3.913万人，比上届增长2%。其中来自美国、法国、日本、韩国、港澳台地区的专业观众有所增加。参展参会规模进一步扩大。本届博览会、商务峰会在服务中国—东盟自由贸易区，务实推动中国与东盟合作方面，取得新成效，体现在六个方面的亮点：

（一）商品贸易成交量再创新高

截至10月24日下午4时，累计交易总额达到17.12亿美元，比2009年增长3.5%。其中，出口额14.28亿美元，同比增长12.3%，东盟出口到中国的贸易额明显增长。

（二）投资合作更富实效

本届博览会举行了46场投资推介活动，共签订国际经济合作项目135个，总投资额66.9亿美元，比上届增长3%。其中，中国与东盟签约的投资合作项目58个，总投资额26.63亿美元，分别占国际经济合作项目的43%和38%。项目数量多，涉及农业、制造业、商贸物流、旅游开发、矿产开采及加工、交通能源设施建设等更多领域，合作质量进一步提升。

本届博览会签署国内经济合作项目156个，总投资674.46亿元，比上届增长9%。

举办地广西壮族自治区在本届博览会期间共签订国际合作项目112个，总投资52.34亿美元，分别比上届增长33.3%和21.4%。

（三）商务与投资峰会取得丰硕成果

本届商务与投资峰会“中国—东盟自由贸易区与区域经贸合作的展望” 为主题，形式更加新颖，交流更加深入。中共中央政治局常委、全国政协主席贾

庆林，印度尼西亚副总统布迪约诺，老挝副总理阿桑·劳里，越南副总理张永仲，中国商务部国际贸易谈判代表兼副部长高虎城，广西壮族自治区党委书记郭声琨，中国外交部副部长张志军，中国贸促会副会长王锦珍等出席开幕式。广西壮族自治区主席马飚主持开幕式。

贾庆林主席、布迪约诺副总统、阿桑·劳里副总理、张永仲副总理发表演讲，郭声琨书记、王锦珍副会长致辞。来自中国、东盟以及世界10多个国家和地区的政府高官、商界领袖、企业精英、区域组织代表、知名专家学者和媒体代表1500人参会。会期举行了东盟国家领导人与中国企业家CEO圆桌对话会，以及中国—东盟商会领袖论坛和行业论坛，进一步推动务实合作。

（四）举办中国—东盟自由贸易区建设成就展，展示自贸区建设成就和美好前景

本届博览会期间举办了自贸区建设成就展。中国商务部官员、东盟国家驻南宁领事馆官员以及中国和东盟各国各界代表500多人出席了开馆仪式。成就展内容丰富，国际性强，以图片、图表、文字、音视频等形式，反映自贸区建设的进程、各方面取得的成就，以及自贸区前景展望，包括反映博览会和商务与投资峰会对促进自贸区发展的成果展示。中国和东盟艺术家以及少年儿童以自贸区及中国与东盟的友好合作为题材，创作了一批书法、美术、摄影、篆刻等作品，艺术地反映了自贸区合作共赢的主题，也很好地反映了中国与东盟在文化等领域合作的成就。共有330位中国和东盟国家书画艺术家参与创作，其中东盟国家艺术家有66位，占20%。

几天来，成就展吸引了十多万各界人士参观，得到各方的赞誉。马来西亚贸工部副部长拿督贾谷·东加·沙甘说，成就展办得很好，可以使人们清楚地了解到自贸区及博览会一步步成长的历程。印尼工商会馆中国委员会副秘书长施锦场说，自贸区建设成就展集中展示了自贸区建设的成果，反映中国与东盟互利共赢，进一步增强了大家共建自贸区的决心。

（五）博览会开幕式继续创新，体现自贸区建设成就，彰显10+1>1的精神

博览会开幕式作为中国和东盟各国政要每年出席的一个重大仪式，今年继续成为亮点，本届博览会开幕式延续了历届博览会“水”的创意元素，以“水润花开，共享硕果”为主题，形象地表达出博览会的“合作之水”从涓涓细流到滔滔江河，浇灌着自贸区的广袤大地，滋润万物，结出了累累硕果的深刻寓意，受到了中国和东盟政府官员、商协会会长、企业家的普遍赞誉。

（六）会期论坛和活动突出“自贸区与新机遇”，体现了各方抓住自贸区建成的新机遇深化多领域合作的共同愿望

本届博览会重点主题为“自贸区与新机遇”，会期前后围绕这一重点主题举办10个高层次论坛，扩大了多领域交流。

中国人民银行、中国银监会、中国证监会、中国保监会（简称“一行三会”）与广西壮族自治区政府共同主办了第二届中国—东盟金融合作与发展领袖论坛。中国“一行三会”领导、东盟国家金融主管部门高官、国际金融机构相关代表、中国及欧美等地区商业金融机构首脑、金融界知名专家学者和企业家出席了论坛。论坛围绕“深化合作机制，构建中国—东盟自由贸易区互利共赢金融发展新格局”的主题，就进一步拓展自贸区金融合作平台，构建自贸区互利共赢金融发展新格局，更好地服务于区域内各领域合作，推动区域经济一体化，进行了深入交流，通过了《论坛共识》。会期还举办了首届中国—东盟银行家圆桌会议，务实推动了跨境金融交流与合作，形成了《中国—东盟银行家圆桌会议倡议》。

中国国家能源局和印尼能源矿产部联合举办了中国—印尼能源论坛，两国政府官员和企业家共同探讨了中国—东盟自贸区建成背景下双方的能源合作，双方企业还围绕加强石油天然气、可再生能源、电力和煤炭等方面互利合作的内容进行了深入讨论，签署了多项合作协议。

此外，国务院扶贫办主办了中国—东盟社会发展与减贫论坛，中国红十字会主办了首届中国—东盟红十字论坛，中国社科院主办了第三届中国—东盟智库战略对话，国家海事总局主办了中国—东盟海事磋商机制第六次会议，中国电力企业联合会主办了第三届中国—东盟电力合作与发展论坛暨中国—东盟电力经贸合作洽谈会。

各场论坛规格高，均有中国和东盟国家部长级官员、国家直属企业负责人、国际知名专家学者出席。博览会后，还将主办中国—东盟农业部长（省长）论坛、2010中国—东盟国际口腔医学交流与合作论坛、“加强国际司法交流与合作，促进区域经济发展与繁荣”研讨会。

博览会期间还举办了南宁国际民歌艺术节暨第七届中国—东盟博览会开幕晚会，以及高尔夫球、网球、汽车拉力赛、青年艺术品创作等丰富多彩的文化体育交流活动，增进了中国与东盟各国人民的友谊。

（七）展会影响力进一步扩大

本届博览会、商务与投资峰会继续受到国内外主流媒体和专业媒体的高度关注。到会采访的记者比往年又有增加，达到199家共1458名记者，比去年增加39名。其中，国外媒体72家共106名记者（含东盟媒体88人）；港澳台媒体16家共41名记者。

中外媒体对博览会、商务与投资峰会进行了全方位、多角度的报道。据不完全统计，中外媒体累计发稿5700多篇；网络报道页面9400多个，网络相关新闻转载与链接页面约85万个。

与会各方对本届博览会、商务与投资峰会给予高度评价：

中共中央政治局常委、全国政协主席贾庆林说，中国—东盟博览会、中国—东盟商务与投资峰会已成为中国同东盟国家对话、交流、合作的有效平台。

印尼副总统布迪约诺说，在自贸区建成之际举办的第七届博览会具有特殊的意义，它不仅为双方商家企业展示产品、宣传形象、结识新伙伴提供了便利，创造了商机，而且也将推动东盟与中国在竞争日益激烈的全球市场中进一步加强经济合作，最终实现共赢。

老挝副总理阿桑·劳里说，中国—东盟博览会和商务与投资峰会的举办十分成功，内容丰富，形式多样，值得我们很好考察和学习借鉴。

文莱工业和初级资源部部长叶海亚表示，每次参加博览会都能感受新发展、新动向。今年文莱的清真食品首次在博览会上展出，将进一步促进友好合作。

本届博览会得到了中外客商的广泛赞誉，普遍认为中国—东盟博览会作为连接中国与东盟各国的经贸合作平台和自贸区建设的“助推器”，发挥越来越重要的作用。

二、加大创新力度，进一步发挥平台作用，让企业更好享受自贸区商机

本届博览会、商务与投资峰会围绕自贸区已签署和实施的《货物贸易协议》、《服务贸易协议》、《投资协议》，加大创新力度，提高服务水平，让企业更好地享受贸易和投资便利化，享受更多商机。

（一）加强自贸区框架下的重点行业合作，展览专业化水平有了新的提高

服务贸易专题作为本届博览会新设的专题，集中了一批实力雄厚的中国和东盟国家金融机构、物流企业、教育服务机构参展，为金融、物流、教育等服务领域合作搭建了平台。

本届博览会新增珠宝展，充分发挥东盟国家丰富的宝石及原材料资源，以及中国在加工设计方面的优势，汇集了区域内一批知名珠宝首饰企业参展，推动了珠宝产业的交流与合作。

本届博览会继续举办农业展，展示了中国、马来西亚、日本、新西兰国家和地区的众多名优产品和品牌企业，特别是台湾岛内企业成规模参展，展位数超过100个，展示了台湾特色水果、茶叶、特色食品等，成为一个亮点。农业展还举办了名优企业推广、花艺表演、茶叶企业推广等一系列现场推介活动，为企业享受自贸区商机搭建了最直接、最有效的平台，推动双方农业合作。

本届博览会在东盟国家展馆内设立了品牌企业展区和食品、木材家具展区，东盟国家参展企业更优，展品进一步向本国优势特色行业集中。

11月19—22日，还将举行中国—东盟博览会木材与木制品展，更好地满足专业客商通过博览会分享自贸区商机的需求。

（二）加强对采购商的服务和经贸配对的力度，让企业充分享受自贸区带来的好处

本届博览会采购商数量和质量较往届有较大提升，采购团组数量比上届

增加50%。除中国和东盟国家的采购团组外，法国、加拿大、德国、澳大利亚和日本等区域外国家和地区也组织了采购团组参会。我们通过组织采购团整团巡馆、组织商贸对接活动，制作采购商和投资商标志徽章等方式，促进供求互动，进一步提升企业参会的实效。

本届博览会贸易配对更有针对性。会期首次在朱槿花厅举办了三场大型贸易对接会，376家企业参与配对。其中，东盟各国采购团在机械设备、电子电器、建材等行业达成一批采购意向。在电力设备采购对接会上，一批越南电力设备采购企业与中国电力设备参展企业进行了有效对接。联合国采购中心首次在会期举办联合国采购推介会，各国企业代表与联合国采购官员开展了洽谈采购活动。会期举办了4场参展商讲坛，为参展企业的品牌推广提供平台。

本届博览会加强了与各国投资促进主管部门的合作，投资促进力度加大。会期投融资项目对接会吸引了100多家中国实力雄厚的对外投资企业、股（权）投资机构、项目咨询机构以及东盟投资促进机构和投资商参会，为500多个投融资项目实现了对接，推动了企业“走出去”。

（三）提高服务水平，为宾客营造良好的洽谈交易环境

第七届博览会、商务与投资峰会继续坚持以客户为中心，不断改善各项服务质量。会期继续开通了南宁至东盟10国首都和重要城市的包机航线。展览管理方面，成立了公安、工商、质监等多部门组成的联合执法组，展馆秩序比往年更好。海关、检验检疫部门采取便利化措施，展品通关快捷便利。证件工作基本实现常态化、规范化、精细化管理，全面实现“人到证到”目标。接待方面加强了对餐饮、住宿、用车等资源的统筹，在节俭的前提下提高了服务质量。对口接待机制进一步完善。我们还开展了“中国—东盟博览会指定接待宾馆”称号、牌匾的核发工作，使宾馆服务更加规范。

（四）创新宣传方式，让更多的企业和民众了解自贸区的好处和博览会、商务与投资峰会的平台作用

我们与中国和东盟及其他国家和地区的150多家媒体建立了合作机制，紧扣重大事件和自贸区建成，策划了“中国—东盟博览会合作媒体广西行”、中国—东盟媒体汽车拉力赛等系列活动，举行了多场新闻发布会和吹风会，大力宣传自贸区建成带来的新机遇以及博览会、商务与投资峰会发挥的平台作用。同时加强面向企业的宣传，帮助企业了解和享受自贸区的优惠政策。

我们在社会宣传上注入更多的文化内涵，将七届博览会的主题词由名人刻成印章。印章是诚信、合作的象征，以此象征建设自贸区过程中各项协议的实施，也突出博览会对促进自贸区建设作出的贡献。我们将印章用于博览会相关活动的T恤衫设计，增添了博览会的文化气息，使自贸区广为人知、深入人心。

三、促进互利共赢，更加紧密了中国与东盟战略伙伴关系，服务了中国—东盟自贸区和区域经济合作

通过本届博览会、商务与投资峰会，中国与东盟各国加深了友谊，深化了合作，巩固了自贸区成果，增强了11国继续共同推进自贸区建设的信心。

（一）进一步密切了中国与东盟战略伙伴关系

本届博览会、商务与投资峰会期间，先后举行了4场国家领导人会见、多场地方领导会见，安排了12个代表团巡馆，举办了博览会和商务与投资峰会2场开幕式，举行了中越友谊手印墙揭幕仪式、中国—东盟商务区各国商务联络部办公楼移交仪式等。主题国印尼举办了国家馆开馆仪式、国家推介会、印尼领导人与中国企业CEO见面会等丰富多彩的主题国活动，通过一系列活动，增进了中国与东盟的了解，达成了新的共识，进一步促进了中国—东盟友好关系。

今年会期各国政要与商界的交流比往届更多，既有东盟国家领导人与中国地方政府领导、企业家的会见、对话，也有中国有关部委领导、各省市领导与中外企业家的会见、交流，推动了各国之间的友好合作，为企业创造更多的商机。另外，新加坡丰隆亚洲有限公司作为首个东盟企业担任博览会首席战略合作伙伴，进一步体现了中国和东盟国家通过博览会平台实现共办共赢的强烈愿望。

（二）进一步服务了中国—东盟自由贸易区

本届博览会、商务与投资峰会进一步把自贸区的投资贸易便利化政策从政府层面推向企业层面。

在展会内容和活动安排上，进一步突出自贸区的主题，更加贴近企业深化商品贸易、服务贸易、投资合作的需求。其中，博览会突出展示零关税商品和降税商品，以及金融、物流、教育等服务贸易内容，开展了一系列务实的投资推介活动，举办了木材、食品农产品、电力、装备制造业等行业对接活动、商务与投资峰会举行了自贸区物流论坛、矿业论坛等活动。这些促进了双方企业在自贸区建成后的行业对接和务实合作。

本届博览会、商务与投资峰会加强了对自贸区投资贸易便利化政策的宣讲、解读。会期举办了中国—东盟自贸区政策与实务研讨会，商务部、海关总署、国家质检总局的有关专家向企业解读了自贸区有关政策。博览会开幕式、布展均突出了博览会对自贸区建设的推动作用，在会期各场活动的致辞、讲话中，突出了自贸区的相关内容，使自贸区被更多的企业所了解。

（三）进一步促进了中国与东盟城市间的合作

本届博览会“魅力之城”丰富更加丰富，形式创新，进一步增进了中国与东盟城市之间的友谊，深化了城市之间的合作。

会期，各国代表团团长分别巡视了“魅力之城”展区，举办了“魅力中国·钦州之夜”宴会，11国魅力之城结为“友谊之城”；举办了“魅力之城”

专场推介会，开展务实合作；推出了博览会“护照”，以民众喜闻乐见的形式介绍11国“魅力之城”；我们为每个“魅力之城”设计了印章，专门举办了第八届博览会中国“魅力之城”移交仪式，体现在充满机遇的自贸区环境下，城市之间友好交流、互利共赢的愿望，也象征着中国—东盟博览会“魅力之城”的传承与发展。会期，东盟各国客商到钦州市进行了考察。

（四）提高了中国与东盟作为一个整体的国际影响力

本届博览会吸引了更多的区域外组织和机构参展参会。日本、法国、德国、澳大利亚、美国、加拿大等国家和地区踊跃参展参会。联合国工发组织执行总干事隋婺出席了博览会。法国马恩河谷省举办了推介会。德国莱比锡国际展览有限公司与博览会秘书处举行了合作洽谈，德国技术合作公司举办了“区域融合与发展国际经验交流会”。区域外组织和机构积极参展参会，大大促进了区域外对中国和东盟的了解与交流，提高中国和东盟作为一个整体在世界的影响力。

（五）为区域经济合作提供有效平台，提高了举办地广西的开放合作水平

会期，中国国内各省区市扩大了与东盟各国的高层交流。海南省副省长李国梁会见了新加坡贸工部兼新闻通讯艺术部政务次长陈振泉，就海南省与新加坡的合作达成了广泛共识。各省区市代表团还举办了一系列的商贸交流活动。例如，宁夏回族自治区在连续七年在博览会上举办推介活动的基础上，今年首次组织10家大型食品类企业参加文莱清真食品推介会，开展了清真食品领域的合作；湖南、河北、陕西、山西、海南、哈尔滨等省区市也举办了推介和交流活动，促进了各省区市与东盟的交流。

会期，广西壮族自治区领导与东盟国家领导人、各国代表团、友好城市代表团等举行了17场会见，就共建广西北部湾经济区，共促泛北部湾经济合作、大湄公河次区域合作、南宁新加坡经济走廊，共同服务中国—东盟自贸区发展，达成了广泛共识。钦州作为本届博览会“魅力之城”，举办了多场活动。会期还举办了中国凭祥—越南同登跨境经济合作区工作商讨会、桂琼战略合作重点工作计划协议签署仪式等，促进了广西与东盟国家和国内省区市之间的合作。

四、第八届中国—东盟博览会、商务与投资峰会的初步考虑

在筹办第七届中国—东盟博览会的同时，我们对第八届博览会和商务与投资峰会的有关问题进行了专题研究，在充分听取东盟和中国国内各组展单位、专业观众、商协会等各方面意见的基础上，经过反复讨论，形成了第八届博览会有关安排的初步意见，并在刚才举行的中国—东盟博览会高官会上获得一致通过。

1. 关于第八届博览会举办时间。为了便于中外领导人活动安排及广大客商参展参会和洽谈业务，从第八届中国—东盟博览会起，将每年博览会开幕的

时间固定在10月份第三个星期的周五。据此，第八届中国—东盟博览会的举办时间是2011年10月21—26日。10月21日是中外领导人巡视展馆、博览会开幕式、商务与投资峰会开幕式、欢迎宴会等活动。10月22日至26日是第八届博览会展览。

2. 第八届博览会主题国是马来西亚，届时将举办主题国活动。

3. 第八届博览会的重点主题是“环保合作”，届时将围绕这一主题举办相关活动。

4. 第八届中国—东盟博览会继续与第八届中国—东盟商务与投资峰会同期举办。

女士们，先生们，

博览会、商务与投资峰会举办七年来，中国和东盟10国政府、东盟各共办方、组委会各成员单位及社会各界给予了高度重视和大力支持。在此，我谨代表组委会和举办地广西向东盟10国共办部门和中国商务部、外交部、贸促会、国家发改委、公安部、中宣部、国务院新闻办等国家部委以及组展单位和参与博览会的安保、接待、宣传等有关部门表示衷心的感谢！向所有支持博览会、商务与投资峰会的各界人士表示衷心感谢！向参与博览会和商务与投资峰会报道的新闻界朋友们表示衷心感谢!

我们相信，在大家的共同努力下，博览会和商务与投资峰会一定会越办越好，越办越有特色，越办越有实效，为促进中国—东盟友好合作，服务中国—东盟自贸区作出新的贡献！

现在，我代表中国—东盟博览会组委会宣布：第七届中国—东盟博览会胜利闭幕！

第七届中国—东盟博览会、第七届中国—东盟商务与投资峰会工作总结

第七届中国—东盟博览会、第七届中国—东盟商务与投资峰会（以下分别简称“博览会”、“商务与投资峰会”）于2010年10月19—24日顺利举办并取得了圆满成功。

2010年是中国—东盟自由贸易区（以下简称“自贸区”）建成第一年，办好第七届中国—东盟博览会、商务与投资峰会意义重大。为此，我们在自治区党委、自治区人民政府的领导下，充分借鉴前六届展会积累的丰富经验，发扬团结协作、迎难而上的精神，围绕“保持政治外交规格、提高经贸实效、扩大多领域合作、提高品牌影响力”这一重点，紧扣自贸区建成新形势，明确办会思路，加大创新力度，强化工作措施，使“两会”筹办工作水平有了进一步提升，在服务国家战略，带动广西发展方面，取得了新的显著成效。

下一步我们将按照10月25日自治区党委常委会扩大会议要求，认真贯彻贾庆林、刘云山等中央领导同志对广西工作的重要指示精神，进一步增强办好博览会和商务与投资峰会的事业心和责任心，进一步完善和健全办好博览会的常态化机制，使明年的第八届博览会和商务与投资峰会办得更精彩更成功。现将第七届博览会、商务与投资峰会有关情况总结如下：

一、基本情况

第七届中国—东盟博览会、商务与投资峰会除保持原有的高规格和共办特色外，还根据自贸区建成的新需求，和《货物贸易协议》、《服务贸易协议》和《投资协议》签订实施的新形势，在已有货物贸易、投资合作内容的基础上，增加了服务贸易专题，同时还新增珠宝首饰展，举办自贸区建设成就展等。通过这些新举措，务实推进中国与东盟友好合作，把自贸区一系列贸易和投资便利化政

策快速传导给企业，取得显著成效，体现了博览会、商务与投资峰会直接为自贸区服务、是自贸区“助推器”的特点。

（一）继续保持较高的政治外交规格

中共中央政治局常委、全国政协主席贾庆林，印尼副总统布迪约诺、老挝副总理阿桑·劳里，越南副总理张永仲出席本届博览会、商务与投资峰会。中国和东盟国家的商务、能源、金融等部门的部长级官员，国际组织代表、各国商协会会长、世界知名企业家出席盛会。出席本届博览会、商务与投资峰会的部长级贵宾有191人。其中，东盟及其他国家部长级贵宾53人。

中国和东盟国家领导人、部长级贵宾、国际组织代表、各国商协会会长、世界知名企业家共同出席本次盛会，表明了各方抓住自贸区建成的重大机遇，发挥博览会、商务与投资峰会平台作用，加强全面合作，深化互利共赢的共同愿望，增强了各方继续共同推进自贸区建设，深化战略伙伴关系，实现共同发展、共同繁荣的信心和决心，也反映出博览会和商务与投资峰会的影响力和吸引力。

（二）务实推动中国与东盟合作，经贸成效进一步提高

本届博览会参展企业2200家，各国大企业和品牌企业比上届增多，展位需求量大，供不应求。本届博览会总展位数4600个，比上届增长15%。其中，中国内地及港澳台地区使用展位3379个，外国企业使用展位1221个，其中东盟10国展位1178个，均创历届新高。印尼、老挝、马来西亚、缅甸、泰国、越南等六个东盟国家包馆。东盟10国均组织本国品牌企业参展，东盟品牌展区成为本届亮点。东盟各国还在本国展区内按行业布展，突出展示农产品食品、木材家具、轻工工艺、珠宝等行业产品，有效提高了本届博览会的专业化水平。博览会市场吸引力和影响力提升反映在几个方面：本届博览会国内外企业重复参展率明显提高，外国展位数连年提升，博览会的外国展位数目前在中国国内展位中居于前列，博览会已经成为东盟等外国企业开拓中国市场的重要渠道。

本届博览会专业观众39130人，比上届增长2%。其中来自美国、法国、日本、韩国和港澳台地区的专业观众有所增加。参展参会规模进一步扩大。本届博览会、商务峰会在服务中国—东盟自由贸易区，务实推动中国与东盟合作方面，取得新成效，体现在以下方面：

1. 商品贸易成交量再创新高。截至10月24日下午16时，累计交易总额达到17.12亿美元，比去年增长3.5%。其中，出口额14.28亿美元，同比增长12.3%，东盟出口到中国的贸易额明显增长。

2. 投资合作更富实效。本届博览会举行了46场投资推介活动，共签订国际经济合作项目135个，总投资额66.9亿美元，比上届增长3%。其中，中国与东盟签约的投资合作项目58个，总投资额26.63亿美元，分别占国际经济合作项目的43%和38%。项目数量多，涉及农业、制造业、商贸物流、旅游开发、矿产开采及加工、交通能源设施建设等更多领域，合作质量进一步提升。

本届博览会签署国内经济合作项目156个，总投资674.46亿元，比上届增长9%。

我区在本届博览会期间共签订国际合作项目112个，总投资52.34亿美元，分别比上届增长33.3%和21.4%。

（三）商务与投资峰会取得丰硕成果

本届商务与投资峰会“中国—东盟自由贸易区与区域经贸合作的展望” 为主题，形式更加新颖，交流更加深入。中共中央政治局常委、全国政协主席贾庆林，印度尼西亚副总统布迪约诺，老挝副总理阿桑·劳里，越南副总理张永仲，中国商务部国际贸易谈判代表兼副部长高虎城，广西壮族自治区党委书记郭声琨，中国外交部副部长张志军，中国贸促会副会长王锦珍等出席开幕式。广西壮族自治区主席马飚主持开幕式。

贾庆林主席、布迪约诺副总统、阿桑·劳里副总理、张永仲副总理发表演讲，郭声琨书记、王锦珍副会长致辞。来自中国、东盟以及世界10多个国家和地区的政府高官、商界领袖、企业精英、区域组织代表、知名专家学者和媒体代表1500人参会。会期举行了东盟国家领导人与中国企业家CEO圆桌对话会，以及中国—东盟商会领袖论坛和行业论坛，进一步推动务实合作。

（四）举办中国—东盟自由贸易区建设成就展，展示自贸区建设成就和美好前景以及广西在其中发挥的作用

本届博览会期间举办了自贸区建设成就展，是博览会的重要组成部分。中国商务部官员、东盟国家驻南宁领事馆官员以及中国和东盟各国各界代表500多人出席了开馆仪式。成就展内容丰富，国际性强，以图片、图表、文字、音视频等形式，反映自贸区建设的进程、各方面取得的成就，以及自贸区前景展望，包括反映博览会和商务与投资峰会对促进自贸区发展的成果展示。中国和东盟国家330位书画艺术家（其中东盟国家艺术家66位，占20%）以及少年儿童以自贸区及中国与东盟的友好合作为题材，创作了一批书法、美术、摄影、篆刻等作品，艺术地反映了自贸区合作共赢的主题，也很好地反映了中国与东盟在文化等领域合作的成就以及广西在其中发挥的重要作用。

会期，数万中国和东盟各界人士参观了成就展，各方高度赞誉。马来西亚贸工部副部长拿督贾谷·东加·沙甘说，成就展办得很好，形象直观地反映了经济快速增长和各方面合作的情况，可以使人们清楚地了解到自贸区及博览会一步步成长的历程。印尼工商会馆中国委员会副秘书长施锦场说，自贸区建设成就展集中展示了自贸区建设的成果，反映中国与东盟互利共赢，进一步增强了大家共建自贸区的决心。

（五）博览会开幕式继续创新，体现自贸区建设成就，彰显10+1>1的精神

博览会开幕式作为中国和东盟各国政要每年出席的一个重大仪式，2010年继续成为亮点。本届博览会开幕式继续以历届博览会的“合作之水”为创意元素，以“水润花开，共享硕果”突出本届博览会适逢自贸区建成的特点，形象地表达

出博览会的“合作之水”从涓涓细流到滔滔江河，浇灌着自贸区的广袤大地，滋润万物，结出了累累硕果。开幕式隆重热烈，主题鲜明，振奋人心，受到了中国和东盟政府官员、商协会会长、企业家的普遍赞誉。

（六）会期论坛和活动突出“自贸区与新机遇”，体现了各方抓住自贸区建成的新机遇深化多领域合作的共同愿望

本届博览会重点主题为“自贸区与新机遇”，会期前后围绕这一重点主题举办10个高层次论坛，扩大了多领域交流。

中国人民银行、中国银监会、中国证监会、中国保监会（简称“一行三会”）与广西壮族自治区人民政府共同主办了第二届中国—东盟金融合作与发展领袖论坛。中国“一行三会”领导、东盟国家金融主管部门高官、国际金融机构相关代表、中国及欧美等地区商业金融机构首脑、金融界知名专家学者和企业家出席了论坛。论坛围绕“深化合作机制，构建自贸区互利共赢金融发展新格局”的主题，就进一步拓展自贸区金融合作平台，构建自贸区互利共赢金融发展新格局，更好地服务于区域内各领域合作，推动区域经济一体化，进行了深入交流，通过了《论坛共识》。会期还举办了首届中国—东盟银行家圆桌会议，务实推动了跨境金融交流与合作，形成了《中国—东盟银行家圆桌会议倡议》。

中国国家能源局和印尼能源矿产部联合举办了中国—印尼能源论坛，两国政府官员和企业家共同探讨了自贸区建成背景下双方的能源合作，双方企业还围绕加强石油天然气、可再生能源、电力和煤炭等方面互利合作的内容进行了深入讨论，签署了多项合作协议。

此外，国务院扶贫办主办了中国—东盟社会发展与减贫论坛，中国红十字会主办了首届中国—东盟红十字论坛，中国社科院主办了第三届中国—东盟智库战略对话，国家海事总局主办了中国—东盟海事磋商机制第六次会议，中国电力企业联合会主办了第三届中国—东盟电力合作与发展论坛暨中国—东盟电力经贸合作洽谈会。

各场论坛规格高，均有中国和东盟国家部长级官员、国家直属企业负责人、国际知名专家学者出席。博览会后，还将主办中国—东盟农业部长（省长）论坛、2010中国—东盟国际口腔医学交流与合作论坛、“加强国际司法交流与合作，促进区域经济发展与繁荣”研讨会。

博览会期间还举办了南宁国际民歌艺术节暨第七届中国—东盟博览会开幕晚会，以及高尔夫球、网球、汽车拉力赛、青年艺术品创作等丰富多彩的文化体育交流活动，增进了中国与东盟各国人民的友谊。

（七）展会影响力进一步扩大

本届博览会、商务与投资峰会继续受到国内外主流媒体和专业媒体的高度关注。到会采访的记者比往年又有增加，达到199家共1458名记者，比去年增加39名。其中，国外媒体72家共106名记者（含东盟媒体88人）；港澳台媒体16家共

41名记者。

中外媒体对博览会、商务与投资峰会进行了全方位、多角度的报道。据不完全统计，中外媒体累计发稿5700多篇；网络报道页面9400多个，网络相关新闻转载与链接页面约85万个。

各国领导人和与会各方对本届博览会、商务与投资峰会给予高度评价：

中共中央政治局常委、全国政协主席贾庆林说，中国—东盟博览会、中国—东盟商务与投资峰会已成为中国同东盟国家对话、交流、合作的有效平台。

印尼副总统布迪约诺说，在自贸区建成之际举办的第七届博览会具有特殊的意义，它不仅为双方商家企业展示产品、宣传形象、结识新伙伴提供了便利，创造了商机，而且也将推动东盟与中国在竞争日益激烈的全球市场中进一步加强经济合作，最终实现共赢。

老挝副总理阿桑·劳里说，中国—东盟博览会和商务与投资峰会的举办十分成功，内容丰富，形式多样，值得我们很好考察和学习借鉴。

文莱工业和初级资源部部长叶海亚表示，每次参加博览会都能感受新发展、新动向。今年文莱的清真食品首次在博览会上展出，将进一步促进友好合作。

本届博览会得到了中外客商的广泛赞誉，普遍认为中国—东盟博览会作为连接中国与东盟各国的经贸合作平台和自贸区建设的“助推器”，发挥越来越重要的作用。

二、主要成效

通过本届博览会、商务与投资峰会，中国与东盟各国加深了友谊，深化了合作，巩固了自贸区成果，增强了11国继续共同推进自贸区建设的信心，服务了区域经济合作，促进了互利共赢。

（一）进一步密切了中国与东盟战略伙伴关系

本届博览会、商务与投资峰会期间，先后举行了4场国家领导人会见、多场地方领导会见，安排了12个代表团巡馆，举办了博览会和商务与投资峰会2场开幕式，举行了中越友谊手印墙揭幕仪式、中国—东盟商务区各国商务联络部办公楼移交仪式等。主题国印尼举办了国家馆开馆仪式、国家推介会、印尼领导人与中国企业CEO见面会等丰富多彩的主题国活动，通过一系列活动，增进了中国与东盟的了解，达成了新的共识，进一步促进了中国—东盟友好关系。

今年会期各国政要与商界的交流比往届更多，既有东盟国家领导人与中国地方政府领导、企业家的会见、对话，也有中国有关部委领导、各省市领导与中外企业家的会见、交流，推动了各国之间的友好合作，为企业创造更多的商机。另外，新加坡丰隆亚洲有限公司成为首个博览会首席战略合作伙伴的东盟企业，进一步体现了东盟国家的企业通过博览会平台实现共办共赢的强烈愿望，也反映出博览会对企业的吸引力。

（二）进一步服务了中国—东盟自由贸易区

本届博览会、商务与投资峰会进一步把自贸区的投资贸易便利化政策从政府层面推向企业层面。

在展会内容和活动安排上，进一步突出自贸区的主题，更加贴近企业深化商品贸易、服务贸易、投资合作的需求。其中，博览会突出展示零关税商品和降税商品，以及金融、物流、教育等服务贸易内容，开展了一系列务实的投资推介活动，举办了木材、食品农产品、电力、装备制造业等行业对接活动、商务与投资峰会举行了自贸区物流论坛、矿业论坛等活动。这些促进了双方企业在自贸区建成后的行业对接和务实合作。

本届博览会、商务与投资峰会加强了对自贸区投资贸易便利化政策的宣讲、解读。会期举办了中国—东盟自贸区政策与实务研讨会，商务部、海关总署、国家质检总局的有关专家向企业解读了自贸区有关政策。博览会开幕式、布展均突出了博览会对自贸区建设的推动作用，在会期各场活动的致辞、讲话中，突出了自贸区的相关内容，使自贸区被更多的企业所了解。

（三）进一步促进了中国与东盟城市间的合作

本届博览会“魅力之城”丰富更加丰富，形式创新，进一步增进了中国与东盟城市之间的友谊，深化了城市之间的合作。

会期，各国领导人和代表团团长分别巡视了“魅力之城”展区，举办了“魅力中国·钦州之夜”宴会，11国魅力之城结为“友谊之城”，推进了中国与东盟国家城市之间的合作； 举办了“魅力之城”专场推介会，开展务实合作，扩大了“魅力之城”与企业的合作；推出了博览会魅力之城“护照”，以民众喜闻乐见的形式介绍11国“魅力之城”；我们为每个“魅力之城”设计了印章，专门举办了第八届博览会中国“魅力之城”移交仪式，体现在充满机遇的自贸区环境下，城市之间友好交流、互利共赢的愿望，也象征着中国—东盟博览会“魅力之城”的传承与发展。会期，东盟各国客商还到本届博览会中国“魅力之城”钦州市进行了考察。

（四）提高了中国与东盟作为一个整体的国际影响力

本届博览会吸引了更多的区域外组织和机构参展参会。日本、法国、德国、澳大利亚、美国、加拿大等国家和地区踊跃参展参会。联合国工发组织执行总干事隋鞏出席了博览会。法国马恩河谷省举办了推介会。德国莱比锡国际展览有限公司与博览会秘书处举行了合作洽谈，德国技术合作公司举办了“区域融合与发展国际经验交流会”。区域外组织和机构积极参展参会，大大促进了区域外对中国和东盟的了解与交流，提高中国和东盟作为一个整体在世界的影响力。

（五）为国内省区市提供了合作交流的有效平台，提高了广西的开放合作水平

中国国内各省区市借助博览会、商务与投资峰会平台，扩大了与东盟各国的高层交流。如：海南省副省长李国梁会见了新加坡贸工部兼新闻通讯艺术部政务次长陈振泉，就海南省与新加坡的合作达成了广泛共识。各省区市代表团还举办了一系列的商贸交流活动。例如，宁夏回族自治区在连续七年在博览会上举办推介活动的基础上，今年首次组织10家大型食品类企业参加文莱清真食品推介会，开展了清真食品领域的合作；湖南、河北、陕西、哈尔滨、山西、海南其他省区市也举办了推介和交流活动，促进了各省区市与东盟的交流。

会期，广西壮族自治区领导与东盟国家领导人、各国代表团、友好城市代表团等举行了17场会见，就共建广西北部湾经济区，共促泛北部湾经济合作、大湄公河次区域合作、南宁新加坡经济走廊，共同服务自贸区发展，达成了广泛共识。钦州作为本届博览会“魅力之城”，举办了多场活动。会期还举办了中国凭祥—越南同登跨境经济合作区工作商讨会、桂琼战略合作重点工作计划协议签署仪式等，促进了广西与东盟国家和国内省区市之间的合作。

三、加大创新力度，筹备工作更加机制化、常态化，让企业更好享受自贸区商机

我们围绕自贸区已签署和实施的《货物贸易协议》、《服务贸易协议》、《投资协议》，加大创新力度，提高服务水平，让企业通过博览会、商务与投资峰会这一平台，更好地享受贸易和投资便利化，享受更多商机。

（一）加强自贸区框架下的重点行业合作，展览专业化水平有了新的提高

本届博览会新设服务贸易专题，集中了一批实力雄厚的中国和东盟国家金融机构、物流企业、教育服务机构参展，为金融、物流、教育等服务领域合作搭建了平台。

本届博览会新增珠宝展，充分发挥东盟国家丰富的宝石及原材料资源，以及中国在加工设计方面的优势，汇集了区域内一批知名珠宝首饰企业参展，推动了珠宝产业的交流与合作。

本届博览会继续举办农业展，展示了中国、马来西亚、日本、新西兰国家和地区的众多名优产品和品牌企业，特别是台湾岛内企业成规模参展，展位数超过100个，展示了台湾特色水果、茶叶、特色食品等，成为一个亮点。农业展还举办了名优企业推广、花艺表演、茶叶企业推广等一系列现场推介活动，为企业享受自贸区商机搭建了最直接、最有效的平台，推动双方农业合作。

本届博览会在东盟国家展馆内设立了品牌企业展区和食品、木材家具展区，东盟国家参展企业更优，展品进一步向本国优势特色行业集中。

2010年11月19—22日，还将举行中国—东盟博览会木材与木制品展，更好地满足专业客商通过博览会分享自贸区商机的需求。

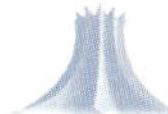

（二）加强对采购商的服务和经贸配对的力度，让企业充分享受自贸区带来的好处

本届博览会采购商数量和质量较往届有较大提升，采购团组数量比上届增加50%。除中国和东盟国家的采购团组外，法国、加拿大、德国、澳大利亚和日本等区域外国家和地区也组织了采购团组参会。我们通过组织采购团整团巡馆、组织商贸对接活动，制作采购商和投资商标志徽章等方式，促进供求互动，进一步提升企业参会的实效。

本届博览会贸易配对更有针对性。会期首次在朱槿花厅举办了三场大型贸易对接会，376家企业参与配对。其中，东盟各国采购团在机械设备、电子电器、建材等行业达成一批采购意向。在电力设备采购对接会上，一批越南电力设备采购企业与中国电力设备参展企业进行了有效对接。联合国采购中心首次在会期举办联合国采购推介会，各国企业代表与联合国采购官员开展了洽谈采购活动。会期举办了4场参展商讲坛，为参展企业的品牌推广提供平台。

本届博览会加强了与各国投资促进主管部门的合作，投资促进力度加大。会期投融资项目对接会吸引了100多家中国实力雄厚的对外投资企业、股（权）投资机构、项目咨询机构以及东盟投资促进机构和投资商参会，为500多个投融资项目实现了对接，推动了企业“走出去”。

（三）提高服务水平，为宾客营造良好的洽谈交易环境

第七届中国—东盟博览会、商务与投资峰会继续坚持以客户为中心，不断改善各项服务质量。会期继续开通了南宁至东盟10国首都和重要城市的包机航线。展览管理方面，成立了公安、工商、质监等多部门组成的联合执法组，展馆秩序比往年更好。海关、检验检疫部门采取便利化措施，展品通关快捷便利。证件工作基本实现常态化、规范化、精细化管理，全面实现“人到证到”目标。接待方面加强了对餐饮、住宿、用车等资源的统筹，在节俭的前提下提高了服务质量。对口接待机制进一步完善。我们还开展了“中国—东盟博览会指定接待宾馆”称号、牌匾的核发工作，使宾馆服务更加规范。安全保卫工作更加周密，确保了展会的安全、顺畅、有序。各方普遍反映本届博览会、商务与投资峰会整体组织、服务水平又比上届有了提高。在闭幕当日举行的博览会高官会议上，东盟10国及东盟秘书处的高官对本届博览会、商务与投资峰会表示满意，东盟各国商协会、企业的满意度也大幅提高。

（四）创新宣传方式，让更多的企业和民众了解自贸区的好处和博览会、商务与投资峰会的平台作用

我们与中国和东盟及其他国家和地区的150多家媒体建立了合作机制，紧扣重大事件和自贸区建成，策划了“中国—东盟博览会合作媒体广西行”、中国—东盟媒体汽车拉力赛等系列活动，举行了多场新闻发布会和吹风会，大力宣传自贸区建成带来的新机遇以及博览会、商务与投资峰会发挥的平台作用。同时加强面向企业的宣传，帮助企业了解和享受自贸区的优惠政策。

我们在社会宣传上注入更多的文化内涵，将七届博览会的主题词由名人刻成印章。印章是诚信、合作的象征，以此象征建设自贸区过程中各项协议的实施，也突出博览会对促进自贸区建设作出的贡献。我们将印章用于博览会相关活动的T恤衫设计，增添了博览会的文化气息，使自贸区广为人知、深入人心。

（五）统筹工作进一步系统化，指挥协调和应变能力增强

本届博览会、商务与投资峰会的重要贵宾、重要人员、重要活动及日程安排变化较频繁，统筹的难度加大，我们完善指挥系统，增强协调应变能力，对国家领导人和自治区领导活动安排、证件、宾馆、车辆调度、机场迎宾、宴会、交通、安保等环节进行了周密安排，不断完善和细化方案预案，多次演练，狠抓细节，做好各场活动的转场衔接，保证了整体工作和具体工作的推进，实现了各场活动有序、顺畅。

中国—东盟博览会、中国—东盟商务与投资峰会广西指挥中心
2010年11月

出席第七届中国—东盟博览会部分贵宾

一、首长及随行

贾庆林　中共中央政治局常委，全国政协主席
支树平　国家质量监督检验检疫总局局长、党组书记
高虎城　商务部国际贸易谈判代表兼副部长、党组副书记
张国宝　国家发展和改革委员会副主任，国家能源局局长
张志军　外交部副部长
王胜洪　全国政协副秘书长
王锦珍　中国国际贸易促进委员会副会长
齐东然　中办警卫局副局长

二、组委会成员单位领导及成员

曹健林　科技部副部长
毕根敬　公安部警卫局副局长
孙毅彪　海关总署副署长
刘金平　国家旅游局党组成员、纪检组长
边振甲　国家食品药品监督管理局副局长
于　平　中国国际贸易促进委员会副会长

三、其他中央国家机关部委领导及特邀省部级领导

楼士礼　北京航空航天大学原党委书记

四、广西籍及在广西工作过的副部级以上现职领导

马庆生　全国政协民族宗教委副主任
彭祖意　全国人大常委、广西法学会会长

罗黎明　国家民族事务委员会副主任
李京文　中国社科院学术委员会委员、北京工业大学经济与管理学院院长
王　涛　中国出版集团党委书记、副总裁

五、中直企业副部级以上领导

熊维平　中国铝业公司党组书记、总经理
罗建川　中国铝业公司总裁
刘振亚　中国国家电网公司总经理
赵建国　中国南方电网有限责任公司董事长
张汝恩　中国通用技术(集团)控股有限责任公司副总经理
罗　涛　中国有色矿业集团有限公司总经理
丁　伟　招商银行副行长
胡望明　武汉钢铁（集团）公司党委常委、副总经理
任建国　中国葛洲坝集团国际工程有限公司副董事长
马传福　中国中信建设有限责任公司副总经理
唐　毅　中国技术进出口总公司总裁
袁　立　中国土木工程集团公司总经理
王旭升　中国机械进出口（集团）有限公司总经理
文　岗　中国路桥工程有限责任公司总经理
梁志东　中国出口信用保险公司副总经理
陆建华　中国中铁二院工程集团有限责任公司副总经理
王　禹　中国水利电力对外公司总经理

六、中国—东盟博览会高级顾问及法律顾问

张蕴岭　博览会高级顾问

七、国内各省(区、市）代表团

王三运　安徽省人民政府省长
程　红　北京市人民政府副市长
王文华　天津市政协副主席
唐登杰　上海市人民政府副市长
刘学普　重庆市政府副市长
布小林　内蒙古自治区副主席
别胜学　吉林省政协副主席
龚　正　浙江省人民政府副省长
花建慧　安徽省人民政府副省长

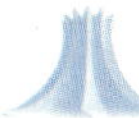

叶双瑜　福建省人民政府副省长
魏小琴　江西省人大副主任
任世茂　湖北省人大常委会副主任
陈肇雄　湖南省人民政府副省长
刘　昆　广东省人民政府副省长
李国梁　海南省人民政府副省长
张作哈　四川省人民政府副省长
黄康生　贵州省人民政府副省长
曹洪兴　贵州省委原副书记、纪委书记，厦蓉高速公路贵阳至水口段建设工作领导小组副组长
顾朝曦　云南省人民政府副省长
罗松多吉　西藏自治区政协副主席、秘书长
景俊海　陕西省人民政府副省长
李　锐　宁夏回族自治区人民政府副主席
崔玉琴　甘肃省人大副主任
于秀栋　新疆生产建设兵团副司令员

八、东盟国家政府代表团

(一)文莱

叶海亚　文莱工业和初级资源部部长

(二)柬埔寨

占蒲拉西　柬埔寨国务兼商业大臣
乌拉本　柬埔寨首相府部长
　　　　财经部国务秘书兼博览会事务部际委员会副主席
苏庆达　柬埔寨首相府部长
　　　　柬埔寨发展理事会秘书长兼博览会事务部际委员会副主席

(三)印度尼西亚

布迪约诺　印尼副总统
达尔温·扎赫迪　印尼能源部长
希达悦　印尼工业部长
冯慧兰　印尼贸易部长
穆斯塔法·阿布巴卡尔　印尼国企部长
杜尔桑迪·埃尔维　副总统办公室秘书长
阿古斯·查哈加纳·维拉古苏马　工业副部长
约赫曼沙·约翰　副总统办公室政治事务副秘书长
迪尔达·希达悦　副总统办公室经济事务副秘书长

穆罕默德·伊赫桑　副总统高级顾问
约比尔·希达悦　副总统高级顾问
马德·孟古·巴斯迪卡　巴厘省省长

(四)老挝

阿桑·劳里　老挝副总理
南·维亚吉　老挝工贸部部长
本格·桑宋萨　老挝外交部副部长
通米·蓬维赛　老挝计划投资部副部长
肯玛妮·奔舍那　老挝工贸部副部长

(五)马来西亚

贾谷·东加·沙甘　马来西亚国际贸易和工业部副部长

(六)缅甸

丁乃登　缅甸商务部部长

(七)菲律宾

克里斯托伯　菲律宾贸易与工业部副部长

(八)新加坡

李奕贤　新加坡贸易与工业部政务部长
陈振泉　新加坡贸易与工业部兼新闻通讯艺术部政务次长

(九)泰国

威拉萨　泰国商业部部长助理

(十)越南

张永仲　越南副总理
乔庭树　办公厅副主任
胡春山　外交部副部长
阮成边　工贸部副部长

九、中国—东盟博览会组委会东盟方副秘书长和联络官

赫斯蒂·英塔　印度尼西亚贸易部出口促进局主席

十、外国驻华使领馆官员

易慕龙　印度尼西亚驻中国大使馆大使

十一、第七届中国—东盟博览会魅力之城

洪　能　柬埔寨磅湛省省长
罗林泰　柬埔寨磅湛省副省长
森柴·费新旺　老挝甘蒙副省长

十二、国外友好城市和友好交流地区团组

杰奎琳·加西亚　菲律宾宿务省省长

蔡文恒　越南义安省人民委员副主席

蒲岛郁夫　日本熊本县知事

小杉直　日本熊本县议会议长

十三、国内支持商协会

刁春和　中国对外承包工程商会会长

十四、全国性行业协会

谢振华　中国电力联合会院党组书记、常务副理事长

何光远　中国机械工程学会名誉会长

陆燕荪　中国机械工程学会荣誉理事长

段正澄　中国机械工程学会中国工程院士

十五、中国—东盟商务与投资峰会

马力强　国务院国有大型企业监事会主席

熊志军　国务院国有大型企业监事会主席

丁俊发　中国物流与采购联合会副会长

十六、出席各论坛活动的副部级及以上部分领导及贵宾

（一）中国—东盟智库战略对话

马久基　印尼国务委员、亚太咨询委员会主席

诺罗敦·西里武　柬埔寨和平合作研究所主席、西哈努克国王私人高级顾问

宋春奔　柬埔寨皇家科学院秘书长

武高潘　越南越中友协副会长

（二）中国—东盟金融合作与发展领袖论坛

朱鸿杰　中国进出口银行副行长

方侨生　柬埔寨加华银行执行总裁

车迎新　农业银行党委副书记、监事长

Bounta Daravy　老挝发展银行兼老挝银行业协会主席

李东荣　中国人民银行行长助理

朱从玖　中国证券监督管理委员会主席助理

华庆山　交通银行监事长

（三）中国—东盟电力合作与发展论坛暨中国—东盟电力经贸合作洽谈会

曹丕玺　中国华能集团公司总经理
刘顺达　中国大唐集团公司董事长
米树华　中国国电集团公司副总经理
云公民　中国华电集团公司总经理
陆启洲　中国电力投资集团公司总经理
孙　勤　中国核工业总公司总经理
陈　飞　中国长江三峡集团公司总经理
张玉卓　神华集团有限责任公司总经理
王炳华　国家核技术有限公司总经理
汪建平　中国电力工程顾问集团公司总经理
晏志勇　中国水电工程顾问集团公司总经理
范集湘　中国水利水电建设集团公司总经理
杨继学　中国葛洲坝集团公司总经理
张炜清　中国广东核电集团公司副总经理
陈继忠　国家开发银行首席审计官
岳　毅　中国银行副行长

（四）第四次中国—印度尼西亚能源论坛

钱智民　国家能源局副局长
吴贵辉　国家能源局总工程师

十七、其他重要贵宾

刘烈宏　中国电子信息产业集团有限公司总经理
杰拉德·雷蒙尼　法国康达勒省副省长、议会副主席
Darmawan Djajusman　印尼投资协调署副主席
Tri Djoko Waluyo　印尼公共工程部部长
LEYMON IE GERARD　法国第15省副议会副议长
赵伟如　柬埔寨总理府总理助理
李晓林　柬埔寨菩萨省政府副省长
LAURENT GARNIER　法国马恩谷省副省长
郑树山　国家行政教育学院院长、党委书记

第七届中国—东盟博览会合作伙伴名单

首席战略合作伙伴

新加坡丰隆集团亚洲有限公司

战略合作伙伴

中国移动通信集团广西有限公司
中国有色矿业集团有限公司
广西投资集团有限公司
广西农垦集团有限责任公司

行业合作伙伴

广西三环企业集团股份有限公司
安徽古井酒业有限公司
中国银行广西分行
上海通用汽车有限公司
广西中烟工业有限责任公司
广西梧州中恒集团股份有限公司
包商银行
广西区农村信用社联合社
广西北部湾银行
广西运德汽车运输集团有限公司

合作伙伴

孔家钧窑有限公司
中国南方航空股份有限公司广西分公司
北部湾国际旅行社
永明珍珠宫（广西永明珍珠商贸有限公司）
海峰珠宝（广西海峰股份投资有限公司）

南宁中达桂宝汽车服务有限公司
广西益强投资管理有限公司
广州统一企业有限公司
广西龙州县人民政府
广西嘉和置业集团有限公司
广西通天香茶业有限公司
广西综路传媒有限公司
山顶会会所
广西中源山泉有限公司
南宁市菱红服饰有限责任公司
南宁聚福隆国际灯具城有限责任公司
广西凌云浪伏茶叶有限公司
南宁历藏文化交流咨询有限公司
武夷山桐木茶叶有限公司
广西中天领御酒业有限公司
桂林康立佳科技开发有限公司
广西福禄寿珠宝有限公司
广西洁宝纸业投资股份有限公司
广西高手商贸有限责任公司
梧州中茶茶业有限公司
太阳黑子企业策划有限公司
广西小海豚职装干洗中心有限公司
广西元之源健康产业有限责任公司
粤珍坊（南宁秦馔餐饮有限公司）
广西瑞康弘中保健会所
广西南宁凤天宝泉饮品有限公司

图书在版编目（CIP）数据

中国—东盟博览会发展报告. 2010第七卷 / 陈武编委会
主任；郑军健主编.
—桂林：广西师范大学出版社，2011.10
ISBN 978-7-5495-0866-2

I. 中… Ⅱ.①陈…②郑… Ⅲ.展览会
－研究报告－中国、东南亚国家联盟－2010 Ⅳ.①G245
中国版本图书馆CIP数据核字（2011）第200928号

图片摄影者及提供单位（排名不分先后）

刘　宇　何运斌　陈宇翔　袁存昭　夏文宁　唐安军　黄　愿
黄大年　梁　春　梁广宁　彭　寰　黎克平　张小宁　雷小华
李伟雄　刘文彪　韦望春　龚晓军　马占成　张　宁　新华社
广西国际博览事务局　广西国际贸易促进委员会
自治区发展和改革委员会　自治区公安厅　武警广西边防总队
自治区对外事务办公室　自治区食品药品监督管理局
自治区出入境检验检疫局　自治区卫生厅　自治区侨务办公室
自治区高级人民法院　广西海事局　共青团广西区委
广西社会科学院　南宁市政府　南宁海关　自治区扶贫开发办公室
广西医科大学附属口腔医院等

策划编辑　李庭华
责任编辑　韦兰琴　黄佳梦　黄　毓
英文编辑　陈俊泉
艺术顾问　张　明　刘　凛
设计总监　梁雪芬
责任技编　沈　明　石玉珏

广西师范大学出版社出版发行
（广西桂林市中华路22号　邮政编码：541001
网址：http://www.bbtpress.com）
出版人：何林夏
服务热线：0771-2092977
全国新华书店经销
广西民族印刷厂印刷
（广西南宁市高新三路1号　邮政编码：530007）
开本：889mm ×1 194mm　1/16
印张：25　字数：330千字　图片：196幅
2011年10月第1版　2011年10月第1次印刷
定价：218.00元